EARLY READING EXPERIENCES FOR YOUNG CHILDREN:

A Book of Selected Readings for Students, Interns and Teachers

Edited by
Heath W. Lowry
Jerry D. King
University of the Pacific

MSS Information Corporation
655 Madison Avenue, New York, N.Y. 10021

This is a custom-made book of readings prepared for the courses taught by the editors, as well as for related courses and for college and university libraries. For information about our program, please write to:

MSS INFORMATION CORPORATION
655 Madison Avenue
New York, New York 10021

MSS wishes to express its appreciation to the authors of the articles in this collection for their cooperation in making their work available in this format.

Library of Congress Cataloging in Publication Data

Lowry, Heath W comp.
Early experiences in reading.

1. Reading (Elementary) I. King, Jerry D., joint comp. II. Title.
LB1573.L66 1974 372.4'08 73-19630
ISBN 0-8422-5148-0
ISBN 0-8422-0366-4 (pbk.)

.... to Doris and Angela for help and encouragement

CONTENTS

PREFACE

In today's rapidly changing educational scene, it seems doubtful that a single author, or even collaborators, in producing a book for reading instruction could adequately present the coverage necessary. So it was that the present editors have sought to bring together many recent viewpoints from the publications of a number of authorities in various areas of reading curriculum and research. Further, the idea of using a single textbook to help the student understand the importance of early reading experiences for the young child can be called suspect. Therefore the current book of readings can be viewed either as a basic introduction to reading instruction or as a valuable reference tool to supplement the more traditional college text.

The editors have planned the learning experiences examined in the current readings to be beneficial in the following settings:

1. For an introductory course in reading instruction for prospective teachers.
2. For the readiness facets of courses dealing with the education of the young child both at pre-school and primary levels.
3. For an accompanying text to be used by student/interns involved in the recently developed module systems of competency based education.
4. For an anthology for basic readings in graduate seminar courses in which particular topics are examined in depth.

The editors selected each reading to bring to the student/teacher an eclectic viewpoint from a rich background of reading persons: Consultants, Specialists, Classroom Teachers, Researchers, and College Personnel. These experts have been and are working at all levels of education, and are concerned with the important topic: "Early Reading Experiences in the Reading Instruction of Young Children." As readers are introduced to the varied authors, they will discover that no one point of view is stressed, but that the editors have sought to introduce the concept that reading is indeed a complex process and its instruction must be approached from a diversified curriculum of many strands of methodology and media.

Professors Heath Lowry and Jerry King
School of Education
University of the Pacific
Stockton, California 95204

SECTION I

READING INSTRUCTION AND TEACHER PREPARATION

How Do You Teach Reading?

Bruce A. Gutknecht

Scenes such as these are repeated in thousands of classrooms in America every day.

Scene 1 Grade 1

"Today, children, we will work on the short sound of *e*. Here on the board are some words which have the short *e* sound: *let, bet, set,* and *pet*. Now let's all say these words together." As the teacher points to each word, the whole class repeats, "Let, bet, set, pet." Tim, who had been sent to the Library corner to find a picture of some sheep for the science lesson, asked, "Teacher, what's this word? It's spelled *e-w-e*."

Scene 2 Grade 4

"Now, class, what important language rule did we learn yesterday?" The whole class answers, pointing to a rule on a chart, "When two vowels go walking, the first one does the talking." Timothy, who loved snakes of all kinds and was looking at a new book on snakes from the library interrupted, "Teacher, what's the right way to say the name of this snake? *k-r-a-i-t*?"

Bruce Gutknecht is on the faculty of the College of Education at the University of North Florida, Jacksonville. He has served as a consultant in several TTT reading projects and has done readability work for Scott, Foresman "Systems" materials.

Scene 3 Grade 2

A small group of children are sitting around the teacher. Timmy is reading. "Then the dog ran down the road with the stick." "Thank you, Timmy. Karen?" Karen was the next child sitting in the circle. There is a pause, "Please read, Karen." There is a longer pause. "Weren't you following along?" There is the longest pause. "Karen, I'll have to speak with your mother about this. You never know the place when it's your turn to read."

Scene 4 Grade 3

The teacher is writing on a large chart. "Now, Rollie, what is the sentence you would like to add to our experience story about our trip to the post office?" Rollie, with much hesitation, says, "The mans taked the mail offa the truck which a mail man drived up." On the chart, the teacher wrote, "The men took the mail off the truck which a mail man drove up." After the whole class had read the sentence, Rollie, looking puzzled, protested, "Teacher, thas not what I said." "But this is the right way, Rollie."

Scene 5 Grade 5

The teacher is pointing to a list of words on the board. "These are the new words in the story which we will read today. Look up the words in the dictionary and write their definitions." As the work begins, the

ELEMENTARY ENGLISH, 1973, Vol. 50, No. 1, pp. 77-80.

class is heard in the background, "Grumble, grumble."

These scenes call attention to practices used by many teachers in reading and language arts instruction which are based on little or no knowledge of what the reading process is all about. The light of recent research into the nature of the reading process needs to be shed on these practices.

Scene 1—The Overemphasis of One Reading Strategy

In many schools, one reading strategy is taught, to the virtual exclusion of any other. This may be phonics, word attack skills, or word recognition. Basal readers, using these grapho-phonic strategies, may be the instructional materials used.

Scene 1 takes place in a classroom where phonics is taught. It is from this type of classroom that the following comment was made by the teacher to a child, "You read well, but you don't sound out your words very well." The notion that a child must sound out each word while reading arises from a misinformed view of the reading process.

The successful reader makes efficient use of not only phonemic and graphic information, but also syntactic (grammar) and semantic (meaning) information.

In fact, research has shown that some children tend to overuse phonics when attempting to read successfully.

Scene 2—Language Should be Taught as a Series of Rules

When teaching language through a series of rules, many a teacher has been led in frustration to comment, "English is so hard to teach because of the exceptions. It just doesn't fit the rules."

English is a composite of many languages. So when the rules of Latin are fit to it, there are many exceptions.

The truth of the matter is that English is quite regular in its structure. In fact it is so regular in sentence pattern for example, that most children use it correctly before they ever set foot inside a classroom. They don't come running into the house shouting, "Toy Billy truck my broke."

In a sense, when language is reduced to sets of rules for purpose of instruction, the child is stifled in his language development.

Scene 3—Each Child Must Follow Along While Another Reads

The child who is forced to follow along while another child reads may not be able to keep up or may read faster and be on the next page already.

The teacher in Scene 3 wants the reading lesson to move right along and so becomes overupset when someone doesn't follow along. What attention is paid to individual differences in this Scene?

Oral reading in a group must be questioned. For whose benefit is this method practiced? The child reading orally is probably nervous and somewhat embarrassed particularly if he has reading problems. Or, the child who reads well, might be more profitably engaged in some other activity than oral reading.

The teacher who must also keep an eye on the rest of the class, can't really diagnose and instruct each child while all of this is going on.

The goal of reading instruction is not the production of orators. Oral reading is not for performance. It should be used for diagnosis of reading problems, evaluation of progress, and alteration of instruction for each child.

The teacher in Scene 3 probably corrects the child immediately when an error is made or supplies the word when a child hesitates a few seconds. This practice causes overdependence on the teacher and does not lead to independent reading. As this dependence grows, the child ceases to try to read unfamiliar words and instead immediately looks to the teacher to supply an unknown word.

Psycholinguistic research has shown that children attempt to correct errors which make no syntactic or semantic sense to them. If the teacher is too quick to supply correction, the child cannot make use of the correction strategy in learning to read. Likewise, if the teacher is impatient enough and supplies the missing word when a child hesitates a few seconds, this child cannot develop his abilities to use syntactic cues and semantic cues in his reading.

This teacher behavior arises from the view that words or their parts are the basic units to be dealt with in reading and ignores the units of meaning and grammar which enable a child to read successfully.

Scene 4—Teachers Must Correct Improper Language of Students

The teacher in Scene 4 is using one of the more successful ways of teaching reading—the language experience approach. This method shows the child how his oral language and the written language are related.

The problem in Scene 4 is that the teacher is not accepting the oral language of the child, which has served his communications needs adequately up until this point. The child is made to feel ashamed of the language that has served him so well. More status is given in the classroom to the so-called standard English. Each teacher seems to assume that the dialect she speaks is standard English. The fact of the matter is that no one speaks standard English, but a dialect of it.

Recent views of dialect indicate it is a social indicator rather than a racial one. Various ways of handling dialect in the classroom have been put forth. One of these involves reading materials written in the dialect of the child. The problem with this is the impossibility of providing materials in all of the dialects in use.

Another suggestion is to teach the speaker of nonstandard English to speak standard English before teaching him to read. This would delay reading even more for children who need to read as early in their education as possible.

Permitting children to read standard English in their own dialects seems to make the most sense. Because in this way the children learn to use standard English while not damaging their self-image regarding their speech.

The fact that Rollie in Scene 4 said *mens* indicates his knowledge of the language convention for forming plurals. His use of *drived* shows that he is familiar with the use of tenses.

Scene 5—Children Must Know All the Words Before Reading

The procedure shown in Scene 5 is used by many teachers to introduce the reading of a new story. The idea is that the student who knows the vocabulary before he reads will have little trouble reading the story.

The theory underlying this practice is that if we provide instruction in each of the areas which make up reading, the child can easily get it all together for successful reading. This theory leads to the practice found in Scene 5 as well as the teaching of the alphabet, letter combinations, sounds, little words, and big words. Once the child has mastered all of these skills, according to this theory, successful reading will follow.

The problem is that it doesn't work as easily as predicted. The teacher may exclaim in frustration, "But he knows his alphabet and his sounds, I can't understand why he can't read."

Research has shown that a child who misses words on a vocabulary list, reads them correctly in the story while he is reading. Students who know the vocabulary before they read, may know the sound of the word and perhaps its lexical meaning. But a word also has a contextual meaning, which can only be learned from reading the story. Even if vocabulary work is a good end in itself, and this idea is questionable too, why waste the time for it before reading the story? Wouldn't it be far better to have the child spend the time with words for which he has no contextual meaning during or after his reading of the story? This vocabulary work will have much more meaning for the child.

The purpose of this article has been to focus on several practices used in reading and language arts instruction which are not based on a theory of what the reading process is all about. It is not intended as an indictment of teachers. Teacher's manuals and reading programs have been advocating some of these practices for years.

To a certain degree, educators have abrogated their responsibilities so that publishers, by default, have dictated the methods and materials to be used in teaching reading.

Each teacher, now held to be more accountable for the success of each child, should take the responsibility again for evaluating and questioning the methods she is instructed to use. She should determine what theory, if any, underlies the instructional methods.

Methods which emphasize only one reading strategy should become suspect, along with overemphasis on grammar rules, oral reading for performance only, the refusal to accept various dialects, and vocabulary work which preceeds reading.

Time is becoming more of a concern as more subjects are added to the curriculum. Accountability is a demand which is becoming louder and louder. Only practices which lead to successful reading deserve to be used.

Recent psycholinguistic research has begun to show what happens when a child reads. It is now our responsibility to take this information and apply it to the teaching of reading.

References

Goodman, Kenneth S. "A Linguistic Study of Cues and Miscues in Reading." *Elementary English*, 1965, Vol. 42.

Goodman, Kenneth S. *Study of Children's Behavior While Reading Orally*. U.S.O.E. Final Report, Project No. S425, Contract No. OE-6-10-136, U.S. Department of Health, Education, and Welfare, March, 1968.

Goodman, Yetta M. *Longitudinal Study of Children's Oral Reading Behavior*. U.S.O.E. Final Report, Project No. 9-E-062, Grant No. OeG-5-9-325062-0046, U.S. Department of Health, Education, and Welfare, September, 1971.

Gutknecht, Bruce A. "A Psycholinguistic Analysis of the Oral Reading Behavior of Selected Children Identified As Perceptually Handicapped," Unpublished Doctoral Dissertation, Wayne State University, 1971.

New Developments in the Teaching of Reading

Doris V. Gunderson

Much is said and written suggesting that the teaching of reading has changed and is changing both rapidly and markedly. Publishers frequently advertise a reading series as a new means of teaching reading. Journal articles herald new methods of teaching reading. A set of physical exercises is proposed which promises to prevent or cure all reading problems. New discoveries concerning the reading process are constantly trumpeted.

Yet, one rarely finds that much of the content of the new reading series is really new. And the old discoveries, more often than not, are simply old wine in new bottles.

However, there are some educational developments, either new or rediscovered, which are influencing the teaching of reading. Some of these developments are external, that is, they deal with the structure of the school or the classroom; others deal with substantive issues.

Two terms which have loomed, frighteningly to some, on the educational horizon are performance contracting and accountability. Frequently, both involve the teaching of reading. Most reports of instructional practices under a performance contract do not appear to indicate that new techniques are used to teach reading; the major difference seems to be that a greater portion of the school day is devoted to reading instruction. The accountability emphasis does not necessarily imply that new approaches are used to teach reading. It may mean, rather, that more time is spent in teaching reading, or it may even mean that time is spent in teaching to a test. Technically, all educational sectors should be accountable—the universities and colleges who prepare teachers, the state department who certify them, and the several levels of personnel in school systems who are engaged in various types of instructional activities.

A relatively new development, which, in some cases, has resulted in change in the classroom structure is the use of more adults in the classroom. Auxiliary professional personnel, such as helping teachers, parents and/or other paraprofessionals may be assigned to a classroom. Increasing the ratio of adults to children enables a teacher to spend more time with individual children; this can change a teacher's approach to reading instruction. Freeing a teacher from busy work should give her time to concentrate on the individual differences of children.

Perhaps the newest influence is television, specifically Sesame Street. The program appears to have had a great impact on young children, and it may have long range influences as yet unmeasured or even unknown. It is too soon to draw conclusions about the Electric Company, the television program designed to teach seven to ten

Doris Gunderson is a staff member of the Office of Education, Department of Health, Education & Welfare, Washington, D.C. This article was originally presented as a talk at the NCTE Convention in Las Vegas, 1971.

ELEMENTARY ENGLISH, 1973, Vol. 50, No. 1, pp. 17-21, 48.

year old children to read, but the techniques and approaches used in the program undoubtedly will have a considerable impact upon children throughout the country. Certainly the skillful use of the medium of television will have some effect on children's reading; hopefully, one of these effects will be that of motivating children to read.

Reports of research rarely mention studies concerned with motivation—encouraging reading as an activity to produce enjoyment or as a means to an end—either of learning to read or of reading to learn. There is little consideration given to establishing reasons for learning to read. What is the motivation for a child to learn to read? Some rationale must be advanced to him as to why he should learn to read, and it must be stated in terms acceptable and reasonable to him. In Nila Banton Smith's summary of trends and implications of research in reading, no research focusing on motivation is reported.[5] Any approach to teaching reading must make learning to read a significant activity for all children; if the child is not motivated to read, he will not read.

The wave of interest in perceptual and motor activities and programs has aroused both discussion and dissension as proponents and opponents debate the value of such training. Some adherents claim great gains, particularly for children with learning disabilities as a result of perceptual motor training. Balow, reviewing the literature in the area, found no research that demonstrated special effectiveness for any of the physical, motor, or perceptual programs claiming to be useful in the prevention or correction of reading or other learning disabilities. Balow suggests, however, that such programs be considered non-specific additions to the curriculum which may be useful in teaching children important general behavioral skills necessary for success in school rather than as replacements for the direct teaching of basic school skills.[1]

The concept of individual differences has been recognized for many years, and teachers have been encouraged, even admonished, to take each child at his particular stage of development and help him to grow. Individualization of instruction should mean that a child is given the opportunity to realize his potential. This, however, is the ideal, not the real world. Individualizing reading instruction should result in universal literacy for the segment of the population enrolled in schools. An examination of the literacy statistics, however, reveals that this goal has not been achieved—the schools are not turning out people who read. Rather, we have a significant number of school dropouts, the majority of whom have reading problems. Apparently individual differences still are not recognized to the extent that each child learns. No scheme has yet been devised for teaching children to read which takes into account their individual characteristics, builds on their strengths, and compensates for their weaknesses although almost every textbook on the teaching of reading stresses the importance of such a provision.

The interest in the British infant schools and informal education has increased since the publication of the Plowden Report in 1967. Articles in professional journals appear frequently in this country describing various aspects of the open classroom or integrated day. Weber defines informal education by saying that it ". . . refers to the setting, the arrangements, the teacher-child and child-child relationships that maintain, restimulate if necessary, and extend what is considered to be the most intense form of learning, the already existing child's way of learning through play and through the experiences he seeks out for himself."[7] The emphasis on allowing children to learn at their own pace and the stress on children's use of oral language have captured the interest of many educators in the United States. At its best informal education has much to commend it—the interest centers, the freedom of movement which as particularly essential for small boys, and the emphasis on children's talking and writing. On a theoretical basis, the integrated day, if properly handled, should allow for individualization of instruction.

One of the most significant developments affecting the teaching of reading is the current emphasis on language and its relationship to reading. Lenneberg listed six characteristics of language:

1. It is a form of behavior present in all cultures of the world.
2. In all cultures its onset is age correlated.
3. There is only one acquisition strategy —it is the same for all babies everywhere in the world.
4. It is based intrinsically upon the same formal operating characteristics whatever its outward form.
5. Throughout man's recorded history these operating characteristics have been constant.
6. It is a form of behavior that may be impaired specifically by circumscribed brain lesions which may leave other mental and motor skills relatively unaffected.[4]

The list reinforces the consensus among linguists concerning language acquisition—by the time a child enters school at six or seven, he possesses a fairly sophisticated language system, or as Venezky says, "he has mastered a system of signals for communicating in a meaningful fashion with other people."[6] The task at the school entrance stage is to teach children to read, to make the transition from spoken language to written language.

The language deficit theory has been discarded by linguists and psycholinguists as well as by many people in reading. However, it must be recognized that the child who speaks a dialect different from the dialect used in the teaching materials or by the teacher may have problems in learning to read which are different from those of the child who speaks the language of the classroom. Goodman hypothesizes that the difficulty of learning to read depends upon the degree of divergence between the dialect of the learner and the dialect of learning.[2]

The language the child brings to school is a part of the culture of his community; he reacts and responds to situations primarily through the medium of his language. If the teacher rejects his linguistic response by inferring that his means of expression is incorrect, the child feels that his cultural milieu has been rejected, and repeated remonstrances by the teacher will soon make him realize that school is not the place for him to express himself.

Several solutions have been suggested for teaching speakers of divergent dialects to read. Goodman says that divergent speakers have a tendency to read in book dialect so that in their oral reading they use phonemes different from those which they use in oral language. He suggests three alternatives for school programs. First, materials may be based on the community dialect, or standard materials such as basal readers may be rewritten in the dialect; second, children may be taught to speak the standard dialect before they are taught to read; third, children may read the standard materials in their own dialect, or in other words, the teacher accepts the language of the learner as the medium of learning. Goodman considers the third alternative the only practical solution and cites several key aspects of the approach.

1. Literacy is built on the base of the child's existing language.
2. Children must be helped to develop

a pride in their language and confidence in their ability to use their language to communicate their ideas and express themselves.
3. The focus in reading instruction must be on learning to read. No attempt to change the child's language must be permitted to enter into this process or interfere with it.
4. Special materials need not be constructed, but children must be permitted, even encouraged, to read the way they speak.
5. Any skill instruction must be based on a careful analysis of their language.
6. Reading materials and reading instruction should draw as much as possible on experiences and settings appropriate to the children.
7. The teacher will speak in his own natural manner and present by example the general language community, but the teacher must learn to understand and accept the children's language. He must study it carefully and become aware of the key elements of divergence that are likely to cause difficulty.[2]

Labov suggests that teachers who work with black speakers of nonstandard English may not have a systematic knowledge of the nonstandard forms which oppose and contradict standard English and may even be reluctant to believe that there are systematic principles in nonstandard English which differ from those of standard English. Of the phonological and grammatical differences between nonstandard Negro speech and standard English, the most important are those in which large scale phonological differences coincide with important grammatical differences.

The result of this coincidence, according to Labov, is the existence of a large number of homonyms in the speech of black children which are different from the set of homonyms in the speech system used by the teacher. Knowledge of this different set of homonyms on the part of the teacher should preclude problems in teaching reading to speakers of nonstandard English. This information may be organized under the headings of the important rules of the sound system which are affected. By using lists of homonyms as examples it will be possible to avoid a great deal of phonetic notation and to stay with the essential linguistic facts. Whether a child says pen or pin is unimportant; the linguistic fact of interest is the existence of contrast.

Labov says that a linguistic orientation will not supply teachers with a battery of phonetic symbols, but rather, it will encourage them to observe what words can or cannot be distinguished by the children they are teaching. In teaching a child to read who has general phonological grammatical characteristics of the nonstandard speaker, the most immediate way of analyzing difficulties is through the interpretation of his oral reading. There are many phonological rules which affect his pronunciation, but not necessarily his understanding of the grammatical signals or his grasp of the underlying lexical forms. The relationships between grammar and pronunciation are complex and require careful interpretation.

Labov lists three basic principles which may be helpful in teaching reading:

1. In analyzing and correcting oral reading, teachers must distinguish between differences in pronunciation and oral reading.
2. In the early stages of teaching reading and spelling it may be necessary to spend much more time on the grammatical function of certain inflections which may have no function in the dialect of some of the children.
3. A certain amount of attention given to

> perceptual training in the early school years may be very helpful in teaching children to hear and make standard English distinctions; such training, however, need not be completed before teaching children to read.

As Labov says, ". . . there is no reason why a person cannot learn to read standard English texts quite well in a nonstandard pronunciation." Although the school may ultimately wish to teach the child an alternative system of English pronunciation, the key to the situation in the early grades is for the teacher to know the system of homonyms of nonstandard English and to know the grammatical differences that separate his speech from that of the child.[3]

Goodman and Labov agree that children who are not speakers of standard English need not experience failure in learning to read, but that the crucial factor is the teacher's acceptance of the child's language, and the teacher's knowledge that there are different language systems. Their suggestions could and should be incorporated into any approach to teaching reading. This is probably the most important factor in reading instruction—it is not an approach to teaching reading, but a constant in reading instruction regardless of the approach that is used.

Venezky, Calfee, and Chapman note that one hears of "psycholinguistic approaches to reading." They comment that sufficient knowledge exists concerning natural language theory and cognitive psychology that needed improvements in reading instruction might be realized. They conclude that until the correspondences between these facts and the acquisition of reading ability are established empirically, a psycholinguistic program of reading will remain an unrealized challenge. Venezky's contention is that certain component skills must be examined if the teaching of reading is to be significantly improved. These skills include task skills, the ability to follow directions and carry out various tasks, oral language skills, and skills related to acquisition of letter-sound relationship.[7]

The teacher must accept the child's language or dialect, and if the child speaks a dialect other than that of the classroom, he must know the differences between the child's language and his. Then the teacher has before him the task of teaching the child to read, and the skills cited by Venezky will have to be incorporated into his repertoire.

What is new in teaching reading? No dramatic scheme which will guarantee instant success for each child exposed to reading instruction has appeared, and such a scheme probably will not appear until we know much more than we now do about the reading process itself. However, we probably know enough, that given properly prepared teachers who like and understand children, we should turn out few children who fail to learn to read.

None of the educational developments mentioned here have changed the teaching of reading to any appreciable extent. The factor which can influence reading instruction, and which perhaps can have a lasting effect on the children we are trying to teach is an improved awareness of language and its relationship to reading. A teacher who has an understanding of language and its structure, and who possesses the requisite skills to understand and to capitalize on a child's particular strengths should be able to provide the proper opportunity for children to learn to read.

Bibliography

1. Balow, Bruce. "Perceptual Motor Activities in the Treatment of Severe Reading Disability," *Reading Teacher.* 24:513-515. March, 1971.
2. Goodman, Kenneth S. "Dialect Barriers to Reading Comprehension," *Teaching Black Children to Read,* Joan C. Baratz and Roger W.

Shuy, Eds. Washington, D. C.: Center for Applied Linguistics. 1969. pp. 14-28.
3. Labov, William. "Some Sources of Reading Problems for Negro Speakers of Nonstandard English," *Teaching Black Children to Read*, Joan C. Baratz and Roger W. Shuy, Eds. Washington, D. C.: Center for Applied Linguistics. 1969. pp. 29-67.
4. Lenneberg, Eric. "On Explaining Language," *Language and Reading: An Interdisciplinary Approach*, Doris V. Gunderson, Comp. Washington, D. C.: Center for Applied Linguistics. 1970. pp. 3-25.
5. Smith, Nila Banton. "Research in Reading: Trends and Implications," *Elementary English*. March, 1971. pp. 320-327.
6. Venezky, Richard, Calfee, Robert C., and Chapman, Robin S., "Skills Required for Learning to Read: A Preliminary Analysis," *Language and Reading: An Interdisciplinary Approach*, Doris V. Gunderson, Comp. Washington, D. C.: Center for Applied Linguistics. 1970. pp. 37-54.
7. Weber, Lillian. *The English Infant School and Informal Education*. Englewood Cliffs, New Jersey: Prentice-Hall, Inc. 1971.

Johnny reads the cues: teacher expectation

CARL BRAUN

Associate professor at the University of Manitoba, Winnipeg, Carl Braun is especially interested in psychological-social factors related to learning problems. Here he reviews research on teacher personality cues and miscues as factors in student achievement. Braun first presented this paper at IRA's 1972 Convention in Detroit.

SITUATION: Principal takes Johnny, a low achieving fifth grader, to the classroom teacher who babysits the collection of intermediate "flunkies".

Principal: (calling Miss Jones to the door) Good Morning, Miss Jones, this is Johnny who is transferring in from Mr. Black's room. (To Miss Jones in less than hushed tones): I assure you Jack is another blank cheque for your collection. Don't worry about him—just keep him in line. He has already made more than enough trouble in Mr. Black's class.

Miss Jones: But, sir, I already have seventeen children in my class. I don't see how I can manage another one.

Principal: Now, now, Miss Jones I have told the superintendent many times, "if there is anyone who can keep our school zoo in order, that is our Miss Jones."

Miss Jones: (pleased) You're very kind. I'm sure I can manage.

Principal: And remember, Johnny hasn't learned a thing in the seven years he's warmed our school seats. We don't expect academic miracles from his type. Remember, he is just another blank cheque.

This nonfictional dialogue portrays one episode in a prolonged school drama in which Johnny too often assumes the role of a defenseless marionette. This particular Johnny came to school with a typical constellation of feelings about his identity as a social being. His assets included an insatiably curious mind, exceptional language skills, and a wild imagination. His kindergarten year was characterized by total boredom

THE READING TEACHER, 1973, Vol. 26, pp. 704-712.

and utter disillusionment. The teacher's recommendation for the first grade teacher included "a pesky brat who needs to be shown his place". In grade one, he became locked into the "dumb group" a membership he held for five and a half years until he was placed with the special class. His declining IQ from 110 in grade three to 89 in grade five confirmed the principal's bias that Johnny was getting "dumber by the year".

Johnny's case, while extreme, represents an example of how environmental cues, particularly those of the teacher, are reflected in his development as a learner. Gergen (1971, p. 49) states that ". . . man . . . seems only a passive agent mirroring the opinions of others, identity becomes a mere reflection of the faces around him." Positions on the influence of external cues in shaping the self include the gamut from total denial to the dismal picture of Johnny as a passive agent trapped in a prison of teacher-class cues.

Recent research, largely triggered by Rosenthal and Jacobson (1968) has attempted to ferret out the impact of these cues. "Teacher expectation", "self-fulfilling prophecy" and "teacher faith" are terms variously used to imply that teachers and experimenters produce their own reality commensurate with their own perceptions. Further, once the teacher/experimenter has created his reality, the child in his charge makes his reality—a reality apparently substantially grounded in the reality of the teacher.

On the basis of earlier studies with rats (Rosenthal and Fode, 1963; Rosenthal and Lawson, 1964), Rosenthal hypothesized that teachers' differential behavior toward pupils is dependent upon how they perceive the pupils as learners. On the basis of these perceptions then, pupils were believed to mirror these expectations in their school performance. In an attempt to test the hypothesis, Rosenthal and Jacobson submitted to elementary teachers a list of randomly selected academic "bloomers" who had been given an unfamiliar standard intelligence test ostensibly to norm the test. According to the researchers, this externally imposed information created expectancies in teachers' minds. The teachers' communication of these expectancies was reflected in significantly greater intellectual gains in "bloomers" than in other children.

Rosenthal's dramatic conclusions stimulated immediate academic criticism as well as wide popular acclaim.

Controversy as to the validity of his results stems from two basic sources: first, methods of collecting test scores, total reliance on TOGA norms considered inadequate for young (Thorndike, 1968) and low SES children (Snow, 1969). Snow suggests, in fact, that some of the reported IQ scores show children to have been functioning at imbecile and low moron levels. Poorly designed sampling procedures, large attrition, misleading graphs and tables, and the teachers' failure to recall the names of "bloomers" cast further doubt on the findings, as does the fact that Elashoff and Snow (1971) found reanalysis of first and second grade scores impossible.

The second source of contention arises from failure of a number of replications of the experiment to demonstrate the self-fulfilling phenomenon (Barber et al, 1969; Claiborn, 1969; and Fleming and Antonnen, 1970).

Typical popular credibility of Rosenthal's findings is reflected in Postman and Weingartner's (1969) expression of surprise to find the self-fulfilling phenomenon rating front page coverage in *The New York Times:*

> The fact that the editors believed that such "obvious" learning occurrence was so newsworthy is evidence of how tragically inept are most of our metaphors of the mind. How many children do you suppose have been driven to stupidity because their teachers believed that they really were "stupid"? . . . There is hardly a school in the country that has not organized children into groups labeled "dumb" so that both teachers and they know exactly what they "are". (p. 94)

This psychological credibility of the self-fulfilling phenomenon is probably one reason why research has continued despite the failure of Rosenthal and Jacobson to provide totally convincing evidence. Indeed, neither Thorndike nor Snow deny the fact that teacher expectation may be a powerful force. Further impetus has been provided by a number of studies that lend convincing support to the phenomenon (Palardy, 1969; Pippert, 1969; Brophy and Good, 1970; Mendoza et al, 1971; Rothbart et al, 1971; Rubovits and Maehr, 1971; and Seaver, 1971).

While the statistical war wages (and some of the battles may well be fruitful in terms of clarifying and refining relevant research techniques) the practitioner cannot blind himself to the stark reality that Johnny does read cues that relate to his view of self as a learner and as a social being. Elashoff and Snow (p. 64) state that "the question for future research is not whether there are expectation effects, but how they operate in school situations."

While conclusive answers await further research, the current thrust on accountability must transcend problems related to programing and gimmickry. It behooves the educator to examine seriously possible channels through which differential expectations are implanted in the teacher's mind and possible mechanisms through which the teacher's expectancy cues become available for Johnny to read and act upon. Psychological and educational literature provides at least some clues.

Teacher reads cues first

While it is vital to consider how Johnny reads the cues and which cues he chooses to internalize, it is of equal importance to consider some of the variables related to the induction of differential expectancies to the teacher. One of the criticisms of research to this point has been the artificial induction or manipulation of expectancies (Elashoff and Snow).

It would appear that teacher personality is a prime factor. Suggestibility or the degree to which the teacher gives credence to externally imposed information would appear from Pippert's study to be a factor. He found a significant difference on all verbal subtests of the *Torrance Tests of Creativity* between pupils whose teachers had not doubted the stated purpose of his study and pupils whose teachers had doubted. Fleming and Antonnen's study suggests that teachers' attitudes towards testing and test scores make a difference. Children whose teachers rated high on a testing opinionnaire showed greater gains in IQ than did children whose teachers rated low on the scale.

The degree to which the external induction learner information generates dissonance and the degree to which the teacher can reconcile this external information with what she has observed of the learner, will determine whether or not she will act on the information.

It is probable that some preconceived expectancies may be more potent than others. There is evidence that race and socioeconomic level of the learner influence what the teacher expects of her charges. Kozol's *Death at an Early Age* (1967) illustrates clearly that some Boston White teachers had differential achievement expectancies for White and Black children. Howe (1972) illustrates how readily these expectancies can result in self-fulfilling prophecies. The teacher who expects "disruptive" behavior in the ghetto school assumes a firm, punitive approach. This, in turn, results in increasing disruptive behavior fulfilling the teacher's expectancy.

Davidson and Lang (1960) found that the higher the social class of children, the more favorable was their perception of the teacher's feelings toward them. Fleming and Antonnen found significant interaction effects of teachers' opinion on testing with socioeconomic status.

There is evidence also that the sex of the learner generates differential cues that the teacher transmits to Johnny. Palardy, in investigating the effect of teachers' beliefs on pupil achievement, concludes that if teachers believe that first grade boys will do as well in reading as do girls, this will in fact happen. The converse was equally true. Meyer and Thompson (1956) found greater teacher approval toward sixth grade girls than boys —a finding corroborated by Davidson and Lang.

Pennock (1971) recommends that teachers in training be sensitized to the fact that sex differences in reading achievement are largely culturally-educationally determined.

What the cumulative files say about Johnny, what the principal says, and what happens in the teacher's lounge may well contribute to the teacher's expectation of Johnny. Even knowledge of performance of siblings appears to be an important variable. Seaver found that younger siblings of good students obtained higher achievement scores if they were assigned to their sibling's former teacher than if assigned to a different teacher.

Elashoff and Snow's statement sums up aptly the impact of teacher impressionability:

> teachers . . . form impressions based on physical appearance and conduct . . . achievement, I.Q. scores, or general characteristics of older siblings or parents. These impressions based on a day's or a week's experience may produce expectations about pupil behavior and future achievement. . . . When teachers characterize pupils they are likely to label them as "good" or "bad". Clean children may be "good", dirty ones "bad"; or they may be "fast" or "slow" learners. (p. 63)

Transmission of cues

Social psychology and operant conditioning models offer some clues as to probable mechanisms which mediate expectancy cues.

Assignment to special classes or learning groups appears to communicate considerable information to the learner. McGinley and McGinley (1970), in a sociometric study, found that significantly fewer than expected low group children chose peers from their own reading group. Middle group children made fewer than expected choices from lower reading groups and more than expected from top groups. The top group made significantly more than expected choices from their own group and fewer than expected from the lower two groups. Group assignment was also found to be related to positive and negative feelings of the teachers toward the children. Stevens' study (1971), while not designed specifically to determine the effects of formal group assignment, ascertained the degree of acceptance of "remedial readers". He found that these children displayed specific behavior mechanisms which are "socially unacceptable". He concludes that remedial readers know how others feel about them.

Additional information on the effects of grouping is provided by Tuckman and Bierman (1971). Randomly selected secondary students who were moved to higher ability groups achieved higher on achievement tests than did control students.

In addition, 54 percent of moved students were recommended to be retained while only 1 percent received transfer recommendations. The authors suggest a possible "inertia" function related to the grouping process, and comment on the frustration and disillusionment of grouping procedures that "lock students in and out."

Rist (1970) describes how kindergarten children were ranked and grouped during their first eight days of school on the basis of mere guesses at their potential. Their assignment to three different tables determined amount of teacher attention given, whether or not they could hear the teacher, and ultimately their performance and group assignment in first and second grade.

Closely related to group assignment is the amount of reinforcement the teacher dispenses to Johnny. Rothbart et al, in a simulated classroom experiment, found no difference in reinforcement given to students of "high" and "low" potential. However, it may be that "reinforcement" was defined too narrowly, as the authors note (p. 52) that the "teachers spent more time attending to the high-expectation than the low-expectation students." Attention is generally viewed as a reinforcer. Further, a one session experiment imposes limitations as to generalizations that can be made for longer range group assignment effects.

Brophy and Good conclude that teachers transmit differential performance cues through varying amounts of praise; these cues encourage responses that confirm the teacher's expectancy. Similarly, Rubovits and Maehr found teacher trainees provided significantly different patterns of reinforcement to "gifted" and "non gifted" junior high students. Mendoza et al also found that low achieving high school students received notably less teacher contact than did high achieving students.

Whether group assignments, labeling or reinforcement comes first, it appears that the amount and quality of pupil-teacher interaction offers crucial insight to the mystery of cues that Johnny reads.

Potency of expectancy cues

Just as teachers differ in acceptance of induced cues about the learner, learners vary in the extent to which they read and internalize cues. There is little reason to believe that all cues are equally potent for all learners.

However, a reminder of the vulnerability of learners even to artificially induced cues should sober even the most insensitive teacher. Peters (1971) describes how third grade children assumed new roles almost without question when the teacher assigned brown eyed children to "superior" and blue eyed children to "inferior" groups.

Peters' study offers at least one clue as to how potent the external induction of cues will be. Credibility of the person transmitting the cues is illustrated by the teacher's statement:

> I have asked each class that has gone through this exercise why they believed me when I said that one group or the other was inferior. The answer has always been the same. They believed me at first because I was the teacher. Later, they believed me because they *saw* it was so. And, of course, they *had* seen it. (p. 102)

It is safe to make the generalization that for many primary school children the teacher's credibility rating is high. If she communicates to Johnny that his performance is poor, this will undoubtedly influence his self-concept and the goals he strives to achieve.

Personalism of the transmitter is also likely to affect the extent to which cues will be internalized. Gergen (1965) suggests that self-esteem is enhanced as the appraisal becomes more personalistic.

The degree of discrepancy between external appraisal of self and the individual's self-view apparently influences the magnitude of change that will occur in the learner's self-view (Gergen). However, an interaction between degree of change and credibility of the appraisal is apparent. Bergin (1962) found that when the source of appraisal is highly credible, the effect on self-image increases as the assessment shows increasing discrepancy from the learner's original self-view.

While research support is limited, there is some evidence that the number of confirmations a learner receives regarding his self-view and the consistency of these confirmations influences change in self-image (Gergen). It is conceivable that the consistency of the bombardment of cues communicating inferiority to the blue-eyed children in Peters' study contributed to the change even in cases where the new image was in total dissonance with the former image.

Implications

While further research is needed, teachers and administrators must be alerted to the reality that Johnny reads even the most subtle cues. Teachers need to be keenly aware that their own beliefs regarding socioeconomic level, test information, or sex of the learner too frequently result in structuring a learning situation which produces behaviors commensurate with their beliefs. Further, teacher educators need to emphasize to prospective teachers the danger of unwarranted labeling and stereotyping.

Teachers need to examine and heed the wide range of cues Johnny can abstract from being cemented into a permanent group—cues that pervade personal, social, and academic realness. Teachers should be aware that the group assignment can, in fact, assign a role difficult for Johnny to change.

The expectancy hypothesis holds important implications for teacher selection, particularly for teachers of kindergarten and first grade children. First, that the teacher at this level holds high credibility dictates careful selection. Second, since this is the time when Johnny develops his image as a learner or nonlearner, the role of the teacher cannot be overestimated.

A further implication relates to the sources of information which impinge upon the teacher to formulate varying expectations for her pupils. The derogatory label communicated by the principal or former teacher may help to fit otherwise unnoticed behaviors into the "predicted" context. Uncritical assessment of cumulative records may plant in the teacher's mind expectations unfavorable to the child. Ignorance of the limitations of intelligence tests can too easily provide diagnostic solace for low performance and result in the teacher behaving toward the child as though he has limited potential, thus fulfilling the biased prophecy made by the intelligence test.

Accounts abound which testify to the importance of faith in children as a crucial variable. Roberts and Roberts (1971, p. 70) attribute the success of the Central Cooperative School in Webster, Louisiana to the attitude of the teachers toward the learners. In explaining why children with IQ's as low as 30 learn skills frequently considered impossible, they state "The best word to describe it is 'expectation'—the expectation that these children will achieve. The teachers believe in them, and for the first time these children believe in themselves."

Another case in point illustrates the impact of lack of teacher faith —a lack of faith at least partially based on bias. In a classroom of educable mentally retarded children a teacher recently stated that four particular children would never develop any number concepts "because children with IQ's that low just don't develop number sense". She hastened to add that she had never done any number work with them; sure fire for a self-fulfilling prophecy. When two psychology students initiated an extended behavior modification program in the classroom, one of the demands included children charting their own earned points. All four children were able to chart and count their own points flawlessly in less than a week's time.

The cues, verbal and nonverbal, communicating faith in Johnny, or lack of faith, likely encompass a spectrum of behavior eluding quantification even for the sophisticated researcher. However, there is sufficient evidence that reinforcement, including attention and approval, aids in enhancing Johnny's self-image as learner and as a social being. How he thinks of himself as a learner is of inestimable importance. Certainly, there is nothing which communicates lack of faith more forcibly than to be given up as in the case of the four "mentally retarded" children mentioned above. How many Johnnys lose faith in themselves because the teacher communicates increasing impatience with wrong answers, choppy oral reading, and messy purple sheets? Particularly devastating is the predictable sequel—asking Johnny fewer questions, suffering his oral reading only frequently enough to appear civil, and generally ignoring him.

Frequent reference has been made to the importance of the learner's self-image. There is considerable evidence that a negative self-image is highly resistant to change (Gillham, 1967). According to Lecky (1945) it may be that part of this resistance results from the fact that the child needs to be faithful to the picture of himself or else be threatened with the loss of selfhood. Making the decision to fail, in fact, becomes a convenient defense—criticism for poor performance can no longer hurt the learner's image (Bettleheim, 1961). Glock (1972, p. 406) states that "A negative self-image is its own best defender". He views the learner's self-image as a boundary which limits his actions. If one learns to think of himself as inferior, his actions will be those of an inferior person confirming to his teacher and peers the legitimacy of treating him as inferior.

The cycle is a vicious one: the teacher for various reasons expects little from Johnny, who in turn, reads the cues—he exhibits behavior to reinforce teacher's expectations. Johnny appears to be a blank cheque; in fact, he likely will be a blank cheque.

References

Barber, T. X., et al. "Five Attempts to Replicate the Experimenter Bias Effect." *Journal of Consulting and Clinical Psychology*, vol. 33 (1969), pp. 1-6.

Barber, T. X., and Silver, M. J. "Fact, Fiction and the Experimenter Bias Effect." *Psychological Bulletin*, vol. 70 (1968), pp. 1-29.

Bergin, A. E. "The Effect of Dissonant Persuasive Communications upon Changes in Self-Referring Attitudes." *Journal of Personality*, vol. 30 (1962), pp. 423-38.

Bettleheim, Bruno. "The Decision to Fail." *The School Review*, vol. 69 (1961).

Brophy, Jere E., and Thomas L. Good. "Teachers' Communication of Differential Expectations for Children's Classroom Performance: Some Behavioral Data." *Journal of Educational Psychology*, vol. 61 (1970), pp. 365-74.

Claiborn, W. L. "Expectancy Effects in the Classroom: A Failure to Replicate." *Journal of Educational Psychology*, vol. 60 (1969), pp. 377-83.

Davidson, H. H., and Lang, C. "Children's Perceptions of Their Teachers' Feelings Towards Them Related to Self-perception, School Achievement, and Behavior." *Journal of Experimental Education*, vol. 29, no. 2 (1960), pp. 107-18.

Elashoff, Janet Dixon, and Snow, Richard E. *Pygmalion Reconsidered: A Case Study in Statistical Inference: Reconsideration of the Rosenthal-Jacobson Data on Teacher Expectancy*. Belmont, California: Wadsworth Publishing Company, 1971, p. 64.

Fleming, Elyse S., and Antonnen, Ralph G. "Teacher Expectancy on My Fair Lady." Paper presented at American Educational Research Association meeting, March 1970, Minneapolis, Minnesota.

Gergen, K. J. "Interaction Goals and Personalistic Feedback as Factors Affecting the Presentation of Self." *Journal of Personality and Social Psychology*, vol. 1 (1965), pp. 413-24.

Gergen, K. J. *The Concept of Self*. New York: Holt, Rinehart and Winston, Inc., 1971.

Gillham, Isabel. "Self-Concept and Reading." *The Reading Teacher*, (December 1967), pp. 270-73.

Glock, Marvin D. "Is There a Pygmalion in the Classroom?" *The Reading Teacher*, vol. 25 (1972), pp. 405-08.

Homze, Alma Cross. "Reading and the Self-Concept." *Elementary English*, vol. 39 (1962), pp. 210-17.

Howe, Michael J. A. *Understanding School Learning*. New York: Harper & Row, Publishers, 1972.

King, Martha, et al. "Observations of Teacher-Pupil Verbal Behavior during Critical Reading Lessons." Paper No. 67-103, Ohio State University, 1967.

Kozol, J. *Death at an Early Age*. Boston: Houghton Mifflin Company, 1967.

Lecky, P. *Self-Consistency: A Theory of Personality*. Island Press, 1945.

McGinley, Pat, and McGinley, Hugh. "Reading Groups as Psychological Groups." *Journal of Experimental Education*, vol. 39 (Winter 1970), pp. 36-42.

Mendoza, S. M., Good, T. L., and Brophy, J. E. "The Communication of Teacher Expectancies in a Junior High School." Paper read at the American Educational Research Association conference, New York, 1971.

Meyer, W. J., and Thompson, G. G. "Sex Differences in the Distribution of Teacher Approval and Disapproval among Sixth-Grade Children." *Journal of Educational Psychology*, vol. 47 (1956), pp. 285-96.

Palardy, J. Michael. "What Teachers Believe—What Children Achieve." *Elementary School Journal*, vol. 69 (April 1969), pp. 370-74.

Pennock, Clifford D. *Student Teacher Expectations for Primary Level Boys' Reading Achievement*. Unpublished doctoral thesis,

University of Illinois at Urbana-Champaign, 1971.

Peters, William. *A Class Divided.* Garden City, New York: Doubleday & Company, Inc., 1971.

Pippert, Ralph. *A Study of Creativity and Faith.* Manitoba Department of Youth and Education Monograph No. 4, 1969.

Postman, Neil, and Weingartner, Charles. *Teaching as a Subversive Activity.* New York: Delacorte Press, 1969.

Rist, Ray C. "Student Social Class and Teacher Expectations: The Self-Fulfilling Prophecy in Ghetto Education." *Harvard Educational Review,* vol. 40, 1970.

Roberts, Nancy, and Roberts, Bruce. "Teaching the Mentally Retarded: Patience and Expectation." *Saturday Review,* September 18, 1971.

Rosenthal, Robert. "Experimenter Expectancy and the Reassuring Nature of the Null Hypothesis Decision Procedure." *Psychological Bulletin,* vol. 70 (6. Part 2), (1968), pp. 30-47.

Rosenthal, R., and Fode, K. L. "The Effect of Experimental Bias on the Performance of the Albino Rat." *Behavioral Science,* vol. 8 (1963), pp. 183-89.

Rosenthal, R., and Jacobson, Lenore. *Pygmalion in the Classroom.* New York: Holt, Rinehart & Winston, Inc., 1968.

Rosenthal, R., and Lawson, R. "A Longitudinal Study of the Effects of Experimenter Bias on the Operant Learning of Laboratory Rats." *Journal of Psychiatric Research,* vol. 2 (1964), pp. 61-72.

Rothbart, Myron, Dalfen, Susan, and Barrett, Robert. "Effects of Teacher's Expectancy on Student-Teacher Interaction." *Journal of Educational Psychology,* vol. 62 (1971), pp. 49-54.

Rubovits, P. C., and Maehr, M. L. "Pygmalion Analyzed: Toward an Explanation of the Rosenthal-Jacobson Findings." Paper read at the American Educational Research Association conference, New York, 1971.

Seaver, W. B. Effects of Naturally-Induced Teacher Expectancies on the Academic Performance of Pupils in Primary Grades, Unpublished doctoral thesis, University of Illinois, 1971.

Snow, Richard E. "Unfinished Pygmalion." *Contemporary Psychology,* vol. 14, no. 4 (April 1969), pp. 197-99.

Stevens, Dean O. "Reading Difficulty and Classroom Acceptance." *The Reading Teacher,* vol. 25, no. 1 (October 1971), pp. 52-55.

Thomas, W. I. "The Relation of Research to the Social Process." *Essays on Research in the Social Sciences.* Washington: Brookings Institution, 1931, pp. 175-94.

Thorndike, R. L. "Review of R. Rosenthal and L. Jacobson, Pygmalion in the Classroom." *American Educational Research Journal,* vol. 5 (1968), pp. 708-11.

Tuckman, B. W., and Bierman, M. L. "Beyond Pygmalion: Galatea in the Schools." Paper read at the American Educational Research Association conference, New York, 1971.

The Politics of Reading

NEIL POSTMAN

Dr. Postman challenges the common assumptions that the literacy process is politically neutral and is the only, or even the best, avenue to jobs and aesthetic riches. He sees a predominantly literacy-based curriculum as obsolete and reactionary in the context of recent advances in electronic communications technology, and recommends broadening the base of school curricula to include "multimedia literacy."

Teachers of reading comprise a most sinister political group, whose continued presence and strength are more a cause for alarm than celebration. I offer this thought as a defensible proposition, all the more worthy of consideration because so few people will take it seriously.

My argument rests on a fundamental and, I think, unassailable assumption about education: namely, that all educational practices are profoundly political in the sense that they are designed to produce one sort of human being rather than another—which is to say, an educational system always proceeds from some model of what a human being *ought* to be like. In the broadest sense, a political ideology is a conglomerate of systems for promoting certain modes of thinking and behavior. And there is no system I can think of that more directly tries to do this than the schools. There is not one thing that is done to, for, with, or against a student in school that is not rooted in a political bias, ideology, or notion. This includes everything from the arrangement of seats in a classroom, to the rituals practiced in the auditorium, to the textbooks used in lessons, to the dress required of both teachers and students, to the tests given, to the subjects that are taught, and most emphatically, to the intellectual skills that are promoted. And what is called reading, it seems to me, just about heads the list. For to teach reading, or even to promote vigorously the teaching of reading, is to take a definite political position on how people should behave and on what they ought to value. Now, teachers, I have found, respond in one of three ways to such an assertion. Some of them deny it. Some of them concede it but without guilt or defensiveness of any kind. And some of them don't know what it means. I want to address myself to the latter, because in responding to them I can include all the arguments I would use in dealing with the others.

In asserting that the teaching of reading is essentially a political enterprise, the most obvious question I am asking is, "What is reading good for?" When I ask

HARVARD EDUCATIONAL REVIEW, May 1970, 40, pp. 244-252.

this question of reading teachers, I am supplied with a wide range of answers. Those who take the low ground will usually say that skill in reading is necessary in order for a youngster to do well in school. The elementary teacher is preparing the youngster for the junior high teacher, who prepares him for the senior high teacher, who, in turn, prepares him for the college teacher, and so on. Now, this answer is true but hardly satisfactory. In fact, it amounts to a description of the *rules* of the school game but says nothing about the purpose of these rules. So, when teachers are pushed a little further, they sometimes answer that the school system, at all levels, makes reading skill a precondition to success because unless one can read well, he is denied access to gainful and interesting employment as an adult. This answer raises at least a half-dozen political questions, the most interesting of which is whether or not one's childhood education ought to be concerned with one's future employment. I am aware that most people take it as axiomatic that the schooling process should prepare youth for a tranquil entry into our economy, but this is a political view that I think deserves some challenge. For instance, when one considers that the second most common cause of death among adolescents in the U.S. is suicide, or that more people are hospitalized for mental illness than all other illnesses combined, or that one out of every 22 murders in the United States is committed by a parent against his own child, or that more than half of all high school students have already taken habit-forming, hallucinogenic, or potentially addictive narcotics, or that by the end of this year, there will be more than one-million school drop-outs around, one can easily prepare a case which insists that the schooling process be designed for purposes other than vocational training. If it is legitimate at all for schools to claim a concern for the adult life of students, then why not pervasive and compulsory programs in mental health, sex, or marriage and the family? Besides, the number of jobs that require reading skill much beyond what teachers call a "fifth-grade level" is probably quite small and scarcely justifies the massive, compulsory, unrelenting reading programs that characterize most schools.

But most reading teachers would probably deny that their major purpose is to prepare students to satisfy far-off vocational requirements. Instead, they would take the high ground and insist that the basic purpose of reading instruction is to open the student's mind to the wonders and riches of the written word, to give him access to great fiction and poetry, to permit him to function as an informed citizen, to have him experience the sheer pleasure of reading. Now, this is a satisfactory answer indeed but, in my opinion, it is almost totally untrue.

And to the extent that it is true, it is true in a way quite different from anything one might expect. For instance, it is probably true that in a highly complex society, one cannot be governed unless he can read forms, regulations, notices, catalogues, road signs, and the like. Thus, some minimal reading skill is necessary if you are to be a "good citizen," but "good citizen" here means one who can follow the instructions of those who govern him. If you cannot read, you cannot be an obedient citizen. You are also a good citizen if you are an enthusiastic consumer. And so, some minimal reading competence is required if you are going to develop a keen interest in all the products that it is necessary for you to buy. If you do not read, you will be a relatively poor market. In order to be a good and loyal citizen, it is also necessary for you to believe in the myths and superstitions of your society. Therefore, a certain minimal reading skill is needed so that you can learn what these are, or have them reinforced. Imagine what would happen in a school if a Social Studies text were introduced that described the growth of American civilization as being characterized by four major developments: 1) insurrection against a legally constituted government, in order to achieve a political identity; 2) genocide against the indigenous population, in order to get land; 3) keeping human beings as slaves, in order to achieve an economic base; and 4) the importation of "coolie" labor, in order to build the railroads. Whether this view of American history is true or not is beside the point. It is at least as true or false as the conventional view *and* it would scarcely be allowed to appear unchallenged in a school-book intended for youth. What I am saying here is that an important function of the teaching of reading is to make students accessible to political and historical myth. It is entirely possible that the main reason middle-class whites are so concerned to get lower-class blacks to read is that blacks will remain relatively inaccessible to standard-brand beliefs unless and until they are minimally literate. It just may be too dangerous, politically, for any substantial minority of our population *not* to believe that our flags are sacred, our history is noble, our government is representative, our laws are just, and our institutions are viable. A reading public is a responsible public, by which is meant that it believes most or all of these superstitions, and which is probably why we still have literacy tests for voting.

One of the standard beliefs about the reading process is that it is more or less neutral. Reading, the argument goes, is just a skill. What people read is their own business, and the reading teacher merely helps to increase a student's options. If one wants to read about America, one may read DeToqueville or *The Daily News;* if one wants to read literature, one may go to Melville or Jacqueline Susann. In theory, this argument is compelling. In practice, it is pure romantic nonsense. *The New York Daily News* is the most widely read newspaper in America. Most of our students will go to the grave not having read, of their own choosing, a paragraph of DeToqueville or Thoreau or John Stuart Mill or, if you exclude the Gettysburg Address, even Abraham Lincoln. As between Jacqueline Susann and Herman Melville—well, the less said, the better. To put it bluntly, among every 100 students who learn to read, my guess is that no more than one will employ the process toward any of the lofty goals which are customarily held before us. The rest will use the process to increase their knowledge of trivia, to maintain themselves at a relatively low level of emotional maturity, and to keep themselves simplistically uninformed about the social and political turmoil around them.

Now, there are teachers who feel that, even if what I say is true, the point is nonetheless irrelevant. After all, they say, the world is not perfect. If people do not have enough time to read deeply, if people do not have sensibilities refined enough to read great literature, if people do not have interests broad enough to be stimulated by the unfamiliar, the fault is not in our symbols, but in ourselves. But there is a point of view that proposes that the "fault," in fact, *does* lie in our symbols. Marshall McLuhan is saying that each medium of comunication contains a unique metaphysic—that each medium makes special kinds of claims on our senses, and therefore, on our behavior. McLuhan himself tells us that he is by no means the first person to have noticed this. Socrates took a very dim view of the written word, on the grounds that it diminishes man's capacity to memorize, and that it forces one to follow an argument rather than to participate in it. He also objected to the fact that once something has been written down, it may easily come to the attention of persons for whom it was not intended. One can well imagine what Socrates would think about wire-tapping and other electronic bugging devices. St. Ambrose, a prolific book writer and reader, once complained to St. Jerome, another prolific writer and reader, that whatever else its virtues, reading was the most anti-social behavior yet devised by man. Other people have made observations about the effects of communications media on the psychology of a culture, but it is quite remarkable how little has been said about this subject. Most criticism of print, or any other medium, has dealt with the content of the medium; and it is only in recent years that we have begun to understand that each medium, *by its very structure,* makes us do things with our bodies, our senses, and our minds that in the long run are probably more important than any other messages communicated by the medium.

Now that it is coming to an end, we are just beginning to wonder about the powerful biases forced upon us by the Age of the Printed Word. McLuhan is telling us that print is a "hot" medium, by which he means that it induces passivity and anesthetizes almost all our senses except the visual. He is also telling us that electronic media, like the LP record and television, are reordering our entire sensorium, restoring some of our sleeping senses, and, in the process, making all of us seek more active participation in life. I think McLuhan is wrong in connecting the *causes* of passivity and activity so directly to the structure of media. I find it sufficient to say that whenever a new medium—a new communications technology—enters a culture, *no matter what its structure,* it gives us a new way of experiencing the world, and consequently, releases tremendous energies and causes people to seek new ways of organizing their institutions. When Gutenberg announced that he could manufacture books, as he put it, "without the help of reed, stylus, or pen but by wondrous agreement, proportion, and harmony of punches and types," he could scarcely imagine that he was about to become the most important political and social revolutionary of the Second Millenium. And yet, that is what happened. Four hundred and fifty years ago, the printed word, far from being a medium that induced passivity, generated cataclysmic change. From the time Martin Luther posted his theses in 1517, the printing press disseminated the most controversial, inflammatory, and wrenching ideas imaginable. The Protestant Reformation would probably not have occurred if not for the printing press. The development of both capitalism and nationalism were obviously linked to the printing press. So were new literary forms, such as the novel and the essay. So were new conceptions of education, such as written examinations. And, of course, so was the concept of scientific methodology, whose ground rules were established by Descartes in his *Discourse on Reason*. Even today in recently illiterate cultures, such as Cuba, print is a medium capable of generating intense involvement, radicalism, artistic innovation, and institutional upheaval. But in those countries where the printed word has been pre-eminent for over 400 years, print retains very few of these capabilities. Print is not dead, it's just old—and old technologies do not generate new patterns of behavior. For us, print is the technology of convention. We have accommodated our senses to it. We have routinized and even ritualized our responses to it. We have devoted our institutions, which are now venerable, to its service. By maintaining the printed word as the keystone of education, we are therefore opting for political and social stasis.

It is 126 years since Professor Morse transmitted a message electronically for the first time in the history of the planet. Surely it is not too soon for educators to give serious thought to the message he sent: "What hath God wrought?" We are very far from knowing the answers to that question, but we do know that electronic media have released unprecedented energies. It's worth saying that the gurus of the peace movement—Bob Dylan, Pete Seeger, Joan Baez, Phil Ochs, for instance—were known to their constituency mostly as voices on LP records. It's worth saying that Viet Nam, being our first television war, is also the most unpopular war in our history. It's worth saying that Lyndon Johnson was the first president ever to have resigned because of a "credibility gap." It's worth saying that it is now commonplace for post-TV college sophomores to usurp the authority of college presidents and for young parish priests to instruct their bishops in the ways of *both* man and God. And it's also worth saying that black people, after 350 years of bondage, want their freedom—now. Post-television blacks are, indeed, our true *now* generation.

Electronic media are predictably working to unloose disruptive social and political ideas, along with new forms of sensibility and expression. Whether this is being achieved by the structure of the media, or by their content, or by some combination of both, we cannot be sure. But like Gutenberg's infernal machine of 450 years ago, the electric plug is causing all hell to break loose. Meanwhile, the schools are still pushing the old technology; and, in fact, pushing it with almost hysterical vigor. Everyone's going to learn to read, even if we have to kill them to do it. It is as if the schools were the last bastion of the old culture, and if it has to go, why let's take as many down with us as we can.

For instance, the schools are still the principal source of the idea that literacy is equated with intelligence. Why, the schools even promote the idea that *spelling* is related to intelligence! Of course, if any of this were true, reading teachers would be the smartest people around. One doesn't mean to be unkind, but if that indeed is the case, no one has noticed it. In any event, it is an outrage that children who do not read well, or at all, are treated as if they are stupid. It is also masochistic, since the number of non-readers will obviously continue to increase and, thereby, the schools will condemn themselves, by their own definition of intelligence, to an increasing number of stupid children. In this way, we will soon have remedial reading-readiness classes, along with remedial classes for those not yet ready for their remedial reading-readiness class.

The schools are also still promoting the idea that literacy is the richest source of aesthetic experience. This, in the face of the fact that kids are spending a billion dollars a year to buy LP records and see films. The schools are still promoting the idea that the main source of wisdom is to be found in libraries, from which most schools, incidentally, carefully exclude the most interesting books. The schools are still promoting the idea that the non-literate person is somehow not fully human, an idea that will surely endear us to the non-literate peoples of the world. (It is similar to the idea that salvation is obtainable only through Christianity—which is to say, it is untrue, bigoted, reactionary, and based on untenable premises, to boot.)

Worst of all, the schools are using these ideas to keep non-conforming youth—blacks, the politically disaffected, and the economically disadvantaged, among others—in their place. By taking this tack, the schools have become a major force for political conservatism at a time when everything else in the culture screams for rapid reorientation and change.

What would happen if our schools took the drastic political step of trying to make the new technology the keystone of education? The thought will seem less romantic if you remember that the start of the Third Millenium is only 31 years away. No one knows, of course, what would happen, but I'd like to make a few guesses. In the first place, the physical environment would be entirely different from what it is now. The school would look something like an electric circus— arranged to accommodate TV cameras and monitors, film projectors, computers, audio and video tape machines, radio, and photographic and stereophonic equipment. As he is now provided with textbooks, each student would be provided with his own still-camera, 8 mm. camera, and tape casette. The school library would contain books, of course, but at least as many films, records, videotapes, audio-tapes, and computer programs. The major effort of the school would be to assist students in achieving what has been called "multi-media literacy." Therefore, speaking, film-making, picture-taking, televising, computer-programming, listening, perhaps even music playing, drawing, and dancing would be completely acceptable means of expressing intellectual interest and competence. They would certainly be given weight at least equal to reading and writing.

Since intelligence would be defined in a new way, a student's ability to create an idea would be at least as important as his ability to classify and remember the ideas of others. New evaluation procedures would come into being, and standardized tests—the final, desperate refuge of the print-bound bureaucrat—would disappear. Entirely new methods of instruction would evolve. In fact, schools might abandon the notion of teacher instruction altogether. Whatever disciplines lent themselves to packaged, lineal, and segmented presentation would be offered through a computerized and individualized program. And students could choose from a wide variety of such programs whatever they wished to learn about. This means, among other things, that teachers would have to stop acting like teachers and find something useful to do, like, for instance, helping young people to resolve some of their more wrenching emotional problems.

In fact, a school that put electric circuitry at its center would have to be prepared for some serious damage to all of its bureaucratic and hierarchical arrangements. Keep in mind that hierarchies derive their authority from the notion of unequal access to information. Those at the top have access to more information than those at the bottom. That is in fact why they are at the top and the others, at the bottom. But today those who are at the bottom of the school hierarchy, namely, the students, have access to at least as much information about most subjects as those at the top. At present, the only way those at the top can maintain control over them is by carefully discriminating against what the students know—that is, by labelling what the students know as unimportant. But suppose cinematography was made a "major" subject instead of English literature? Suppose chemotherapy was made a "major" subject? or space technology? or ecology? or mass communication? or popular music? or photography? or race relations? or urban life? Even an elementary school might then find itself in a situation where the faculty were at the bottom and its students at the top. Certainly, it would be hard to know who are the teachers and who the learners.

And then perhaps a school would become a place where *everybody,* including the adults, is trying to learn something. Such a school would obviously be problem-centered, *and* future-centered, *and* change-centered; and, as such, would be an instrument of cultural and political radicalism. In the process we might find that our youth would also learn to read without pain and with a degree of success and economy not presently known.

I want to close on this thought: teachers of reading represent an important political pressure group. They may not agree with me that they are a sinister political group. But I should think that they would want to ask at least a few questions *before* turning to consider the *techniques* of teaching reading. These questions would be: What is reading good for? What is it better or worse than? What are my motives in promoting it? And the ultimate political question of all, "Whose side am I on?"

For Johnny's reading sake

J. MICHAEL PALARDY

ONE DOES NOT HAVE to venture far, into either the literature or the grass roots of the classroom, to find support for the contention that boys very often do less well in beginning reading than girls. Although the reasons for the failure of many boys to achieve as well as girls have not been definitely established, the difference in achievement is usually explained in one of three ways.

First, the claim is made that boys mature physically at a slower pace than girls. If mental development accompanies physical development, as child growth and development specialists say, "then the teacher of young children might expect that more boys than girls in her class would have some difficulty in learning to read" (Smith, 1963). Second, the instructional content found in many basal readers is said to be less appealing to boys than to girls (Smith and Dechant, 1961). And third, the school procedures of many teachers in the early grades, practically all of whom are women, are said to conflict more with the personality traits of boys than with those of girls (Smith and Dechant, 1961).

EXPECTATION AND ACHIEVEMENT

Without denying the validity of these explanations, there is, it would seem, another possibility. It is that some boys are less successful than girls in beginning reading because their teachers believe that they will be less successful. If this *is* a possible explanation, then its converse would also be true; namely, that other boys are as successful as girls in beginning reading because their teachers believe that they will be as successful.

In a 1967-68 study conducted in an Ohio city (Palardy, 1968), statistical support was found for this last explanation. In this study, five first-grade teachers who reported in December that they believed that boys are as successful as girls in learning to read (Group A) were matched with five teachers who reported in the same month that they believed that boys are far less successful than girls in learning to read (Group B).

In early May, the reading achievement scores of fifty-three boys and fifty-four girls whose teachers made up Group A and of fifty-eight boys and fifty-one girls whose teachers constituted Group

READING TEACHER, May 1969, vol. 22, pp. 720-724.

B were obtained from the four reading sections of the *Stanford Achievement Test*, Primary Battery Form X. Four of the variables which might have contributed to a difference in the achievement among these four groups of pupils were accounted for. First, no first-grade repeaters were included in the sample. Second, all the pupils' ages, as of January 1, 1968, ranged between six years and three months and seven years and three months. Third, only those pupils were used as subjects who scored in the average and the superior ranges on *Ginn and Company's Pre-Reading Test,* which was administered by their teachers in late September. Fourth, all the pupils attended schools which were said to be located in middle-class neighborhoods.

In Group A, which was made up of the five teachers who reportedly believed that boys are as successful as girls in learning to read, it was found that the boys did achieve as well as the girls, with the former having a mean reading achievement score of 96.5 and the latter, 96.2. In Group B, composed of the five teachers who reportedly believed that boys are far less successful than girls in learning to read, it was found that the mean score of the boys, 89.2, was in fact considerably lower than that of the girls, 96.7. When, finally, the mean scores of the four groups were compared by a two-way analysis of covariance with the IQs of the pupils controlled statistically, a significant difference ($F = 4.075$, $p < .05$) was found among them.

SELF-CONCEPT

The hypothesis is not particularly new that the achievement of pupils is affected significantly by what their teachers believe concerning the pupils' ability to succeed. Increasing attention has been given, in the literature, to this idea. However, relatively little research has been done with the expressed intention of testing it. This does not mean, however, that a rationale has not developed over the years to explain why teachers' beliefs do affect pupils' achievement. This rationale, which draws heavily on self-concept theory, involves three sequential stages.

First, when teachers believe for any of a number of reasons that certain pupils have a relatively good or poor chance of succeeding academically, over a period of time they will communicate these beliefs to their pupils. The communication of these beliefs, whether it be verbally or non-verbally, need not involve some dramatic episode, such as a first-grade teacher informing Johnny in front of the entire class that he is most certainly the poorest reader in the room. Rather, Johnny will receive the message when his teacher repeatedly gives him exasperated looks after he has rendered such a reading as "Sally *was* Spot;" or when, even in the bottom group, he seems to be asked to read less and less frequently; or when he perceives that teacher is becoming more concerned with how he holds his book than with how he pronounces the words. Even in these latter ways, then, teachers, however unintentionally and however subtly, do communicate to pupils their beliefs.

The second stage is when pupils begin to perceive and value themselves in the same way they think their teachers perceive and value them. Johnny, who thinks now that his teacher believes he is a poor reader, begins to become convinced of this himself. At this point, it can be said that Johnny's self-concept, at least as it relates to his ability to read, is fast becoming negative.

There is no lack of research to support the contention that pupils do perceive and value themselves in the same way they think their teachers perceive and value them, or, stated in a slightly different way, that pupils' self-perceptions to a considerable extent are formed through interaction with their teachers. Davidson and Lang (1965), for example, report finding a significant correlation between the self-appraisals of over 200 elementary-school pupils and their perceptions of their teachers' feelings toward them. Foshay (1953), Morse (1964), Perkins (1958), Staines (1965), Slobetz and Lund (1956), and Washburne and Heil (1960) are only a few among many other investigators whose findings reveal that teachers do have an impact, both positive and negative, on the development of their pupils' self-concepts.

The third and final stage of the rationale explaining how teachers' beliefs affect the achievement of their pupils is the logical culmination of the preceding stages. It occurs when pupils' self-perceptions regarding their ability to succeed in a curriculum area become positively associated with their actual performance in that area. Johnny, whose self-perception of his reading ability is now negative, actually begins, or in some cases continues, to underachieve in reading. This happens because he loses much of his interest in learning to read. Why should he be interested in something that makes him feel negatively about himself? Concurrent with his loss of interest is a lessening in motivation. Why should he continue to try to learn to read when practically every experience he has with reading results in real or perceived failure? Finally, Johnny begins whenever and wherever possible to avoid reading. He avoids, in other words, doing the one thing that might eventuate both in increased reading skills and in an improved reading self-concept. What is most unfortunate, of course, is that as a result of this he falls further behind in his reading skills and develops an even more negative view of his reading self.

Once again, there is much research confirming the association between the self-concept of pupils and their academic achievement. In studies published just within the past two decades, Borislow

(1965), Roth (1959), and Stevens (1956) report finding this relationship among college students; Combs (1964), Fink (1965), Lowther (1962), and Brookover, Thomas and Paterson (1965) report finding it among pupils of junior and senior high school age; and Bledsoe (1967), Hallock (1958), Spicola (1961), Walsh (1956), and Wattenberg and Clifford (1962) report its existence among elementary-school pupils.

IMPLICATIONS

If teachers' belief about their pupils' potential for learning does affect these qualitative and quantitative dimensions of that learning, as the research and the rationale presented here would seem to indicate, the implications for educators at all age levels and in all curriculum areas would certainly be more than a few. Yet it is recognized that there is still much to be learned about the relationship between the two.

Data are needed, for example, to pinpoint the different processes by which teachers communicate their beliefs to pupils. Do these processes vary according to the personality traits of teachers, according to the socioeconomic status of the schools in which they are employed, according to the methods and materials they use in the classroom, and/or according to the age levels of the pupils they teach? Of an equally important nature, when and if answers are found to the above questions, empirically validated procedures need to be devised and implemented at the pre-service and in-service levels to help teachers formulate more positive beliefs and expectations about the academic potential of some, if not all, of their pupils.

These, very briefly, are some of the tasks that lie ahead. Granted, they are ambitious. But when thought is given, for example, to the possible cumulative effects on Johnny of having consecutively three teachers who believe that he will be less successful in reading than Sally, the tasks seem worthy of pursuit. Indeed, for Johnny's sake, they must be pursued.

REFERENCES

Bledsoe, J. C. Self-concepts of children and their intelligence, achievement, interests, and anxiety. *Childhood Education*, 1967, 43, 14-18.

Borislow, B. Self-evaluation and academic achievement. In D. E. Hamachek (Ed.) *The self in growth, teaching, and learning*. Englewood Cliffs: Prentice-Hall, Inc., 1965. Pp. 464-476.

Brookover, W. B., Thomas, S., and Paterson, Ann. Self-concept of ability and school achievement. In D. E. Hamachek (Ed.) *The self in growth, teaching, and learning*. Englewood Cliffs: Prentice-Hall, Inc., 1965. Pp. 477-485.

Combs, C. F. Perception of self and scholastic underachievement in the academically capable. *The Personnel and Guidance Journal*, 1964, 43, 47-51

Davidson, Helen H., and Lang, G. Children's perceptions of their teachers' feelings toward them related to self-perception, school achievement, and behavior. In D. E. Hamachek (Ed.) *The self in growth, teaching, and learning*. Englewood Cliffs: Prentice-Hall, Inc., 1965. Pp. 424-439.

Fink, M. B. Self-concept as it relates to academic underachievement. In D. E. Hamachek (Ed.) *The self in growth, teaching, and learning*. Englewood Cliffs; Prentice-Hall, Inc., 1965. Pp. 486-492.

Foshay, A. W. Considerateness and agression: an action research study. *Educational Research Bulletin*, 1953, 32, 85-112.

Hallock, G. A. Attitudinal factors affecting achievement in reading. *Dissertation Abstracts*, 1958, *18*, 2061-2062.

Lowther, M. A. A comparison of the educational motivation, self-evaluation and classroom conduct of high and low achieving eighth grade students. *Dissertation Abstracts*, 1962, 22, 2290.

Morse, W. C. Self concept data. *National Association of Secondary Principals Bulletin*, 1964, 48, 23-27.

Palardy, J. M. The effect of teachers' beliefs on the achievement in reading of first-grade boys. Unpublished doctoral dissertation, The Ohio State University, 1968.

Perkins, H. V. Factors influencing change in children's self-concepts. *Child Development*, 1958, *19*, 203-220.

Roth, R. M. The role of self-concept in achievement. *Journal of Experimental Education*, 1959, 27, 265-281.

Slobetz, F., and Lund, Alice. Some effects of a personal development program at the fifth grade level. *Journal of Educational Research*, 1956, 49, 373-378.

Smith, H. P., and Dechant, E. V. *Psychology in teaching reading*. Englewood Cliffs: Prentice-Hall, Inc., 1961.

Smith, Nila B. *Reading instruction for today's children*. Englewood Cliffs: Prentice-Hall, Inc., 1963.

Spicola, Rose F. An investigation into seven correlates of reading achievement including the self-concept. *Dissertation Abstracts*, 1961, *21*, 2199.

Staines, J. W. The self-picture as a factor in the classroom. In D. E. Hamachek (Ed.) *The self in growth, teaching, and learning*. Englewood Cliffs: Prentice-Hall, Inc., 1965. Pp. 404-425.

Stevens, P. H. An investigation of the relationship between certain aspects of self-concept and students' academic achievement. *Dissertation Abstracts*, 1956, *16*, 2531-2532.

Walsh, Ann Marie. *Self-concept of bright boys with learning difficulties*. New York: Bureau of Publications, Teachers College, Columbia University, 1956.

Washburne, C., and Heil, Louis M. What characteristics of teachers affect children's growth? *The School Review*, 1960, 68, 420-428.

Wattenberg, W. W., and Clifford, Clare. *Relationship of the self-concept to beginning achievement in reading*. (Cooperative Research Project No. 377) Washington, D.C.: United States Office of Education, 1962.

SECTION II

THE READING PROCESS: "WHAT IT'S ALL ABOUT!"

A paradigm: current approaches and programs in reading

HEATH W. LOWRY

THE DEVELOPMENT of curriculum models has become a popular and valuable means to help the teacher view the structure of a particular discipline or teaching area. At a glance, he can see *1*] the various components and facets making up an instructional rationale, 2] the implementation of a specific program, and *3*] the teaching strategies consistent with the entire plan. Such schematic devices have been developed for many of the current teaching fields.

Contemporary reading instruction is probably as complex in theory and structure as any single area of elementary curriculum. Yet, little has been done to help the classroom teacher or the graduate student visualize the over-all scope of the entire program. As a result, a blurred picture and a confused hesitancy often cloud the total clear focus needed in today's teaching of reading. With this need in mind, the author has attempted to plot the basic levels of a schema to show as clearly as possible the *1*] modalities of learning through which reading takes place, 2] the strands of methodology of reading instruction, *3*] the current approaches to the teaching of reading, and *4*] the administrative schedules by which the instructional program is implemented. The following paradigm reflects chiefly the early years of reading instruction, beginning reading through the primary grades. Some implications and practices, however, may be traceable through the whole continuum of instruction.

LEARNING MODALITIES

Authorities have described reading as having a sensory as well as a perceptual process. Both ideas involve the impinging of sensory stimulii and the reaction of the organism to awarenesses of these stimuli. These responses are naturally affected by the experience, knowledge, and condition of the individual in his present "life space" as he views the total.

THE READING TEACHER, 1970, Vol. 24, pp. 120-123.

The concept most relevant for reading teachers in this first level of the model is that instruction can be successfully channeled through any one, or combination of several, of the modalities as shown in the paradigm: the visual, the auditory, and/or the kinesthetic-tactile. It should be noted, however, that research has indicated that there are strengths of modality through which the process takes place more easily and permanently in various learners. This implies that it is important for teachers to know that modality and make use of the open channel for effective instructional approach and practices.

CURRICULUM MODEL FOR BEGINNING READING INSTRUCTION

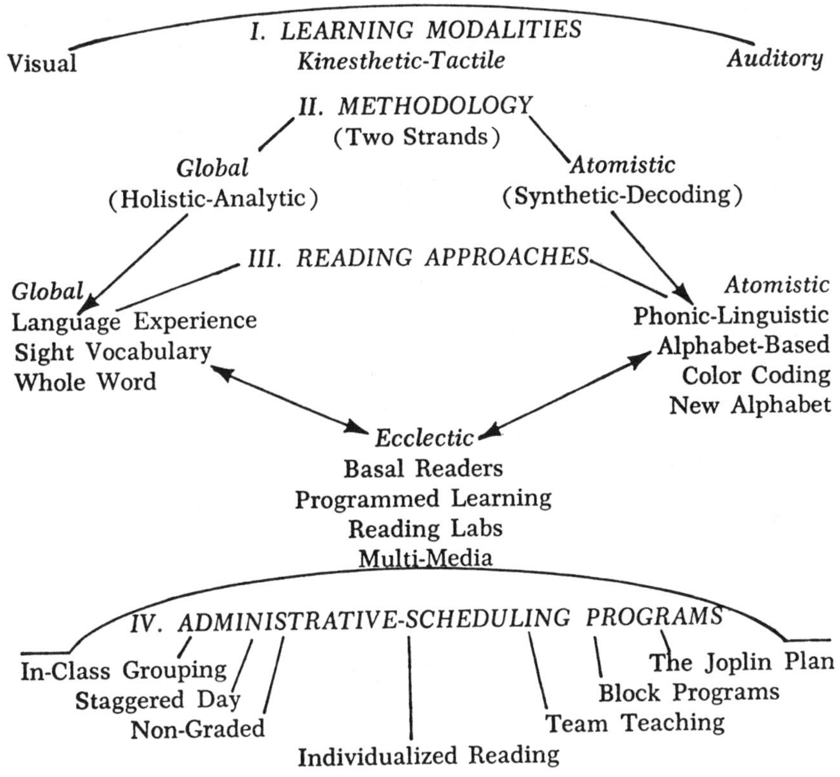

READING METHODOLOGY

The second level of the schema deals with the two strands of methodology in reading instruction. These represent either a gestalt, holistic method, or in contrast, a "from fragment to total" method, an artificial, atomistic technique. This means that, in beginning reading, the teacher will make use of materials and strategies using *1*] whole words, meaning segments, or complete sentences, or 2] the building blocks of language, the graphic symbols or phoneme combinations which make up the structure of language sounds and words.

Because English is not a particularly phonemic language, and with a sincere desire to make reading instruction a meaningful experience, American teachers have, in general, for some decades used a global, whole word, approach to beginning instruction.

On the other hand, reading has been traditionally taught for centuries in many areas via a synthetic methodology in which words were learned not by memory from seeing them a sufficient number of times to recognize them but by learning the phoneme-grapheme relationship and thus being able to unlock unfamiliar reading words. The child has learned the graphic symbols of his particular orthography and has then assembled them in proper sound sequence to form known words. This is reading from small parts and building toward the complete whole word, then phrases, and then sentences.

CURRENT READING APPROACHES

The third phase of the model covers those current approaches to beginning reading which are representative and reputable. It is often difficult to identify a particular reading approach as to its belonging to either pure category or methodology: holistic or atomistic. Those who have developed programs of reading instruction have frequentlv made use of a combined or eclectic method of teaching reading. However, several approaches can be specified as being oriented chiefly in one or the other of the two main strands.

Global approaches

The Language Experience Approach to reading makes use of a total language learning, hence can be placed in the holistic family. Any teaching of reading which makes use of a strategy dealing primarily with whole words and/or sight vocabulary methodology belongs in this strand. Many of the well-known basal reader programs have been global in their beginning of formal reading instruction.

Atomistic approaches

Any alphabet-based approach in beginning reading, including some of the new alphabets such as i.t.a., takes a parts-to-whole tack. There are also several phonics-linguistics programs of instruction which belong in this atomistic category. Any of the coded systems which make use of color and diacritical markings should be included under this heading as well.

Eclectic approaches

Four combination types of reading instruction are identified in the model. These make use of both global and atomistic methodology early or throughout the development of their programs. They are basal reading programs, programmed learning approaches, developmental reading labs, and multi-media programs which make use of all varieties of visual and auditory and manipulative educational materials and devices. Generally speaking, these four types of reading approaches make use of a combination of learning modalities as well as strands of methodology.

ADMINISTRATIVE SCHEDULING

The fourth level of the paradigm is concerned with the implementation of the first three phases. Through the years various plans, programs, and schedules have been developed to improve or enhance the reading instruction being undertaken. Seven such plans have been identified. These are chiefly involved in providing for individuation. Although they have frequently been referred to as "approaches to reading," the term is a misnomer, for they are mere scheduling conveniences for carrying out learning programs.

The mechanics of these devices fall into four groupings: *1*] those which group students—heterogeneously or homegeneously—by ability or reading level; 2] those which provide for numbers of students to be taught at various periods of time, *3*] those which allow students to progress through levels of difficulty or time periods, and *4*] those which make for additional personalized and self-selective reading programs. Some of these plans are modified and combined to meet needs of particular school districts or areas, but can be recognized as implementive, organizational plans developed to facilitate the reading program.

CONCLUSIONS

At best the Model is an attempt to clarify current trends and innovative practices by helping the reading person to view the total program. Within the structure, there is ample scope for additional curriculum modifications, combinations, and implementations. The person interested in his own philosophy of education or learning theory will see possibilities of interjecting practice and theory consistent with the skeletal outline, and will be able to identify and relate current practices with specific or eclectic educational theory.

Let's throw out reading!

ROBERT J. IRELAND

After elementary and college level teaching, Robert Ireland now serves as coordinator of language arts for the Metropolitan Separate School Board, Toronto. Having read this article, one reviewer responded, ". . . he certainly challenges me to think about my way of doing things."

A FEW years ago, Jerome Bruner (1960) caused many rut-bound educators to shake themselves out of a long slumber. His alarm clock was this hypothesis: "Any subject can be taught effectively in some intellectually honest form to any child at any stage of development." Many have since pulled the blankets of educational jargon over their heads and gone back to sleep. One of the words in that jargon is "reading" and its misuse is harming many children. This article will hopefully reawaken those whose verbalism is keeping them from thinking effectively.

Though no equal to Bruner's insight, intelligence, and experience, my hypothesis about reading is "Assuming word recognition skills, any child can read any book with some degree of comprehension."

What would happen if teachers took this hypothesis to heart? Teachers in universities, secondary schools, and the upper divisions of elementary schools would have to stop saying, "The students can't read the textbooks." Instead these teachers would say, "These students can't read the textbooks with the degree of comprehension that I expect."

The difference between the two statements is that the teacher puts himself into the latter. This could be the start of a self-examination. Perhaps we expect too much from reading. It is, after all, only one of several methods of gathering information.

Every author has his own definition of reading, carefully written to indicate his own biases. And all definitions are suitable to a point. For example, Albert Harris' definition: "Reading is the meaningful interpretation of verbal symbols." (Harris, 1961) This is a precise, workable definition of

THE READING TEACHER, 1973, Vol. 26, pp. 584-588.

the process but it does not answer the critical question for teachers whose children are beyond beginning reading: "How much meaning?"

The answer to that question depends on the teacher himself and his pupils. The amount of meaning children derive from a printed page greatly depends on their purpose for reading, which is related to their experience and motivation. The teacher must clearly state the purpose for which he wants the children to read until they can set their own purposes.

Here again the teacher becomes involved in his pupils' reading and takes some responsibility for their success or failure. This is not the case if the teacher simply says, "They can't read." This point of view leaves the teacher out and merely specifies pupil failure.

Positive self-concept

We should treat a child's learning to read the way we treat a child's learning to walk. Think of what happens with the latter. When he takes that first staggering step, the rest of the family is ecstatic. "He's walking!" The word flashes through the neighbourhood: "He's walking!" And from that moment on, we never say he can't walk. Even though he continues to propel himself by crawling 90 percent of the time for a while, we are confident that he can walk. We heap praise upon him, rearrange the furniture so that he can go from piece to piece successfully, and never doubt his future achievement. He catches this from us and works diligently at his new ability. When he is ten years old, if he slips and falls on ice, or trips over a curb, or gets tangled up in his own feet, we don't get all excited and say he can't walk. We buy him skates or shoes that fit and encourage him on his way.

A similar analogy could be made with the development of speech, but not with listening. We do accuse children of not being able to listen. Isn't it strange that, although the fault may well be with the initiator of the message, we blame the receiver?

For example, a nonreader looks at the first word of this paragraph, is unable to identify the marks even as letters of the alphabet. A reader sees the first word of this paragraph and says "for." He can make nothing else out of the whole paragraph, but he has read in the same way that a tottering infant walks.

To measure this child's ability, first present him with an instructional objective that he can achieve: *Given a paragraph beginning with "for," the child will correctly say the first word of the paragraph.* Secondly, present a question that this child can successfully answer: *What is the first word in this paragraph?*

Ridiculous? Only if it's ridiculous to define objectives so precisely that we can see every bit of achievement a child makes and only if it's ridiculous to ask a child a question that he can successfully answer.

Rather than define "reading," then, we can say that only a child who gets absolutely nothing from a printed message is a nonreader. If he can do anything more than that, he is a reader; the onus is on the teacher to adapt his expectations of success to suit the child's ability. And if we expect him to gain a lot of information from material for which he has little experience and/or motivation to read, we will be sadly disappointed.

Most children beyond the primary level have developed word recognition skills. They have not mastered them, to be sure, but they have learned some word attack skills. By the earlier definition, then, they are readers. If the teacher asks the right questions, these children can read any book. And it need not be on a simple level.

For example, an intermediate division teacher has a class of children for whom English is a second language. They have been in an English language school for several years but language has been a continuing struggle for them. Not surprisingly, they detest reading. Their teacher is in her first year and hasn't yet learned all the "no-no's" about reading. She still thinks these children can read, so she decides they will read Dickens. She gathers up all the Dickens stories she can find and the books pass through the class like wildfire.

How do the children do it? The teacher asks only one question. "Find out who the people are and what they are like." In discussions she asks how the students know what the people in the books are like. Their understanding and, most of all, their enjoyment is shown in drawings of characters and scenes, dramatizations of incidents, and informal sharing of ideas from the books.

Many experienced teachers would have looked at this class and started searching for high interest/low vocabulary books, reading comprehension exercises, reading labs, skill development workbooks—and the children would have continued to resist reading. But the young teacher capitalized on what her children knew about people and on their adolescent curiosity about how people behave.

Reading in the content subjects

Often the child who tries the hardest suffers most in reading textbooks. He knows he must read carefully and remember all the information. He starts into a textbook chapter on the Plains Indians. The first paragraph names nine different tribes. He rereads and "studies" trying to memorize all nine. The second paragraph names five rivers and two mountain ranges. Again, "study," memorize. By this time he's getting pretty well fed up with the Plains Indians and with reading in general. The next paragraph describes the buffalo. It is high shouldered, shaggy. He thinks it looks like his brother and then goes on. The buffalo has hair like a lion and a hump like a camel. Picture that! By this time, he has been reading for fifteen minutes and has covered three paragraphs. The teacher now orders the books closed and the following dialogue takes place.

Teacher: *Describe the homes of the Plains Indians.*

Pupil: They lived in tepees.

Teacher: *Well, of course. You knew that in Grade Three. What else can you tell me about them?*

Pupil: *I can't think of anything else.*

Teacher: *Why not? Didn't you read the book?*

Pupil: *I didn't get that far.*

Teacher's conclusion: *He can't read the textbooks.*

Pupil's conclusion: *I can't read.*

They are both wrong. Since the teacher's first question had to do with the Indians' homes, let's assume that that was the thing she really wanted to discuss.

Suppose she had asked that question *before* the pupil started to read. When he read about names of tribes, rivers, and mountains, he would not have stopped to memorize. He would have reached the portion of the text dealing with homes and would have read more carefully then. And if the teacher had given a bit of information or had asked some stimulating questions about Indian homes the pupil would have done even better. This is not a new idea. It's just the guided reading lesson applied to a textbook.

Textbook problems

No wonder children have trouble reading textbooks. In the primary division they have a reader with a controlled vocabulary. In the junior division and above they have a reader in social studies, a reader in math, a reader in science, and so on. The further they go in school the more "readers" they have. Each subject has its own specialized vocabulary and some have their own specialized formats for presenting informa tion. Pupils need help in learning these new vocabularies and new methods of organizing information.

The teacher's aim when using a textbook should be merely to emphasize the main ideas. There may be only one main idea in several pages of text, probably not more than three or four in an average chapter. In helping pupils find the main idea, the question "What is the main idea of this section?" is useless. The teacher must decide the main idea according to his purpose in teaching the lesson. He then asks a question, the answer to which is the main idea of the portion of text at hand. Details, inferences, and implications are arrived at through discussion of the main idea, and what a pupil doesn't get from the printed page is learned from his classmates.

The young teacher previously mentioned asked her class one question about the Dickens stories. They had read for that purpose only, skipping and skimming parts that seemed irrelevant. Their understanding was shared and enlarged through discussion with their classmates.

We don't deny a child the chance to listen to Mozart or Brahms because "he won't understand it" or because "it's above his listening level". We let him listen and let him get from it what he can. The phony exactitude of reading tests has made us think we can really measure reading ability. We cannot any more than we can measure what a child gets from a Mozart sonata or a Simon and Garfunkel song. That word "reading" is making many deny children the chance to learn from and enjoy the printed word.

Reading and thinking

Many articles state the close interrelationship of reading and thinking. The two are inseparable as any uses of language and thought are inseparable. But if we are sure children can't read, then we often give up and say they can't think either. We take the attitude of an uncle of mine who lived in a cabin in Northern Ontario. When he was thinking about what to have for breakfast, he liked to say, "If we had bacon, we could have bacon and eggs. But there's no eggs." Our tendency is to say,

"If these kids could read, they could read and think. But they can't think."

Every child can think. Every child who can listen and speak can learn to read. Focus on what children can do and adapt programs to that. Give success a chance to accumulate and watch the results in a child's total personality and especially in his motivation to read. We can't change the children overnight nor can we change the textbooks overnight. But we can change our expectations of the children we teach. We can turn our attention to motivation and experience and away from "reading skills". Give it a try and discover some Pygmalions in the classroom.

Let's throw out "reading" and "reading levels" and "reading exercises". Let's talk instead about "degree of comprehension" or some such term that will force us as teachers into every bit of experience that a child has with the printed page. Then we will look on reading as only one way of learning—giving, listening, speaking, touching, smelling, and tasting their proper place in the learning situations we create. We will more carefully consider a child's experience and motivation and set purposes for him and with him in his encounters with written materials. Then, if we ask the right questions, we'll realize that, assuming word recognition skills, any child can read any book successfully.

References

Bruner, Jerome S. *The Process of Education.* New York: Vintage, 1960.

Harris, Albert J. *How to Increase Reading Ability*, 4th ed. New York: McKay, 1961, p. 8.

IMAGINATION AND EXPERIENCE IN LEARNING TO READ

BARBARA ARNSTINE

Once upon a time there was a little boy who reached the age for learning how to read. Now this little boy did not know that he couldn't read—in fact, he thought he read every day. He read his mother's face for storm warnings when he asked for a third cookie. He read the coins his grandfather gave him, since coins were tricky (the biggest wasn't necessarily the best). He read "NBC" and "CBS" and "My Favorite Martian" as they were flashed on the television screen. He thought he knew how to read but evidently he didn't, because he was going to learn it in school, and everybody was very excited about it—his mother, his teacher, his schoolmates.

So one day the little boy was given a book. And he worked very hard. For one thing, he sat still, which is a very hard thing to do. It seems that this "reading" business required sitting still, although the little boy did not understand that at all. In his view nothing required sitting still except doctors, dentists, and church—all very suspect activities. For another thing, all the children were to do this thing called reading together—although it was a very queer kind of together where they were not allowed to talk to one another or tickle or punch. It was a very unfriendly together.

But he managed to do all this work, and to hold the book right side up, and to find the word on the bottom of the page and to be told, or recognize or discover (whichever you prefer), that the word was "Look." Now the little boy was a very obedient boy, and when he was told to look, he looked. Only there wasn't much to see—just an ordinary face very much like every other face, but not moving or anything. So he tried the next page. And it said "Look" again. And so did the third.

Then the teacher asked him to read to the rest of the class. This was exciting, because he was allowed to get up. He was moving at last. So he held the book and said very loudly, "Look Look Look." But in his excitement he forgot to turn the pages. Alas, it seems that turning the pages is part of reading, so the little boy did not do well at all. He was very sad. But the teacher smiled brightly and said he was a Bluebird. Many of his friends were Bluebirds. It meant that they would have to do the reading thing again.

* * * * * * * *

This little boy did not live happily ever after. Yet you notice that this little boy had really very few problems in settling down to read. He had problems that we smile indulgently about, rather than take seriously—like sitting still. Nevertheless, the work involved in overcoming these problems was sufficient to make the boy doubt the advisability of any future effort at reading. Because the reading simply wasn't worth it. It wasn't exciting, interesting, meaningful—all those things we value in the material *we* read. Another way of putting it would be to say that the material was not "imaginative." It is this problem of imaginative material, or imagination in reading which we will consider in this paper.

The problem of imaginative reading material grows in proportion to the difficulties that children have in settling down to read. Our example involves simple diffi-

EDUCATION, 1972, Vol. 92, No. 3, pp. 81-86.

culties—obstacles that teachers are often able to eliminate through careful planning. But teachers are not able to cope with the difficulties that many children face when they are asked to learn to read—difficulties such as a hunger headache from no breakfast, exhaustion from being up too late at night where there is no privacy or peace for sleep, and a teacher who talks and looks like she is from another planet.

It is a serious social question whether some of the difficulties that children face can be overcome—whether we can expect children to learn anything, given the conditions under which they are asked to learn it. And it could be argued that that problem is as much the responsibility of the teacher as anyone else. But whatever the conditions, teachers are expected to help children to learn to read in a very direct way, every school day. To focus our professional attention on that immediate problem is not to ignore the conditions that sometimes make it insurmountable. Difficult conditions are not to be used as an excuse for poor teaching. If we focus on the difficulties that well-fed, well-rested and verbally astute children have in learning to read, we may find that we can better teach children who come from different environments as well. To note that any child has difficulty when he encounters the strange activity we call reading, is not an invitation to list the difficulties and lament the lack of social change that could ameliorate the worst of them. It is rather an opportunity to investigate the characteristics of reading that might make overcoming those difficuties seem like a worthwhile effort to the child. For it seems reasonable to suppose that in the best of worlds, children will have habits and desires that will have to be changed when they learn to read. If what they are reading does not seem worthwhile, then chances are they will not learn to read with ease or enjoyment. We cannot make a society in which children can learn to read dull and useless books. While our responsibilities to society are debatable, our responsibilities to children in schools are quite clear. If the books they are reading are not worth reading, it is no one's fault but our own.

Our notions about how to make reading material worthwhile have been very crude indeed. Two alternatives have been offered us. The first is that reading is worth it when it is fantastic, exciting, removed from the realities of everyday life. Advocates of this point of view feel that a child's reading should offer him heroes, danger, and lots of imagery. We shall call this the "Dragon" point of view. The second alternative is that reading should have "meaning," and this meaning is found in the record of the child's present experiences. It is familiar and comfortably ordinary—in tune with the everyday happenings of the child's world. We will call this the "Backyard" position.

Both views have a great deal to offer, but in their narrow and mutually exclusive character, it seems that they misconstrue the problem. If we consider the limitations of the Dragon view, and then the Backyard view, we will see how an exclusive attention to one position would seriously limit our use of reading materials. Our understanding of these limitations may enable us to see other bases on which we can select reading materials for children.

The Dragon camp is bent on entertainment at any cost—and it bases its decision on an important hypothesis: if people are going to do any reading at all, they are going to do it because they enjoy it. In our anxiety over counting vocabulary lists, determining the appropriate "common" words, and disputing over phonics, sight-reading, and I.T.A., we often forget that reading is fundamentally a pleasure for those who do it. Of course we can torment children through fear of failure and thereby pressure students into reading dull and unimaginative text books for a number of years. But if the test of schooling is what people do when they leave school, then we have evidence to show us that as soon as the artificial restraints of grades and college are lifted, a great many people happily give up the distasteful activity of reading. Thus, if reading is not intrinsically enjoyable, no amount of skill will induce a person to read once the external pressures are removed. And if a person does not believe that the external pressures are appropriate, or apply to him, then no amounl of skill-training is going to get him to learn to read unless he likes it. If a student is black and poor, and already tracked into oblivion by our "expert" testing, then no amount of skill-training is going to get him reading, unless we also provide the opportunity for personal enjoyment.

But the Dragon camp can have a very narrow view of what constitutes enjoyment. Pleasure can be viewed as mere pleasure, as an appeal to interests and desires at their present immature level, as we see in most television shows and comic books. If schoo's had no responsibility to the young, except to keep them enclosed and intact nine months of the year, then we could let this kind of pleasurable entertainment baby-sit for us. But schoo!s are places that are supposed to "educate." And of all the things that we might mean by that term, one of the ideas it conveys is some sort of change in the learner. Mere pleasure leaves us exactly where we are—it doesn't take us any place. It makes no change in us, whether in our outlook, our information or our values. A passing excitement *is* exciting, and that is important —but it's not educative.

It is this educative concern that motivates the Backyard camp. Their purpose is to get the student reading so that he can get on to the important tasks of acquiring information and skills. The watchword of this camp is efficiency—how to help the child acquire a useful and large vocabulary in the shortest time possible. The key to this method is to give the child stories about familiar things—to teach him the names of his environment. But this practical aim is achieved in a very prosaic way, since the aspect of our personal environment that we find most interesting is the one which is unique and different. The Backyard camp looks for things which are common, and finds things which are dull. A dog who could be anybody's dog is not a real dog. A real dog is particular, unusual, not ordinary at all. Poor Spot has a name, but no character—no child misses him or wonders about his future. It takes great artistic talent to make the familiar sufficiently dramatic for our attention—lacking that art, many basal readers are merely prosaic and dull.

Do people ever read for practical reasons? Of course they do. My cookbooks are not great art, but I read them very carefully. The reason is quite simple: because I am doing something, or about to do something. Practical reading is very important in the context of our practical activities. But the Backyard camp has taken practical reading and placed it in an activity—less setting. Reading carefully, reading familiar words, reading quickly, these are efforts that make sense when one is engaged in some purposeful activity. But if you are just sitting and reading, then care, swiftness and familiarity are all artificial restraints imposed by the teacher.

One result of practical reading can be seen in many elementary schools. Children try to find a purpose for the activity, since its content provides no intrinsic purpose. So children adopt whatever adult purpose is available, and the on'y adult purpose they know about is "learning to read" which means getting into a high reading group, increasing your vocabulary, etcetera. Many children know *how* they are doing in reading (i.e., their scores, their report cards), but they don't know *what* they are doing—they don't go home to tell Mother about the latest story. Consequently we have a situation where children are learning to read, not because they like it, or it is worthwhile, but because adults want them to learn to read. When the adults no longer can control their purposes, the children (who will be older) will surely stop "learning to read."

But the sins of the Dragon camp and the Backyard camp are not sins of incompatibility. It is quite possible to devise reading that is pleasurable and practical, enjoyable and meaningful. We can do it if we investigate children's experience a little more closely.

When a child experiences something he can be confused and disorganized in his responses. When he does this he looks so much like all the other animals of the world, we call animal efforts by a similar name—trial and error behavior.

In other situations, a child's experiencing can be merely routine. He does something the same way—as a mechanical act, like tying your shoes. When children read aloud, it is striking how mechanical they sound, and how often they search for the next word in a trial and error fashion, with no sense of what has gone before,

But a child has still another way of experiencing that is significantly different from random or habitual behavior. This responsiveness grows out of the child's ability to use his past as he copes with his present world. Now everyone immediately gets a past—but it takes continuous learning to know how to use it. First of all, in order to use it, you have to remember it. Secondly, you have to organize it—to remember selectively and coherently. Language is the great medium by which we remember and organize our past. Thus, as a child learns language, he learns a vehicle through which he can select from, remember, and use his past experience.

The past is important, however, only as it comes into play when we deal with an immediate present. The present can be obstinate and difficult, or it can be delightful, depending on our desires. But what gives meaning to the present is our power to shape it through the use of our past. The absence of a past that is rich and useful would be like waking up in a two dimensional world. Our past breathes life into the present, so that we can shape the present into the practical effort that our future hopes require, or, if we are freed from future purposes, we can enjoy the present for its own sake.

The effort that organizes the past so that we can use it to deal with problems in the present, or simply to enrich the present in a pleasurable way, is commonly called imagination. For when we think of activities that we call imaginative, we can find an array of efforts, from children's play to the creative responses of adults in problematic situations. We usually applaud the imaginative response, whether it be charming, as children involved in an elaborate game of make-believe, or useful, as a solution to a difficult problem.

Whether make-believe or art or practical effort, the imaginative response is one that organizes the past so that the present is enriched with meanings. These meanings can be delightful or useful, or both, depending upon the situation.

When we speak of a child's imagination, we sometimes deride it as a fantastic, unrealistic response, such as the claim that there are ghosts in the closet. But even our derision is tempered with the understanding that to identify ghosts in the closet is to define and locate ones fears in such a way that they can be dealt with. The explanation is given to Mother, and Mother has her own methods for exorcising ghosts. A claim of ghosts in the closet may be far-fetched, but it is a claim that promotes action and help from others. It is a social communication. A child that is namelessly, wordlessly afraid cannot help himself by giving place and location to the problem. And we cannot help him because he has not communicated.

Thus a child's imagination can often be understood as a form of social response. He learns through contact with others, to deal with the world imaginatively. "Tomorrow" is a very imaginative word. A child who faces it as a response to his requests needs a past of waiting for things to know how long tomorrow will be in coming. He must project his desires into the future. And he must decide if this is tolerable. All this happens in the moment of exchange. Mother says, "No, we will go to the park tomorrow." The child doesn't think it all out, decide what "tomorrow" is, and then decide how he feels about it. He reacts instantly. The meaning of tomorrow *is*, right there, what he thinks and feels about it. A five-year-old told me very seriously that "tomorrow is a bad word." For him, that is part of its meaning. He responds imaginatively to it.

If we can see a child's imagination as a social effort, then the imaginative response is one that involves the person's past in helping him to understand the present and to shape it into a future. Reading expands our pasts in a pleasurable way, by making the familiar new and sometimes beautiful —but always dramatic. Reading gives the child a new present to refer to—whether it is a present set of directions for the model airplane he sees in the future, or the vicarious present of being a hero in a new and exciting place. The child reshapes his future through what comes to him from this present—he now knows how much wood to buy for the plane, or he knows that being an Indian is a difficult and oppressive burden in 20th century America. Thus reading, whether pleasurable or practical, or both, has social consequences. The child's imagination is affected—his future reshaped, his past enriched. No mechanical test of vocabulary words is a substitute for this experience and no amount of coercion can create it.

As we bring our two camps together, we can conclude that any book in order to be an experience must be somewhat familiar. But the familiar as social is not common or prosaic. Does this mean that every child has to have his own unique book, based on his own unique experiences? Not if our common experiences can be seen as interesting ones. For humans can be said to share very exciting commonalities—exciting in that although situations are unique, we can experience love, hate, fear, pride, and other similar emotions. The *things* we share in common—like shoelaces —may be very dull. But the emotions that we socially experience and commonly share in our language are exciting and meaningful to all of us.

This does mean that every child has to have a past that is sufficiently rich in experiences for us to draw on them. The sad truth is that some children are coming to school with a set of experiences that are either too different or too limited for us to draw on. If the past is not there, then we have to make it for these children. To put it quite bluntly, perhaps we should abandon our dismal efforts at remedial reading instruction and instead get some remedial experiences going for children.

These "remedial" experiences will have to be social and emotional in character, however. It is not enough to teach children to manipulate middle-class objects, such as expensive silverware in an elaborate restaurant. Chances are they won't want to read about it afterwards, either. The kind of experiences that are rewarding are those that draw on our common store of emotions and the social contexts that produce them. Children need to talk to one another, to give and receive physical affection from adults and from peers. Whether at a restaurant or a baseball game, the child has to be in a setting that he wants to talk about, to exclaim over, to ask questions about. When we talk about children who are "deprived," we are usually referring to the luxurious objects that fill our middle-class environments. But what interests us in reading is a deprived imagination. If a child's imagination is limited, looking at objects after the fashion of a tourist will not improve it. As we have already discussed, imagination develops in social contexts that are pleasurable and rewarding, rich in emotions and the language we hold in common. Children stuffed in a bus and told to sit quietly while they are taken out to the country to stare at cows are not having the kind of experience that contributes to a rich or remembered past. Indeed, they are getting little more "experience" than the cows get who stare at *them*! We may think we are increasing their vocabulary, but the mere seeing of objects, however concrete, is not enough. The part of the world we remember is the part we *do* something with, in a practical way, or the part we enjoy and value. Our past is made up of things we used and things we loved—not things we looked at.

If we cannot provide the appropriate experiences then we'd better find some other books. No experience is going to turn a black child into a white child, so we have to have books about black children. No experience is going to change a child's house, his family, his peers—so we have to have books about street gangs, tenements, and mothers without fathers. If we want kids to read about justice, and freedom, and honesty, and love, and clear lakes, and polar bears, then we have a lot to come up with in the way of experiences.

If these are all familiar, and part of the past of the child, why read about it? Simply because something new is said, something that makes all these experiences either more beautiful and dramatic, or more useful. So dogs which are seldom useful must become more beautiful, with names like Horatio and a mysterious habit of guarding bridges. And that which is practically written must become immediately useful in shaping the child's purposes like having a chance to build a model airplane after you read about it.

Thus, if we want a child to read carefully, precisely, with maximum retention of selected material, then we must give him an opportunity to do something with what he has read, something he wants to do. And if we want to capture him in the immediate enjoyment of a story, then we must find the art that enhances the familiar, and that familiarity must have roots in the child's own experiences and our common emotions.

The same rules apply to all children when we teach them to read. Unfortunately, rich children probably haven't been learning to read any better than poor ones. They have simply been more dutiful and obedient to our external pressures. The poor child, with nothing to lose, is telling us the truth when he won't do it for those external goals. If he reads, he will read forever, for its own sake, and, in the doing, for much more. The stubborn, unruly, disrespectful child is our greatest asset. His interests will suggest to us activities that are useful through which we can promote careful and practical reading. Through him we will find the stories that are exciting, pleasurable and intrinsically worthwhile. Perhaps we can encourage a reconsideration of reading to the point where we will fill our classrooms with books that relate to children's ongoing activities and that give him pleasure. If we do so, we may find that our adult concerns with grouping, phonics, and vocabulary lists are really of secondary importance in achieving our aims. For if children continue to read after they grow up, then this monumental success will far outweigh the carefully researched discriminations that we have found in the teaching of words and syllables. It would be wise not to let our present concerns with the minutiae of research distract our attention from our primary goal.

Linguistically speaking, why language experience?

MARYANNE HALL

MaryAnne Hall is an associate professor in the University of Maryland's Department of Early Childhood-Elementary Education, and an officer in IRA's Language Experience interest group. Not content simply to list benefits, she presents seven "statements of linguistic rationale" for using this well-known approach with beginning readers.

THE language experience approach has increasingly been employed for initial reading instruction in the last decade. In recent years, there has been growing interest in the implications of linguistic study for the teaching of reading. The term "linguistics" as related to reading instruction often signifies a beginning approach based on phoneme-grapheme correspondence through the presentation of a carefully controlled vocabulary illustrating selected spelling patterns. However, linguistics is used here with a broader application. Since reading is communication through written language, all reading, therefore, is linguistic. Knowledge about language supplied by linguists should lead to reading instruction based on accurate information about the reading process.

The relationship of reading to spoken language is basic to a linguistic definition of reading. This relationship is also basic to teaching reading through the language experience approach. Seven statements of the linguistic rationale for the language experience approach are expressed below in terms of the beginning reader.

The beginning reader must be taught to view reading as a communication process. Language experience reading is communication-centered. Attention is on communication through the medium of print just as in speaking and listening the emphasis is on communication through the medium of speech. In beginning reading, children should feel a need to communicate naturally through print just as before learning to read they had felt the need to

THE READING TEACHER, 1972, Vol. 25, pp. 328-331.

communicate through speech. A creative and competent teacher must provide the stimuli and opportunities for children to communicate in reading and writing.

The content of personally composed stories involves concepts within the scope of children's background knowledge and interests. Communication is present as children react while discussing their ideas, as they write or watch the teacher write those ideas, and as they then read their ideas. Comprehension is present since children do understand that which they first wrote.

The beginning reader is a user of language (Goodman, 1969). The spoken language which the child possesses is his greatest asset for learning written language. The normal child from an adequate home environment has mastered the patterns of his native language by the time of school entrance. This is not to overlook the fact that his linguistic facility is by no means complete. He has much to absorb in language flexibility and elaboration; still, he has more than sufficient linguistic ability to learn to read.

In discussions of reading readiness, great attention has been given to the experience background of children, and less to their language background. When attention has been given to language factors, usually that attention has been to the extent of vocabulary and general language facility in expressing and understanding spoken language instead of how this facility operates in learning to read. The child who learned spoken language in the preschool years displayed an amazing feat of linguistic performance. We should make it possible for him to learn to read with equal ease and to draw upon his existing linguistic background in doing so.

The beginning reader should understand the reading process as one of consciously relating print to oral language. As the beginning reader works with print he changes the unfamiliar graphic symbols to familiar oral language. Goodman (1968) defines reading as the processing of language information in order to reconstruct a message from print.

In the language experience approach the child finds translating print into speech greatly simplified since he is reading that which he first said. The message is easily reconstructed when the reader is also the author. In the beginning stages reading instruction must be geared to ensure success for the learner. The ease with which children can read their language should be capitalized on in language experience instruction.

Downing (1969) reports in studies of five and six year olds' views of reading that their conceptions of language are different from those of their teachers. Terminology such as "word," "sentence," "sound," and "letter" was unclear to the children in his research. He comments on the need to provide ". . . language experiences and activities which (a) *orient* children correctly to the true purposes of reading and writing, and (b) enable children's natural thinking processes *to generate understanding* of the technical concepts of language."

The beginning reader should incorporate the learning of writing with the learning of reading. Relating the written language code to the spoken code was discussed earlier as the task of the beginning reader. Learning the written code involves decoding — going from print to speech—and encoding—

going from speech to print. In the language experience approach, writing is a natural corollary of reading as a child first watches the recording of thought he has dictated and as he progresses gradually to writing independently.

The integration of decoding and encoding should provide reinforcement in both processes. In studies of preschool readers, Durkin (1970) reported that interest in writing often preceded interest in reading. Dykstra (1968) reported in the National First Grade Studies that a writing component added to reading programs enhanced achievement in reading.

The beginning reader should learn to read with materials written in his language patterns. The language experience approach does use materials written with the language of the reader for whom they are intended. Reading materials should always convey meaning to a child in natural language phrasing which sounds right and familiar to him—not necessarily "right" to the ears of a Standard English speaker. For children who do not speak Standard English, the language of standard materials does not match their spoken language. While there are special materials written in nonstandard dialects, these materials are not available to all teachers of nonstandard-speaking children. Also, these materials may not fit all children in a group where they are being used. An often overlooked fact is that the limited preprimer language is also unlike the oral language of a child who does use Standard English.

The point to be remembered here is that the nonstandard speaker is a user of language. The absence of mastery of Standard English need not delay the beginning reading instruction when language experience materials are used. The teaching of oral Standard English will be another part of the total language program.

It is recommended that the teacher record the syntactical patterns of the children as spoken but using standard spelling. For example, if the child says "des" for "desk," the word will be written "desk," but if the child says, "My brother, he . . . ," this pattern will be written. The language communicates, and there is sufficient language to be used for teaching beginning reading.

The beginning reader should learn to read meaningful language units. In language experience reading, children are dealing with thought units from the flow of their speech. They are not dealing with a phoneme-grapheme unit or a word unit, but with a larger piece of language. From the total running flow of speech of others in their environment they learned to talk. The child gradually learned to pick words of very high meaning, "Mommy," "Daddy," "me," and others. From one-word utterances the child progressed to two-word patterns and built his linguistic knowledge from hearing natural speech around him.

In reading from language experience, children learn to read using the meaning-bearing patterns of language. They will be exposed to reading material which is not controlled in vocabulary and which does not distort language in an effort to limit vocabulary or to emphasize phoneme-grapheme relationships. They gradually acquire a reading vocabulary by identifying words from stories which represent the natural flow of written language. Perhaps with the first experience story, children learn to read one story, perhaps two or three from the next one, and so on until their word banks represent a respectable stock of known words. These words were presented and learned, not in isolation, but in meaningful sentence and story units.

The beginning reader should learn to read orally with smooth, fluent, natural expression. The language experience approach provides oral reading situations in which children can truly "make it sound like someone talking." In the language experience approach, word-by-word emphasis in oral reading should not be permitted to occur. The teacher's model is important in illustrating fluent natural reading in the first pupil-dictated stories. In their concern that children learn vocabulary, some teachers may tend to distort the reading of experience stories with overemphasis on separate words.

Lefevre (1964) maintains that "single words, analyzed and spoken in isolation, assume the intonation contours of whole utterances. Single words thus lose the characteristic pitch and stress they normally carry in the larger constructions that comprise the flow of speech and bear meaning." He emphasizes that the sentence is the minimal unit of meaning, and that children should develop "sentence sense" in reading. In the language experience way of learning to read the beginner does learn to supply the "melodies of speech" as he reads.

The relationship of oral and written language can also be shown as punctuation signals are pointed out incidentally, with emphasis on function and meaning. For example, after a number of experience stories have been written the teacher may casually say, "This is the end of your idea—so we put a period. The next word goes with the next idea so we start this part with a capital letter."

Summary

The linguistic rationale for the language experience approach gives theoretical support to the teacher who is concerned with the implementation of this approach in teaching beginning reading. Language experience reading is truly a linguistically-based method since the relationship of oral and written language is the key to teaching children to read through the recording and reading of their spoken language. The beginning reader is a user of language who must relate graphic symbols to the oral language code he already knows. Understanding the process of language communication through language experience reading should enable the teacher to facilitate the task of learning to read for the beginner through use of relevant material which reflects *his* language. The most important consideration is how language communicates meaning — in language experience reading, *communication is the central focus.*

References

Downing, John. "How Children Think about Reading," *The Reading Teacher,* 23, December 1969, 217-230.

Durkin, Dolores. "A Language Arts Program for Pre-First-Grade Children: Two Year Achievement Report," *Reading Research Quarterly,* 5, Summer 1970, 534-565.

Dykstra, Robert. "Summary of the Second-grade Phase of the Cooperative Research Program in Primary Reading Instruction," *Reading Research Quarterly,* 4, Fall 1968, 49-70.

Goodman, Kenneth S. "Pro-Challenger Answer to 'Is the Linguistic Approach an Improvement in Reading Instruction'?" *Current Issues in Reading.* Conference Proceedings of 13th Annual Convention, Ed. Nila B. Smith, 268-276. Newark, Delaware: International Reading Association, 1969.

Goodman, Kenneth S. *The Psycholinguistic Nature of the Reading Process.* Detroit: Wayne State University Press, 1968.

Lefevre, Carl A. *Linguistics and the Teaching of Reading.* New York: McGraw-Hill, 1964.

THE DOLCH BASIC WORD LIST—THEN AND NOW

Jerry L. Johns

Historical Background

Around the 1930's, controlled vocabularies in basic reading series became the vogue. This practice created a need to find out which words appeared in practically all reading matter. A list of such words could then form a core of words which children should be taught to recognize instantly. Knowledge of these basic sight words should help make a child's reading easier and more fluent. Although a basic sight vocabulary list was considered so necessary, there was considerable doubt as to which words should comprise such a list. Dolch sought to resolve the problem by finding a reasonably small number of words which were so common in all reading materials that children should know all these words instantly by sight.

To secure a core of high frequency words, Dolch (1941) assumed that the most essential words needed by pupils in reading were contained in three basic word lists. All these lists were published at least forty years ago. The first list Dolch considered was published in 1928 by the Child Study Committee of the International Kindergarten Union. This list was a summary of many studies which contained words children knew and used before entering first grade. The list was based on detailed observations in kindergarten classrooms. It contained 2,596 words which were the most frequent of 7,000 different words known to children before entering grade one. Many of these 7,000 words were not, according to Dolch, common words. Since the most important words were wanted, Dolch chose only those with a frequency of one hundred or more. This process of selection resulted in a list of 510 words that were spoken often in the kindergarten. This list contained about the same number of words as the remaining two lists which Dolch used.

JOURNAL OF READING BEHAVIOR, Fall 1971, vol. 3, no. 4, pp. 35-40.

The second list was the first 500 words of the Gates (1926) list which has been used as a basis for many studies in reading vocabulary. This list is generally recognized as containing words of first importance for children's reading. Gates developed his list from several sources. He began with Thorndike's (1921) 2500 words of highest frequency. Next, Gates added those words not in the 2500 from Thorndike's list which were among the thousand words of highest frequency found by Moore (unpublished) in her count of words in a selection of young children's literature. Gates then included additional words from the most frequent words in a series of first-grade readers (Packer, 1921). Finally, Gates consulted Horn's study (1925) and chose additional words from the thousand most frequent words in the spoken vocabularies of young children up to and including six years of age.

The third list was that compiled by Wheeler and Howell (1930). It consisted of the 453 words most frequently found in ten primers and ten first readers published between 1922 and 1929. This list represented the actual reading vocabulary used in grade one and presumably the vocabulary upon which all later reading was built in those basic reading series. Dolch, then, used each of the three lists described above to compile his basic list of service words which should be recognized instantly by children.

The basic list was arranged according to parts of speech. If Dolch would have rigidly adhered to the criterion of appearance of each word on *all* three lists, twenty-seven of the words would have been cut from the list. According to Dolch, this elimination would have been unfortunate since the twenty-seven words appeared in the first 510 of the International Kindergarten Union list and in the first 500 of the Gates list. Dolch felt that these words "obviously" belonged with the other 193 words. In addition, the words for the numbers under ten which did not appear in the original three lists were added to the basic list thereby resulting in a list of 220 basic sight words.

The Dolch list, as the name implies, is a short list of basic words which children should recognize "at sight" since they are used in all writing regardless of the subject matter. It should be noted that the Dolch list contains conjunctions, prepositions, pronouns, adverbs, adjectives, and verbs. There are no nouns included on the list since each noun, according to Dolch, is tied to special subject matter. A casual perusal of the Dolch list reveals, however, that several words (fly, work, today, show) may function as nouns depending upon the context in which they appear.

Dolch also believed that nouns were not as difficult to teach or learn as basic sight words. In addition, he found that the historical or longitudinal reliability of nouns was far below that of the 220 basic sight words. The nouns seldom appeared on lists generated by student usage in sufficient frequency to warrant teaching them as sight words. He did, nevertheless, offer a list of 95 common nouns which could be taught to students who failed to get a good start in reading.

The basic character of the Dolch list was demonstrated by their use in numerous textbooks. Based on a thousand-word sampling in each book (ten samples of one hundred words each, taken at equal intervals throughout the book), Dolch determined what percentage of all the running words in textbooks used in the elementary school were sight words. A sampling of four basic reading series revealed that for first-grade readers 70 per cent of the running words were words from the Dolch list; for second-grade readers, 66 per cent were Dolch words; for third-grade readers, 65 per cent; for fourth-grade readers, 61 per cent; and for fifth- and sixth-grade readers, 59 per cent were Dolch words. These percentages, supported by comparable percentages for similar word counts in arithmetic, geography, and history textbooks, emphasize the importance for every child having mastery of the Dolch list.

A study reported by Zintz (1966) checked the vocabularies of five primary readers (pre-primer through the third grade) against the Dolch list. It was reported that over 200 of the 220 words contained on the Dolch list had been presented in *each* of the basic reading series by the end of the third-grade reader. Although no date is given for this study, it is probably twenty years old because of the particular basic reading series used.

Problem

The Dolch list is commonly accepted today as the basic core of sight words children should be able to recognize instantly. The study reported here was undertaken to check the vocabularies of currently published basic reading series against the Dolch list of words. Such a comparison should determine whether or not the Dolch list is still the core of words that comprised 50 to 70 per cent of the words in basic reading series published over three decades ago.

Procedure

For this investigation, a group of undergraduate students in a professional education course in the teaching of reading checked the vocabularies of five basic reading series against the Dolch list.

In the pre-primers and primers, all pages in each book were checked for Dolch words. Each time a Dolch word appeared in a book, it was marked on a prepared sheet which contained an alphabetical list of all 220 Dolch words. To determine the percentage of Dolch words in the pre-primers and primers, the total frequency of Dolch words was divided by the total number of words in the books.

To determine the percentage of Dolch words found in the first through sixth readers, a slightly different procedure was used. In each book a selection of 300 words was chosen at random from each third of the book. Each time a Dolch word appeared in the selections for that particular book, it was marked on a prepared sheet which contained an alphabetical list of all 220 Dolch words. To determine the percentage of Dolch words for each book level, the total frequency of Dolch words for that particular sample was divided by the total number of words (in each case 900) for that particular book level.

Results

Using the procedure described above, the percentage of Dolch words in each book was calculated. The major question that prompted this investigation was whether or not the Dolch list of 220 basic sight words still comprises 50 to 70 per cent of the words in basic reading series published in the last few years. Table 1 contains the various percentages of Dolch words for each reader level.

Table 1

Percentage of the Dolch Basic Sight Words Found in Five Series of Basic Readers

Basal Reading Series	Reader Levels							
	PP	P	1	2	3	4	5	6
Allyn and Bacon	69	70	64	60	52	53	54	54
Ginn	77	64	73	63	53	57	56	58
Lippincott	40	44	56	61	52	49	56	51
Macmillan	55	63	64	57	53	56	54	55
Scott Foresman	79	72	75	65	51	58	56	57

From the figures in this table, it can be noted that Dolch's word list is still very accurate for the basic reading series published in recent years. Only the percentages in the pre-primer, primer, and first-grade readers from the Lippincott reading series depart noticeably from those of the other series. At the remaining levels, however, the figures for the Lippincott series are similar to the percentages obtained in the other series. Although variations exist between the basic reading series at the various levels, these variations are not as great above the third-reader level.

Perhaps one of the most interesting findings concerns a comparison of the results of this investigation with the results of Dolch's original findings. The various percentages in Table 2 show that there is generally close agreement in the two investigations.

Table 2

A Comparison of the Percentage of Dolch Basic Sight Words in the Present Investigation with Dolch's Original Findings

Investigator	Number of Reading Series	Reader Levels					
		1	2	3	4	5	6
Johns	5	66	61	52	55	55	55
Dolch	4	70	66	65	61	59	59

The table shows a remarkably high percentage of Dolch words for books in grade one and, as might be expected, a gradual decrease through the remaining grades. For all reader levels, however, the Dolch list made up more than half of the reading matter.

The consistently lower percentages in the present investigation compared to Dolch's original findings is probably due to the fact that Dolch included inflected forms of the basic sight words whereas the present investigation did not.

A second explanation for the differences may be due to the fact that this investigation represents only text demand and one edition of each basic reading series. The original investigation by Dolch represented text demand *and* pupil usage. In addition, Dolch used various editions of each basic reading series which added historical or longitudinal reliability to his findings.

Concluding Statement

The present investigation cannot be considered flawless since most studies involving frequency counts have some degree of error associated with them. The results of this investigation, nevertheless, agree remarkably with Dolch's original study. It seems reasonable to conclude, therefore, that the Dolch basic sight word list is still essentially up-to-date and useful in the teaching of reading. Classroom teachers should stress recognition of these 220 service words from the early stages of reading instruction so that the average child knows the words by the end of third grade. Remedial reading teachers should also find the Dolch list useful for older children who have not yet acquired a basic sight vocabulary. The child who gains recognition of these 220 basic sight words should acquire confidence in his reading and be better equipped to use context in unlocking unknown words.

References

CHILD STUDY COMMITTEE OF THE INTERNATIONAL KINDERGARTEN UNION. *A study of the vocabulary of children before entering first grade.* Washington, D.C.: The International Kindergarten Union, 1928.

DOLCH, E. W. *Teaching primary reading.* Champaign: The Garrard Press, 1941.

GATES, A. I. *A reading vocabulary for the primary grades.* New York: Teachers College, Columbia University, 1926.

HARRIS, A. J., *et al. The Macmillan reading program.* New York: The Macmillan Company, 1967.

HORN, E. Appropriate materials for instruction in reading. In G. M. Whipple (Ed.) *Report of the national committee on reading, twenty-fourth yearbook of the national society for the study of education, part I.* Bloomington, Illinois: Public School Publishing Company, 1925.

MC CRACKEN, G. and WALCUTT, C. C. *Basic reading.* New York: J. B. Lippincott Company, 1965.

PACKER, J. L. The vocabularies of ten first readers. In G. M. Whipple (Ed.) *Report of the society's committee on silent reading, twentieth yearbook of the national society for the study of education, part II.* Bloomington, Illinois: Public School Publishing Company, 1930.

ROBINSON, H. M., *et al. The new basic reading series.* Chicago: Scott, Foresman and Company, 1965.

RUESSELL, D. H., *et al. Ginn basic readers: 100 edition*. Boston: Ginn and Company, 1966.

SHELDON, W. D., *et al. Sheldon basic reading series*. Boston: Allyn and Bacon, Inc., 1968.

STONE, C. *Progress in primary reading*. St. Louis: Webster Publishing Company, 1950.

WHEELER, H. E. and HOWELL, E. A. A first grade vocabulary study. *The Elementary School Journal*, 1930, *31*, 52-60.

ZINTZ, M. V. *Corrective reading*. Dubuque, Iowa: Wm. C. Brown Company Publishers, 1966.

Do they read what they speak?

BY DR. YETTA GOODMAN and CAROLYN BURKE

THERE ARE FOUR linguistic principles to keep in mind when teaching reading or dealing with children's reading problems:

- Children can be sophisticated about the grammatical structure of the language of their speech community.
- Children bring their knowledge of language to the task of reading.
- Reading is a process which involves the interaction of language and thought.
- Reading is not an exact letter-by-letter, word-by-word decoding process. Rather, it is a "psycholinguistic guessing game," a process which involves the integration of the child's grammatical system with his knowledge of the world and the printed page.

Now these four principles may seem obvious enough, but really they signal a radical change in our concept of what the reading process is. Since every response a child makes in reading is cued by his sophisticated knowledge of language, his personal experiences and the printed material, it's not simply a case of a child making a mistake when he comes up with responses which are not the same as the printed material. In fact, we don't even use the word "mistake" to describe such responses—we prefer the term "miscue."

A teacher must look at a miscue as a piece of evidence, not as something bad or wrong which must be immediately corrected or eradicated. With careful evaluation of a child's miscues, a teacher can zero in on his problem and help him become a more proficient reader.

Mary Jo, a first-grader, was reading to her teacher:

THE GRADE TEACHER, 1968, vol. 86, pp. 144-150.

Old Mother Hubbard
Went to the Hairdresser
To get her poor dog a wig.

Mary Jo read everything correctly except the last line which she read:

"to get her poor dog *play hair.*"

In this situation Mary Jo's teacher can correct the child and insist she reread the phrase exactly as it appears, or she can try to discover what is happening when Mary Jo reads. She attempts the latter by asking herself two questions concerning miscues:

—*Do miscues fit into a pattern?*

—*How does each miscue relate to the grammatical structure of the language and the meaning of the reading passage?*

Mary Jo has to know a great deal in order to produce the miscue *play hair* in place of *a wig.* She must have some level of comprehension to substitute *play hair* for *a wig.* Her teacher might want to help Mary Jo understand the difference of meaning between *play hair* and *a wig,* but Mary Jo has given no evidence that she is experiencing difficulty with reading skills. She is bringing her own understanding of *wig* to her reading.

We have found that a particularly good way for a teacher to evaluate a child's reading profile and at the same time gain an insight into the reading process itself is through the occasional use of worksheets such as those shown.

The teacher asked Pat and Fred to read a story which had sufficient theme and plot to provide some level of interest. The material was at a level of difficulty that would cause some reading problems, but would not cause frustration to the point of task rejection. The children were told that the purpose of the reading passage and the marking by the teacher was to help evaluate reading strengths and weaknesses in order to plan for a more individualized reading program. They were, therefore, not given any help. Any difficulties they encountered had to be worked out by each child individually. The children read from a book while the teacher marked the miscues on an accompanying worksheet.

Evaluating the miscues

When the teacher evaluated the children's miscues by applying the two questions mentioned earlier—Do miscues fit into pattern? How do they relate to grammatical structure and meaning?—she was able to come up with valuable insights into the reading problems of each child *and* with a wealth of information about reading in general. Here are some examples of the kind of information she developed:

Question 1: Do the miscues fit into patterns? Every miscue seems to relate to some pattern, even though the patterns are complicated and variable.

Corrections. Children attempt to correct those miscues which upset the grammatical structure of the meaning of the passage they are reading. Fred corrected the substitution of *I* for *A* in the sentence "A man doesn't have to be big to be a river man" (line 21 on worksheet). He also corrected the omission of *they* in the sentence "Are you all right, they asked" (line 17).

Children do not often correct

miscues when they result in passages where the meaning or grammar is acceptable. Pat was content with the substitution of *wet* for *right* in the sentence "Are you all right, they asked" (line 17). Fred was also content not to correct *Joan* and *coming* for *John* and *climbing* in "Soon Big John was climbing back into the boat" (line 14).

Corrections demonstrate that children are aware of many of their own reading problems and that they have adequate information and strategies to make the corrections acceptable ones.

Grammatical function: When a child makes a miscue it will often be the same part of speech or have the same grammatical function as the word or phrase in the printed material. All of Fred's miscues retained the same grammatical function as the word or phrase in the printed material: *Joey* for *George; does* for *doesn't*. Out of Pat's 31 miscues, there were only three instances where the grammatical function of the miscue was different from the grammatical function of the printed material: *thought* for *through; on* for *no; around* for *another.*

Habitual association: Sometimes children develop habitual associations between words. For example, a child may read *happy birthday* whenever he sees either *happy* or *birthday* in printed material. Research shows that this phenomenon seems to be of low level functioning and disappears or diminshes as children become more proficient readers. Sometimes habitual associations last during one story only. Other habitual associations, however, may be more lasting. Pat had two habitual associations: *were* for *was;* and *on* for *no*. Fred had none.

Dialect: Research has also shown that as children become more proficient readers, dialect miscues tend to increase, although they do not seem to affect comprehension. This suggests that children begin to slip into their mother tongue in oral reading when they are more at ease with their reading.

Dialect miscues often result in passages which are acceptable grammatically within the reader's dialect and in which the meaning is left unchanged. Neither Pat nor Fred produced any dialect miscues which resulted in unacceptable meaning or grammar. Both of them had the same pronunciation miscue which is related to regional dialect: What sounded like *rowed* for *rolled,* and what sounded like *cawed* for *called.* Pat substituted *don't* for *doesn't* and was confused about the use of *was* and *were.*

Graphic and phonemic relationships: Research indicates that as children become more proficient readers, their miscues are more similar to the printed material in sound-symbol relationship than the miscues made by less proficient readers. Fred's miscues *Joan* for *John, Joey* for *George,* what sounded like *kwitch* for *catch,* and *coming* for *climbing* involved both sound and symbol relationships. He was responding to beginning, medial and final sounds and symbols.

On the other hand, examples of Pat's miscues included *Gregory* for *George, thought* for *through, hurry* for *hold, our* for *your, around* for *another,* and *right* for *river.* These miscues suggest that she was paying attention to initial letters and occasionally to final letters, but that she did not sense strong sound-symbol relationships.

Reading Miscues: How to chart them

Fred

All the men on the boat had to work.
George worked right along with them.
The boat rolled on through the wind
and the rain. Then it gave a big roll.
As the water ran off the boat,
it took Big John into the cold river!
No one but George saw him fall.
"Help! Help!" called Big John.
"What shall I do?" George thought.
He wanted to call for help, too.
But there was no time.
There was just one thing to do.
"Catch!" George called. "Catch and hold on!"
Soon Big John was climbing

Pat

All the men on the boat had to work.
George worked right along with them.
The boat rolled on through the wind
and the rain. Then it gave a big roll.
As the water ran off the boat,
it took Big John into the cold river!
No one but George saw him fall.
"Help! Help!" called Big John.
"What shall I do?" George thought.
He wanted to call for help, too.
But there was no time.
There was just one thing to do.
"Catch!" George called. "Catch and hold on!"
Soon Big John was climbing

18 "Yes, I am," said Big John.

 Gregory

19 "But without George, I would not be

 ready

20 here at (all). Now I know he is a river man."

 (C)I *don't*

21 Then Mr. Long said, "(A) man doesn't

 right

22 have to be big to be a river man."

 Our *Joe*

23 "Your uncle will (be pleased)," Big John

24 said to George.

25 "I know what he will say," said George.

26 "He will say that we have

 around right

27 another river man in the family."

18 "Yes, I am," said Big John.

 Joan *Joey*

19 "But without George, I would not be (I)

20 here at all. Now he is a river man."

 (C)I

21 Then Mr. Long said, "(A) man doesn't

22 have to be big to be a river man." *Joan*

 (C)u—

23 "Your (uncle) will be pleased," Big John

 (C)the *Joey*

24 said to George.

 Joey

25 "I know what he will say," said George.

26 "He will say that we have

 (C)I—

27 (another) river man in the family."

KEY TO WORKSHEET MARKINGS

(H)) Regression or rereading for change in intonation.

(C)) Regression or rereading for purposes of correction.

(John) Part of word, word, or phrase circled was omitted.

John Word over printed text indicates substitution.

Question 2: How does each mistake or miscue relate to the grammatical structure of the language and the meaning of the material?

A very large percentage of miscues seems to be explained by their relationship to the grammatical structure of the language of the children. Children's miscues are strongly influenced by their knowledge of their grammatical system. As children become more proficient readers, a greater percentage of their miscues leaves the grammar of the resulting passage unchanged.

As was mentioned earlier, none of Fred's miscues changed the grammatical structure of the reading matter in any way. Pat not only had miscues in which the grammatical functions were different from the printed material, but she sometimes produced unacceptable grammatical passages. She read, "Our uncle will please Big Joe said to George," instead of "Your uncle will be pleased, Big John said to George" (line 23); and she read, "He will say that we have around right man in the family," instead of "He will say that we have another river man in the family" (lines 26 and 27).

As children become more proficient readers, a greater percentage of their miscues causes only slight changes in the meaning of the reading materials. Fred was vitally concerned with meaning. Whenever he produced a miscue which might have resulted in unacceptable meaning, he corrected it. He corrected *I* for *A* in the sentence, "A man doesn't have to be big to be a river man" (line 21). He also corrected *the* for *to* in the sentence, "Your uncle will be pleased, Big John said to George" (lines 23 and 24). However, he did not correct the substitution of *coming* for *climbing* in "Soon Big John was climbing back onto the boat" (line 14), where the two words were synonyms.

Pat did not generally use correction strategies. She seemed content simply to provide a response to the printed material and did not view the reading process as one of gaining meaning from printed symbols. Pat made no distinction between acceptable and unacceptable miscues. She seemed as satisfied to say, "Our uncle will please," for "Your uncle will be pleased" (line 23), as she was to say, "Are you all wet?" for "Are you all right?" (line 17.) The latter miscue was of "better" quality because it indicated that Pat was comprehending some level of the story.

Counting the number of miscues is less important than looking at the quality of these miscues and how they change as children become more proficient readers. For example, Fred made 34 miscues including five intonation corrections and eight word corrections. Pat made fewer total miscues—31 including one intonational correction and one word correction.

Real differences begin to show only when the miscues are analyzed for quality and type. It becomes evident that the miscues of more proficient readers are more complex. They involve more integration of the meaning, the grammatical and sound systems of the language with the graphic input and the experience and background of the child. Miscues made by less proficient readers tend not to be overly complex and include more miscues which respond to the graphic field or to habitual association.

As children become more proficient readers, they make "better" miscues than they did at earlier stages. By "better" we mean more productive or more demonstrative of complex processing.

In summary, in analyzing the miscues of these children we have made the following discoveries:

The individual reader. We have learned that Pat was very dependent upon the use of initial consonant sounds and graphic similarity in attacking reading material. She paid little attention to context clues or to meaning, although she showed evidence of using them occasionally. Fred integrated meaning, context and sound-symbol relationships in his reading.

Readers at particular ages or developmental levels. For all their individual differences, both Pat and Fred proved to be proficient in handling grammatical structures and sound-symbol relationships. The major difference between them was that Fred was able to integrate the skills as he read, while Pat generally made use of one skill at a time.

Construction of reading materials. One passage in the text gave both readers difficulty. In the sentence, "Then Mr. Long said, 'A man doesn't have to be big to be a river man' " (lines 21 and 22), both children substituted *I* for *A*. This kind of occurrence suggests that the structure of the reading material is sometimes the cause of miscues.

Helping the children

Pat's main attack skill is initial consonant sounds. She is also aware of grammatical structure as she reads. Integrating the use of context clues, sound-symbol relationships, grammatical function and meaning are instructional objectives beneficial for her. These objectives can be achieved by providing her with material that has language in appropriate context rather than isolated units.

Pat will probably benefit from dictating experience stories which can become a part of her reading program. She needs to develop self-evaluating and self-correction strategies as she reads. Pat needs to learn that reading involves concern for the intent, outcome, significance and relationships within a story.

Pat's language materials should deal with concepts within her experience. Her reading should be encouraged only when what she reads sounds like language and makes sense to her.

Fred seems to be developing well rounded and fully integrated reading techniques and skills. He makes appropriate use of self-correcting strategies. He simply needs to read more widely. He can deal with conceptually more complex materials, so long as they are interesting to him.

Fred should be encouraged to read orally—in order to prove a point, for example, or to share something he likes with others. This will help him become conscious of differences between oral and silent reading.

SECTION III

READINESS: PRESCHOOL-KINDERGARTEN EXPERIENCES

Classroom Diagnosis of Reading Readiness Factors

B. Betty Anderson, Ed.D.

This article describes the results of a research study on the validation of a teacher checklist for diagnosis of reading readiness. The purpose of the study was to provide classroom teachers with a diagnostic tool for evaluating specific strengths and weaknesses in visual perception and auding. Such diagnostic information serves to assist teachers in planning a readiness program based on specific needs.

A major task for all first grade teachers is to determine the reading readiness of their pupils. Reading readiness testing is usually included as an integral part of the beginning reading program. Many authorities (Heilman, 1961; Carroll, 1964) view readiness for beginning reading as a complex of many factors, and evaluation of readiness for beginning reading as a process of assessing those factors in individual children. This evaluation is used diagnostically for planning the readiness instructional program. If classroom teachers are to make this assessment, they need a valid and reliable measuring instrument to provide information for each factor of reading readiness. At present such an instrument is not available for classroom teachers, although the Murphy-Durrell Reading Readiness Analysis does give diagnostic information on the readiness factors of auditory discrimination and knowledge of letter names.

Standardized reading readiness tests are commonly used to determine the child's readiness for beginning reading. These tests usually provide a global score which is considered helpful in predicting the child's probable success in the beginning reading program. But such a global score does not provide the teacher with specific diagnostic information on the separate factors of reading readiness.

Teachers are frequently urged to use subtest scores or part scores of standardized readiness tests for diagnostic assessment of the pupil's needs in the various areas of reading readiness (Heilman, 1961; Tinker and McCullough, 1962; Gunderson, 1964). The practice of using the subtest scores in this manner has been discouraged by the designers of one of the most widely used tests on the basis of weak reliability (Hildreth, Griffiths, and McGauvran, 1965) and by Dykstra (1967) on the basis of weak validity. A check of the 16 reading readiness tests listed in *Tests in Print* (1961) reveals that reliability and validity information on the subtests as measures of separate factors of reading readiness is indeed lacking in most cases. For those tests that provide reliability and validity information for the subtests, the

JOURNAL OF LEARNING DISABILITIES, May 1970, vol. 3, no. 5, pp. 260-263.

TABLE I

CHECKLIST

Item	Rating
ORAL LANGUAGE	
Metropolitan Word Meaning[1]	1 2 3
Can the child:	
T – Retell a story after hearing it[2]	1 2 3
T – Follow oral directions	1 2 3
T – Identify objects in a picture	1 2 3
T – Follow a group discussion	1 2 3
VISUAL PERCEPTION	
Eye Motor	
Metropolitan Matching	1 2 3
Metropolitan Alphabet	1 2 3
Metropolitan Copying	1 2 3
Can the child:	
T – Dress himself (outer clothing)	1 2 3
T – Cut with scissors	1 2 3
T – Skip	1 2 3
Observation of Metropolitan Copying for:	
* – Broken lines[3]	1 2 3
Figure Ground	
Metropolitan Matching	1 2 3
Metropolitan Alphabet	1 2 3
Metropolitan Copying	1 2 3
Can the child:	
T – Change from one visual task to another easily	1 2 3
T – Find an obvious object such as his pencil among several similar objects	1 2 3
T – Attend to visual tasks at his seat	1 2 3
Form Constancy	
Can the child:	
T – Discriminate size of objects of same shape	1 2 3
T – Recognize sameness of shape with different sized objects	1 2 3
T – Locate circular objects in room	1 2 3
T – Locate rectangular objects in room	1 2 3
Position in Space	
Metropolitan Draw-a-Man	1 2 3
Can the child:	
T – Follow body movement directions (as in exercises)	1 2 3
T – Use location words correctly (such as behind, beside, up, down, left, right	1 2 3
Spatial Relations	
Metropolitan Matching	1 2 3
Metropolitan Copying	1 2 3
Can the child:	
T – Rotate hand rather than paper in printing or drawing	1 2 3
Observation of Metropolitan Copying for:	
* – Positioning of drawing	1 2 3

[1] *Metropolitan subtest items are rated as follows:*

	1	2	3
Word Meaning Score	0-6	7-10	11-16
Matching Score	0-4	5-10	11-14
Alphabet Score	0-5	6-13	14-16
Copying	0-4	5-9	10-14
Draw-a-Man	E-E	C	A-B

[2] *Task Mastery items (T) are rated as follows:*
1 = Inability to perform the task
2 = Incomplete mastery and inconsistent performance of the task. The child is still learning the task.
3 = Complete mastery of the task. The child can and does do it consistently.

[3] *Miscellaneous items (*) are rated as follows:*
Broken lines (Metropolitan Copying)
1 = Broken lines are consistently used in the drawing.
2 = An occasional broken line in the drawing.
3 = One-stroke lines without breaks, false starts or drawing over of lines.

levels are generally below those suggested as acceptable by Guilford (1956).

Specific skill tests are now available for separate factors of reading readiness such as visual perception and auding. These specific skill tests measure one factor in detail and have established reliability and validity. However, these tests either require special training for their administration or interpretation or they must be given to children individually. These requirements present serious disadvantages for their use by classroom teachers. However, these specific skill tests could be used for validating a measurement instrument designed for classroom use. I have used this in an attempt to develop an instrument to measure the separate reading readiness factors of visual perception and auding. Following is the study undertaken to validate the checklist test (see Table I).

HYPOTHESES

Two major hypotheses were investigated. They were (1) that the auding section of the Checklist is an effective instrument for a classroom teacher to use in place of the Peabody Picture Vocabulary Test for measuring auding ability in beginning first grade pupils, and (2) that the visual perception section of the Checklist is an effective instrument which a classroom teacher can use in place of the Frostig Developmental Test of Visual Perception to measure visual perception skills in beginning first grade pupils.

PROCEDURE

The population consisted of the pupils in 35 first-grade classrooms in a suburban location near a large state university. One pupil was randomly selected from each classroom for the sample.

The Checklist consisted of items of informal appraisal by the teacher of the child's performance in specific task situations. The tasks were selected from the literature as behaviors indicative of achievement in visual perception (Frostig and Horne, 1964; Kephart, 1960) and in auding (McKim and Caskey, 1963; Barbe, 1961). Other items were added to include the subtests of the Metropolitan Reading Readiness Tests, which were selected on the basis of the descriptions of content validity given in the Manual of Directions for the test. I then developed rating scales (1968) to measure the task items and to convert the subtest scores.

All testing was completed between the second and fifth weeks of school. The Frostig Developmental Test of Visual Perception was used as the criterion to establish validity for the visual perception section of the Checklist; the Peabody Picture Vocabulary Test was used for auding.

STATISTICAL ANALYSIS AND FINDINGS

A Pearson product-moment correlation was computed between each section of the Checklist and the appropriate criterion test. A positive correlation of .40 or above was established as the level to determine effectiveness of the instruments which were being validated (Guilford, 1956). Each computed r was converted to a z statistic and then subjected to a z test using the .05 level of significance. A correlation of .53 was obtained between the auding section of the Checklist and the Peabody test. This was not sufficient to indicate significance when subjected to the statistical analysis described above. The visual perception section of the Checklist and the Frostig test did indicate significant results. The correlation computed between these measures was .74.

In addition a test retest reliability check was provided for the Checklist items rated by the classroom teacher. A correlation of .93 was obtained in this procedure.

CONCLUSIONS AND IMPLICATIONS

The conclusions drawn from the findings were that the hypothesis regarding the auding section of the Checklist was not supported, and the hypothesis regarding the visual perception section of the Checklist was supported.

If the visual perception section of the Checklist is to be used by classroom teachers, replication of the study would be needed with larger and more representative populations to establish validity. In addition, further research is recommended to refine the items, particularly those requiring task performances to be rated by the teacher for visual perception. The items in the auding section need to be improved and expanded before use of this section can be recommended to classroom teachers. Continued research in the area of assessment of readiness for beginning reading is needed. For example, research studies which provide validation information on the subtests of the standardized reading readiness tests are needed if teachers are to use these tests diagnostically. It is hoped that this study will help provide direction for further research in this area.

REFERENCES

Anderson, B.B.: Evaluation of a Checklist to Measure Specific Reading Readiness Factors in Beginning First Grade Pupils. Unpublished doctoral dissertation, University of Maryland, 1968.

Barbe, W.B.: Educator's Guide to Personalized Reading Instruction. Englewood Cliffs, N.J.: Prentice-Hall, 1961.

Buros, O. (ed.): Tests in Print. Highland Park, N.J. Gryphon Press, 1961.

Carroll, J.B.: The Analysis of Reading Instruction: Perspectives from Psychology and Linguistics. In Ernest R. Hilgard (Ed.) Theories of Learning and Instruction. Sixty-Third Yearbook of the National Society for the Study of Education, Part 1. Chicago: NSSE, 1964.

Dykstra, R.: The Use of Reading Readiness Tests for Prediction and Diagnosis: A Critique. In Thomas C. Barrett (Ed.) The Evaluation of Children's Reading Achievement. Perspectives in Reading No. 8. Newark, Del.: Internat. Reading Assn. 1967.

Frostig, M., and Horne, D.: The Frostig Program for the Development of Visual Perception. Chicago: Follett, 1964.

Guilford, J.P.: Fundamental Statistics in Psychology and Education, 3rd ed. New York: McGraw-Hill, 1956.

Gunderson, D.V.: Research in Reading Readiness. U.S. Dept. of Health, Education, and Welfare, U.S. Office of Education, 1964.

Heilman, A.W.: Principles and Practices of Teaching Reading. Columbus, Ohio: Charles Merrill, 1961.

Hildreth, G.H., Griffiths, N.L., and McGauvran, M.E.: Manual of Directions: Metropolitan Readiness Tests. New York: Harcourt, Brace and World, 1965.

Kephart, N.C.: The Slow Learner in the Classroom. Columbus, Ohio: Charles Merrill, 1960.

McKim, M.G., and Caskey, H.: Guiding Growth in Reading in the Elementary School, 2nd ed. New York: Macmillan, 1963.

Tinker, M.A., and McCullough, C.M.: Teaching Elementary Reading, 2nd ed. New York: Appleton-Century-Crofts, 1962.

World of work and early childhood

THOMAS D. YAWKEY
EUGENE L. ARONIN

Thomas D. Yawkey is assistant professor of Early Childhood Education at the University of Maryland, College Park. Eugene Aronin is a child development specialist with the Harford (Maryland) County Schools. They contend that much greater emphasis is needed on introducing young children to the world of work, through realistic vocational orientation programs.

DR. HAROLD Shane, at a recent AAEKNE-NEA colloquy on Early Childhood Research, contended that there is a great need for teaching children ages three to eight about the world of work. Other leading educators have also noted a paucity of emphasis on occupational information and vocational alternatives in early education.

> . . . a need (exists) for information in early grades to develop wholesome attitudes toward all fields of work, to make children aware of the wide variety of workers, to help children answer questions about occupations, and to bring out the varying rewards of work (Arbuckle, p. 14, 1968).

Additional authorities, Simmons (1968), and Wrenn (1967), have also supported the contention that development of positive values and an expanded frame of reference toward the world of work cause should be developed at an early age.

Other authorities such as Gunn (1968), Norris (1963) and Wellington (1968) have researched conceptions of the "world of work" held by children ages three to eight. Gunn (1968), Norris (1963), and Wellington (1968) have all noted that in early childhood, youngsters have little idea of the realities connected with specific job settings, except for stereotypes associated with a few limited glamorous professions or popular heroes. Gunn (1968) further contended that youngsters have limited and, in many cases, ambigu-

THE READING TEACHER, 1971, Vol. 25, pp. 253-256.

ous vocational aspirations. Gunn (1968) also found that first graders assigned highest ratings to vocations of parents while fourth graders designated "most highly regarded" vocations according to importance to the community, state, or nation. Beginning in third grade, Gunn noted that children began placing vocations in some sort of prestige hierarchy, often agreeing with adults as to the prestige assigned to specific occupations.

The need for vocational exploration activities in early childhood years was further accented by recent findings on the significance of early experience on later vocational behavior. Both family experiences (Burrow, 1964) and the formation of self-concept (Wrenn, 1967) were described as being crucial to later vocational activity. Burrow (1964) for example, in speaking of vocational choice, noted that vocational interests were a function of the self-concept and occupational stereotyping. Super (1957) also stated that vocational development is an aspect of personal development, an implementation of the self-concept.

Curricula in kindergarten to third grade provide many opportunities for exploring the world of work and perhaps simultaneously enhancing the growth of self-concept and building "realistic" notions of vocations.

The World of Work: Retrospect

Approaches to the world of work through social studies and science in early childhood curricula have been attempted. Reading was chosen for this attempt because of its extreme importance in early childhood curricula. The language experience approach, which has traditionally emphasized the child's own experience, was employed, and found to be effective in improving self-concept as well as reading skills because of its emphasis upon the child's own experience (Hall, 1969). This "experiment" was conducted by the Baltimore County Schools, Baltimore, Maryland and it involved 240 children ranging in age from four to nine years for a period of ten consecutive weeks.

The recording of experience stories was considered to be of extreme importance. Verbal responses elicited after certain experiences (for example, a trip to the supermarket) were usually written on large sheets of paper mounted on an easel or chalkboard. After the experience story was completed each child was required to read his contribution. Words from these stories were studied and led to learning of other words as well. The language experience activity tended to contribute to the child's feeling of accomplishment and worth because his own ideas were used. The language experience served the purpose of utilizing work exploration experiences, building and improving reading skills and tended to build healthier self-images than the traditional book oriented reading program.

The World of Work: Prospect

The physical organization of the learning groups in the Baltimore program was of extreme importance. The three types of learning groups employed were:

The initial experiences group. All children in one or two or three classes or the primary grade unit of the elementary school comprised this learning group. Group experiences centered on occupations and vocations through field trips, rescarch persons and visual presentations. The Baltimore County program involved six groups of forty children. These initial experiential groups were not essentially age related and proved extremely flexible in transferring children from one to another group.

The recording groups. These were a number of rather small groups in each initial experiential group. Each of these recording groups was to synthesize and graphically symbolize the children's experiences, through written records. The children would then proceed to the Language Development Center, where activities concerning comprehension, vocabulary development, and word attack skills were conducted. Experiences at the Language Reading Center and the Language Development Center were alternated.

The multisensory groups. The three Language Development and three Language Recording Groups were divided into smaller multisensory learning groups based on interests. These learning centers were to provide a variety of ways of self-expression through sense modalities—i.e., seeing, hearing, feeling, touching, and smelling. Each child would rotate through the interest centers requiring him to employ numerous sense modalities in learning. Groups included:

- Drama Center — Children discussed feelings and experiences related to the program, vocationally related interests, hobbies, and characteristics of the vocational settings they had visited.
- Arts and Crafts Center—Children painted, modeled, structured crafts, and made drawings concerning vocations.
- Story Time Center—Within this center, children could listen to or read stories representing various occupational fields. The stories also centered on vocabulary, and reinforced specific skills introduced earlier.
- Music Center—Here the children wrote, or listened to songs emphasizing specific vocations. They also received a chance to practice rhythm on instruments which they built themselves.
- Creative Writing Center — The children were encouraged to express themselves freely through stories dealing with their present experiences and vocational ideas.
- Book Binding Center—All stories the children composed, including vocabulary and skills each child had mastered, were duplicated. Each child made a book of his own experiences. This activity illustrated a vocation and provided the children with a sense of success and achievement. A classroom newspaper could be easily built into this center.
- Physical Education Center — This center emphasized physical skills and motor development within and outside of the area of occupations.
- Skills' Center—Here children received perceptual skill development using equipment such as tape recorders, overhead projectors, and language masters.

The six large experimental groups emphasizing vocational aspects were given the name of major companies in the area. The names of the companies were changed as needed to allow occupational emphasis throughout the entire program to shift. Upon entering school, the children proceeded to the "board room" part of the multipurpose classroom. They took attendance themselves by moving "time cards" from a card holder labeled "out" to a card holder labeled "in." All students gathered in the large groups for experiential programs, field trips, and to hear resource persons from neighborhood commercial establishments and industries. After each initial group experience half the children proceeded to the Language Recording Center and half to the Language Development Centers. The recording and developing activities were alternated to provide practice in expression and skill development. The recording groups were then divided into six to eight smaller units based on the children's inclinations. The large experimental groups were again convened for socializing and snack time, and the children returned to their smaller multisensory groups to continue working on their projects. At final "reconvening of the boards," the groups were asked to summarize their experiences and accomplishments. At dismissal the children "checked out."

Program Evaluation

A reading skill checklist noting specific deficits was completed at the beginning and end of the program. Much improvement between pre and post measures was noted by the teachers. Standardized reading tests were also administered to preschool youngsters. The results tentatively illustrated that reading progress was made by a majority of students.

An ongoing evaluation was made by the teachers through post session discussion of the program's progress. At these regular meetings, teachers discussed ideas to use in activities, modifications of procedures, progress of individual students, and ways of dealing with specific learning situations.

The following statements by the students perhaps show their own feelings about the programs:

I like to sing in the morning.
I like to read.
It is fun to work.
I like to go in the gym.
I like to watch films.
It helps me for next year.
I like coloring and writing. It is fun.
I like to go outside and make stuff.
We get to go on trips. We like to play games.
I like school.

References

Arbuckle, D. S. "Occupational Information in the Elementary School." *Guidance in the Elementary School: Theory, Research, and Practice.* Ed. E. D. Koplitz. Dubuque, Iowa: William C. Brown, 1968.

Burrow, H., Ed. *Man in a World of Work.* Boston: Houghton Mifflin, 1964.

Gunn, B. "Children's Concepts of Occupational Prestige." *Guidance in the Elementary School: Theory, Research, and Practice.* Ed. E. D. Koplitz. Dubuque, Iowa: William C. Brown, 1968.

Hall, M. *The Language Experience Approach.* Columbus: Charles E. Merrill, 1969.

Norris, W. *Occupational Information in the Elementary School.* Chicago: SRA, 1963.

Simmons, D. D. "Children's Rankings of Occupational Prestige." *Guidance in the Elementary School: Theory, Research, and Practice.* Ed. E. D. Koplitz. Dubuque, Iowa: William C. Brown, 1968.

Super, D. D. *The Psychology of Careers.* New York: Harper & Row, 1957.

Wellington, J. A. and Olechowski, N. "Attitudes toward the World of Work in Elementary Schools." *Guidance in the Elementary School: Theory, Research, and Practice.* Dubuque, Iowa: William C. Brown, 1968.

Wrenn, C. G. *The Counselor in a Changing World.* Washington, D.C.: American Personnel and Guidance Association, 1967.

Goals of first grade

JUDITH S. BRIDGES
KEN LESSLER

SUCCESS in first grade is an illusive achievement. It might seem at first that success should be measured by the acquisition of certain academic skills. However, the literature concerning the goals of primary education points to a much different emphasis.

According to Dottrens (1962) there should be a minimum of material to be mastered in primary school and the stress should be placed on the capacity to understand and adapt, on curiosity, and on the ability to observe, judge, and reason. Similarly, at a UNESCO meeting of educators in 1968 there was agreement that in the first phase of primary education, children should be taught how to learn. Children should learn how to acquire information, to express themselves, and to cooperate with group members. Although Platt (1966) includes the skills of reading, writing, and arithmetic as goals of first grade, she asserts that the establishment of a healthy self-concept based on success and good study habits is equally important.

The fact that reading readiness tests are the single best predictors of first grade performance, as defined by teachers' ratings, (Lessler, Schoeninger and Bridges, 1970) suggests there is a possible contradiction between the goals represented by the UNESCO document and those perpetuated in actual practice.

A questionnaire was devised to determine 1) which goals were considered most important in first grade, and 2) the actual basis for performance evaluation. The study

THE READING TEACHER, May 1972, vol. 25, no. 8, pp. 763-767.

compared the goals and evaluative standards adhered to by first grade teachers, by other teachers and administrators in the same school system, and by other professional educators in North Carolina.

Method

Questionnaires were sent to first and second grade teachers, principals, and supervisors in a rural county school system in North Carolina, and education and school psychology faculty in three North Carolina universities. The resulting sample was composed of nineteen first grade teachers, twenty-two second grade teachers, fourteen principals and supervisors and ten faculty members.

The questionnaire consisted of a list of nine skills and attitudes (reading skills, curiosity, desire to learn) which the respondent was asked to rank-order according to importance as goals of the first year of school. Next, the respondent was requested to rank-order the same goals according to importance as reasons for promotion or retention in first grade. The goal rankings are assumed to reflect ideal goals. Skills and attitudes indicated as reasons for promotion or retention would appear to be skills actually used as criteria of performance.

Top priorities

Which skills or attitudes are thought to be important both as goals and as reasons for promo-

Table 1

Frequency distribution of ranks given to each skill as a goal of first grade

Skill	Ranks	Teachers 1st Gr.	Teachers 2nd Gr.	Prin. & Superv.	Univer. Faculty
Ability to understand instructions	1-3	14 (74%)	19 (86%)	10 (72%)	2 (20%)
	4-6	4 (21%)	3 (14%)	3 (21%)	7 (70%)
	7-9	1 (5%)	0 (0%)	1 (7%)	1 (10%)
Adjustment to other children	1-3	10 (53%)	6 (27%)	8 (57%)	3 (30%)
	4-6	7 (37%)	12 (55%)	2 (14%)	6 (60%)
	7-9	2 (10%)	4 (18%)	4 (29%)	1 (10%)
Desire to learn	1-3	13 (69%)	17 (77%)	8 (57%)	8 (80%)
	4-6	5 (26%)	5 (23%)	4 (29%)	2 (20%)
	7-9	1 (5%)	0 (0%)	2 (14%)	0 (0%)
Curiosity	1-3	4 (21%)	6 (27%)	8 (57%)	7 (70%)
	4-6	7 (37%)	3 (14%)	2 (14%)	2 (20%)
	7-9	8 (42%)	13 (59%)	4 (29%)	1 (10%)
Reading Skills	1-3	6 (32%)	8 (36%)	2 (14%)	3 (30%)
	4-6	8 (42%)	12 (55%)	8 (57%)	4 (40%)
	7-9	5 (26%)	2 (9%)	4 (29%)	3 (30%)
Writing Skills	1-3	3 (16%)	0 (0%)	2 (14%)	0 (0%)
	4-6	4 (21%)	4 (18%)	2 (14%)	2 (20%)
	7-9	12 (63%)	18 (82%)	10 (72%)	8 (80%)
Oral Language Skills	1-3	5 (26%)	5 (23%)	3 (21%)	7 (70%)
	4-6	9 (47%)	14 (64%)	9 (64%)	3 (30%)
	7-9	5 (26%)	3 (14%)	2 (14%)	0 (0%)
Arithmetic Skills	1-3	1 (5%)	1 (5%)	0 (0%)	0 (0%)
	4-6	6 (32%)	7 (32%)	5 (35%)	3 (30%)
	7-9	12 (63%)	14 (64%)	9 (64%)	7 (70%)
Discipline	1-3	1 (5%)	4 (18%)	2 (14%)	0 (0%)
	4-6	7 (37%)	6 (27%)	6 (42%)	1 (10%)
	7-9	11 (58%)	12 (55%)	6 (43%)	9 (42%)

Total N: First Grade Teachers = 19; Second Grade Teachers = 22; Principals and Supervisors = 14; University Faculty = 10.

tion or retention? Tables 1 and 2 present, for each group of educators, the frequency distributions of ranks given to each skill and attitude as a goal of first grade and as a reason for nonpromotion. As is indicated in Table 1, first grade teachers, second grade teachers, and administrators rate the ability to understand instructions as the most important goal for children in the first grade. The university faculty believe that the desire to learn is the most important goal. The skill which is considered least important by first grade teachers and administrators is arithmetic skills; second grade teachers choose writing skills; and the university faculty rank discipline as least important.

In contrast, (Table 2) reading skills are considered the most important criterion for determining promotion or retention by first grade teachers and administrators. Reading is also considered very important by second grade teachers, although ability to understand instructions is ranked slightly higher by this group. University faculty rank oral language skills as somewhat more important than reading. Discipline is considered the least important reason for retention by all groups.

Differences and correlations

Are these skills or attitudes (thought to be important both as goals and as reasons for retention)

Table 2

Frequency distribution of ranks given to each skill as a reason for non-promotion

Skill	Ranks	Teachers 1st Gr.	Teachers 2nd Gr.	Prin. & Superv.	Univer. Faculty
Ability to understand instructions	1-3	13 (68%)	15 (68%)	7 (50%)	4 (50%)
	4-6	5 (26%)	7 (32%)	6 (43%)	3 (38%)
	7-9	1 (5%)	0 (0%)	1 (7%)	1 (13%)
Adjustment to other children	1-3	3 (16%)	1 (5%)	2 (14%)	4 (50%)
	4-6	8 (42%)	10 (46%)	8 (57%)	3 (38%)
	7-9	8 (42%)	11 (50%)	4 (29%)	1 (13%)
Desire to learn	1-3	6 (32%)	14 (64%)	3 (21%)	4 (50%)
	4-6	7 (37%)	7 (32%)	5 (35%)	2 (25%)
	7-9	6 (32%)	1 (5%)	6 (43%)	2 (25%)
Curiosity	1-3	1 (5%)	3 (14%)	2 (14%)	2 (25%)
	4-6	3 (16%)	1 (5%)	3 (21%)	2 (25%)
	7-9	15 (79%)	18 (82%)	9 (64%)	4 (50%)
Reading Skills	1-3	16 (85%)	15 (68%)	12 (86%)	4 (50%)
	4-6	2 (10%)	6 (27%)	2 (14%)	3 (38%)
	7-9	1 (5%)	1 (5%)	0 (0%)	1 (13%)
Writing Skills	1-3	5 (26%)	3 (14%)	4 (29%)	0 (0%)
	4-6	11 (58%)	10 (46%)	6 (42%)	5 (63%)
	7-9	3 (16%)	9 (41%)	4 (29%)	3 (38%)
Oral Language Skills	1-3	6 (32%)	6 (27%)	9 (64%)	5 (29%)
	4-6	11 (58%)	11 (50%)	4 (29%)	3 (38%)
	7-9	2 (10%)	5 (23%)	1 (7%)	0 (0%)
Arithmetic Skills	1-3	6 (32%)	6 (27%)	3 (21%)	1 (13%)
	4-6	8 (42%)	9 (41%)	7 (50%)	2 (25%)
	7-9	5 (26%)	7 (32%)	4 (28%)	5 (63%)
Discipline	1-3	1 (5%)	2 (9%)	0 (0%)	0 (0%)
	4-6	2 (10%)	5 (23%)	2 (14%)	1 (13%)
	7-9	16 (85%)	15 (68%)	12 (86%)	7 (88%)

Total N: First Grade Teachers = 19; Second Grade Teachers = 22; Principals and Supervisors = 14; University Faculty = 8.

Table 3

Correlations by subgroup between each skill as a goal and as a reason for non-promotion

Skill	Teachers 1st Gr.	Teachers 2nd Gr.	Prin. & Superv.	Univer. Faculty
Ability to understand instructions	.26	.70***	.55	.75*
Adjustment to other children	.21	.40	.27	.71*
Desire to learn	.33	.13	.33	.20
Curiosity	.22	.63**	.40	.50
Reading Skills	.38	.60**	.33	.85**
Writing Skills	.38	.39	.65*	.15
Oral Language Skills	.67**	.37	.60*	.69
Arithmetic Skills	.43	.49*	.60*	.83**
Discipline	.47*	.53*	.06	.52

N: First Grade Teachers = 19; Second Grade Teachers = 22; Principals and Supervisors = 14; University Faculty = 8.

* p .50 ** p .01 *** p .001

consistent across different groups of educators? All three groups of local educators each rank the ability to understand instructions as the most important goal of first grade. However, the university faculty members rank this skill quite low. More specifically, as is revealed in Table 1, 74 percent of the first grade teachers, 86 percent of the second grade teachers, and 72 percent of the administrators give the ability to follow instructions a high ranking (from 1 to 3) but only 20 percent of the university faculty assign it such a priority.

A second difference between the groups of educators was found in relation to curiosity as a goal. Both the administrators and the university faculty rank this skill as more important than do either the first or second grade teachers. As Table 1 indicates, 57 percent of the administrators and 70 percent of the faculty give this goal one of the three top places, versus only 21 percent of the first grade teachers and 27 percent of the second grade teachers.

Are these skills or attitudes (thought to be important as goals of first grade) the same as those believed to be important as reasons for promotion or nonpromotion? Table 3 presents the correlations between the skills and attitudes as goals and as reasons for nonpromotion for each group of educators. As can be observed in this table, in most cases the relationships between the skills and attitudes as goals and as reasons for retention are quite low. Correlation between the skills as goals and as reasons for retention is lowest for the first grade teachers and highest for the university faculty.

Some important discrepancies are highlighted by this data which should give pause to university professor and teacher alike. Are we saying one thing and doing another? Are we talking about curiosity, desire to learn and following instructions but evaluating reading? Or is it reading which is the interest and do we feel some professional necessity to ascribe to what seem to be higher values?

Pressures of the classroom

The data might be viewed in terms of the demands of the classroom. The further from the classroom and the further from any performance criteria the rater is, the more likely he is to ascribe to more general goals of learning such as the desire to learn or to be curious. The teacher, on the other hand, while not denying the importance of these goals for the overall development of the child, must work with large numbers of students in a group setting.

It is therefore not surprising that she would rate the ability to follow instructions as a very high priority. It is also true that the teacher often feels evaluated by the child's actual performance, not his enthusiasm for learning. Achievement tests at the end of a year are a usual part of the educational cycle, and the teacher whose children do poorly, especially in reading, believes she is doing a poor job. This belief is, of course, often supported by parents and administrators. In addition, when a teacher sends a child on to the next grade there is the clear feeling that her product is being evaluated according to his basic educational survival skills, and primarily his reading ability.

In this context it is little wonder that teachers want children to follow instructions and yet evaluate him by his reading ability. It is only those removed from the day to day task of teaching who apparently can afford the luxury of a more longitudinal view of the child, a view which clearly places learning skills, curiosity, and language ability on the top of the stack.

The situation is further complicated by the current emphasis on establishing and measuring behavioral objectives for the classroom. While efforts to remove academic pressures such as nongrading and individualized instruction are becoming increasingly popular, there is a concurrent emphasis on measuring the effectiveness of the classroom program by measuring the achievement of the children in academic subjects. Durost (1971) describes the potential difficulties succinctly:

> That freedom of mind which permits the individual to try but fail and yet count his failure as a success, provided it shows the way to some new and better procedure, is in danger of being seriously eroded. (page 292)

What is clear is that changes are needed wherever contradictory situations are observed. It is believed that the situation described here is the rule rather than the exception. If the goal of the first year is to be curiosity, or the desire to learn, then the evaluative system and the value system needs to be congruent. If the goal is to be reading, the teacher needs to be duly supported and spared the crossfire of being told one thing by her professors and supervisors and receiving a very different message from an unyielding though hidden "agenda."

References

Dottrens, R. *The Primary School Curriculum.* Paris: UNESCO, 1962.

Durost, W. N. "Accountability: the task, the tools, and the pitfalls." *The Reading Teacher,* 24, 4 (1971), 291-304, 367.

"Goals of Primary Education," *School and Society.* UNESCO, 96 (Summer 1968), 295-96.

Lessler, K., Schoeninger, D. W., and Bridges, J. "Prediction of First Grade Performance," *Perceptual and Motor Skills,* 31 (1970), 751-56.

Platt, E. M. "The Child Is the Father to the Man." *School and Community,* 53 (1966), 38.

A look at early reading

ARTHUR M. ENZMANN

READING HAS BEEN INTERPRETED in the light of the ability of the reader to comprehend the ideas offered by the author. This interpretation implies that the reader understands what he is reading and is able to relate the ideas to his knowledge and level of intelligent action. A second interpretation of *reading* considers it to be an action in which the emphasis is upon decoding. Reading becomes a process of breaking the code. The key word here appears to be the word *process*. Once the proper process, that of decoding skills, is learned, the child may be classified as a reader. In this interpretation, the work on the many comprehension skills is left until later.

Obviously, this second interpretation stresses the performance of a feat of "reading" orally irrespective of the meaning of what is read. Proponents of the second interpretation would have children work to gain the approval of others, that is, to gain a literal or figurative pat on the head. On the other hand, working toward helping children grasp the meaning of written material, with its many subtitles and nuances, without providing them with the opportunity to develop adequate word-attack skills, results in frustration since the child's ability to grasp meaning will soon outstrip his ability to read the individual words. Consider now two areas concerning the kindergarten reading program. The first area is the timing or pacing of the reading program; the second area, the materials and techniques available to foster reading ability.

TIMING AND PACING

Basic to any discussion of the timing of the introduction of a focused reading program is the recognition that children vary in readiness for reading as widely as they vary in other areas, both physical and mental. Thus the determination of when to begin the reading program rests on the readiness level of the individual child rather than on a calendar date in the school year for all children. Children should begin a reading program at various times during the school year. Optimally, the teacher should di-

THE READING TEACHER, April 1971, vol. 24, no. 7, pp. 616-620.

agnose each child's readiness using continuing observation, informal inventories, and objective tests on an individual basis and then schedule the reading program at the most appropriate time for the child. Unfortunately, most teachers must face so many students each day that as a matter of practical necessity, they cannot provide individual programs. Rather teachers must sort the children into groups on the basis of teacher judgment of student capacities. Within this framework, it is possible to make adjustments in curriculum offerings that will go a long way in meeting the reading instruction needs of pupils.

At what level does this first diagnosis take place? In Michigan, it is fortunate that almost all children have an opportunity to attend kindergarten. In almost all cases, kindergartens enroll children in a one-year experience which begins in September. A random selection of kindergarten children would reveal that they have an age range of almost a full year, a maturity range of more than a year, and an experiential range that is not measurable but is extensive.

A major issue in early childhood education revolves around the question. "Shall we teach reading in the kindergarten?" There are, of course, pro and con positions. However, the problem can be satisfactorily resolved by focusing attention on the variability of children. Some children at the kindergarten level are completely ready and eager to become involved in the complex and interesting business of reading. In fact, there are children with a natural inclination toward reading which results in their coming to the kindergarten already able to read. To be sure, the number of such children is small; but they do exist. For most kindergarten children, however, the joys of reading are still in the future.

In view of the variability, school systems should be prepared to offer some kindergarten children a program of reading and language activities for a specified period of time every week. Selection of the children who will participate in the program should be a professional responsibility of the teacher, with no restrictions on the maximum or minimum number of participants.

One of the most publicized and well documented programs for teaching reading in the kindergarten is that in Denver. The Denver program was designed to offer . . . "planned, sequential instruction in skills basic to beginning reading instruction for twenty minutes each day" (Bond and Dykstra, 1966). Children were screened for readiness and placed in special part-time groups. If a child reacted negatively to the program or gave signs that he was not able to cope with the program immediately, he was allowed to drop out of the group.

A less structured plan for moving children into a reading

program is basic to kindergarten instruction in the Detroit Public Schools. Emphasis is placed on a variety of activities which strengthen skills involved in reading. Two curriculum guides titled *Kindergarten-Readiness in Action* and *Let's Teach Phonics . . . NOW!* are available to help teachers focus on the specific outcomes that are essential to beginning reading. These outcomes are as follows:

1. Good listening habits.
2. Better oral expression.
3. Vocabulary development.
4. Immediate recall.
5. Delayed recall.
6. Identification of rhyming words.
7. Classification skills.
8. Knowledge of the letters of the alphabet.
9. Ability to see the relationship between sound and symbol.

An important aspect of both the Denver and Detroit approaches is that the teacher exercises a high quality of professional judgment as she determines the scope and depth of the child's instructional program. The determination is not made in a routine, mechanical fashion. This characteristic of the program makes the difference between tailoring students to fit the curriculum and tailoring the curriculum to fit the students.

MATERIALS AND TECHNIQUES

As children move beyond the introduction to basic reading, teachers and school administrators must make a decision as to which reading instruction program should be instituted. Teachers and superintendents are drawn to and fro as they are barraged by the proponents of various instructional approaches and the exuberant claims sometimes made for them. Recently instructional materials in reading have received tremendous amounts of research attention. The amount of *inconclusive* data now available would probably fill the Empire State Building to overflowing. Much of this reading research suffers from the common faults of most educational research; namely, it is loosely structured, not rigidly controlled, done in a short interval of time, and is carried on with a small sample population. It is natural to wish that clear-cut answers could be given by the researchers which would relieve teachers and school officials of having to make the decision concerning how to proceed. Unfortunately, such help does not appear imminent.

However, guidelines rather than answers are obtainable. The U.S. Office of Education sponsored a series of studies in beginning reading instruction which appear to offer some much needed rational guidance (McKee, Brzlinski, and Harrison, 1966). The results of these large-scale studies support a basic theory that the crucial factor in the teaching of reading is the quality of the instruction rather than the particular reading approach used. The twenty-seven first-grade studies indicate there is no single "best way" to teach beginning reading. The studies also indicate that the range of student achievement within a medium is as great as that between media.

The lack of consistent support for one teaching methodology results in a tacit acknowledgment that one can neither blame the material for failures nor praise the material for successes. Rather, the bright spotlight focuses upon the real agent of the change—the classroom teacher.

The teacher who receives children directly from the kindergarten must recognize that the kindergarten year has not ironed out their variability. On the contrary, the better kindergarten programs widen the differences. As a result, the first grade teacher receives a group of students with many different strengths and weaknesses and with many different learning styles. The pupils will also have experienced a differentiated instructional program and thus will be at different achievement levels. It is up to the teacher to adapt her teaching methodology to the children, using whatever material is available which meets the students' needs as she diagnoses them.

The failure of specific material to do the whole job thrusts a heavy burden on the teacher of beginning reading. She must become knowledgeable as to different approaches and media so that she may orchestrate a program of reading instruction which draws its quality from the flexible, creative use of many teaching methods. However, if she lacks the necessary knowledge, she can be effective only if she assumes personal responsibility for her own inservice education and actually seeks the knowledge she knows she has to have.

It seems that the best way to diagnose student achievement and student weaknesses is by means of oral tests. Paper and pencil tests do not offer as clear a picture to the teacher of the specific lacks in student achievement or the specific kinds of errors being made. This is why the testing program in the City Schools Reading Series, written by a team of Detroit teachers, has emphasized the need for a continuous oral testing program. Certainly individual oral tests are more time consuming than silent-reading tests and sometimes administratively cumbersome; but in the long run, the results offer so much more knowledge about the child that the time used is very well spent.

It is impossible in a brief article to spell out a complete reading methodology, but two emphases seem to be important.

First, entrance into reading should be natural and meaningful to the child. For example, kindergarten children may begin by learning to read their names in order to take their name cards from a counter and place them in the rack that shows who is "present today." Or, they may learn the letters in their names so that they can respond to directions such as: "Stand up when the initial of your first name is called" or "Line up at the door if your name starts with 'C'."

The important point is that the child has a right to see a reason for learning and not be considered a captive participant in a meaningless drill program. There are many legitimate ways to offer opportunities for young children to learn basic reading skills and to use the printed word as a communication tool.

A second emphasis is that the basal reader should not be considered the entire reading program but rather a tool in the program. A basic reader offers a framework upon which teachers must construct a reading program designed to meet the needs of a particular class and an individual youngster. The goal is ability to draw meaning from printed words, not the ability to read a certain story in a basal reader. There are many avenues leading to this goal and many separate starting points. The professional teacher makes use of the avenue most appropriate to the student's starting point and moves him along only as fast as he is able to proceed.

SUMMARY

Early reading can be considered along two dimensions, timing and methodology. It would seem that the key words to be kept in mind are "some children." Some children are able to read before they start school; some children are developmentally ready to begin reading during the kindergarten; some children will not begin reading until well beyond kindergarten. Some children will learn to read best by means of strong phonetic training; some will learn to read best by a strong emphasis on comprehension and meaning. Some children will learn to read despite all we may do as teachers to confuse and discourage them!

REFERENCES

Bond, G. L., and Dykstra, R. The role of the coordinating center in the cooperative research program. *The Reading Teacher*, 1966, *19*, 565-568.

McKee, P., Brzlinski, J. E., and Harrison, Lucile M. *The effectiveness of teaching reading in kindergarten.* (Cooperative Research Project No. 5-0371) Washington, D. C.: United States Office of Education, 1966.

Are Deficient Readers Born or Created?

R. Baird Shuman

Everyone who has observed young children closely has surely recognized that language development is startlingly rapid between ages two and five. The child progresses almost overnight from monosyllabic baby talk to the building of intelligible sentences. With no formal instruction in the structure of language, the pre-schooler learns to communicate with considerable effectiveness, employing virtually every sentence pattern available to speakers of English and handling such matters as juncture and intonation as the situation demands.

Before he enters the primary grades, the child has, according to Ruth Strickland, "learned the basic phonology of a language and also its basic syntax. . . . he has learned to give his attention to sound and schemes of operation. He is deeply interested in language and recognizes its worth in his daily living."[1] The child at this stage is articulate and he uses language naturally, learning new words and phrases so quickly that adults often feel that they must be very careful of what they say in front of four- or five-year-olds, who are known to repeat everything they hear.

For many children, the first exposure to formal education leads not to greater articulateness and freedom of expression but rather to the development of linguistic or communicative inhibitions. The development of such inhibitions in some children appears to be directly related to their learnng to read.

Baird Shuman is Professor of Education at Duke University, Durham, North Carolina.

Teachers of young children have long been at a loss to explain the processes by which children learn to read. The mechanical processes are to a large extent physiological and ophthamological. The questions of readiness and comprehension are more psychological and linguistic. People from an assortment of academic disciplines have attempted to come to an intelligent, scientific understanding of how children learn to read while the less scientific—among them most parents and primary school teachers—have worked more or less intuitively toward helping children learn to read in a broad variety of ways. In some manner or other, an estimated 97% of our adult population has developed reading skills sufficient for their daily needs; that is, they can read newspapers, labels on cans, road signs, and time tables, even though they might be unable to read James Joyce or William Faulkner with any real comprehension.

Leonard Bloomfield was concerned that teachers have characteristically known relatively little about linguistics, his own academic discipline: "In view of our schools' concentration on verbal discipline, it is surprising to see that they are utterly benighted in linguistic matters. How training is best imparted must be for the pedagogue to determine, but it is evident that no pedagogic skill will help a teacher who does not know the subject which is to be taught."[2] Bloomfield took an active concern in the area of reading instruction and in 1940 pro-

ELEMENTARY ENGLISH, 1973, Vol. 50, No. 1, pp. 22-26,48.

duced *Teaching Children to Read,* which was updated by Clarence L. Barnhart and published for the first time in 1961 under the title *Let's Read: A Linguistic Approach.*[3] Bloomfield's 1942 article, "Linguistics and Reading,"[4] also remains a landmark in the literature concerning reading which is available to teachers today.

Bloomfield takes a categorical stand against teaching reading by use of phonic methods: "The letters of the alphabet are signs which direct us to produce sounds of our language. A confused and vague appreciation of this fact has given rise to the so-called 'phonic' methods of teaching children to read." He goes on to point out that those who would employ phonic methods "confuse writing with speech." He reminds the reader that the proponent of phonic methods is guilty "of isolating the speech-sounds" by expecting the child to say a letter like *t* "either all by itself or else with an obscure vowel sound after it." He correctly asserts that "English-speaking people . . . are not accustomed to make that kind of a noise. The sound *(t)* does not occur alone in English utterance." And he concludes that "If we insist on making the child perform unaccustomed feats with his vocal organs, we are bound to confuse his response to the printed signs."[5]

Bloomfield proposes a *word-method* approach to the teaching of reading and would begin with simple monosyllables "in which the letters have the sound-values assigned at the outset."[6] He would include such words as *hat, pat, man, pin,* and *tap* at this first stage, but would exclude words with double consonants; words such as *gem* and *get,* since the initial sound in each is spelled the same but pronounced differently; words with semi-irregular spellings such as *line* or *shine* in which the final vowel, while not pronounced, affects the preceding vowel; words which are spelled irregularly such as *right* or *enough* or *knit;* and words containing the letters *q,* which occurs only with *u,* and *x,* which represents two phonemes, (*ks* or *gz*).

At stage two, Bloomfield would introduce "regular spellings in which double consonants and other digraphs appear in consistent uses, e.g. *ll* as in *well, th* as in *thin, sh* as in *shin, ch* as in *chin, ee* as in *see, ea* as in *sea, oa* as in *road, oo* as in *spoon.*"[7] He would also introduce a limited number of words of irregular spelling—*is, was, the*—so that the content of reading material might be more varied. However, Bloomfield would not rush into this second stage; he would be very sure that the student had mastered the first stage before broaching this new material.

At the third stage would be introduced the semi-irregular spellings—*line, shine,* etc. —; two-syllable words with assigned sound-values—*winter, summer, butter,* etc.—and such common irregular words as would facilitate the expansion of reading materials. The fourth stage would take up irregularly spelled words—*rough, though, night,* etc.

In terms of linguistics, Bloomfield's suggestions make considerable sense. However, from a practical viewpoint—a very necessary viewpoint for the teacher at the primary level—Bloomfield probably errs by trying to make generalizations about the learning process which are valid for only some students who are learning to read. The method which Bloomfield suggests is overly compartmentalized and highly restrictive.

When a child is learning to *speak,* he is not protected from polysyllabic words, from variances in pronunciation, or from any of the components of human utterances. He is surrounded by a noise environment which increasingly comes to be meaningful to him; it is by imitating elements of this noise environment that he ultimately learns to speak, progressing rapidly from the rudimentary *ma-ma/da-da* stage to the point that he is able to communicate quite fully, using, by the time he is five years old, about fifteen hundred words of varying degrees of complexity to fashion utterances which must be meaningful to others. If they are less than meaningful, the child fails to communicate and isolates himself by this failure. Motivation for language learning is never greater than in the first five years of a child's existence.

Certainly I do not mean to imply that learning to speak is wholly comparable to learning to read or learning to write. Each area of communication is unique and the learning problems involved in mastering each are peculiar to the individual area; nevertheless, there is *some* interrelationship among these three basic areas and this interrelationship cannot be so completely ignored as it sometimes has been. Nor can one who works with children ignore the fact that different children learn in different ways. Given a single school environment, one child teaches himself to read, another is still a nonreader at age eight, another has mastered the mechanics of reading simple material, but he reads it with such difficulty that he cannot comprehend the meaning of what he is reading, hence is virtually a nonreader, and yet another can read with good comprehension but is unable to read aloud. When one finds himself working in such a situation as this, it should rapidly become apparent to him that (1) he can adopt no single method of teaching his twenty or twentfy-five students to read and (2) he cannot realistically expect anything even vaguely resembling uniform results from his teaching.

The primary classroom—and hopefully it will be an ungraded classroom in which everyone proceeds at his own pace—should offer its children both the incentive and opportunity for learning to read and write. The spontaneous verbal fluency with which the child enters school should be encouraged in every way for it is the foundation upon which the other skills of communication must necessarily be built. Achievement must be measured individually rather than comparatively for, as Albert J. Harris has astutely observed in regard to standardized reading tests, "Because they show how a child compares with other children rather than exactly what he can do with specific kinds of reading materials, standardized tests are somewhat less useful for instructional guidance than has often been assumed."[8] This statement can really be extended to include any sort of comparative evaluation of one's achievement in learning basic skills. It is as patently absurd for teachers to grade primary students in reading and writing as it would be for parents to grade two year olds in speaking. And fortunately, few schools now exist in which letter or numerical grades are given to youngsters at the primary level.

Primary teachers must give considerable thought to what they mean by *reading.* Is a child reading if he can vocalize correctly from symbols on the page? Is he reading if, on seeing the letter *b,* he can say *bbbb-* or *bee*? Is he reading if he can pronounce the words in a short sentence, but if he does so with such difficulty and so slowly that he does not know what the sentence means? If one is referring merely to the mechanical process of reading, the answer to these questions is yes. And for many teachers, reading at the primary level refers to a mechanical process rather than to a process involving comprehension.

The danger in this is that the child who is taught to look carefully at each word and pronounce it may well develop into the teenager who pronounces each word under his breath and reads with such arduous slowness that reading can never be a pleasure to him. Certainly there is danger in generalizing; some youngsters who learn to read by pronouncing each word eventually develop into excellent readers. However, I am convinced that many deficient readers are deficient because they have never progressed beyond the first stage of reading which in most schools has involved the conscious articulation of words from the printed page. In other words, some youngsters have been turned into deficient readers by the training they have received.

The young child who is placed in an enriching environment will generally learn, with little formal instruction, by exploring that environment. Both Montessori and Piaget have stressed the importance of providing the young child with objects which he can handle and with which he can experiment. The three year old who begins to throw things or who slowly pours his milk from his cup is experimenting, for example, with some basic rules of physics despite all that his mother might say about his being a naughty child. The child who separates blue beads from red beads is, without instruction, engaging in a process of differentiation. It is important that the child do these things; and it is equally important that, when he enters school, he be surrounded by an informal environment filled with materials which will be interesting to him. Maria Montessori has discussed in some detail how teachers might, at minimal expense, provide such materials.[9]

The classroom should provide an active word environment. Pieces of furniture and parts of the room should be labeled with large, lower case block letters: *door, desk, chair, window,* etc.[10] Reading material of the most enticing sorts should be abundant and should be readily available within the classroom. The child who reads a book by merely looking at the pictures is growing used to seeing print on pages; the child who pours through the frames of a comic strip is learning an important lesson in reading: that of moving from left to right, from top to bottom, a requisite in learning to read English. To the adult mind this may seem trivial; however, to the child just becoming acquainted with printed media, this represents a great stride forward.

Children should be encouraged to tell very brief stories which the teacher or an aide will write down and either ditto or type. The child whose story is translated into written form is often able to "read" his own story, truly recognizing some of the words and remembering from his telling most of the others. It often happens also that other students in a primary class will be able to read stories told by some of their classmates.

Obviously, when this technique is used in the early stages of reading instruction, many of Bloomfield's principles of teaching reading are violated—words like *elephant, hippopotamus, light, mother, father, grandmother, rough, quiet, fix,* etc. will creep in. But the student will ultimately come to recognize these words if they are presented through his own story. They are already part of his vocabulary else he would not have used them.

Children are intrigued by machines. They will spend happy hours playing with such machines as typewriters and cassette players. The teacher can capitalize on this interest if he can beg, borrow, or steal a few old typewriters for his classroom and if he can obtain a few cassette players. The latter should be used in part for him to record readings of his youngsters' favorite books. He should read the text into the cassette clearly but not too slowly. He should include the direction "Turn the page," every time it is necessary to turn a page. The student who listens to the cassette while following the pictures in his book will eventually come to recognize the words below the pictures and will soon be able to read the book—or at least major portions of it—on his own. Such listening activities probably are most effective if they are individual or small group activities rather than whole class activities. To succeed best, they should also be voluntary, for the question of readiness again arises here.

One of the few whole class reading activities I would suggest would be essentially a reading game. The teacher or aide would letter simple commands on cards: "Sit down," "Stand up," "Turn around," "Say, 'Hi.'," etc. The cards with the simplest commands (linguistically speaking) would be shown first and read aloud. The next day the cards would be shown again in the same order but would not be read unless no one obeyed the command. In subsequent days, the cards would be scrambled, and ultimately more difficult words would be used in the commands. Some cards would have full sentence commands on them. However, for variety, the teacher might say "Point to" and then hold up cards with only the determiner and the noun—*the door, the desk, the book, the pen.*

The virtue of this sort of exercise, which Bloomfield mentions briefly in "Linguistics and Reading,"[11] is that it encourages rapid reading for content rather than the slow perusal of each individual letter or word. At the beginning, relatively few children will actually read the command; most will be following the leads of another child; however, in time, many of the students will be reading the commands. This exercise, which has to be repeated several times to be effective, should not last for more than five to seven minutes each time or it will become boring.

When children are first learning to read, they may have difficulty recognizing on one page a word which they were able to read on another. This often surprises adults, but it should not. John Holt tells of obtaining samples of Oriental writing from a British printer and of the difficulty that he, a trained adult, had in recognizing the same symbol when it occurred in different places.[12] Try it with Arabic or Chinese, and you may understand better some of the problems which face your beginning readers.

Often, when a child is beginning to read, he will approach the teacher and ask what a given word in the text is. Many teachers ask the child to sound the word out or to guess what it is. John Holt questions the effectiveness of this widely used practice:

> On this day she [the little girl he was teaching] found such a word. Slowly she climbed out of her chair and, holding the book, came toward me. I looked at her as she came. She had a set, stern expression on her face. Pointing to a word in her book, she asked, "What does it say?" Her look seemed to say, "Now please don't ask me a lot of silly questions, like: 'What do you think it says?' or 'Have you tried sounding it out?' or anything like that. If I could do those things, I wouldn't be up here asking. Just tell me what the word says: that will be enough." I told her. She nodded, went back to her chair, and continued to read.[13]

In discussing this exchange with the little girl's mother, Holt asked whether Linda often asked for such help. The mother said that she did this only once or twice a week, but that she never forgot the words which she had asked about.

Every child must be allowed to develop his own best style of reading. The fact that he cannot read well aloud might point to a significant reading deficiency. On the other hand, it could indicate that he is able to read rapidly and with good comprehension without focusing on each letter or word. The fact that he might be slow in beginning to read does not necessarily mean that he is destined to be a deficient reader. The role of the teacher in the teaching of reading in the primary grades is to provide an atmosphere in which the child's curiosity will be piqued, to provide materials which will lead the child toward learning to read, and to provide specific instruction *when the child is ready for it.* The teacher who insists that children read each letter carefully and sound it out may well be leading the child into the development of habits which will forever interfere with his becoming a rapid, efficient reader.

Notes

1. "Building on What We Know," in J. Allen Figurel, ed., *Reading and Realism*, XIII (Newark, Delaware: International Reading Association, 1969), p. 59.
2. *Language* (New York: Holt, Rinehart and Winston, 1961), pp. 499-500.
3. (Detroit: Wayne State University Press, 1961).
4. *The Elementary English Review*, XIX (1942), pp. 125-130, 183-186.
5. *Ibid.*, pp. 130, 183.
6. *Ibid.*, p. 185.
7. *Ibid.*, p. 186.
8. Albert J. Harris, "Key Factors in a Successful Reading Program," in Eldonna Evertts, ed., *Aspects of Reading* (Champaign, Illinois: National Council of Teachers of English, 1970), p. 6.
9. Maria Montessori, *The Montessori Method* (New York: Schocken Books, 1970), pp. 271-309, particularly pp. 296-307.
10. See Charles E. Silberman's suggestions in *Crisis in the Classroom* (New York: Random House, 1970), p. 245.
11. *Loc. cit.*, p. 183.
12. John Holt, *How Children Learn* (New York: Pitman Publishing Company, 1969), p. 95.
13. *Ibid.*, pp. 92-93.

Readiness tests: implications for early childhood education

ROBERT T. RUDE

University of Wisconsin doctoral candidate Robert Rude is a reading specialist for the university's Research and Development Center for Cognitive Learning. He has criss-crossed the United States for presentations of the Center's Wisconsin Design for Reading Skills Development.

INCREASED interest in the cognitive development of preschool children has been evident during the past decade. Bruner's (1960) statement that any subject can be taught in some intellectually honest form to any child at any stage of development, and the current interest in Piagetian psychology have resulted in a profusion of studies focusing on early childhood education. Unfortunately, many investigations appear to be intent on proving a point or reinforcing the investigator's personal bias about the issue under study. This is especially true in considering the feasibility of teaching three, four, or five year olds to read.

Two distinct schools of thought prevail regarding this issue. The first, decrying the dangers of teaching young children to read, is generally espoused by the child development experts. Hymes (1958), for instance, makes an emotional plea for not introducing reading before the child enrolls in first grade. Writing about perception, he states: "Those eyes must have grown enough so they can quickly see, when they are taught, that *c* and *e* and *o* are different" (p. 23). Robison and Spodek (1965) caution that reading should not be introduced into kindergartens for want of anything better.

The second school of thought insists that reading instruction begin as early as possible. Fowler (1964, 1971), for example, describes the structural dimensions of the learning process in early reading and then delineates a pro-

THE READING TEACHER, 1973, Vol. 26, pp. 572-580.

gram designed to teach preschoolers to read. Bereiter and Engelmann (1966) contend that the preschool teacher, rather than the first grade teacher, is generally in a better position to assure successful and enjoyable first encounters with academically oriented instructional programs.

Understandable confusion

Preschool and kindergarten teachers have good reason to be perplexed when trying to decide if they should teach reading. It is difficult to determine which course to follow when each side argues convincingly for its instructional philosophy. Regardless of which position is advocated, however, the concept of readiness plays an important part in determining when instruction will commence. The term *readiness* connotes different meanings to individuals, however.

Durkin's (1970) thorough historical review of the term illustrates how changing psychological beliefs affect the educator's perception of the concept of readiness. The belief that readiness is an assessable commodity, however, has been held since the early 1920's. Durkin (1967) contends that many of our readiness paper and pencil assessments ". . . are leftovers from an earlier era that was characterized by a very naive faith in the validity and so-called 'objectivity' of test scores" (p. 28). Dykstra's (1967) critique of assumptions implicit in readiness test usage is in general agreement with Durkin's position. And yet the fact that reading readiness tests have been published for over half a century implies a certain degree of credibility and worth.

It is easy to understand, then, why some preschool, many kindergarten, and most first grade teachers have turned to reading readiness tests to help them determine pupil readiness for reading. These tests are believed to add reliability to teacher judgment. Additionally, the tests provide objective data for administrative personnel who need to be concerned with policy decisions regarding the desirability of teaching reading to young pupils.

A fundamental question needs to be raised, however, before readiness tests are chosen and administered. Specifically, what skills are prerequisite to successful reading, and are they measurable?

Lack of knowledge

Unfortunately, little is known about this area. Calfee and his associates (1970), however, describe a series of prereading skill tests that covered five areas of cognitive functioning: matching of visual forms, auditory-phonetic identification, letter-sound association, vocabulary knowledge, and general achievement. The tests are purported to assess necessary skills a child must master before he can read adequately.

A similar diagnostic/instructional program is developed and described by Venezky (1970). Six skills are considered essential prerequisites to successful beginning reading: attention to letter order, attention to letter orientation, attention to word detail, picture sound learning, sound matching, and sound blending. Data obtained from field tests should provide needed insights into constituent components requisite for successful performance in reading.

In another study examining reading readiness skill prerequisites, Jeffrey and Samuels (1967)

Table 1

Reading readiness batteries, subtests, and subtest titles*

	Metropolitan	Murphy-Durrell	Clymer-Barrett	Gates-MacGinitie	Harrison-Stroud
vocabulary develop.	word meaning				
listening	listening			listening comp. and following directions	using the context and using context and auditory clues
letter recognition	alphabet	letter names	recognition of letters	letter recognition	giving the names of the letters
numbers	numbers				
visual-motor coordination	copying		shape completion and copy-a-sentence	visual-motor coordination	
rhyming words			discrim. of ending sounds in words		
phoneme correspond.		phonemes	discrim. of beginning sounds in words		making auditory discrim.
learning rate		learning rate			
auditory discrim.				auditory discrim.	
auditory blending				auditory blending	
word recognition				word recognition	
matching	matching		matching words	visual discrim.	using symbols and making visual discrim.

*Subtest titles are given in the appropriate cells

used a task analysis to determine what subskills are required to independently decode a set of four words. They found that when first grade subjects combined left-to-right visual scan, phonic blend training, and letter-sound training, they out-performed a control group which did not receive the training.

While the Venezky and Jeffrey-Samuels studies are not identical, both focus on at least three of the following skills: grapheme perception, left to right visual scan, understanding of grapheme-phoneme relationships, and phoneme blending ability.

Assuming that these skills are indeed requisite to reading, it is interesting to examine the content of major reading readiness batteries to determine which specific skills are assessed and what techniques are employed in their measurement. While Barrett (1970) attempted to explicate the content of five major reading readiness batteries, he listed and tabulated only the readiness factors measured. There was no indepth analysis of subtest content and evaluation techniques—factors that must be considered if teachers and administrators are to make intelligent decisions concerning which, if any, readiness battery should be administered.

Reading readiness batteries

This study examines five major reading readiness batteries: the *Metropolitan Readiness Tests; Murphy-Durrell Reading Readiness Analysis; Clymer-Barrett Prereading Battery; Gates-MacGinitie Reading Test—Readiness Skills;* and *Harrison-Stroud Reading Readiness Profiles.* These instruments were assumed to represent current attempts to measure reading readiness.

Interestingly, there is lack of consensus among test authors as to which skills should be assessed as well as the techniques employed to assess them. The *Gates-MacGinitie Reading Test—Readiness Skills* for example, includes seven separate subtests while the *Murphy-Durrell Reading Readiness Analysis* consists of only three subtests (see Table 1). Disagreement is also apparent in the labeling of the subtests, even though tests are essentially similar. The broad category entitled Matching, for instance, included the following subtest labels: Matching, Matching Words, Visual Discrimination, Using Symbols, and Making Visual Discrimination. Additional labeling ambiguity is found between other similar subtests in each battery.

Subskill categories

To better understand the content of the five batteries, each subtest was examined to determine which skills were assessed. Twelve specific subskill categories were listed. Techniques used to assess each skill were then identified.

Word meaning. Only one of the five batteries, the *Metropolitan Readiness Test,* measures word meaning. According to Hildreth et al (1965) this subtest measures the child's store of verbal concepts. They assert that since the test measures oral vocabulary acquisition, it is an index of general mental maturity. The skill is assessed by having the child mark one picture from a three item array. The teacher identifies orally each picture in the array and asks the child to mark one of them. There are sixteen items.

Listening. Three tests purport to measure listening ability. Two of the three tests, the *Gates-MacGinitie Reading Test—Readiness Skills* and the *Harrison-Stroud Reading Readiness Profiles* include two subtests within each battery to measure this skill. With the exception of the Using the Context and Auditory Clues subtest of the *Harrison-Stroud Reading Readiness Profiles,* the tests typically require the child to mark the picture that depicts the sentence or paragraph read by the teacher.

The Using the Context and Auditory Clues subtest, however, introduces an important variable not found in other subtests. Specifically, the child was asked to select the correct response based on his understanding of grapheme-phoneme relationships as well as overall listening ability. An example of test directions from the *Harrison-Stroud Reading Readiness Profiles* teachers' manual:

> Move your finger down to the blue box under the green box. Find a basket, a balloon, and a wagon.... Listen: Bob brought the things

> home from the store in something. What Bob used begins like his name. Draw a line under the picture of what Bob used to bring the things home from the store . . . (p. 20)

Letter recognition. All batteries include a subtest measuring letter recognition. This is not surprising when one considers that letter recognition ability consistently correlates highly with later reading achievement (Chall, 1967). A closer examination of the subtests reveals, however, that four batteries assess letter recognition by having the child identify a letter named by the examiner from a multiple choice array. The *Harrison-Stroud Reading Readiness Profiles* subtest assesses the skill by asking the child to name the letter shown by the examiner. Nicholson (1958) shows the latter task to be more difficult than the former. It is interesting to speculate what effect this might have on test reliability. One serious drawback with the naming letter test is that it must be administered individually whereas the former subtests are all group administrable.

Numbers. Only the *Metropolitan Readiness Test* includes a numbers subtest. According to its authors, this battery measures a child's stock of number concepts, number knowledge, ability to manipulate quantitative relationships, recognition of and ability to produce number symbols, and related knowledge, such as the subject's concept of money. Since this test is not a reading assessment, per se, but an overall readiness assessment, a description of the assessment procedures will be omitted. It is interesting to note, nonetheless, that the numbers subtest in earlier versions of the test proved repeatedly to be the most powerful single predictive subtest of later academic achievement.

Visual-motor coordination. Three batteries include a subtest measuring visual-motor coordination. Each measure is unique, however. The *Metropolitan Readiness Test* requires the child to reproduce the entire stimulus item in a blank space. Included in the fourteen item subtest are two uppercase letter items, one lowercase letter item, one two digit number item, and ten geometric shapes.

The *Clymer-Barrett Prereading Battery* includes two subtests measuring visual-motor coordination. The first, Shape Completion, is a twenty item test requiring the subject to complete partially drawn responses until they replicate the stimuli, which are geometric shapes. The other subtest, entitled Copy-A-Sentence, requires the child to reproduce the sentence "The black dog jumped over the box." This task is designed to determine the subject's perception and ability to reproduce whole words in a given sequence.

The *Gates-MacGinitie Reading Test—Readiness Skills* subtest includes only seven items measuring visual-motor coordination. All items measure the child's ability to reproduce either upper or lowercase letters. The child supplies the remaining strokes to a partially completed letter, thereby matching the stimuli.

Rhyming words. The *Clymer-Barrett Prereading Battery* is the single battery found to contain a subtest measuring understanding of rhyming words. The subtest is entitled Discrimination of Ending Sounds in Words. While its authors contend that this task places the same requirements on the pupil and the teacher as Task 3 (Discrimination of Beginning Sounds in Words), the majority of items assess rhyming sound as well as ending sounds. It is conceivable, therefore, that a subject could score highly on the test because of his ability to discriminate rhyming sounds rather than his ability to discriminate nonrhyming ending sounds, per se.

Phoneme correspondence. Understanding phoneme relationships is an important skill in learning to read. It is surprising, therefore, to find this subtest included in only three batteries: *Murphy-Durrell Reading Readiness Analysis, Clymer-Barrett Prereading Battery,* and the *Harrison-Stroud Reading Readiness Profiles.*

The Phonemes subtest of the *Murphy-Durrell Reading Readiness Analysis*, a twenty-four item section, measures the most frequent consonant sounds in their initial position, with a few (five) in the final position. The test is divided into two sittings. Each sitting requires the examiner to teach the sound for each test item prior to assessment of the item. After the short teaching session, the subject marks two of the four choices which begin with the same sound. According to Murphy and Durrell, this procedure assures successful identification of the easiest sounds, and makes clear to the child what he is to do on the test.

The Clymer-Barrett battery evaluates knowledge of consonant sounds somewhat differently than the Murphy-Durrell test. The former twenty item subtest, Discrimination of Beginning Sounds in Words, requires the subject to select from a three item picture array the response matching the consonant stimulus.

The *Harrison-Stroud Reading Readiness Profiles* subtest, Making Auditory Discriminations, a sixteen item stimulus-response pairing assessment, requires the child to identify which of a two choice pic-

Table 2

Prereading skills as measured by five reading readiness batteries*

	Metropolitan	Murphy-Durrell	Clymer-Barrett	Gates-MacGinitie	Harrison-Stroud
grapheme perception	alphabet (matching)	letter names (learning rate)	recognition of letters (matching words) (copy-a-sentence)	letter recognition (visual discrimination) (visual-motor coordination) (word recognition)	giving the names of the letters (using symbols) (making visual discriminations)
left-to-right visual scan	(matching)	(learning rate)	copy-a-sentence (matching words)	(visual discrimination) (word recognition)	(using symbols) (making visual discriminations)
grapheme-phoneme relationships		phonemes (learning rate)		(word recognition)	
phoneme blending		(learning rate)		auditory blending (word recognition)	

*Parentheses indicate subordinate subtests measuring skills in a limited manner

ture array begins with the same initial consonant as the stimulus. It is similar to the Clymer and Barrett subtest with the exception of a two choice rather than a three choice response array.

Learning rate. The Murphy-Durrell Reading Readiness Analysis is the only instrument which contains a learning rate subtest. The rationale for including this subtest is based on the assumption that if a child can learn words easily at the time of school entrance, there is no reason to delay reading instruction or to give reading readiness practice. Nine words, including nouns, verbs, and adjectives, are taught to subjects. One hour later, subjects are asked to identify each word in two multiple choice situations.

Auditory discrimination. One subtest, Auditory Discrimination, found in the *Gates-MacGinitie Reading Test—Readiness Skills*, assesses auditory discrimination. The label, strictly speaking, is somewhat of a misnomer. Actually, the test is best described as a "listening" or "following directions" assessment rather than an auditory discrimination test. From a two choice, twenty-one item picture array, subjects mark the object named by the examiner. A portion of the test administrator's manual directions follows:

> Now look at the first box on this side of the page, the box where I'm pointing. There you see some money and a monkey. Take your pencil, ready to work. Put one finger of your other hand on the first box. Listen: MONEY, MONKEY. Put an X on MONKEY. Make the X a big one so that it is easy for me to see (p. 6).

Auditory blending. Only the *Gates-MacGinitie Reading Test—Readiness Skills* includes an auditory blending subtest. This test purportedly measures the child's ability to join the parts of a word, presented orally, into a whole word. The test manual instructs the examiner to say:

> I will ask you to put an X on one of the three pictures in this box. I will say the name of the picture in two or three parts. You listen carefully and see if you can put an X on the picture that I name. Put an X on RAB-BIT (p. 12).

Word Recognition. The *Gates-MacGinitie Reading Test—Readiness Skills* assesses word recognition through a subtest of twenty-four items, each consisting of three words. In each item subjects mark the word that is read by the teacher. Whole word recognition is measured. This and the Learning Rate subtest are the only measures in the twelve subtests categories which actually require subjects to read.

Matching. Matching subtests are found in four of the five batteries. As was the case with many of the other subtest categories, a variety of techniques are used to measure the skill.

The *Metropolitan Readiness Test* uses a fourteen item stimulus-response pairing assessment. Upper and lower case letter words and geometric shapes constitute the test. Subjects match the correct response, from a three choice array, with the stimulus item. The *Clymer-Barrett Prereading Battery* uses essentially the same technique with two exceptions. First, only lower case letter words are used, and secondly, a four item response array is used instead of the three item array. Twenty items are included in the *Clymer-Barrett Pre-*

reading Battery instead of fourteen items as in the *Metropolitan Readiness Test.*

The Matching subtest of the *Gates-MacGinitie Reading Test—Readiness Skills,* Visual Discrimination, uses still another assessment technique: oddity selection. Twenty-four items constitute the subtest. Each item contains four lower case letter words; the child marks the word which is different from the remaining three.

The *Harrison-Stroud Reading Readiness Profiles* includes two subtests to assess matching ability. The first, Using Symbols, measures the subject's ability to understand the use of symbols (words) to represent familiar pictures. Subjects match lower case letter words with pictures. The other subtest, Making Visual Discriminations, is administered in two parts. Both require the correct matching of lower case letter words in a four item stimulus-response pairing array. The first portion of Making Visual Discriminations is paced by the examiner; the latter half is done independently.

The value of this analysis becomes apparent when a comparison is made between the composite Venezky and Jeffrey-Samuels prereading skills list and the reading readiness batteries. This is especially evident when categorizing the subtests of each battery to determine whether they measure grapheme perception, left-to-right visual scan, understanding of grapheme-phoneme relationships, and phoneme blending.

Only eight of the twenty-nine battery subtests can be classified unequivocally as measuring the four specified prereading skills (see Table 2). Nine other subtests measure the four skills in a less straightforward manner and were therefore classified as subordinate measures—that is, they could be construed as measuring the skill but only in limited manner.

Most striking is the fact that twelve of the twenty-nine total subtests measured abilities other than the four identified prereading skills considered necessary for competent reading. Interesting too is the fact that grapheme perception is the most frequently assessed skill, followed by left-to-right visual scan, grapheme-phoneme relationships, and phoneme blending. Evidently, the latter two skills are not deemed important, are difficult to assess, or have been overlooked by reading and measurement specialists.

Discussion

What implications are evident for teachers and administrators in early childhood education? First, reading readiness test authors disagree as to what constitutes reading readiness skills. Investigators are only beginning to discover the constituent elements of reading readiness. Levin and his associates (1963), Gibson (1970), and Samuels (1970) provide some of the data needed to better understand the beginning reading process. Meanwhile, educators must define reading readiness operationally as best they can, being aware of limitations inherent in the definition.

Secondly, personnel who instruct young beginning readers must realize that reading readiness tests measure a limited number of readiness skills. Attention span, cognitive learning style, and experiential background are only three important factors which are not measured in the five batteries examined.

Third, while this paper investigates the specific content and format of five popular reading readiness batteries, there is ". . . almost no evidence that the increased teaching of these skills will ensure success in learning to read (Farr, 1969, p. 154)." An important point often overlooked by teachers is that most test authors report their reading readiness tests to be *predictive*, not *diagnostic*, in nature. The limited number of items in most subtests and the high correlations often found between subtests within the same battery prohibit diagnostic interpretation.

References

Barrett, T. C. "Predicting Reading Achievement through Readiness Tests." *Measurement and Evaluation of Reading*, Ed. R. Farr. New York: Harcourt, Brace & World, Inc., 1970.

Bereiter, C., and Engelmann. *Teaching Disadvantaged Children in the Preschool.* Englewood Cliffs, New Jersey: Prentice-Hall, Inc., 1966.

Bruner, J. S. *The Process of Education.* New York: Vintage Books, 1960.

Calfee, R. C., Chapman, R. S., and Venezky, R. L. *How a Child Needs to Think to Learn to Read.* Technical Report No. 131. Madison, Wisconsin: Wisconsin Research and Development Center for Cognitive Learning, 1970.

Chall, J. *Learning to Read: The Great Debate.* New York: McGraw-Hill Book Company, 1967.

Clymer, T., and Barrett, T. *Clymer-Barrett Prereading Battery.* Princeton, New Jersey: Personnel Press, 1969.

Durkin, D. "Informal Techniques for the Assessment of Prereading Behavior." *The Evaluation of Children's Reading Achievement*, Ed. T. C. Barrett. Newark, Delaware: International Reading Association, 1967.

Durkin, D. *Teaching Them to Read.* Boston: Allyn and Bacon, Inc., 1970.

Dykstra, R. "The Use of Reading Readiness Tests for Prediction and Diagnosis: A Critique." *The Evaluation of Children's Reading Achievement*, Ed. T. C. Barrett. Newark, Delaware: International Reading Association, 1967.

Farr, R. *Reading: What Can Be Measured?* Newark, Delaware: International Reading Association, 1969.

Farr, R., and Anastasiow, N. *Tests of Reading Readiness and Achievement: A Review and Evaluation.* Newark, Delaware: International Reading Association, 1969.

Fowler, W. "A Developmental Learning Strategy for Early Reading in a Laboratory Nursery School." *Interchange* 2 (1971). pp. 106-25.

Fowler, W. "Structural Dimensions of the Learning Process in Early Reading." *Child Development*, Vol. 35 (1964), pp. 1093-1104.

Gates, A., and MacGinitie, W. *Gates-MacGinitie Reading Test—Readiness Skills.* New York: Teachers College Press, Teachers College, Columbia University, 1968.

Gibson, E. "Learning to Read." *Theoretical Models and Processes of Reading*, Eds. H. Singer and R. Ruddell. Newark, Delaware: International Reading Association, 1970.

Harrison, M. L., and Stroud, J. B. *The Harrison-Stroud Reading Readiness Profiles.* Boston: Houghton Mifflin Company, 1950.

Hildreth, G., Griffiths, N., and McGawran, M. *Metropolitan Readiness Tests.* New York: Harcourt, Brace & World, 1965.

Hymes, J. L., Jr. *Before the Child Reads.* New York: Harper & Row, 1958.

Jeffrey, W. E., and Samuels, S. J. "The Effect of Method of Reading Training on Initial Learning and Transfer." *Journal of Verbal Learning and Verbal Behavior*, Vol. 6 (1967), pp. 354-58.

Levin, H., Gibson, E., Baldwin, A., Gibson, J., Hockett, C., Ricciuti, H., and Suci, G. *A Basic Research Program on Reading.* Cooperative Research Project No. 639. Ithaca, New York: Cornell University, 1963.

Murphy, H., and Durrell, D. *Murphy-Durrell Reading Readiness Analysis.* New York: Harcourt, Brace & World, 1965.

Nicholson, A. "Background Abilities Related to Reading Success in First Grade." *Journal of Education*, Vol. 140 (1958), pp. 7-24.

Robison, H. F., and Spodek, B. *New Directions in Kindergarten.* New York: Teachers College Press, Teachers College, Columbia University, 1965.

Samuels, S. J. "Letter-Name versus Letter-Sound Knowledge as Factors Influencing Learning to Read." Paper read to American Educational Research Association, Minneapolis, 1970.

Venezky, R. L. "The Prereading Skills Program." Unpublished manuscript, Wisconsin Research and Development Center for Cognitive Learning, 1970.

THE CHILD FROM THREE TO EIGHT, WITH IMPLICATIONS FOR READING

FRANCES ILG

ALL TOO OFTEN, I fear, we are prone to neglect the developmental aspects of a child's growth. We are likely to make our judgments according to where we think he *should* be. Or we try to push him along, to teach him, so that he will progress to where we *think* he should be.

It would be far better if we studied the child, determined his present development and achievement, and related them to what has gone on before. Then we could glimpse the future and could more readily provide what he needs and is capable of absorbing right now. Growth is, to be sure, a complex of three forces—age, individuality, and environment. Each must be considered both separately and together with the other two. Only then are we in a position to help a child grow in his own unity.

The ability to read is a case in point. This ability does not appear suddenly. It does not appear merely in response to a learning situation. The organism's preparation for reading is long and elaborate. Without the early nascent stages, the basis has not been laid for reading readiness; the beginnings go far back in infancy. The patting of a picture in a picture book at 15 months is an initial, crude step that includes both recognition of form and meaning. This response is refined into pointing at a picture by 18 months and, finally, to naming the picture at 2 years of age.

Dr. Ilg, a recognized authority on the psychology of children, is director of the Gesell Institute in New Haven, Conn. Her publications have been widely read both at home and abroad, and she speaks from many years of close association with and careful study of boys and girls of all ages.

Dr. Ilg believes that educators must pay greater attention to the developmental needs of children, not pushing them into situations and tasks for which they lack readiness. She warns that such children may seemingly achieve quite well in grade one when the constant stimulation of new beginnings carries them along. Some children, says Dr. Ilg, might profitably wait until the age of 9 or even 10 before receiving formal reading instruction.

TEACHING YOUNG CHILDREN TO READ, H.E.W, Proceedings: Nov. 14-16, 1962, pp. 21-30.

This ability to look at pictures is an important step in recognizing a symbol of reality on the page. The young child not only shows his response by pointing and naming, but he also shows significant changes in his visual mechanism. We test these changes by throwing a beam of light from a retinoscope into the child's eye. We find that the eye shifts into a minus projection as high as −1.00 to −2.00 D., especially in the process of search. There is a definite release into less minus as the child points or names. This indicates that he is focusing well within the page. At an older age when the child is beginning to read, we find that the good readers shift their focus on a retinoscopic finding to −.50 to −.75 D. When this does not occur and when the scoping reveals a +.25 to +.50 D. finding, we know the child is focusing beyond the page. Children who focus beyond the page are more often than not poor readers.

Preschool Years

The early language ability of a child also gives us many clues to his expected progress in reading. Rapid, early language development suggests rapid early reading. Slow language development is very often correlated with slower progress in reading. If the combination of words into sentences is slow, you would also expect slow development in the reading of sentences. With children who wait as late as 2 or 3 years to acquire a vocabulary of single words, it is my opinion that we should expect very slow progress in reading.

Early interest in books and letters also portends early and good reading. A 9- to 12-month infant who picks up his baby books in preference to toys is, perhaps, disclosing an interest in being read to. This interest in books does not mean that he will not gaily tear up a paper book if he gets the chance, nor should we be alarmed over such destructive behavior. This paper tearing, which is enhanced by the paper being assembled in a book, is characteristic of his age. It does not mean that he will be disrespectful of books at a later age. I have seen a number of these young children who both loved books and loved to tear them who later became very fine book collectors.

The 2- to 2½-year-old often likes tiny things, tiny pellets, tiny cars, tiny books. You may find him walking around with a tiny edition of Kate Greenaway or Peter Rabbit, not because he is interested so much in the book as in its minuteness. And he loves tiny pictures. That is why he often likes a picture ABC book filled with little, separate colored pictures.

A more specific item that correlates more directly with reading is a child's interest in letters. As early as 2 to 2½ years, a child may go up to a bookshelf and point to the letters on the back of the books asking, "What dat?" I have found that the chances are good that a child with such a pronounced, early interest in letters will teach himself to read before he enters first grade.

The sustained ability to sit and listen to a story at 2 and 3 years of age offers a further clue to later good reading ability. When a child of 6 or 7 years is having difficulty in reading, it may be helpful to probe back into this earlier period to find out if he was able to sit still long enough to have a story read to him. My guess would be that he was not able to do so, that he bolted after a few minutes, and that he was a very active child. If we examined such a child with a retinoscope, we would probably discover that he was failing to register a good minus projection as he identified objects on a page; more than likely he would be scoping beyind the page into a +.25 to +.50 D. This is the type of child who has trouble with near vision—with near-point tasks. The child who has trouble in listening to a story is more likely to respond to a factual book, a book with good pictures of things he knows about and is interested in, such as trains, cars, trucks, and fire engines. The potentially good reader, on the other hand, likes not only these factual books, but also the more imaginative story in which he needs to project beyond the pictures, in which he needs to hold on to the thread of a plot.

Memorizing whole stories or especially nursery rhymes in the 3- to 3½-year-old period gives us a clue that good auditory recall may well be followed by good visual recall. The good memorizers, the ones who *seem* to be reading at around 5½ until they are checked on single words and are found to be memorizing the story, later become the good readers.

Learning Letters and Words

A fairly common age to begin to recognize letters is at 3½ to 4 years of age. It is interesting to watch the different patterns of learning characteristic of different children. Some recognize and choose only the round letters, as the *O*, *C*, *D*, or *G*. Others prefer letters with vertical and horizontal lines, such as the *T* and *H*. And some learn best by associating a letter with a word that has meaning for them such as *M is for mommy*, *D is for daddy*. The alphabet may already be gathering meaning for some. At least they enjoy singing the song about the alphabet, and they may know it by heart without knowing the letters separately.

When a 3½-year-old insists on looking at the page being read to him, he is beginning to relate pictures and words. This becomes a part of his listening and enhances his grasp of the story. This same child at the later age of 5 to 5½ can move from pictures to the recognition of single words. He likes to pick out or be shown words of strong impact such as *wow* or *oh boy*. He likes to pick out proper names that he has heard in the story especially because they begin with a certain capital letter.

Five adores anything to do with letters. He spells out words: *n-o*, *y-e-s*, or even a longer word like *m-o-m-m-y*. He intersperses these spelled-out words in his sentences and does this with such relish that he seems to feel that he possesses some marvelous new secret code. He is indeed at the gateway of a whole new world.

The child's progress in recognizing single words moves more rapidly at 5½ to 6 years. He is now beginning to recognize selected words on a page. But he is not interested in following a line of print. He prefers to move his eyes vertically. And he is interested in picking out certain words at random, ones which have meaning for him, ones which he has picked up in the context of the story as it has been read to him. He can read the word *Washington* as easily as *Jane* if the story is about Washington, and he can recognize this word because it begins with a *W*.

Immature Vision at 6

Six overcomes his unstable visual mechanism by keeping his place with his fingers. Sometimes as his eyes drop to the next line, he may drop too far and thus skip a line. He would profit by the use of a ruler as a marker. It is hard for me to understand why some teachers outlaw the use of a finger to keep the place, especially for 6-year-olds. When this habit still occurs at 8 and 9, of course, something is amiss and it may suggest the need for a visual examination.

As Six reads he often inserts words he has just read, especially adjectives, even though they do not recur. He loves repetition, often providing it for himself. This is why he finds repetitive primers so congenial to his temperament.

Six often gets his clues about a word from its initial letter and from its relative length. A word such as *mother* is recognized easily because it begins with an *m*. Six wants to know the sound of the initial letter. Everything about him shows an interest in beginnings. He is constantly making good starts. He wants to be first. But he cannot sustain his interest very long, and he is very poor at finishing. *It is important for a teacher to recognize that a child may do quite well in the first grade when the constant stimulation of new beginnings carries him along. But, alas, when the need for finishing at 7 is demanded of him, he may fail.*

Six still loves to be read to. Listening, I feel, is as much a part of learning to read as the actual act of reading itself. Unfortunately, parents stop reading to their children when they think it will hamper them from learning to read by themselves. The opposite is probably true; the more experience the child has with language and the written word, the faster will be his progress in reading.

A Look at 7-Year-Olds

The 7-year-old can fix his eyes more steadily on a page. He has developed marked improvement in his acuity and can read little letters with ease—in fact, preferring them. This is the time to introduce small letters. He is still likely to reverse certain letters such as *b* and *d* when he writes or reads them, but he almost always recognizes his errors and corrects them.

Seven is what we call a mechanical reader. His voice sounds mechanical as he reads aloud. He reads almost in a monotone with very little inflection as he links one sentence to the next and one paragraph to the next, not wishing to stop and work over a word he does not know. That is why he likes to be told a word when he does not know it. This is no time to interrupt his flow of reading, although he might guess at a word, since guessing is a quite typical 7-year-old response. Seven wants especially to hold on to the meaning of what he is reading, and this might be lost if he stopped to work over a word. This desire for meaning is so strong that he might read the word *surprise* as "birthday". There is a relationship here but not a visual one.

Seven drives to reach the end, to finish a task, even though it may be the hardest thing for him to do. Notice Seven's favorite words—*end*, *finish*, and *last*. Notice how he will even choose to be last in line in preference to being first as when he was 6.

8-Year-Olds Surge Forward

The release, relaxation, and flexibility that come at 8 years of age is a welcome change and so striking that it is as if a child had shifted to a higher gear. This change is soon evident in his reading. He develops a new capacity to attack words, new words which he has never seen. He can work them out phonetically, for he now knows the sounds of letters and combinations of letters and is able to put them together. He also sees the word as a whole in a flash. He not only sees the beginning and end of a word, but the middle too. He no longer has trouble with vowels. But the complications of double vowels and double consonants still may elude him.

Eight reads with expression. He knows how to pause, how to drop his voice at the end of a sentence. He no longer links sentence to sentence and paragraph to paragraph as he did at 7. He can now stop and work over a word in the middle of a sentence without losing the thread of the story. He can even stop to discuss what he is reading without losing his relationship to the story. He loves to read out loud to a group. He reads with greater speed.

Changes are also evident in his visual mechanism. He is now pushing out into space with a more flexible, totally operating mechanism. He has greater resiliency. He likes school, often for the first time. He is adjusting well to the group. He often considers his teacher a part of the group. If she can be caught in a mistake such as a misspelled word on the blackboard, she becomes one of the group. (A teacher should recognize this close potential tie and sometimes make a mistake deliberately, just so Eight can catch her on it. She is then really appreciated.) Eight often for the first time is reporting more fully about what is happening at school. Parents report that they no longer feel left out. This indicates that there should be closer communication between school and home, especially in the earlier grades when a child is a poor reporter.

Although this paper is primarily concerned with the child from 3 to 8, it is important for us to consider some characteristics of older children in order to understand more fully the younger child.

One of the outstanding forces that is operating at 8 is power of attack. This leads to very real changes at 9 and 10 years. Nine is an age that makes great demands on a growing child. His reading ability often advances rapidly. He now is more on his own. He is capable of going to the dictionary to look up the meanings of words. He comes to realize through the table of contents that a book is broken up into parts. He is beginning to know when he can skim and when he needs to read more thoroughly. He often prefers to read silently, although he still needs to be checked orally. Boys who have been slow or poor readers up to now, though they have earlier shown high interest and good comprehension, may now become good readers. Nine is eager for more and more information and is definitely interested in the different subjects at school.

By 10 a child is normally a proficient reader. He may also be a ravenous reader, sneaking books to bed and reading under the covers by flashlight. This behavior usually hits its peak at 11. Ten enjoys reading to his younger siblings and does so with good expression. He especially enjoys biographies and, most of all, stories about the childhoods of great men. He is beginning to read the newspaper and to keep up with daily events.

Symptoms To Study

In studying the process of learning to read, it is interesting to see if we can relate any outward manifestations of posture and behavior with the inner workings of the mind. Watching the child work with pencil and paper, watching his eye movements as he thinks, or his tongue movements as he writes, makes us aware of patterns related to age and quality of response.

Let us consider the 5-year-old. He sits erect. He moves his head mainly vertically. He does not shift his paper. His nondominant hand is flat, with fingers close together. This nondominant hand moves along beside the dominant hand as he writes. His eyes stare into space as he thinks. Notice how often older children who have difficulty in reading hold on to the restricted patterns of the 5-year-old. Their bodies do not take on new patterns of behavior. They are, as it were, sitting on a point with blinders on.

By 5½ the head starts moving from side to side, the eyes are more fluid, and the tongue sweeps from side to side over the lips almost in a contorted way. This breakup that begins at 5½ begins to gather a direction more surely in six. His head is more often tilted to the nondominant side as he writes. The paper is often tilted slightly. The nondominant hand is still flat, but now with fingers spread. The tongue is beginning to inhibit itself, but often pushes against the lower lip or cheeks. The eyes have wide lateral sweeps as Six thinks.

By 7 the shift of both paper and body is more evident. The whole nondominant side is more tense. The head is more tilted, often far over and down, almost touching the table surface. The nondominant hand is usually more relaxed and may pin down the corner of the paper with thumb and index finger. The tongue no longer projects. Rather, the lower lip is drawn in. Often this movement is so frequent that the lip becomes chapped. The eye movements shift obliquely upward. It is interesting to try to pick out the good readers in a second-grade class. My observation has been that they reveal eye movements sweeping obliquely upward as they calculate in their head, that they bend their head, far over to the side as they write and, most telling of all, that they have that pathognomonic sign of the good 7-year-old reader—a chapped lower lip.

By 8 the child's posture is less extreme. He is now working opposite the shoulder on his dominant side as he writes. His head is tilted to the opposite side but he sits erect. His mouth may be slightly open as he works. His eyes often roll as he thinks. This may well indicate his newly found sense of totality, his ability to take in a situation in one sweep. He also uses this rolling to enhance his dramatic tendencies.

A significant and interesting change takes place at 9 years of age. Nine may shift his paper almost a full 90°, until the vertical side is parallel with the table edge. His entire trunk is shifted to the nondominant side so that his feet are often placed to the side, even in the aisle. It becomes quite natural to trip others as they pass by.

Nine's dominant shoulder is thrust forward and his head is tilted to the nondominant side. He anchors his paper quite naturally halfway down the vertical edge. As he writes, his head moves through an arc from the nondominant to the dominant side, then back again as another line is traversed. His eyes have lost their roving and their rolling. Rather, they fixate a point with a sharp perceptual edge. This is not the staring into space that characterizes the 5-year-old. Five's outer space is vague as he stares. But Nine often says he likes to fixate his eyes on a point so he can think more clearly.

With this type of highly differentiated mechanism is it any wonder that Nine is so ready to achieve, is so penetrating in his search for knowledge? And is it not sad that a child who has not come into this stage, or whose mechanism is not capable of differentiating to this point, is expected to achieve with energy and enjoyment as does the highly differentiated Nine? No wonder the nonready child "falls flat on his face." No wonder nearsightedness is often the price a child must pay.

Interpretation and Application

We must learn how to use this developmental knowledge. But first this information needs to be documented and studied. Teachers and parents alike need to be made aware of these stages and manifestations. A short developmental examination could be administered to each child each year to find out where and how a child is operating. This would be most valuable in the early years—kindergarten, first and second grades—when much could be revealed about a child. An interview with the parents could give us valuable information about the child's growth in the early years. With this knowledge of and respect for the past, along with facing the realism of the present, there is no reason why we cannot plan more successfully than we now do for a child's future.

If, for example, we have a child who has been slow in his language development, who would never sit long enough to listen to a story in the preschool years, and who was always on the go, we are not facing reality if we expect him to sit down, pay attention, and follow directions in first grade, especially when he is only 6 or 7. He simply clutters up the classroom and becomes confused by all the meaningless instruction he is receiving.

We might also find that such a child has never shown any interest in letters, that as often as you direct his attention to road signs, his mind wanders away to something else. We might also find that his body, hands, and eyes do not make the shifts expected as he moves from 5 to 9 years. Often he has trouble with the oblique. Wholes are broken up into parts, and parts are often seen as wholes. His 5-year-old flat hand stays with him as he writes, through 6, 7, and 8 years. He quickly spots a bird on the wing but he cannot hold to near-point tasks.

Give him a machine and his mind works with facility and penetration. His electric train set is no longer a maze of switches, tracks, and complicated setups by 7 or 8 years of age. He manipulates a tractor with ease by the age of 8. But, he does not see those letters on the bus he has been riding day after day until he is 9 or 10.

Might it not be wise to delay formal reading for this type of child until he is 9 or 10, when there is something to work with? This does not mean that nothing is to be done during this 5- to 10-year period, but such children should be treated as though they were going through all the stages from 2 to 5 which they have not yet traversed. Above all, they should be read to or, better yet, be exposed to selective television at a 2- to 5-year-old level, but lifted to his realm of interest. We find that these boys, for they are mainly boys, learn their letters at 9, read words at 10, sentences at 11, and are doing a reasonably good job by 13 years of age. With them 13 is comparable to 7, when we normally expect a child to be well on his way in the art of reading.

My main plea is to learn first about the child. Know him, both in relation to his age and his individuality, and his unique way of growing. Place him in an environment in which he can move. Then, I feel, we cannot fail; nor can the child.

For the present, however, much research still needs to be done. This does not mean we are not already well on our way. With proper placement in school and emphasis on respect for the child, many of our questions will be answered. I feel that curriculum changes will then come normally, determined in large measure by the forces of natural growth and development.

SECTION IV

READING: THE SKILLS INVOLVED

Make a reading skills kit and each child will get

PRACTICE WHEN IT MEANS THE MOST

BY DONNA CROLL

Students help themselves to drill needs when you categorize skillsheets by type and difficulty

BECKY IS A good reader. But right now she needs extra practice in syllabication. With an individualized reading program that is working properly, you should be able to provide Becky or any child—no matter what his or her need—with the necessary practice materials at the proper level. What's more, you should be able to give it to her the moment her need becomes evident and she's receptive.

Often ideal moments for learning pass by because immediate help is not available. It is stalled either by a lack of materials or by a lack of time to search for appropriate materials. But a reading skills kit organizes the materials already in your classroom so that worksheets to reinforce specific reading skills at a range of difficulty levels are at your fingertips. Syllabication sheets for Becky and for Jerome, who needs the same kind of practice but on a different level, can be quickly pulled out of the kit. These can be used again by others and can be corrected by the students themselves.

Basically a reading skills kit is a collection of two copies of all the worksheets you can get, filed according to the main skill being practiced on each pair. To make a kit take the following steps:

1. *Determine the specific reading skills to be included in your reading skills kit* (see box). In addition to general knowledge and observation, an outline or chart of skills introduced in the core material you are using is helpful. Such charts are available from most publishers. Be sure to include skills introduced below and above your students' actual grade placement. You may wish to begin with broad skill categories and then subdivide each category as your collection increases.

2. *Get a cardboard box.* A box from the grocery store makes a fine place to file folders. Paint or cover it with contact paper.

3. *Begin collecting pairs of worksheets.* In addition to the many skillsheets you already have, ask other teachers at different grade levels to save you pairs of skillsheets they have duplicated. The pages of published workbooks can be separated and the teacher's edition used as the answer key. Care should be taken in selecting skillsheets. They should be legible, have a good format, emphasize one specific skill and have directions that are easy to understand or do not require written directions. Read over each skillsheet and delete any item that may confuse the student. If there are no written direc-

GRADE TEACHER, 1972, Vol. 90, pp. 52-54.

tions, provide students with a model by working the first item.

Some suggested published materials which are well suited for a reading skills kit are: *Phonics We Use Workbooks* (Lyons and Carnahan), Readiness–Gr. 6, and *Specific Skills Series* (Barnell Loft), Gr. 1-6.

4. *Label a file folder for each skill.* Depending upon the degree to which you subdivide each skill area, you may wish to add cardboard dividers in addition to the folders. For example, if the area *vowels* has several subdivisions, make a cardboard divider labeled "Vowels" followed or preceded by one folder each for "Short," "Long," "Digraphs," etc. As I said, you may want to start with broad categories and subdivide later.

5. *Decide how you will make the sheets reusable.* There are several ways to do this.

–Back the skillsheets with heavy paper and either tape or laminate a sheet of acetate over them. Processed x-ray film can also be used. The children record their responses right on the film with grease pencils, felt-tip pens or the kind of crayons that will write on acetate. After the papers are corrected, the markings can easily be wiped off with a damp paper towel. I have found the processed x-ray film to be the least expensive transparent material. Sometimes a local hospital will give it to you or it can be purchased in 8 x 11 sheets for about three cents a sheet.

–If you don't attach the plastic sheets permanently, the children can paperclip a transparent sheet over the skillsheet and record their answers on it. After they have checked their answers they can erase them, as above.

–The student numbers a sheet of notebook paper so that it corresponds with the numbers on the skillsheets and then writes his answers beside the appropriate number on the notebook paper.

–The child paperclips a sheet of onionskin paper over the worksheet and writes his responses on it.

6. *Determine how you will file the answer keys.* I have found attaching the answer sheet to the worksheet to be the most efficient method. There is very little copying of answers when the students realize the purpose of the activity. I also do some informal testing when I review a

READING SKILLS—WHICH COUNT MOST TO YOUR CLASS?

A reading skills kit allows your students to practice in needed areas in their own time and at their own pace. To construct one, you will have to identify important reading skills in some way. The teacher's manual of your basal reader may have a scope and sequence chart that will help you or the publisher may be able to send one. What follows are some suggestions for basic topics that might be included. Of course they will have to be broken down further, i.e., you might divide the vowel section into: short, long, digraphs, diphthongs, "r" control, variants and generalizations.

1. Word and structural analysis—visual discrimination, letter names, consonants, vowels, phonograms, root words, compound words, contractions, structural changes, affixes, syllabication, accent, dictionary usage.

2. Comprehension—vocabulary development, factual recall, locating answers to specific questions, following directions, sequence, main idea, summarizing, predicting outcome, critical reading, creative reading.

student's work with him.

The answer keys can be filed separately and placed at a "checking station." When a child completes his assignment he brings his work to the "checking station" and corrects the papers.

7. *Prepare an answer key for each skillsheet.* This is perhaps the most time-consuming step. Some time-saving suggestions:

–If workbook pages are used, use pages from the teacher's edition as answer keys.

–Get help from a group of upper elementary grade students, high school clubs or teacher aides.

8. *Classify and file the skillsheets according to skills.*

9. *Color code the sheets according to difficulty level.* Assign a color for each grade or difficulty level and put a small colored mark at the upper right-hand corner of each sheet.

10. *Have an orientation session for your class.* The children learn how the materials in the reading skills kit are to be used–how to locate the sheets you designate and the procedure for checking their work.

Now, on that Monday when you want to give Becky immediate practice in syllabication, you'll be able to ask her to do green (third-grade level) skillsheets one, three and five from the syllabication folder. Jerome's assignment from the same area will be from the purple (sixth-grade level) group of worksheets. You'll be organized so that you won't have to let those ideal moments for learning pass by.

Primary Children's Recognition of High-Frequency Words

Dale D. Johnson
Richard J. Smith
Kenneth L. Jensen

The value of the widely used Dolch List has been challenged. Johnson has questioned the list. It was constructed from studies done in the 1920's and has not been updated, though almost half a century has passed since the list was compiled. (1). The vocabulary of the English language changes. The frequency with which certain words are used changes. The need to keep word lists for beginning readers current seems apparent.

Most reading programs introduce children to reading by teaching them words that are part of their oral language usage. After the children have developed some basic skills, most reading programs encourage beginning readers to include functional and recreational materials in their reading activities. It would seem logical in constructing a basic vocabulary list for beginning readers to choose words that children use in their oral language and words that are frequently found in materials other than materials for teaching basic reading.

Johnson relied on two sources in compiling his word list for beginning readers (2). One source was the Kučera-Francis analysis of present-day English, which provided a rank-order tabulation of 50,406 distinct words occurring in a body of 1,014,232 words representing the full range of subject

THE ELEMENTARY SCHOOL JOURNAL, 1972, Vol. 73, pp. 162-167.

matter and prose styles, from sports pages to scientific journals and from romantic fiction to philosophical discussions (3). The other source Johnson used was Murphy's tabulation of the frequency of occurrence of 6,318 words from a running count of 1,195,098 words in the oral language of kindergarten and first-grade children (4). From the Kučera-Francis study Johnson selected the five hundred most frequently used words and, of these, retained the 306 that had a minimum frequency of fifty occurrences according to the Murphy study.

Johnson's basic vocabulary, then, is built on three criteria. It is current in that words were selected from studies done in the 1950's and the 1960's. It contains words that are among the five hundred most frequently occurring words in printed English, and it contains only words that are also in the spontaneous speaking vocabularies of kindergarten and first-grade children.

Words were not selected on the basis of occurrence in basal reading series or because of grammatical function.

Johnson's list was used to test the word knowledge of beginning readers in different school settings. The intent was to determine the varying abilities of pupils in different schools and at different grade levels to identify words from sources other than basal readers. Only 28 of the 306 words in Johnson's list occur in the first-grade materials of ten popular basic reading series, and fewer than half occur in the same ten series at either first- or second-grade level.

The present study reports the results of the initial testing of the 306 words with first- and second-grade children in four schools in Madison, Wisconsin. Two of the schools serve low socioeconomic populations, and two serve upper-middle to high socioeconomic populations. The testing was done at the end of the school year in May. In each school the subjects came from classes that were heterogeneous in reading ability. Two half-days were spent in each school. During that time three examiners tested as many pupils as the time permitted. The pupils came from two first-grade and two second-grade classrooms that were randomly selected. In all, 118 first-grade subjects and 92 second-grade subjects were individually tested to discover how many of the 306 words they could recognize within a maximum five-second time limit per word. (Each word was typed on cards eight and a half inches by eleven inches.) The subjects were tested on half of the words the first day and on the other half of the list on the following day. Test sequences were rotated for different subjects to minimize the effects of ordering.

The data in the present study were collected from schools that served populations from high and low socioeconomic levels. Three of the schools used a three-group approach in reading in a heterogeneous, self-contained classroom. Each ability group used a different basal reading series. This approach, the tri-basal approach, is used in most primary classrooms in Madison. A fourth school participating in this study used a programmed decoding approach with all pupils. In the tables, this school is listed as School 3.

Because of the preliminary nature of the testing, the data collected were not treated statistically. Therefore, con-

TABLE 1. *Median Scores and Ranges for Subjects from Four Schools*

School	Number of Pupils	Socioeconomic Status	Median	Ability Range for Upper Half	Ability Range for Lower Half
			GRADE 1*		
1	40	High	92	92–99	59–91
2	34	High	76	76–99	45–74
3	26	Low	69	69–95	21–67
4	18	Low	57	57–97	35–53
			GRADE 2†		
1	18	High	86	86–99	27–66
2	25	High	44	44–95	18–40
3	26	Low	40	40–92	7–31
4	23	Low	36	36–99	1–34

*Clymer-Barrett Prereading Battery
†Gates-MacGinitie Reading Test (Level B)

clusions must be viewed as tentative. Table 1 shows the differences among the first-grade subjects according to their performance on the Clymer-Barrett Prereading Battery administered the preceding September. Table 1 also shows the differences among the second-grade subjects according to their performance on the Gates-MacGinitie Reading Test (Level B) administered the preceding fall.

As Table 1 shows, there were substantial differences among the first-grade subjects in the four schools in their readiness to begin formal reading instruction. There were similar differences in the reading ability of the second-grade subjects. The rank orderings by school are the same at both grade levels, favoring the two schools with high socioeconomic enrolments.

Table 2 reports the number and the per cent of the correct and the incorrect responses to the 306 words made by all

TABLE 2. *Number and Per Cent of Correct and Incorrect Responses to List of 306 Words by All First-Grade Subjects and All Second-Grade Subjects in Each School*

School	Number of Pupils	Socioeconomic Status	Correct Responses		Incorrect Responses	
			Number	Per Cent	Number	Per Cent
			GRADE 1*			
1	40	High	8,106	76	2,589	24
2	34	High	6,072	68	2,850	32
3	26	Low	5,180	67	2,612	33
4	18	Low	2,421	44	3,026	56
			GRADE 2†			
1	18	High	5,279	96	214	4
2	25	High	6,536	87	964	13
3	26	Low	5,731	91	542	9
4	23	Low	6,011	87	871	13

*Mean per cent correct: 64
†Mean per cent correct: 90

first-grade subjects and all second-grade subjects in each of the four schools.

As Table 2 shows, for the subjects in Grade 1, the ordering of the schools remains the same as the ordering in Table 1, though there is almost no difference between School 2 and School 3. As Table 2 shows, the second-grade subjects had mastered a considerably larger per cent of the 306 words (64 per cent in Grade 1, 90 per cent in Grade 2). Again, the difference between School 2 and School 3 was slight. One could speculate that the decoding program used in School 3 serves to offset the advantages typically associated with high socioeconomic status. The speculation is particularly inviting when School 3 is compared with School 2.

The data were further examined to

TABLE 3. *Per Cent of Correct Responses to List of 306 Words by First- and Second-Grade Subjects in the Upper Ability Half and the Lower Ability Half of Their Groups*

		Per Cent of Correct Responses			
		Grade 1		Grade 2	
School	Socioeconomic Status	Upper Half	Lower Half	Upper Half	Lower Half
1	High	91	60	99	94
2	High	78	58	91	83
3	Low	83	51	95	87
4	Low	65	23	97	72

TABLE 4. *Johnson List—First-Grade Words**

1. the	28. an	55. two	82. us	109. big
2. of	29. they	56. may	83. old	110. four
3. and	30. one	57. then	84. off	111. children
4. to	31. you	58. do	85. come	112. help
5. a	32. her	59. my	86. go	113. it's
6. in	33. all	60. like	87. house	114. name
7. that	34. she	61. over	88. home	115. today
8. is	35. there	62. man	89. went	116. having
9. was	36. we	63. me	90. say	117. car
10. he	37. him	64. did	91. school	118. I'm
11. for	38. when	65. back	92. don't	119. tell
12. it	39. who	66. your	93. away	120. keep
13. with	40. will	67. just	94. something	121. street
14. as	41. no	68. people	95. water	122. boy
15. his	42. if	69. Mr.	96. put	123. love
16. on	43. out	70. how	97. think	124. girl
17. be	44. so	71. too	98. took	125. six
18. at	45. said	72. little	99. night	126. mother
19. by	46. what	73. good	100. end	127. run
20. I	47. up	74. very	101. called	128. top
21. this	48. its	75. make	102. going	129. black
22. had	49. into	76. see	103. look	130. play
23. not	50. them	77. men	104. ask	131. soon
24. are	51. can	78. work	105. next	132. red
25. but	52. new	79. get	106. days	133. book
26. from	53. some	80. here	107. let	
27. have	54. time	81. day	108. room	

*These 133 words were read correctly by at least 75 per cent of the first-grade subjects.

The 289 words identified correctly by 75 per cent or more of the 92 second-grade subjects tested are the 133 words listed in Table 4 and the 156 words listed in Table 5.

TABLE 5. *Johnson List—Second-Grade Words**

134. or	166. each	197. does	228. want	259. close
135. which	167. those	198. got	229. done	260. turn
136. were	168. still	199. left	230. open	261. full
137. would	169. own	200. number	231. God	262. an
138. their	170. long	201. until	232. kind	263. wife
139. been	171. both	202. always	233. different	264. wanted
140. has	172. under	203. almost	234. door	265. front
141. more	173. never	204. hand	235. whole	266. sometimes
142. about	174. same	205. far	236. above	267. feel
143. them	175. another	206. head	237. hands	268. music
144. only	176. know	207. yet	238. show	269. party
145. other	177. last	208. better	239. five	270. short
146. could	178. might	209. set	240. gave	271. town
147. these	179. great	210. told	241. feet	272. morning
148. first	180. year	211. nothing	242. across	273. outside
149. any	181. came	212. why	243. past	274. art
150. now	182. right	213. didn't	244. seen	275. leave
151. our	183. used	214. eyes	245. really	276. plan
152. even	184. take	215. find	246. together	277. sound
153. most	185. three	216. knew	247. money	278. believe
154. made	186. use	217. city	248. sure	279. says
155. after	187. again	218. give	249. real	280. mean
156. man	188. place	219. face	250. behind	281. table
157. before	189. around	220. things	251. miss	282. road
158. must	190. small	221. early	252. air	283. gone
159. years	191. found	222. need	253. making	284. idea
160. where	192. Mrs.	223. saw	254. office	285. women
161. much	193. thought	224. best	255. brought	286. started
162. way	194. part	225. church	256. change	287. cut
163. well	195. high	226. light	257. board	288. down
164. should	196. every	227. thing	258. west	289. point
165. because				

*These words together with those in Table 4 were read correctly by at least 75 per cent of the second-grade subjects. The seventeen words not recognized by 75 per cent of the second-grade subjects are listed in Table 6.

TABLE 6. *Johnson List—Residual Words**

290. through	294. American	297. present	300. already	303. able
291. world	295. enough	298. ever	301. whose	304. hard
292. between	296. group	299. company	302. heard	305. alone
293. while				306. America

*These seventeen words were not read correctly by 75 per cent of first-grade or second-grade subjects.

find the per cent of correct responses made by the first-grade subjects in each school who had scored in the upper and the lower halves of their group on the reading readiness tests. A similar analysis was made of the second-grade subjects, based on the reading achievement tests (see Table 1). Table 3 reports the results of these analyses.

As Table 3 shows, the first-graders who scored in the upper half on the reading readiness test and the second-graders who scored in the upper half on the reading achievement test performed considerably better on Johnson's word list than pupils in the lower halves.

Finally, an item analysis for each word was done. A separate analysis was made for each grade—first and second. From the results, preliminary word lists by grade level were developed. The lists included all words recognized by at least 75 per cent of the subjects in each grade. As Table 4 shows, 133 words were correctly identified by 75 per cent or more of the first-grade subjects. As Tables 4 and 5 show, 289 words were identified correctly by 75 per cent or more of the second-grade subjects. Of the 306 words on Johnson's list, only 17 were not correctly identified by at least 75 per cent of the subjects tested. The words are listed in Table 6.

The results of the study reported here, though obtained from a relatively small sample, suggest that the ability of pupils to identify high-frequency words varies from school to school and from grade to grade. The results also suggest that the development of a child's reading vocabulary is influenced by factors other than the developmental materials he or she uses in school. It might well be that basal readers that attempt a high degree of vocabulary control in initial reading instruction do not limit the child's vocabulary. Children who are exposed to a variety of printed materials and who have other advantages that contribute to learning may move beyond the limitations of their basal reader sooner than expected. The tentative findings of this study argue for instructional reading programs that incorporate printed materials other than basal readers. The findings also suggest that further research is needed to assess the size and the source of the recognition vocabulary of children in the primary grades.

References

1. Dale D. Johnson. "The Dolch List Re-Examined," *The Reading Teacher, 24* (February, 1971), 449—57.
2. Dale D. Johnson. "A Basic Vocabulary for Beginning Reading," *Elementary School Journal, 72* (October, 1971), 29—34.
3. Henry Kučera and W. Nelson Francis. *Computational Analysis of Present-Day American English*. Providence, Rhode Island: Brown University Press, 1967.
4. Helen Murphy and Others. "The Spontaneous Speaking Vocabulary of Children in Primary Grades," *Boston University Journal of Education, 140* (December, 1957), 3—105.

ILSE MATTICK

The Teacher's Role in Helping Young Children Develop Language Competence[1]

Supposing teachers provided human communication instead of "language treatment"?

My interest in the language development of young inner-city children has two sources: my own intensive study of and work with poor urban children and my numerous observations in classrooms.

There is much controversy and much confusion in the field today about programs fostering cognitive processes (and thus communications skills) about "the whole child," about directive strategies, structured-cognitive or permissive-enrichment strategies, to use Joan Bissell's terminology.[2] We know by now which of those teach Stanford-Binet's better than the others, i.e., which one has more easily identifiable quick results in terms of specific tests.

I have real difficulties with these trends and concerns because I cannot imagine a separation between the cognitive domain and that of interaction between people. I cannot imagine such a separation for my own life; so how could I possibly for children? My ideas on the teacher's role in helping children develop language competency represent a developmental-interaction approach.[3]

1 This article is a version of a talk by the author for a panel on "Programs for Promoting Language in Early Childhood," Courtney Cazden, Chairman, at the NAEYC Conference in Boston, November 19, 1970.

2 See Joan Bissel's paper: "The Cognitive Effects of Pre-School Programs for Disadvantaged Children," National Institute of Child Health and Human Development, June 1970, Mimeo.

3 This term and its underlying conceptual framework for understanding the learning/teaching process are derived from the work of Barbara Biber, Roger Cartwright, and Edna Shapiro. However, they are not responsible for my own inelegant definition used here, specifically, in relation to language development.

YOUNG CHILDREN, 1972, Vol. 27, pp. 133-142.

I assume that there is an interdependence between cognitive and affective development and that the growth of intellectual functioning, such as the acquisition and organization of information, the ability to solve problems and to engage in symbolic representation cannot be divorced from interpersonal and intrapersonal growth processes. From this it follows that the ability to *relate* to others goes hand in hand with *talking* to others and that the development of self-esteem, self-assertion, self-confidence and self-control are inextricably intertwined with growth in cognitive functioning and thus with competency in communication.

We should question both the celebration of the higher test scores produced by some preschool programs designated as cognitively oriented, and the educative value of the teaching procedures these programs are preparing the children to deal with. A high score on instruments predicting success in an authoritarian, asocial context that denies human variety and invalidates differential needs and responses is a poor indicator of a child's ability to learn about, cope with and have an impact on his environment. Surely, you can teach most four-year-olds to answer in long sentences, even to read—with or without the use of cleverly constructed machines or "precooked" teaching sequences. But does *this* assure a reading, comprehending, thinking, questioning, communicating person, capable of socially meaningful action?

It is of course not to a concern with intellectual growth that I object, but to a stated intent of widening the children's cognitive field when instead children are closed off from the exploratory learning processes; and skill acquisition is mistaken for knowledge. But let me also state clearly that I wish neither to denigrate, dismiss nor ignore the rich knowledge that comes to us from some innovative programs. Obviously we need to learn from each other and to continually modify our methods in the light of new findings and insights. However, in my scheme of priorities, I find references to "mean length of utterances" far less fascinating or even useful than the content and affect of in-depth human communications.

The other kinds of pronouncements that concern me are those which allow people to assert that poor kids need and profit most from controlled, directive teaching. The reasons given for this kind of teaching are that poor children have fewer inner resources, difficulties in focusing, low frustration tolerance; and are not accustomed to making choices. Quite aside from the stereotyping and patronizing aspects of such statements, the consequent reasoning seems to me like saying "Let's brick up his windows, it's dark in his apartment anyhow."

Now, I am *not* saying that didactic teaching has no place in the classroom. It does—in any classroom. In fact, it must be admitted that an even quite controlled program in which children are introduced to a rich variety of offerings will have a better chance to do something for them than one which promotes chaos and is without plans for any learning whatever to take place. It should be clear to educators by now that neither the teacher nor the children must call all the shots if the operation is to be fruitful. There must be a balance, with delib

Ilse Mattick is Associate Professor of Education and Co-Director of the Therapeutic Tutoring Project at Wheelock College. Together with Lois B. Murphy she wrote *Cognitive Disturbances in Young Children.*

ate action taken by the teacher for pecific purposes, in the context of her nderstanding of the children.

If we wish to help children become ore competent communicators on a riety of subjects, in a variety of con- xts, it won't do to just sit back and wait r things to happen and it won't do to drill." The process is much more sub- e, but also much more pleasant and uman. It is not even particularly diffi- ılt, given a bit of good will, some imagi- ation and the teacher's ability to over- me some unfortunate "habits."

For teachers there are a few important cts to keep in mind to help ensure eaningful communication and then ere are some specific things each teach- needs to watch for. First the facts:

1. Even the most quiet child, the one ho communicates chiefly with pleading oks or eager nods or scowls is capable using language, certainly of under- anding it. I have yet to discover a onverbal" child, unless there has been definite physical handicap; and as we ow, such handicaps occur across all cial classes.

2. By the time children enter school, ey already have some language; it is t something you find yourself teaching om scratch, even to a two- or three- ar-old.

3. The teacher can be expected to ve a considerable impact on language velopment. Language competency es not emerge full-bloom all of itself an atmosphere that is a verbal or ective vacuum; it requires the experi- ce of back and forth communication d this calls for conscious action on the rt of the teacher.

4. Language development does not ean only language production; it also eans language comprehension. To a certain extent language comprehension precedes language production. However, language production is not a clear indication of language comprehension. To assume that a child understands everything he says can be misleading. He may talk as he heard others talk and not necessarily understand the meaning of the words. I recall a four-year-old, for example, who walked about the classroom smiling at people and saying "Do me a favor." When the teacher said, she would be glad to, the child looked utterly bewildered and just repeated the phrase. The teacher explored further to find out just what the child had in mind and discovered that the little girl did not have the slightest understanding of the term but simply liked the friendly response it evoked from people. Children easily pick up affectively important phrases without necessarily understanding them at all. (Cursing frequently goes under this heading.) Also, children like to please and poor children in particular, learn very early that adults are apt to be nicer if you agree with them. So, just because a child nods his head when you speak to him doesn't mean that he understands what you have said to him. Unless he can deal functionally with whatever he is told, we cannot be sure he understood.

For instance, I observed a three-year-old girl standing in front of the sink and saying over and over to herself, "Turn the handle of the faucet, make the water run," making no move to do so herself but looking pleadingly at the teacher to produce some water. Even when the child does deal functionally with the teacher's pronouncements it could mean he understood the words, but it could also mean that he understood just the context.

Another example is little Janice, almost five, who was sitting at the table stringing beads. One of the beads rolled off the table. She wondered where it was and I, her teacher at the time, told her that it was "under the table." Since she immediately dived under the table and recovered her bead I assumed that she understood what I had said. However, it later occurred to me that as I said "under the table" I looked under the table and pointed with my finger. So I made a little experiment. Every day when Janice came to school she was in the habit of making a drawing with chalk on the easel chalk board. There was a box of chalk on the easel tray. Before Janice came in the next time, I took the tray and put it on the window sill right next to the easel. Needless to say, Janice noticed that "her" chalk was not in its proper place and set up a howl. I said that the chalk was right behind her on the window sill, restraining myself from either pointing to or looking at that place. Janice looked me straight in the eye, smiled and said, "Yes, but where is it?" I found out subsequently that she was just as unable to find something "under the table" when I did not give other than language cues.[4]

5. Children will use language more fully if there is something of importance to them to communicate, that is: of importance to *them*, not to the teacher. This is a crucial issue and one most frequently ignored by teachers, investigators, program planners. I observed only recently a teacher trying her very best to get children interested in a sto she was reading to them. It was a pe fectly lovely story and it was reasonab for her to assume that it would catch t children's interest. However, the ch dren's responses were meager; a fine e ample of the monosyllabic language pr duction researchers are fond of quoti as typical of poor children. Then t teacher, who didn't seem to give in frustration and become irritable but w remained sensitively aware of her ch dren's reactions, discovered that a nu ber of children were straining to list to something outdoors. The teach switched from the topic of her story the topic of the noise outside. Imme ately the children launched into linguistically complex discussion abo the garbage truck they heard outsi The difference between the levels of t responses to the two topics was striki It is well known that back and fo verbal interactions are more likely to prolonged if initiated by the child, contrast to those that are thrust upon child to extract teacher-specified conte

6. It is much harder for a teacher interact verbally with children whose sponses she either doesn't understand who do not give clear signs of what p of her message they have understo Often in classrooms where there is socioeconomic mix of children, ver interactions tend to be most prolon and varied between the teacher and children who are most tuned in to c versing with adults, i.e., those who n it the least. However, just because i harder is no excuse for the teacher "cop out." It is her responsibility initiate interaction and to bring child to the point where they themselves interact spontaneously.

7. While the quality of the inte

[4] For a more detailed discussion of the above, see my descriptive passage on Language and Cognitive Development in *The Drifters*, (E. Pavenstedt, ed.) Little Brown, 1967, pp. 71-80, and Adaptations of Nursery School Techniques to Deprived Children, in the *Journal of the American Academy of Child Psychiatry*, Vol. 4, No. 4, October 1965, pp. 670-700.

on is far more important than the uantity; still, *prolonged* back and forth iteraction contributes to the growth of inguage complexity, particularly if it is aried and rich. And this takes us back the fifth point concerning communica-on which is of importance to the child.

This is just an introduction to the iscussion of language development in lation to a preschool program. I have ot even mentioned the factual knowl-dge available concerning dialects and her specific linguistic dimensions lated to social life styles.[5] We are just eginning to be aware of their precise nplications for communication attain-ents and/or mismatches; and it is cer-in that teachers will want to become nsitive to and knowledgeable about ese facts as well. But the above seven oints hopefully may serve as a guide for spelling some of the bewilderment at teachers may have experienced in e face of the barrage of prescriptive otions about "language treatment" in cent years.

What about the teacher's tasks, ferred to as "teaching strategies," or nteraction-skills," or whatever term is n" for you? If language is to be used as means of finding solutions to problems, showing interest and concern, of elicit-g thinking responses, of presenting in-rmation of interest to the children, of uiding children into elaborated activi-es and more complex cognitive organi-tion and as a means of helping them ntrol their own behavior then I would ggest that a teacher ask herself the llowing questions when interacting rbally with children:

[5] For further information on these important nensions of communication and linguistic compe-cy see the findings by Baratz, Bernstein, Cazden, bov.

Is this a back and forth interaction, or a monologue on my part? Do I encourage the children to engage me in conversation; i.e., is the topic of relevance to the child and does it therefore give better chances for rich and complex language expression? Who does most of the talking, the child or me?

Are my questions open or close-ended: i.e., are they thought-inducing. (such as, "What do you suppose the boy did with the bird?") or are they correct answer questions (such as, "What did the boy find?") ? The former encourages *thinking responses* and these lead to much more complex communicative skills and to much better chances for fluent conversation than the latter which are apt to produce one-word responses—"bird," or—bewildered looks if the child has forgotten or is not sure what answers the teacher wants, or—perhaps even contemptuous looks if it occurs to him, as it often does to kids, that the answer is self-evident and therefore the question is silly.

It can be assumed that the child offers the answer to a close-ended question to satisfy the teacher, period. This does not mobilize his communicative abilities. Thought-provoking questions, on the other hand, can lead to greater clarity in thinking and expression; at least they open up this possibility. At the very least they signal to the child that the teacher respects his thought, rather than that she is putting him on trial. It isn't really difficult to show this respect (providing the teacher feels genuine respect for children) and to promote thinking responses.

In a classroom recently I watched two children fighting. Each of the two boys was pushing a small car along the floor; they were practically tripping each other to get ahead of one another and both of them were screaming at the top of their lungs, "cheating, cheating." To the teacher's calm query, "What seems to be the trouble?," both shouted "He's cheating." The teacher asked, "In which way?" with real interest in her voice. One boy went into a long complicated explanation of the race they were having and the other boy expressed in a complex sentence his frustration that he could not get ahead of the first boy. The teacher commented that in races people usually had a starting line. This triggered a discussion between the boys about where and how they might make a starting line as well as a finish line. A little later in the same classroom a girl asserted to the teacher that another girl's drawing was "no good." Again the teacher asked, with real interest, "How do you mean?"; thus encouraging the girl to be more specific about her reaction to the drawing. On each of these two occasions the teacher elicited verbalizations borne of further thinking.

As a teacher I would watch for the *specificity* of my responses. If we want to move children from a global, nonspecific mode such as the familiar "lookit teach" or "gimme dis" to focused communication, it is incumbent upon us to provide a model of highly specific verbalizations. Here are two examples that are illustrative of the difference.

In one setting a five-year-old boy ran out of the classroom with a stapler in his hand. In the hallway he encountered the director. The boy smiled, thrust the stapler out at the director and said, "Here, take it." The director smiled and said, "Oh, you're done with this." The child nodded and returned to his room. Contrast this episode with the following excerpt from a tape recorded observation in another classroom. The teacher said, (to a five-year-old) "Oh, Ronny, do me favor. I borrowed this stapler from Mi Brown's desk to fix the book Lar made, so that we could see the word You give this stapler back to Mi Brown, please, and tell her she was n there when we borrowed it; and that sh did not know that we borrowed it. Te her thank you for the stapler, okay Naturally I was curious to observe wh would happen and so I followed th child to the director's office. Ronny n only conveyed the message in long com plex sentences, but he used different e pressions rather than recalling the teac er's words verbatim. I cite this examp in detail because it shows that specifici does *not* imply feeding a child pap, i.e simplifying language to meaningless a tificial structures that a child would ne ther use nor normally encounter in th real world, (as in "jump, Spot, jump, s Spot jump."). It does mean, howeve that factual information embedded in meaningful interactional context nee to replace nonspecific interchanges abo "it" or "this."

Also, one might ask oneself: "Am moralizing, i.e., am I telling the chi how he should be thinking and feeli instead of accepting the way he does, says he does? It is hard for teachers resist preaching and moralizing;—it's o of the guaranteed ways to turn off ba and forth verbal interactions and to re der the child unsure of himself and his own opinions. It also invites defia responses.

Do I really listen to children? Or do jump in with an answer as soon as think I have guessed what he means even with an answer that fits my ow preconceptions or needs for control. Re search findings have confirmed what chi dren have known for a long time; nam

' that teachers tend to pay scant atten-
on to their, the children's, efforts at
ommunicating. Sometimes not even the
rbalizations themselves are attended
. More often there is a facile response
the words, but not to the message the
ild is trying to convey. The teacher
en has "listened"; but her response is
terms of her own rather than the
ild's intent. While the resultant comunication mismatch is prevalent be-
een middle-class teachers and children
working-class parents it is by no means
stricted to this group.

The following is one example of many
at demonstrates nonlistening to a high-
pertinent communication: The teach-
walked to the easel where a five-year-
l had been painting for some minutes
th energy, concentration and wild
andon. The paper was dripping with
ight reds and yellows, as were the
y's hands and arms. He had just
pped back and surveyed his picture
th a frown. With the teacher next to
n he again reached for a brush, made
vide sweeping stroke over the paper
l the easel frame and said softly:
ye, bye, bus." With a disdainful look
the dripping paint the teacher retort-
"Bye, bye painting. Georgie, go wash
ır hands." The teacher here "lis-
ed" to the boy's words; they gave her
opening to terminate his messy activi-
in an overtly friendly manner. She
sed completely, however, his intend-
communication (easily solicited by
observer) about his mother going
away on a bus.

t is even more common for teachers
ut off genuine curiosity and a spirit
nquiry by not "listening": I observed
oup of children working with mirror
ls; one girl was holding the mirror
ard the window and as she "caught" the reflection of the sun she called excitedly: "Lookit, it's burning!" The other children looked up and one girl asked: "Why it burn, teach?" The teacher's verbatim response was: "What's my name, Louise? My name is Miss Jenks, not "teach"; if Nancy would be using the mirror the right way it would not burn." This type of inappropriate and inaccurate as well as chilling response is all too common, particularly in programs dedicated to furthering cognitive skills.

There is little reason for children to make the effort to solicit information, to state their intentions, their quests or vague notions in a distinct manner or, for that matter, to speak much at all if nobody *listens*. It is only on the basis of really listening that the teacher can a) request more details; b) help children identify the issues, ideas, feelings, and give them names; c) project various alternatives for the children to consider; in other words, create the possibility for a sequence in language proficiency and expressiveness.

Is my language production geared to the children's understanding and at the same time expanding the child's existing language, giving them new words for more complex operations? Many teachers talk down to children while at the same time communicating thought-associations that cannot possibly make sense to children. For example, I recently heard a child complain to the teacher, "I got no scissors." The teacher's response in a "cute" voice was "Oh, I wish our scissors would hurry up and come." I wonder if the child shared my vision of scissors marching up the stairs into the room? Of course, while indulging in this fantasy, resulting from taking the teacher's actual words at face value—as kids usually do—I also understood that the teacher had ordered new scissors and was awaiting their arrival. It is not reasonable to expect a young child to make this assumption.

Do I finish my sentences or do I leave the children hanging in mid-air? Recently, I heard a teacher say to her class: "Put your name on your picture because when it's time to go home. . . ." On another recent visit, the teacher said to the children, "Let's see what I can do for you." She said this on seven different occasions during one morning without ever following through with one more word or action.

Do I avoid using pat phrases over and over again? There is a kind of stereotyped early childhood education lingo that is deadly for developing communicative competency in children. For example, using the phrase, "What's the matter?," each time something goes wrong as opposed to varying it with, "What is happening over here?" or "How are you getting along?" etc. Do children hear, "It's time now to wash hands, it's time now for music," etc., every day, or are a variety of expressions used that are designed to help children think about solutions or about some concept?

Do I involve children in activities that lend themselves easily to promoting—and might even necessitate—verbal interactions? Just to name a few: word games, cooking (involving verbal choices and instructions), puppets, grocery store, dramatic play, etc., aside from the obvious ones of story telling, "making my own book" projects, putting captions to pictures, describing a trip or other special occasion, writing to a friend, etc.

Is there maximum chance for children to converse with each other? It is amazing how frequently children are prevented from talking to each other. The most prevalent teacher vocabulary ite
that I hear in classrooms, is "Sh-Sh." F
some reason it seems to make teache
nervous to have children converse free
with each other. I believe this is main
due to the extraordinary reluctan
shared by many adults, but especially b
a great many teachers, to refrain fro
exerting arbitrary control over childre
There is also, of course, the complete
erroneous but persistent assumption th
children learn better when they are q
et. Such assumptions, although long d
proved, die slowly because we tend
replicate that which happened to us, ju
as the children will be apt to replica
that which they experience. To say th
children need the freedom to converse
not to say that we should promote be
lam or chaos. On the contrary, the ki
of organization where rich interactio
can take place is of real importance.
staggering amount of opportunities
lost for engaging children in meaning
verbal interaction if there are no p
dictable and accepted ground rules
conduct and/or if the children fi
themselves in a generally unpredictab
environment. In other words, unl
teachers encourage the development
an organization of classroom life t
reflects their well thought out conc
tions about education, their efforts
likely to fail. But let us return to
specific teaching strategies that prom
and enhance language development.

Do I, the teacher, take action to
volve children in verbal communicati
when there is the opportunity? W
talk among children is apt to deve
naturally in familiarly experienced
roundings (as you can check by listen
to children playing in the street),
the school setting the teacher freque
needs to do far more than just wait

ildren to talk to her (or him) or even each other in a group. Many middle-ass children may not need nearly as uch deliberate effort on the part of the acher to get a conversation rolling and keep it going, as do some of the ner-city children. This can be observed ring comparable program periods ch as snack times in a suburban nur-y school and a Head Start center.[6] For e teacher to wait beyond a reasonable ne for the inner-city child to approach r is to abdicate her teaching role. In t, chances are that many of the chil-en will have approached her far more n do most of the suburban children, t frequently with either less verbaliza-ns or verbalizations with which she is t familiar and therefore tends to misun-rstand or ignore. It is her job to assist children in organizing their learning periences via the tools of symbolic rep-entation, i.e., play and language. For mple, a teacher asked a boy, almost e years old, to tell her about his block ilding. He looked up, smiled, pointed the last block he put on top of the ucture and said, "De block on top." e teacher nodded and walked off, ac-ting his limited "concrete" answer hout making any attempt to help this verbalize the relevant information out his activity and thus be aided in anizing his experience for himself.

urthermore, a teacher needs to consider the following: Is verbal interaction related to the real world and more importantly to the child's real world? The distinction to be made here is between a teacher engaging a child in verbalization, (perhaps of measurements related to water play or cooking) as it fits meaningfully into the child's activity, and a teacher who artificially imposes "learning tasks" quite remote from the children's priorities, in the contexts she selects. An example for the latter is this scene, observed in a classroom: The children were eager to have their milk and cookies. The teacher poured their milk for them. I wondered why these five-year-old capable children were not allowed to pour their own milk; but I quickly noticed that the teacher poured differential amounts of milk into several of the glasses. She then proceeded to launch into a "language and math lesson" on the amounts of milk in different glasses. Billy's glass is 3/4 full, Jimmy's glass is 1/2 full, Sarah's glass is 1/2 empty, Jane's glass is 1/4 full," etc. Her lesson was certainly related to the "real world" but was it the children's "real world" at this time? They clearly were concentrating on getting their snacks as well as reacting to the teacher giving some children less milk than to others. I have never seen as much milk gulped, spilled and noisily slurped, nor as many ears closed.

Drilling children in linguistic forms can turn the kids off in a hurry, just as quickly as asking them to produce correct answers to questions. You can teach a child to use the correct words in the right places, such as for instance "under," "over," "around," "into," "or." But if you want more than a mechanical repertoire of words, if you want understanding and transferability, be sure the

Reasons for observable differences are obviously ed to life styles, priorities (who in a family ggling for survival has the time and energy for chat or lengthy explanations?) and preferences lternate ways of communicating—they are *not* ed to "capacity" or "ability." I hope it is rstood that when I refer to differences among ps I am of course talking of tendencies, not of lutes. The very wide range existing in any p of children cannot be ignored by any but the obstinate stereotypers. On the other hand, to that different tendencies exist is to deny the macy of adaptational patterns.

words are attached to action or demonstrations of what the words actually mean in the context of the child's experiential field and are not imbedded in abstractions.

It is no accident that words like "or" are usually missing from the vocabulary of children who have had few options to choose between. How often during the course of the day, do we as teachers give children legitimate choices? I stress "legitimate" because a child dripping with finger paint is not being given a choice if he is asked, "Do you want to wash your hands now?" How often do you hand a child a piece of construction paper, of whatever color happens to come into your hands; and how often do you ask him which color he prefers? Opportunities for legitimate decision-making b children, affecting their own increasin ability to act upon the real world, const tute significant learning experiences o value far beyond the gains in linguist maturation.

There is one last question that a teach er needs to ask herself, and it is the mo important one when communicatin with young children: Does the intera tion take place in the context of mutu trust and respect; a mutual trust and r spect based on the teacher's genui friendliness, unconditional acceptan warmth, empathy, interest? It is *this* th makes language flow, that makes it wort while and exciting for the children talk freely and motivates them to acqui communication competency.

Expansion of Meaning Vocabulary: Strategies for Classroom Instruction

Susanna W. Pflaum

In our zeal to isolate essential reading skills and to provide systematic instruction, we may be neglecting vocabulary expansion. Of course, teachers are aware of the importance of building a sight vocabulary, and word attack skills are very much a part of beginning reading programs. The aspect of vocabulary growth which concerns this writer is the expansion of meaning vocabulary. Unfortunately, textbooks on reading and language do not stress development of meaning vocabulary sufficiently. Further, visits to classrooms and talks with teachers reveal that this aspect of vocabulary growth is slighted in practice.

There are a number of reasons why we must re-examine our priorities with respect to expansion of vocabulary. We intuitively know that the ability to comprehend reading material depends in large measure on ability to understand the vocabulary used. Also, word meaning consistently appears as an important factor in reading ability.[1] Measures of difficulty of reading material have shown that readability levels are in large part determined by word difficulty.[2] Further, vocabulary knowledge is strongly related with measures of general academic ability. For example, the Peabody Picture Vocabulary Test, a test of passive vocabulary knowledge, correlates with the 1960 Binet at .83.[3] Since meaning vocabulary is related with reading and general academic success, it must not be left to chance.

There are really two aspects to be included in an instructional program intended to increase students' meaning vocabularies. One aspect stresses the acquisition of new vocabulary items. The other attends to the extension of meaning of items which are already part of a student's vocabulary. School programs should promote both acquisition of new terms and the deepening of understanding of partially or superficially known terms. Where classroom instruction does include a meaning vocabulary component, usually it concentrates on the acquisition of new vocabulary items rather than the furthering of in-depth understanding of words already in use. But in-depth understanding is necessary so that students can actively use items in speaking and in writing as well as being able to passively recognize them as they listen and read. And, of course, for thorough understanding of reading material key terms must trigger more than partial recognition. For example, a student's comprehension of a passage about westward expansion will be dependent on his in-depth understanding of such terms as *desert*, *mountain*, and *thirst*. Or, his comprehension of rain in terms of the water cycle will be enhanced by in-depth knowledge of liquid and vapor forms of water.

Susanna Pflaum is Asst. Professor at the University of Illinois at Chicago Circle.

ELEMENTARY ENGLISH, 1973, Vol. 50, No. 1, pp. 89-93.

To explore further what is meant by "in-depth" understanding of vocabulary items, it is helpful to look at concept development. *Concept* is defined as "an idea comprehending the essential attributes of a class or logical species."[4] Or, a concept is a collection of attributes assigned to it by convention. In classroom practice, to determine whether a student has a certain concept or not, he must consistently identify instances of that concept. In addition, he must be able to identify instances which do not belong. For example, a student who always calls a *river* a *river* and never calls it a *lake* and, in addition, never calls a *lake* a *river* understands the concept *river*. On the other hand, the toddler who calls all hairy, four-legged creatures *doggy* does not have the concept *dog*. He has acquired some attributes which apply to the mature concept, but he has not yet parcelled out the attributes which do not belong. In due course, with sufficient experiences with animals, he will learn the unique attributes which belong with *cat, horse, cow,* etc. And, as he acquires these new words and associates unique attributes with them, his original concept of *dog* becomes greatly modified so that he can correctly identify only dogs, even small ones, as *dog*. In other words, he has acquired a more specified list of the positive attributes as well as negative attributes, the attributes which do not belong, to the concept *dog*. Although this is a very early example of vocabulary or concept acquisition, the process is in some ways paralleled in later acquisition. In many cases when they are first acquired, concepts are understood only vaguely; not all attributes are present, and some attributes are present which will be abandoned later. This kind of gradual learning has been called horizontal acquisition of concepts.[5]

By contrast, some items are acquired vertically. This occurs when a person already has a categorical understanding of a related group of concepts so that a new member of the group is acquired with its full complement of attributes. For example, a youngster who has learned the attributes correctly for *dog, cat, horse, cow,* and *sheep,* let us say, and in addition has a general categorical understanding of domestic animals, can acquire all the attributes of *goat* at once. The distinguishing attributes of *goat* will probably be sufficient when the real or pictured animal is observed, identified, and discussed. Both horizontal and vertical learning continue through the school years even though the experiences necessary for acquisition change.

Young preschool children need direct sense experiences in order to acquire most concepts. Later, during elementary school, many concepts are acquired through verbal explanation. When a young child is relying on direct experiences to provide the material for concept acquisition, he is using an inductive learning procedure. When the older child has to rely on verbal explanation, often his learning is deductive. While instructional strategies used to introduce new vocabulary items in elementary school will often be deductive, in-depth analysis of partially understood concepts should probably be inductive in approach. The activities described below are designed to outline strategies for verbal analysis of concepts so that inductive as well as deductive learning will take place. Close personal attention to words and their meanings ought to help students learn key concepts to further their reading comprehension and general language growth.

Strategies for Acquisition of New Vocabulary Items

Most of the techniques recommended in pre-service reading and language texts for vocabulary extension apply to the acquisition of new items. Because of this, the reader should think of this section as a review of practices already in use in many classrooms. The most important ingredient is for the teacher to provide a climate which encourages vocabulary extension. Students should feel comfortable enough to say, "I don't know what gravity really means." Or ask "What is a rhinocerous?" Unfortunately, however, one of the first things a young child learns in school is that he should not appear to be "dumb." Children learn, probably from our reaction to them, that questions illustrating ignorance are not appreciated. Teachers can create an atmosphere conducive to vocabulary growth through enthusiastic interest in words and their meanings and by full, honest encouragement and appreciation of students' admission of ignorance or misunderstanding of words.

A second important general consideration is that in introducing new words for a reading selection, the teacher must attend to the meaning as well as the pronunciation of the words. Recently, this writer observed second graders in a large city school "reading" a story which took place in a meadow. After their reading class I asked two children to tell me all they knew about a meadow: where one could be found, what it might look like, what farmers would use it for. Not surprisingly, the children could only respond in terms of a city park. The significance of the story setting was lost to them. Many key words in reading texts are unfamiliar to young readers. Teachers should attend to the meaning of the "new words" by pictures, use in context, explanation, dictionary, and by relating the words to more familiar ones.

Other techniques for helping students acquire new words are reviewed.

—Not only should one teach dictionary skills, but one ought to provide for natural use of the dictionary. Teachers should encourage students to jot down words they do not understand and look up and discuss them later. Further, rather than have students look up words assigned to them, let students explore the dictionary for new interesting words to share with classmates.

—Since use of context is a major means for vocabulary extension, teachers should make explicit techniques for full use of context. Important context clues are: experiences built up in a passage, comparison or contrast within a paragraph, synonyms provided, use of familiar language associations, summaries, and clues from the mood or unique setting. Ability to use context to figure out word meaning can be enhanced through use of nonsense words inserted in a passage which illustrate the meaning. Class discussions using examples of each kind of context clue may help. Students can write their own paragraph to illustrate a word.

—Many teachers use affix study to expand vocabulary. Written worksheets which ask students to circle prefixes and suffixes are much less worthwhile than exercises which build up new words. For example, students can take one root word and build up as many new words with affixes as possible. And, instead of telling the meaning of each affix, students can figure out the meaning from two or three familiar words which have that affix.

—Older elementary students enjoy study of word derivation. Attention needs to be paid to the meaning of the word parts, however.

—Since practice and use in various settings increases understanding of words, teachers should make a point of reviewing new terms periodically.

—Such techniques as use of charts and development of individual student dictionaries, etc. already being used by teachers should be continued.

Strategies for Development of In-Depth Knowledge of Known Words

There are fewer techniques used in classrooms which provide for in-depth understanding of known terms than there are techniques in use to teach new ones. Since much of our vocabulary is acquired horizontally, the strategies recommended below will apply to terms partially understood. The most appropriate terms to be analyzed in depth are the key words which have been selected from the subject matter units.

Basically, what is recommended is that inductive learning should be applied to extend understanding of these terms so that they become true members of student's reading, listening, speaking and writing vocabularies. Although the dictionary definition is often a good place to start, the discussion and analysis of concepts recommended here will go beyond the dictionary definition. The goal is to help students become aware of word groups and categories; further, it is important that students become conscious of the distinguishing attributes of the individual terms. Students can begin with discussion of the essential attributes of words which they know well. An example would be *woman*. Probing questions encourage students to identify the following attributes: *human, female,* and *adult*. Next, the teacher can begin discussing less well-known words. As students identify the attributes of these words, the teacher will become aware of missing or overlapping attributes and can plan activities for further learning.

It is important that care be taken so that expectations do not exceed the cognitive level of the students. For example, before a child understands the principle of conservation, he cannot be expected to understand the relational meaning of terms such as *heavy*. For the preschooler *heavy* is an absolute term and no amount of verbal explanation will help him understand its relative meaning. The strategy of explicating concept attributes to extend vocabulary knowledge can be realized in classrooms in the following ways:

–Begin with individual concepts which are well-known. Students list the essential attributes, and add to the original word other words which are related to it.

–Next, teachers can select terms from content area study. Probing questions are used to elicit student's awareness to develop a beginning list of essential attributes. Often, verbal experiences will help students add to a list of attributes when some are missing.

–Teachers can present related words to students for analysis: for example, *tourist* and *immigrant*.[6] Students then identify those attributes which both words share, such as: people, people who travel, new space and experiences, particular location and transportation problems. Then students identify the attributes which distinguish these concepts. For *tourist:* a temporary visit, pleasure seeking, observation of surroundings. For *immigrant:* permanent move, job seeking, and ultimate absorption into culture. Younger students could do the same activity with *lake, stream, river, pond, ocean* which so often are confused. Comparison of opposite terms such as *aunt* and *uncle* reveal that they are opposites in terms of only one attribute. Students can work individually developing attributes if the teacher wants to diagnose each student's concept level. It is better if small groups of students develop the list of attributes together in order to provide for more active learning.

–Class concept dictionaries can be produced over time. The grouped words and individual terms can both be included.

–Students can be presented with categorical terms with lists of mixed words to be grouped under each given category.

—Students can be given words which first must be categorized and then the categories named.

—Students can be presented with groups of four words, some of which share a relationship. Students will select the words which share a relationship and then they are to name the relationship.

—Present students with a descriptive phrase and a long list of possible accompanying terms. Students should select only those terms which might apply to the description.[7]

—Multiple meanings of words strengthen in-depth understanding. Although young children use words with different meanings, they are often unaware of multiple meanings. Begin to build this awareness by using common words with strongly contrasting meanings. The dictionary can be the source. Students can then attach attributes to each meaning.

—A word which has many meanings can be presented in several contexts so that each one shows a different meaning. Students can identify and describe the meanings in their own words.

—Students can build up their categorical groupings. For example, children can begin to relate animal names which share one attribute. Perhaps they begin a list of all animals they can think of which are hairy. Then they examine their list of animals for other attributes which are shared. The list of shared attributes is further expanded as the teacher asks probing questions until students have identified the essential attributes for *mammal.*

In conclusion, it is suggested in this article that school programs provide more instruction in vocabulary than is presently the case. Growth in meaning vocabulary occurs when new words are regularly added to existing vocabulary. Growth is also dependent on increasing the in-depth understanding of words only superficially understood. While much instruction which aims at increasing the size of vocabulary is deductive in nature, it is recommended that teachers employ inductive exploratory techniques to expand knowledge of partially known terms.

Notes

1. Roger T. Lennon, "What Can Be Measured," *The Reading Teacher*, XV (March, 1962), 326-337.
2. Edgar Dale and Jeanne S. Chall, "The Concept of Readability," *Elementary English* (1949).
3. Lloyd M. Dunn, *Expanded Manual for the Peabody Picture Vocabulary Test* (Minneapolis, Minn.: American Guidance Service, Inc., 1965).
4. *Webster's Third New International Dictionary* Unabridged. (Chicago: Encyclopaedia Britannica, 1966).
5. David McNeil. *The Acquisition of Language: The Study of Developmental Psycholinguistics* (New York: Harper and Row, 1970), 116.
6. John B. Carroll, "Words, Meaning and Concepts: Part II. Concept Teaching and Learning," *Harvard Educational Review*, XXXIV (1964), 191-202.
7. The four preceding activities are adapted from Harold L. Herber *Teaching Reading in the Content Areas* (Englewood Cliffs, N.J.: Prentice-Hall, 1970), Chapter Eight.

Critical Reading in the Primary Grades

by Helen W. Painter

In her book *I Will Adventure* Elizabeth Janet Gray (*4*) has her main character, Andrew, scorning study and school. He expresses his feelings to his new friend, an actor and playwright named William Shakespeare. Shakespeare says to him: "Ignorance is a curse, Andrew, knowledge the wing by which we fly to heaven. If you get a chance to pluck a feather from that wing, make the most of it."

Surely in our world today the informed individuals who can read and think are of vital importance. Kathleen Hester (*6*) writes about a boy in second grade in Puerto Rico. He read: "We wish to read good books, in order not to be ignorant, in order not to be slaves." What better reasons do we need for critical reading?

What is critical reading and how early can we teach it? Dr. Nila B. Smith (*8*) has pointed out the popularity of the term critical reading today and the fact that many people are using the term to refer to many skills in reading. She sees three types of thought-getting processes: (1) literal comprehension, getting the primary meaning from words; (2) interpretation, getting a deeper meaning from words in addition to simple, literal comprehension; and (3) critical reading, including the first two but going further in involving personal judgment on and evaluation of the "quality, the value, the accuracy, and the truthfulness of what is read." Critical reading involves critical thinking.

How early can we start teaching critical reading? Is it possible in elementary school, particularly in the primary grades? Research findings reveal that critical thinking can be taught from kindergarten through college. Dr. Leo Fay (*3*) points out: "Actually children at ages well before those at which they enter school are able to make valid judgments in relation to their experiences and their maturity levels."

Critical reading *in its highest form* is complex, and a young child usually would be unable to do such involved reading. Second graders may be critical readers, Heilman (*5*) says, but "no one would suggest that their interpretation of the Constitution is adequate for our society." But they can evaluate in terms of their maturity, their backgrounds, and experiences. Stauffer (*10*) tells of a six-year-old questioning how three ducks in a story could be "long parade of ducks." The child knew ducks, had seen them walk in single file, had reached a reaction to *long* and *short,* and could figure out what a parade was. He obviously was doing critical thinking.

Are teachers teaching the skills of critical reading? In the Harvard

THE READING TEACHER, October 1965, vol. 19, pp. 35-39.

report of reading in elementary schools, *The First R* (*1*), the staff reported that not until Grades 5 and 6 did school systems estimate "considerable" attention was given to critical reading, a situation "very much in keeping with the prevailing opinion among administrators and teachers that only older children are able to think and read critically." More than half of the school systems devoted "little" or "no" time to such skills in Grades 1 and 2. In observations in the classroom, the field staff rarely found teachers trying to help children in those activities that contributed to critical reading. Therefore, among their recommendations the authors proposed that "a definite program be initiated in which all children are taught critical and creative reading skills appropriate for their development, and that teachers find ways to stimulate thinking beyond the literal meaning of passages read."

It is apparent that critical reading skills do not appear automatically but must be taught. All authorities agree that a teacher must so direct the reading of children that they can think critically. A teacher herself must be a critical reader and thinker. She must give practice in the skills. She must remember that "critical thinking abilities are difficult and they are slow agrowing" (*7*). She must help children gain background and experiences. She must encourage critical thinking and be pleased by the questioning of children, not annoyed by it. She must create the setting for critical reading. Too often a teacher asks merely for simple recall.

A teacher must be skillful in teaching critical thinking: we want to develop questioning attitudes in children, but we do not want teachers or classes always to be unduly suspicious, to question everything and thus deny themselves opportunities to lead lives full of satisfaction (*2*). A teacher must use logic in promoting sound and proper attitudes.

Exactly how, then, can critical reading and thinking be taught? Probably the best way is to guide classroom discussion as it occurs. Dr. Smith writes (*8*):

> Rarely should a teacher plan to "give a lesson" in critical reading, particularly in the primary grades. More direct work can be done at times in the upper grades. Leads into critical reading activities usually arise from discussion of reading content.
>
> Children themselves often offer leads to critical reading. The wise teacher keeps herself ever on the alert for such leads, encouraging them with commendation for good thinking and stimulating further research for facts with tactful questions or remarks.

Surely, the primary school curriculum provides a fertile field for critical thinking. Basal reading selections and individual books, as well as materials in content fields, offer many opportunities to a teacher. Critical reading may be taught to a large or small group or to an individual pupil.

It is obvious, therefore, that critical reading is possible with young children, but that the amount and kind of such activity rest upon the teacher. To assist teachers, here are some examples and applications of critical reading at the primary school level.

Primary school children can question whether a situation is truth or fantasy. Russell (7) mentions first graders making such distinctions after hearing "The Day It Rained Cats and Dogs." Primary grades include the age for the start of interest in fairy tales, and children can be led to distinguish between fantasy and truth. Could someone sleep for a hundred years? Could a pumpkin become a coach? Could such events take place? Why or why not? We can help children to look for clues that signal a fairy story, such as the once-upon-a-time beginning and the fairy prince and princess.

A child may decide if action is plausible in stories not labeled fairy stories. Look at Phyllis McGinley's "The Horse Who Lived Upstairs." Have you ever heard of a horse living upstairs? It is possible? How does the author make the situation seem plausible? Are animals, insects, and birds able to talk, as Wilbur, Charlotte, and Templeton do in *Charlotte's Web?* Why or why not? Is there a land where the wild things are?

Young children can be led to judge the competence of an author. Chibi could distinguish the cry of crows under different circumstances. Can this be? Laura Ingalls Wilder in *The Little House in the Big Woods* tells of Ma and Laura going out to milk the cow after dark and finding a bear in the barnlot. Did bears come to farms then? What would your clothes, your house, or your parents' work have been a hundred years ago? Why did not Laura's father take an automobile or jet plane?

Such materials call for checking on an author. Is the author writing about what he or she actually knows? How can we find out? It is unfortunate that notes about authors and how they happen to write their stories do not appear somewhere within the covers of books to offer quick proof of competency.

Children can judge how fair and just another is. Should Peter Rabbit have been punished, or should Ping have gotten a smack for being last? Is an author right to make such things happen? Why do you think so?

Characters can be judged as lifelike or real. Does Fern do things that you would if you owned Wilbur? Is Templeton just what a greedy, selfish rat ought to be? Why does the little old man set out to find a cat? Why did he want to please the little old woman?

Perhaps discussion can lead to some understanding of the motives of characters, why a giant was bad and why a hero's deeds are good, for example.

Sometimes a title can be appraised. Children can judge such a title as *The Courage of Sarah Noble.* Does it seem a good one? Why? How do you think Sarah will show her courage? Was she brave? Would *you* have been? Children might judge a title by deciding whether it gives the idea of the story and sounds interesting.

Children can judge pictures. Children can do some critical thinking about the pictures in a book, though they are too immature yet to evaluate the technical quality of the art. They can see if a picture is true to the story. Most children are very much aware of details and catch discrepancies before adults do. One first grader was much disturbed at a picture of a little girl in a clean dress, because on the previous page the girl had fallen into a mud puddle. How, then, could her clothes be clean? As Lynd Ward once said, illustrations should be part and parcel of a book.

By being exposed to good illustrations, even young children can begin to build standards of art appreciation. They can offer some good reasons for their preferences.

Children can judge likenesses and differences in books dealing with children of other lands. Why did the boys and girls make fun of Chibi? Why did Ping live on a houseboat? Why did Pelle take a boat to the store and pay for the dye for the wool with a shilling? Family stories of people of other countries or races may lead to animated discussion and serious thought.

Various types of comparisons can lead to critical thinking. A child may compare biographies about the same person for details and authenticity, for example, the d'Aulaires' *Abraham Lincoln* with another book or TV program about Lincoln. A book, *Little Toot,* may be checked against a film or filmstrip in deciding how much the two are alike. Different versions of a story (or song) may be compared, as *Frog Went A'Courtin'* and "The Frog He Would A'Wooing Go." Some very capable children may check the original copy of a book against a simplified copy and try figuring out why the story has been made easier to read. The popularity of book clubs, even for young children, also leads to critical evaluation.

A child should be ready to evaluate his own oral or written reports. Even a young child, under guidance, can be taught to look up material for a report and judge what material is pertinent and what sources are best. Second and third graders are reading more widely than ever for information, and they must be led to dictionaries and encyclopedias. They must learn to check on accuracy. Even small children must be led to examine copyright dates in order to determine if material is up-to-date, an aspect of critical evaluation particularly important in content areas. With dictionary work a teacher must lead her class to develop awareness of multiple word meanings, that the right meaning may be chosen for the material being read.

A teacher may teach children to detect propaganda. One of the most common means of propaganda is television. According to David Russel (7), many children before starting school have developed critical thinking abilities with regard to this medium. He cites the five-year-old saying with a smile, "*All* the TV ads say they have the best breakfast cereal." While more chances are offered in the upper grades, probably we can teach children to detect propaganda as early as Grade 3 and help them recognize some of the techniques (8).

The child must be alert to figurative language. Figurative language is common. Many such expressions as "It's off the record" constantly confront the child. The young reader who has been taught to think critically will ask what the material really means.

A child can become alert to words that arouse emotions. A child may find a poem about rain personally pleasant. If he wants to play in the yard he may be dismayed by rain, however, just as may his mother who wants to hang the washing outside. He can be led to realize that a man whose fields are drying up may be delighted with rain. Words arouse emotions. Some understanding comes when meaning can be brought into the critical thinking of the child.

Finally, a child will select books according to his preferences. How does a child choose reading materials outside school? Spache (*9*) say that children begin as early as the primary grades to offer comments about their enjoyment of books. They can compare events and experiences in a book with their own. They can be led to think critcially about the author, what he wants them to see as his purpose, what words he uses, and what his characters are like. Evaluative skills and appreciation call for the personal involvement of each individual.

In summary, children of primary grades will be able to think critically about those situations which are a part of their own experiences or can be related to them. Many children will not do critical reading or thinking unless the teacher directs or challenges them. Surely critical reading by children calls for teachers who are critical thinkers themselves.

References

1. Austin, Mary, and Morrison, Coleman. *The First R*. New York: Macmillan, 1963.
2. Dallmann, Martha. "Critical Evaluation," *Grade Teacher,* 75 (Sept. 1957), 46-47.
3. Fay, Leo. *Developing the Ability to Read Critically*. Reading Promotion Bulletin No. 28. Chicago: Lyons and Carnahan, n.d.
4. Gary, Elizabeth Janet, *I Will Adventure.* New York: Viking, 1962.
5. Heilman, Arthur W. *Principles and Practices of Teaching Reading*. Columbus, Ohio: Charles E. Merrill, 1961.
6. Hester, Kathleen B. "Puerto Rico—Leader in a Spanish-American Reading Program," *Reading Teacher,* 17 (Apr. 1964), 516-521.
7. Russell, David H. "The Prerequisite: Knowing How to Read Critically," *Elementary English,* 40 (Oct. 1963), 579-582, 597.
8. Smith, Nila B. *Reading Instruction for Today's Children.* New York: Prentice-Hall, 1963.
9. Spache, George D. *Reading in the Elementary School.* Boston: Allyn and Bacon, 1964.
10. Stauffer, Russell G. "Children Can Read and Think Critically," *Education,* 80 (May 1960), 522-525.

The newspaper: resource for teaching study skills

NANCY G. WHISLER

Interested primarily in offering workshops, demonstration lessons, and courses to help teachers construct and use their own instructional materials in reading, author Whisler is on the extension staff of the University of California at Berkeley. After reading this article, any teacher better think twice before she uses yesterday's newspaper simply to wrap today's garbage.

MANY excellent innovative reading programs are currently on the market. Now available are a parade of fantastic machines that are able to perform just about every classroom task short of replacing the teacher. However, high costs of mechanized teaching equipment and other reading materials combined with shortages of money leave many classrooms with inadequate supplies to educate our youngsters.

The readily available American newspaper, still a dime in some areas, can, with a little ingenuity and time be recycled into innovative reading activities designed to teach and practice many study skills.

Teachers are continually searching for a wide variety of high interest contemporary reading materials. The newspaper offers this diversity. The teacher's task is to adapt the articles, columns, and ads into reading materials for her own unique teaching situation. Care should be taken to adjust these materials to meet the needs of individual students. The lessons may be developed in line with a student's reading level, rate of learning, interests, special difficulties, and need for enrichment. The activities, once constructed, are nonconsumable and may be reused many times, thus making optimum use of teacher time. Adaptable for independent or group use, these newspaper lessons may be assigned as a follow-up to a teacher directed lesson or freely selected as an independent activity.

THE READING TEACHER, 1972, Vol. 25, pp. 652-656.

Often, little formal instruction is provided to teach, or time allowed to practice, study skills before their application and mastery is expected on difficult assignments. Frequently children are assumed to possess prior knowledge of study skills and are thus given only incidental teaching treatment. Although skill in finding the main idea, skimming, summarizing, outlining, analytic reading for specific purposes, reading graphs and tabular material, elaborative and critical thinking may seem obvious and clear, most children need direct instruction in how to implement them in different reading tasks. Just as important as the sequential and developmental nature of beginning reading skills is the slow careful organization of a graded program to develop study skills. Initially each skill should be taught at the lowest level of difficulty, gradually increasing in complexity by using a wide variety of activities. Utilizing the newspaper for these lessons enables the teacher to construct materials exactly suited to her specific teaching objectives. Following are fourteen suggestions for using the newspaper to develop study skills.

Rim rat's dilemma. The purpose of the first activity, called *Rim Rat's Dilemma,* is to help students to understand the main idea of a reading selection. (A rim rat is a newspaper man who writes headlines.) The teacher cuts a number of articles from the newspaper, then separates the text of the article from the headline. The student's task is to read each article and locate the most suitable headline for it. Provision for differing levels of difficulty may be achieved by varying the number or similarity of the articles. Matching articles and headlines about completely different subjects, for example, is much easier than matching all articles and headlines concerning only one topic.

Editor's choice. As a beginning step to outlining, *Editor's Choice* is an activity which involves classification of newspaper articles under specific headings. A number of articles relating to three topics are put in an envelope. The task of the editor (student) is to organize them according to which section of the newspaper he feels they will best fit—sports, financial, social, or whatever. This activity may be made more difficult by making the discriminations more subtle and fine by using headings that are more closely related—national, international, and local politics, perhaps. This same exercise done on a timed basis is an excellent way to practice skimming skills.

Top of the news. On top of the front page of some large newspapers is a section wherein brief two or three line synopses of some of the major news stories of that day are located. *Top of the News* gives students a chance to make use of beginning summarizing skills. These summaries as well as the full text of the articles are cut out of the newspaper. (Headlines may be removed so that the student may not depend on the headline to match it to the summary.) Later, as the students become proficient at matching the summaries to the articles, they may read the articles and write their own two or three line summaries. They can then check the real summary from the newspaper to see if they included the pertinent main points.

Captive captions. The ability to comprehend material read may be practiced with the activity *Captive Captions*. For this lesson, captions are separated from the pictures they describe and the student's task is to correctly rearrange the captions by the pictures they describe. Difficulty may be increased by using more similar pictures: nothing but sports pictures, for instance, or even pictures of just one sport.

The funny order. The Funny Order makes use of the comic section of the newspaper to practice sequence of events. Frames of a comic strip are cut separately and placed in an envelope. By reading the text of each frame, the student's job is to place them back in the correct sequential order. Adapting to different levels can be easily done. For lower levels the first or first and second frames of the comic strip may be left in place to give the student the clue as to how the story begins. For more advanced readers, longer cartoon serials may be used where it is necessary to collect the funnies from several days' newspapers. In this case you may either have the student arrange each frame individually or reorganize sets of a whole week's strips together as long as it is just from one comic strip.

What happens next? What Happens Next? is an activity to help students learn to anticipate outcomes. Assemble a group of articles and remove the last paragraph from each selection. As the student reads each article he selects the most appropriate ending for the article.

Set the type. One of the most important jobs related to reading for the intermediate grade teacher is to develop a wide meaningful sight vocabulary. *Set the Type* is an activity designed to give practice in word recognition and meaning. This lesson may use whole page advertisements or sales ads large enough to be featuring several items. The teacher needs to cut and remove the pictures of all the items for sale. Cut the pictures all the same shape and size so configuration of the pieces will not be a clue when the student sets the type to reconstruct the page as it was printed. The student's task then is to read the descriptions of the sale items and match the picture that goes with the description.

Proofread the galley. Proofread the Galley, as its name implies, involves the student in locating and correcting punctuation, spelling, or even informational errors. Frequently newspaper articles contain mistakes. The teacher needs to collect a number of such articles over a period of time as she encounters them in her reading. She may make this assignment easier by telling the student the number and nature of the errors or make it more difficult by merely requesting him to correct any mistakes he can locate.

Wire service review. The ability to note and recall details can be practiced with the activity *Wire Service Reveiw.* Cut and mount entire articles on tagboard. For these lessons the teacher needs to write comprehension questions about the article on the reverse side of the news stories. The student reads and answers the questions either individually or with a partner. This can easily be adapted to a team learning situation where one student reads the article orally to the group. The group listens carefully and may take notes as a news reporter would. When the student is finished reading, members of the group ask him a number of comprehension questions relating to the material he just read. They may refer to their notes as guides for questions. For this exercise there is no need for teacher constructed questions to appear on the back of the article.

Press conference. Skimming or partial reading for different purposes is an essential skill for many study assignments. The entire front page of a newspaper is the only material needed for the activity called *Press Conference.* Students are told they will hold a press conference in a certain number of minutes. They are to then skim and try to remember as many facts as they can about the news that appeared on the front page. (As students become more proficient decrease the time allowed for skimming.) One half of the group act as reporters and do the questioning and the other half are the people who are being interviewed and they answer the questions at the press conference. The teacher may act as the interviewer and divide the class into teams who alternate answering her questions for score points.

Nonverbal material. Specific provisions need to be made in the reading program to teach students how to use nonverbal reading materials such as maps, charts, graphs, tables, and figures. The newspaper provides a good source, not only for different subject areas but also related to practical everyday situations. It may be necessary to collect these graphics over a period of time because they may not appear in the newspaper every day. Mounted on tagboard with questions on the back, they offer excellent practice in interpreting and understanding this type of reading material.

Scavenger hunt. Knowing where to locate different kinds of information is an important study skill. Practice exercises in the beginning stages of this skill can be made from the newspaper. In preparation for *Scavenger Hunt,* the teacher makes a list of different general topics—travel or the stock market, for instance. She may be even more specific on the list and write references to specific articles—new charter trips to Europe or drop in stock market prices. Working from the teacher's list, the student locates the articles that match the references on the list. He writes the page number and column number to indicate where he found the articles.

Want ads. Elaborative and critical thinking skills, which involve the student in evaluation of material or making judgments based on his experiences can be practiced by several activities using the newspaper. *Read the Want Ads Carefully* is a lesson which can be made by selecting eight ads of one type. These eight ads are then mounted on a single sheet of tagboard—for example, eight ads for "positions available." The student reads all the ads and decides which position he would like to apply for and why. Another example might incorporate eight "house for sale" ads; the student must evaluate the information and make a decision as to which house he would like to buy and why. A third example might have the student read eight ads for lost items. The student is then to judge which item is most or least valuable and suggest reward amounts for each item. Each of these activities requires the student to evaluate and judge in terms of his own experiences.

Point of view. Activities called *Which Point of View?* can be made from editorials or opinionated columns. This is a more sophisticated task where the student reads the selection and chooses from several alternatives the point of view that the author held. Suppose he reads an editorial about an antismog bill in Congress. The student selects one of three possible answers: The author favors passage of the bill. The author urges defeat of the bill. The author discusses the advantages and disadvantages and has no opinion regarding passage of the bill.

Supplementary materials to any commercial approach to reading are often necessary to service the individual needs of youngsters. The newspaper activities described in the preceding paragraphs have tremendous potential in the developmental reading program and can be effectively used in conjunction with any reading series or method of instruction. Certainly the proponents of any reading system will agree that it is the teacher who makes the program function successfully. If she is enthusiastic, well prepared and has the confidence in the materials she is using, in this case the newspaper, success is imminent.

References

Ashley, Rosalind. "Linguistic Games and Fun Exercises." *Elementary English*, XLIV (November 1967), 765-67.

Durrell, Donald D. *Improving Reading Instruction.* New York: Harcourt, Brace & World, 1956.

Durrell, Donald D., and McHugh, Walter J. "Analysis of Reading Services in Intermediate Grades." *The Reading Teacher*, XIV (September 1960), 26-29.

SECTION V

READING PROGRAMS AND APPROACHES

HOW TO TEACH READING?

by John F. Savage

Today's teacher has a lot to choose from in deciding how to teach reading. Never before have we been buffeted by such an array of suggestions and an overabundance of advice from many directions: the basal reader, individualized reading, the language experience approach, the linguistic method, i/t/a, programmed reading, words in color. Which brand should we choose? What's the best approach to use?

The variety of approaches offered as solutions to help alleviate the reading problem in our schools often confuses teachers. Each approach sounds like a panacea when one of its fervent advocates advances arguments, introduces evidence and quotes research to prove that his approach is *the* best way or at least better than all other ways.

One source of the current confusion is our frequent failure to distinguish between approaches, methods and materials. We are brainwashed by the phonics vs. whole word (or the decoding vs. meaning, to use newer terminology) debate. We see each of these approaches as dichotomous, when often they are not. A linguistic or i/t/a approach, for example, is usually presented within the structure of a basal reading series. Different approaches exist side by side. Most can be integrated and used in a well-balanced reading program. There are, of course, some very basic differences between certain approaches. But even where there are basic differences in the thinking behind two different approaches to reading instruction, mixed marriages can exist in the classroom (for example, where the basal is used for skill development in a so-called "modified individualized approach").

When we talk about these different approaches to teaching reading, we are often talking about apples and elephants. This is fine, as long as we realize it and know what we're talking about.

This article is an attempt to separate the apples from the elephants. It aims at an objective and dispassionate description of the various approaches to reading instruction now being used. Perhaps it may unmuddy the waters and help teachers sort out features of some of the more popular modern approaches to teaching reading.

THE BASAL READER

In the champion's corner is the "good old" basal approach. From Colonial times, the basal has been the chief tool used to teach reading. Basals still constitute the reading staple in nine-tenths of our classrooms.

The basal is often misnamed a "method." The basal is more precisely a *tool* for teaching reading. A basal program consists of a series of reading materials that are carefully graded for continuous progress from the prereading level to the upper grades of elementary school. Along with the readers, the basal program includes a series of workbooks designed to develop and reinforce skills in conjunction with the basal texts, manuals to guide the teacher in the use of the materials, and other devices like charts and tapes intended to supplement the basic part of the program. The "method" for teaching with basal materials is suggested in the teacher's manuals.

The two major components of basal reading programs are content and skills. The content of stories provides the reading material which children use to learn and practice the skills needed for reading competency. The skills to be learned with each story are identified and built into the lessons in the manual, and extra practice is provided for in the workbooks.

All basal programs are not the same. Different series place different emphases on different skills at different levels. Traditionally, the most common emphasis in most basal programs was on the *look-say* or *whole word* methods. Children were taught to read words by sight, using picture and configuration clues to build a large store of words they could recognize at a glance. After this sight vocabulary had been built, the basic skills of context clues, structural analysis and phonetic analysis were gradually developed. Getting meaning from the printed page was emphasized from the beginning of reading instruction.

Basals of more recent vintage place greater emphasis on the decoding process. Printed language is viewed as a code representing the language that children already know how to speak. The emphasis in early instruction is on helping children break the code by associating language sounds, or phonemes, with symbols, or graphemes, used to represent these sounds. Children are taught to read only the most necessary phonetically irregular words by sight. Reading for meaning is reserved until the basic decoding skills have been developed.

Basal programs have been developed by experts after years of careful study and experience. These programs give many teachers the structure they need in planning reading instruction for their classes. Most teachers group their children according to ability, since a single book fails to meet the range of needs in any class.

The most common criticism leveled against the basal has been directed at the content. Stories are said to hold no appeal or interest for children, not even for the "average child" for whom the basal is purportedly designed. The upper middle-class children in the basal—doing such nice things in ideal surroundings and circumstances—are too unreal and unbelievable.

The manner in which the content is presented has also come under fire. Basals are typically written in an artificial language style that is not found anywhere but in the basals. It has been facetiously referred to as "primerese." Decoding experts have criticized the criteria in choosing words that are used for initial reading instruction.

The skills program of a basal series is well planned, too well planned according to critics. The skills program is both comprehensive and balanced. Each item in the total inventory of basic skills for all phases of reading is identified, introduced, developed, reinforced and reviewed at appropriate levels. The program is often said to be so inflexible, regimented and confining that children lose all desire to read. Also, depending on one's point of view in the decoding vs. meaning debate, the specific skills emphasized at dfferent levels may be questioned.

It is fair to say that publishers of modern basals have tried to overcome these frequently identified shortcomings. Many recently published programs use more interesting and realistic content, improved illustrations, more natural language patterns and greater emphasis on decoding skills early in the program. Enough of the old remains, however, to make many of the traditional criticisms valid.

Basal programs usually constitute the major part of the reading program in classrooms where they are used. As the name indicates, however, basal programs are designed to develop *basic* skills. Where best used, the basal does not constitute the total program. Rather, it serves as the foundation of a balanced reading program that includes recreational reading, content reading, research, news reading and other reading activities that are carried on apart from the basal.

Despite the blast of recent criticism leveled at basals, the majority of American children have learned to read through the extensive (or exclusive) use of basals. The tragedy, however, is that many children have not learned to read, and many more have not learned to make reading a life-long interest. When the traditional basal programs were found wanting, new programs cropped up to challenge the supremacy of the champion in providing solutions "to solve the reading problem" in our schools.

INDIVIDUALIZED READING

The individual is at the heart of the American heritage and philosophy. Any approach to teaching that emphasizes the individual is bound to have appeal. Individualized reading is a working plan that provides one answer to the long-sought-after goal of individualizing instruction.

The individualized approach does not have the rigid structure of the typical basal series. The essential characteristics of an individualized program are:

1. *Self-selection of reading materials.* A large selection of reading materials from different sources—library books, magazines, books from children's personal collections, and collections of books designed specifically for individualized programs by a growing number of publishing companies—are made available in the classroom. From this collection the child chooses material according to his own needs and interests. The child keeps a record of the books he has read for use during his individual conference time.

2. *Individual conferences for skill development.* The teacher plans individual conferences with each pupil to hear him read, discuss content, check on comprehension, note progress, determine what basic skills need im

provement and development and help him select further reading material. The skills that are taught during conference time are related to the child's specific reading needs.

3. *Groups organized for instructional purposes.* Most skills teaching is done during individual conferences. From time to time, however, when common needs become apparent, the teacher forms groups to teach certain basic skills to those children with a common need. These reading groups are formed on the basis of skills and needs, not on the basis of ability or proficiency as in a typical basal program. Occasional whole class sessions are planned for shared activities related to reading.

Other language activities or projects, such as sharing, discussion, dramatization, story writing, are usually part of the reading program as well.

In an individualized approach, the pupil is allowed to progress at his own pace without pressure to keep up or wait for the rest of the group to catch up. Allowing children to choose their own reading material has built-in motivational power.

Individual conference times provide a mutual advantage for both pupil and teacher. The child profits from the one-to-one teaching situation aimed at his own specific reading problems. The teacher gets to know the child, his interests, his ability and his needs a little better than in a regular classroom situation.

A successful individualized reading program demands a knowledgeable and skillful teacher who has an encyclopedic knowledge of children's books, a thorough familiarity with her pupils, a sound knowledge of how to teach reading, and the ability to put all this information to work effectively. Reading doesn't just "happen" in an individualized approach.

While an individualized program avoids the rigidity of a basal program, it also abandons the organization and structure of the basal. Individualized reading requires a teacher who can organize 30 or more individual programs and create structure out of a situation with limitless possibilities for chaos. The teacher must provide an efficient method for circulating books, activities to go along with the books, and practice exercises and worksheets for skills that different children need at different times. Yet, as overwhelming as these demands seem to be, thousands of teachers, convinced of the values of the individualized approach, are doing this in their classrooms every day.

The individualized approach is often supported in some measure by the basal program, either through the skills program of the basal or through supplementary use of basal readers themselves.

Many references on individualized reading programs are available, but the standard one is *Individualizing Your Reading Program,* by Jeanette Veatch (Putnam, 1959).

LANGUAGE EXPERIENCE APPROACH

Another approach to reading that abandons the rigidity and structure of the basal program is the language experience approach. This approach uses the child's own language as the stuff of the reading program.

The language experience approach begins with dictation. The children, either individually or in groups, dictate stories. The stories are usually accounts of firsthand experiences, or they can be retold versions of stories that the children have heard. The teacher, teacher aide or other adult records the children's stories on charts, on large sheets of paper or on the chalkboard to be later transferred to experience charts. The children see and learn to read their own language in written form.

When the children can read their own stories, they are encouraged to read them aloud to other children, to the class, to the principal or to the janitor. Frequently stories are illustrated and class booklets are made for children and parents to read. From this, children progress to books — "talk" that has been produced and written by someone else.

Skill development takes place within the context of these reading activities in the daily program. As the teacher helps children read their stories, she consciously calls attention to letter names and sounds, familiar words and word elements, punctuation and the other basic skills and elements that the children need.

By its very nature, the language experience approach provides children with interesting and meaningful reading material. Children learn to read about things that are important to them in their own world. Stories are about their own pets, not Dick's dog Spot. By recording the child's personal thoughts and words, this approach takes advantage of the unique background of each individual. There is often pride when the child sees that what he has to say is important enough to be recorded in print.

In the reading material, the words that the child reads are familiar and rich in meaning because they come from the child himself. Language patterns are more natural because they are taken from spontaneous talk.

The language experience approach builds on the interrelationships among all the language arts: reading, writing, speaking and listening. Estimates of the number of words that a child understands and uses by the time he starts to learn to read vary from less than 5,000 to over 20,000. But whatever the exact vocabulary size, one thing is certain: children know a lot more words than the 20-odd typically presented in the basal preprimer. In the language experience approach, writing usually begins early, thus breaking the artificial barrier that has kept reading and writing apart for instructional purposes in the early grades.

When a child learns to read through the language experience approach, there is a tendency to develop further awareness of and sensitivity to his own out-of-school environment, since this is the content that he is reading about. This approach also creates the necessity for a rich classroom environment with lots of things in the room to stimulate language and many arranged experiences to talk about.

Finding enough time to carry on a language experience program is a problem. Listening to and recording the stories of each child and helping him read his own story is time consuming. Many teachers have made effective use of teacher aides and other paraprofessionals to help solve this problem.

Another problem arises with children who are shy, who come from a deprived language background or who have a meager speaking vocabulary. Teachers report that patient guidance and group stories usually draw these children out. Rare is the child who has absolutely nothing to say, especially when he realizes that what he has to say is worth saying. Vocabulary enrichment is an important part of any approach to reading.

A serious question often raised about the language experience approach is how to broaden children's reading horizons. Children need to read words that are outside their own vocabularies and be exposed to the world of ideas and experiences beyond their own. Broadening reading experiences is handled by skilled teachers as children's reading skills advance.

The language experience approach was designed to be used as the major way of teaching beginning reading. It is used as the sole approach and in conjunction with other aproaches. It has been reported as a particularly effective technique for teaching children who fail with more conventional approaches, even in the upper grades.

Learning to Read Through Experience by Doris M. Lee and Roach Van Allen (Appleton-Century-Crofts, 1963) is a good source for finding out more about the language experience approach to teaching reading.

LINGUISTICS APPROACH

The approach fast gaining popularity in schools today is the linguistics approach. During the past decade the effect of linguistics on the language arts curricula has been revolutionary. More and more linguistic readers are appearing on the market, and even the most traditional basals have the name of a "linguistic advisor" attached to the team of authors.

Linguistics is the scientific study of language. It has produced new insights into the way our language is structured and functions. A linguistic approach to reading is based on certain principles arrived at through the scientific study of language. Methods and materials for teaching reading are consistent with this linguistic thinking.

In discussing linguistics, it is important to realize that there is no one linguistic approach to reading. All linguists do not look at language in the same way and linguistic programs differ in certain respects from one another. There is, however, an accepted body of linguistic knowledge and some consensus on how this knowledge should be applied in teaching reading.

The linguistic approach begins with a strong foundation of oral language. Speech is the primary form of language. Many fully developed languages have been found without any writing system at all. Young children and even some adults who cannot read or write, use language—that is, they receive and transmit messages through speech. When the child begins to learn to read, he has a knowledge of the sound, meaning and syntactical systems of the language. Reading instruction—teaching children how to deal with the written symbols used to represent spoken language—draws upon this knowledge that children already possess.

In linguistic approaches, learning to read is viewed as a process of learning to decode printed language. Language is the main code humans use to transmit their thoughts and ideas to one another. Before he comes to school, the child can both encode and decode messages in spoken language. In learning to read, he must break the written code that is used to represent speech.

English is an alphabetic language. In other words, English language sounds called "phonemes" are represented by written symbols called "graphemes." In some languages graphemes represent syllables or whole words, but in English graphemes represent individual speech sounds. English, however, does not conform perfectly to the alphabetic principle. There are about 44 phonemes and only 26 letters of the alphabet used to represent these sounds. The same sound is represented in different ways (as in the initial sounds of *fun* and *phone*), while the same grapheme represents different sounds (as in the vowel sounds of *fat*, *father* and *fate*). While English is not perfectly regular, the linguistic approach builds on the extensive regularity that does exist.

About eighty per cent of our English words have a regular sound-symbol (phoneme-grapheme) relationship. Beginning reading materials systematically control vocabulary according to this sound-symbol regularity. In the typical traditional preprimer sentence *Stop and go, Mother*, the vowel *o* represents three different sounds. In the typical linguistic preprimer sentence *Hop on the log* the vowel *o* represents the same sound each time it is used. This systematic control and patterning of consonant-vowel-consonant combinations is why we find sentences like *Dan ran to the tan man* in some linguistic readers.

After the most regular phoneme-grapheme relationships have been established, other less regular patterns are systematically introduced. Some phonetically irregular words (for example, *of* which ends in a *v* sound) occur so frequently in our language that they must be introduced early as sight words or through some other device.

Linguistic approaches emphasize oral reading as a means of checking the child's mastery of the sound-symbol relationships. In oral language, words alone do not give the full meaning of what we have to say. The way in which the words are said—the pitch, stress and juncture we use—can change the whole meaning of an utterance. Thus, linguistic programs give great attention to intonation patterns in oral reading.

Comprehension and the many uses of reading are usually not stressed until later stages of reading instruction, after the sound-symbol relationships have been firmly established. The syntactic relationships between words and other elements in sentences are emphasized in developing comprehension skills. Most of us can remember trying to translate a sentence in a foreign language when we knew all the words but just couldn't put them together to make any sense. In reading, the child must know the meaning of each word, but since most words are within his speaking vocabulary, this is usually not a problem. In addition to knowing the meaning of each word, the child must also see the relationship between words and word groups in a sentence. Seeing these syntactical relationships in the arrangement of words in a sentence is the key to comprehension.

Linguistic programs focus on reading as part of language. Some series avoid the use of pictures in the books, since pictures are non-language clues to meaning.

All of these characteristics and elements of the linguistic approach are neither unique to linguistic programs nor equally strong in all linguistic series. Technically, since learning to read is the process of learning to deal with language in its printed form, any approach to reading might be termed "linguistic." All approaches must emphasize the left-to-right sequence in reading. The linguistic approach emphasizes initial knowledge of letter names, but the importance of this was proven by non-linguistic researchers many years ago. Oral language is the starting point in the language experience approach as well as in the linguistic approach. What sets the linguistic approach apart from all the others is its attention to the alphabetic principle and the concern with building on the regularity that exists in our language.

With the recent emphasis on linguistics, several books and articles have appeared within the past few years describing the linguistic approach to reading. One of the earlier ones that is an excellent reference is *Linguistics and Reading*, by Charles C. Fries who is considered by many to be the dean of American linguists (Holt, Rinehart & Winston, 1962).

INITIAL TEACHING ALPHABET

Another approach to reading instruction that attempts to regularize language is Sir James Pitman's Augmented Roman Alphabet, commonly known as the Initial Teaching Alphabet or i/t/a.

A language that conforms perfectly to the alphabetic principle has a one-to-one sound-symbol relationship. English, with its 40-odd phonemes and 26 letters of the alphabet, is less than perfect. In i/t/a, Pitman revised traditional orthography to achieve more consistency in the language used to teach beginning reading.

The i/t/a alphabet has one symbol for each language sound. Of the 44 characters used in i/t/a (see chart), 19 consonant letters and five vowel letters, representing the short vowel sounds, have been retained from traditional orthography. The letters *q* and *x* have been discarded since they have no unique sounds in the language. Long vowel characters are created by adding *e* to the short vowel form. Eight characters are combinations of traditional letters, and there are seven new characters.

In a concession to traditional orthography, which children would eventually have to read, Pitman included *c* and *k* to represent a single phoneme. As another concession, he included double letters (in words like ***letter***) to retain similar word patterns. The major strength of i/t/a is that it provides a consistently alphabetic representation of the English language.

The 44-character Initial Teaching Alphabet

Even though English is written from left to right, the child has to break the left-to-right sequence with some words in traditional orthography. For example, he has to look at the final *e* in *ride* before he decides that the *i* represents the long *i* sound. In i/t/a this problem is eliminated.

Many teachers are bothered by the additional odd-looking characters in the i/t/a alphabet. How, some ask, can i/t/a purport to ease the process of learning to read when it requires learning more than the 26 standard symbols of the alphabet? Advocates of i/t/a are quick to point out that in the traditional orthography, with capital and lower case letters, the child must learn more than 26 symbols. i/t/a symbols are always the same. Where capitalization is needed, the lower case character is merely enlarged.

When he devised i/t/a, Sir James did not intend to follow in his grandfather's footsteps as a spelling reformer. i/t/a is intended as a temporary medium, a beginning reading alphabet. As soon as the child has learned to read with fluency, he makes the transition to materials written in traditional orthography.

The transition period produces the major question mark in most people's minds. Teachers are concerned that children will become confused when it comes time to read words in traditional orthography. But tests have shown that the transition takes place rather easily. The transition is not started until basic skills have been developed and the child is confident of his ability to read. Many of the i/t/a symbols are exactly like or similar to letters of the standard alphabet. Also, while he is learning to read with i/t/a in school, the child is surrounded outside of school with traditional orthography in magazines, signs, labels and other printed materials. Reading materials in i/t/a provide for a smooth and gradual transition.

Research experiments involving i/t/a, both in Great Britain where it was originally tested and in this country, usually report tremendous growth in children's reading abilities. One side effect of i/t/a that is frequently reported is significant improvement in children's writing abilities as well. John Downing, Pitman's associate and co-worker, calls i/t/a a writing system, not a teaching method.

The i/t/a approach is well explained in *The Initial Teaching Alphabet,* by John Downing (Macmillan, 1964).

PROGRAMMED READING

Programmed reading is not a way of teaching reading. It is a way of organizing and presenting materials used to teach reading.

Programmed learning is the learning approach of a technological age. Programmed materials are being increasingly used in elementary schools, and programmed texts and machines are available to teach reading skills all the way down to the prereading levels.

In a programmed approach to learning, subject matter is broken down into very small pieces called "frames." Frames are arranged in careful sequence and presented in steps to the learner. Each frame is based upon or related to previous ones, so that later learning is often dependent upon what has gone before.

In using programmed materials, active response is demanded. The student reacts to a question or statement by writing an answer or pressing a button. He knows if his answer is right or wrong through immediate feedback. If right, the learner can move along through the program. If he is wrong, he immediately checks his answer, learns the correct response, and thus insures that he knows each step as he progresses.

More sophisticated programs have built-in provisions for diagnosis and/or remedial work. The learner's moves are dictated by the responses he makes. If he makes correct responses on certain items, the learner is directed to skip the parts of the program designed to teach him what he already knows.

A program can be contained in a book, in a relatively simple and inexpensive plastic box, or in a sophisticated piece of electronic equipment. In book form, the child uses a card to cover the answers that are presented in the margin. In the simple mechanical devices there is usually provision for a multiple choice response and the learner cannot progress until he has pressed the right button. The design of more highly technical devices containing programmed materials are limited only by the ingenuity of the designer and the nature of the program.

Many currently popular reading materials contain certain elements from programmed learning—the self-correcting, self-directing aspects, for example—but technically they are not programmed materials.

The major strength of programmed materials in reading lies in the sound learning principles upon which the whole theory of programmed learning is based. Programmed materials are self-instructional. A child can work independently and move through the program as quickly as his learning rate will allow. The pupil is actively involved in his learning. With immediate feedback, right answers are reinforced and wrong answers can be immediately corrected.

Programmed learning tends to be rote. Programmed materials can well be used to develop certain basic skills but hardly those involved in the critical, interpretative and creative aspects of the reading act. Programmed materials are more efficient, if somewhat less personal. The impersonality is what bothers many teachers most. Programmed materials feature all the mechanical efficiency of a machine without the human weaknesses of the teacher. But they also have all the weaknesses of a machine without the human strengths of the teacher. Both man and machine are needed.

In more conventional reading programs, the programmed approach is used as a supplementary device for many skill-building materials. Programming is used more extensively in systems using computer assisted instruction.

For those interested in principles and practices of programmed learning, Edward Fry's *Teaching Machines and Programmed Instruction: An Introduction* (McGraw-Hill, 1963) is a worthwhile reference.

WORDS IN COLOR

While not yet widely popular, an interesting approach to beginning reading that is getting some attention of late is Words in Color, another attempt to create regularity in early reading materials. As the name indicates, the program uses color as a device to help teach sound-symbol correspondences. Beginning with the five short vowels, each sound is represented by a letter presented in a distinct color. For example, the short sound of *a* in a word is represented by a letter printed in white; the short sound of *e* is represented by a blue letter. Letters are designated by their color names. Consonants are added to build words. Games are an important part of the program in helping to develop skills of visual discrimination, auditory discrimination, word recognition and word building.

Since it is a phonics program, Words in Color has many of the same strengths and weaknesses attributed to any phonetic approach to teaching beginning reading. While there has been serious question as to whether the use of color coding makes any significant contribution in helping children learn to read, the approach has been reported as successful in some places where it has been tried.

Where used, this approach is usually employed as a supplementary device to help develop initial reading and phonics skills.

The program is explained by its originator, Calib Gattegno, in *Words in Color* (Learning Materials, 1962)

WHICH APPROACH IS BEST?

Now comes the inevitable crucial question: Of all these approaches to reading instruction, which one is best?

Fame and wealth await the person who proves conclusively that *his* approach is the best way to teach reading. While we await the coming of this educational King Arthur, however, we are still faced with the job of deciding which approach to use in our classrooms today. We're still faced with doing our best with the best we have.

No one method is guaranteed to abolish reading failure in our schools. There's merit in each of the approaches described. If it has been advanced, then it must have been tried and found successful for some children. All approaches have the same aim—reading success—but no one approach will meet the needs of all pupils nor solve all our reading problems.

Despite all the research that has been done to determine which approach is best, no conclusive answer has been found, mainly because not all children are alike and not all teachers are alike.

All children do not learn in exactly the same way. It has long been recognized that some children learn best through visual means, others, through aural means, and still others need kinesthetic help. An eclectic approach is often suggested as a means of providing for all these individual differences.

A teacher who uses an eclectic approach selects the sucessful features of those approaches that best meet the needs of children in her own class. But the eclectic approach is more than a cafeteria style of teaching reading. Using color coded i/t/a symbols to record phonetically regular words on individualized experience charts is a bizarre consideration. Some children will learn to read with any approach. The secret is to find out what aspects of which approach will work best with children who *aren't* learning to read. Many successful classroom reading programs are hybrids of two or more approaches.

An eclectic approach not only allows for individual differences in children, it allows for individual differences in teachers as well, since it allows the teacher to use her own special talents. The answer to the question Which is the best way to teach reading? is more often found in the teacher than in the approach itself.

Research efforts to find out which

approach is best are usually colored by the teacher's enthusiasm for, and commitment to, the particular approach being tried. An approach is found to be successful because the teacher believes in it, wants to see it work, and works hard to see that it *does* work. In the final analysis the teacher's preference for an approach is most often the major factor in determining its success.

A. Byron Callaway
Director, Reading Clinic
The University of Georgia

Oscar T. Jarvis
Curriculum and Instruction
University of Texas at El Paso

Program and Materials Used in Reading Instruction: A Survey

Among the important factors contributing to the success of the reading program in the elementary school are: (1) the type of reading program, (2) the supplementary materials used in reading instruction, (3) the types of equipment used, (4) the methods used in selecting textbooks and supplementary materials. A survey of these factors was made recently in Georgia where elementary principals were asked to complete a survey questionnaire while attending an in-service workshop on reading. One hundred and four elementary principals completed the survey form. A discussion of the findings follows.

It was indicated by 62 per cent of the principals that the reading program basic to their schools was a combination of two or more approaches such as basal readers and packaged kits as Part A of Table I shows. A basal series was part of all but one of these programs; that being indi-

TABLE I

Type of Reading Programs Employed in Elementary School

Part A Type Program	Number of Schools	Per Cent of Schools	*Part B* Combination of Programs	Number of Schools	Per Cent of Schools
a. Basal Readers	38	37	a & b	2	2
b. Programmed Reading	0	0	a & c	5	5
c. Individualized Reading	1	1	a & d	27	25
d. Packaged Kits	0	0	a & f	1	1
e. Language Experience	0	0	a,b,c & d	2	2
f. i/t/a	0	0	a,d, & e	2	2
g. Combination	65	62	b,c, & d	1	1
h. Other	0	0	a,c, & d	15	14
			a,c, & e	1	1
			a,b,c & e	1	1
			a,b, & c	2	2
			a,c,d,e	3	3
			a,b,d	2	2
			a & other*	1	1

*One school used "Words In Color"

ELEMENTARY ENGLISH, 1972, Vol. 49, pp. 578-581.

vidualized reading in the instance of one school as Table I shows. An additional 37 per cent listed a basal series as the program basic to their school. Many combination programs were used as Part B of Table I indicates. The frequent combinations were: basal readers and packaged kits (25 per cent); basal readers, individualized reading, and packaged kits (14 per cent); and basal readers and individualized reading (5 per cent). Other combinations were used by only one, two, or three per cent of the schools.

A wide variety of supplementary materials was used by schools in reading instruction. Eighty-nine per cent of the schools had a central library, 60 per cent also used classroom libraries and several schools reported that additional materials were furnished by regional libraries.

Additional series of readers, other than the basal series, were used by 88 per cent of the schools to supplement reading instruction as can be seen in Table II. Likewise, 88 per cent of the schools used the workbooks that accompany the basal series while 14 per cent utilized other workbooks. Packaged kits were used in 75 per cent of the schools as supplementary material for reading instruction. Reader's Digest Skill Builders were employed in 40 per cent, programmed materials in 18 per cent, and the Reading Spectrum in 29 per cent of the schools responding to the survey questionnaire.

Special book groups were utilized in a number of schools. Of those listed, the Owl Series* was employed by 27 per cent, the Torch Series* and the Invitation to Personal Reading Series* were each listed as being used in 13 per cent of the schools as Table II further depicts.

Selection of basal material for reading instruction in the elementary school was of major importance. This survey study attempted to determine who selected this type material.

In the vast majority of school systems (80 per cent), textbook materials for basal reading instruction were selected by a system wide committee composed of teachers and administrators as Table III shows. In 11 per cent of the schools, a teacher committee made the selection. Curriculum

*These series are collections of previously published books selected by publishers and distributed in sets.

TABLE II

Supplementary Materials Used for Reading Instruction

Type Supplementary Materials	Numbers of Schools	Per Cent of Schools
Series of Readers Other Than Basal	91	88
Workbooks That Accompanying Basal	91	88
Other Workbooks	15	14
Packaged Kits	78	75
Reader's Digest Skill Builders	42	40
Programmed Materials	19	18
Reading Spectrum	30	29
Owl Series	28	27
Torch Series	14	13
Invitation to Personal Reading	14	13
Games	43	41
Literature Sampler	7	7
Others	13	12

TABLE III

Basal Reading Textbook Material Selection Process

Selected By	Number of Schools	Per Cent of Schools
System Wide Committee (Teachers & Administrators)	83	80
Teacher Committee	12	11
Curriculum Director	5	5
Individual Teachers	1	1
Reading Coordinator	2	2
Other	1	1

Directors made the selection in five per cent of the schools.

In conducting the survey study, it was also determined how reading materials other than the basal textbooks were selected. Selection of nontextual materials was made jointly by teachers, principal, and librarians in 77 per cent of the schools responding as Table IV sets forth. Teachers and librarians made the selections in seven per cent of the schools; and teachers, principal, and curriculum directors had the responsibility in six per cent of the schools.

Many types of equipment were available for teacher use in the schools to aid in reading instruction. The filmstrip projector and phonograph were the most frequently reported types of equipment available for use in the schools as can be seen in Table V. The tape recorder was available in 95 per cent of the schools and the overhead projector in 85 per cent of them. Also, available was the primer typewriter in 45 per cent and the controlled reader in 38 per cent of the school systems reporting.

Several types of equipment were available for diagnostic purposes in reading as Table V also shows. Forty-one per cent of the schools had the audiometer available for checking hearing. However, less than seven per cent had equipment for checking vision. Fifty-four per cent of the schools had access to the Snellen Chart for checking vision, a questionable practice.

TABLE IV

Selection Process for Materials Other Than Basal Textual Material in Reading

Selected By	Number of Schools	Per Cent of Schools
Teachers, Librarians, and Principals Jointly	81	77
Teachers and Librarian Jointly	7	7
Teachers Alone Select	4	4
Teachers, Curriculum Director and Principal	6	6
Reading Coordinator	2	2
Librarian and Principal	1	1
Teachers and Curriculum Director	1	1
Teachers and Principal	1	1
Curriculum Director	1	1

Summary

In the group of schools surveyed, the basal reader predominated in reading instruction. However, it was noted that most systems used a variety of approaches and materials for reading instruction. Most schools utilized a variety of supplementary

TABLE V

Availability of Equipment

Type Equipment	Number of Schools	Per Cent of Schools	Type Equipment	Number of Schools	Per Cent of Schools
Telebinocular	6	6	Shadowscope	1	1
Orthorater	1	1	Skimmer	1	1
Snellen Eye Chart	57	54	Tachistoscope	13	12
Audiometer	43	41	Craig Reader	4	4
Tape Recorder	99	95	Language Master	17	16
Phonograph	101	97	Reading Eye Camera	0	0
Over-head Projector	88	85	Audio Notebook	0	0
Filmstrip Projector	101	97	Perceptomatic	4	4
Tach-X	14	13	Viewlex	15	14
Controlled Reader	39	37	Primer Typewriter	47	45
			Other	7	7

materials to assist in the teaching of reading. Basal textbooks and supplementary reading materials were generally selected jointly by teachers and administrators. Many school systems reported the availability of a wide array of equipment such as the filmstrip projector and phonograph for teaching reading.

What's <u>Right</u> with Basal Readers

John F. Savage

Of all the teaching tools and learning resources used in the elementary classroom in recent years, the one that has come under the most severe criticism is the basal reader. Taking a pot shot at the basal has for some time been a fashionable pastime for journalists, psychologists, sociologists, college professors and even a few teachers. Despite the widespread (and sometimes valid) criticism, however, the basal reading program remains the backbone of reading instruction in America. Basals are the major tools used for teaching reading in about 90 per cent of our schools.

The argument against basal programs usually goes something like this: "Basal readers do not provide a totally adequate reading program for children. Therefore abolish their use in schools." No serious reading teacher would argue with this premise. To reach this conclusion based on the premise, however, is like throwing the baby out with the bath water.

As the name indicates, *basal* programs are designed to develop the *basic* skills children need for reading competence. When the basal serves as the total reading program, it is inadequate. When it serves as the foundation for a well-balanced developmental program, it has an important place in reading instruction.

The two major components of the basal series are content and skills. The whole basal program—including the pre-reading materials, teachers' manuals, workbooks, supplementary books, charts, filmstrips, audio tapes, and other supplementary materials and devices—is set up to develop children's basic reading skills using the content of the basal texts. Let's take a careful look at each of these components.

Content

The content of the typical basal reader has been the main focus of the criticism leveled against it over the years. Since the days of McGuffey, children have been forced to face a ". . . series of horrible, stupid, emasculated, pointless, tasteless little readers, the stuff and guff about Dick and Jane or Alice and Jerry visiting the farm and having birthday parties and seeing animals in the zoo and going through dozens and dozens of totally unexciting middle-class, middle-income, middle-I.Q. children's activities." (from Flesch's *Why Johnny Can't Read*, published by Harper & Row).

Anybody who takes time to examine some of the basals of the late 1960s knows that it's a whole new ball game. While much of the "stuff and guff" remains, today's readers are markedly improved over those of the past. Not only is the art work more attractive, but the content is often more sophisticated. Characters are less stereotyped and more believable. More stories are set in an urban environment. Many stories and illustrations are apt to be racially mixed. Episodes which fall within the experience of all children (for example, watching TV or shopping in a supermarket or just plain dreaming) are included. While families still take trips to the zoo and to the farm, family life is generally presented more realistically. Today's readers contain more plays and poems with genuine juvenile appeal. The content of the basal still has a long way to go, but it has started to move.

The manner in which the content is presented has also been the object of heavy criticism. Rigid vocabulary control and the systematic introduction of new words results in a language style that is not found anywhere but in the basal. The style is typified by the story of the first grade teacher who, upon discovering a dent in her car in the school parking lot, responded with, "Oh, oh! Look, look! Damn, damn!"

New linguistic research is just beginning to change this artificial style. Studies of children's language show that youngsters employ a variety of sentence patterns in their speech by the time they come to school. In even the most modern basal, one still finds sentences of the "See Spot run" variety. But lately, one is apt to find sentences like "Have a good day," or " 'Some fire!' says the girl." (from *People Read*, part of the Bank Street Series published by The Macmillan Co.). Contractions, which were anathema in the traditional lower grade basal, are found in the pre-primers of today, as in "Tuggy can't get the bug," (from *Pepper*, part of Linguistic Readers, published by Harper & Row). The writing style found in the basals is beginning to approach children's natural way of speaking.

'Flick the tick off the chick'

Linguistic research, however, has created another source of criticism about the sentence patterns in early basals. The linguistic approach, which emphasizes the regularity of sound-symbol relationships in beginning reading, often produces sentences like "A cat is on a mat" or "Flick the tick off the chick with a thick stick, Nick." These sentences, it is argued, are as artificial as the traditional "Oh, see Spot jump!" But if one accepts the criterion of phonetic regularity instead of frequency of use in choosing vocabulary for beginning readers, then one can accept the Seuss-like sentences that result. This kind of sentence is characteristic of the beginning reading stage, and more natural sentence patterns are introduced soon after the initial essentials have been mastered.

The literary quality of the basal's content is also criticized. This criticism is often unwarranted. "Looking down the list of authors (of an upper grade basal reader), the teacher does not find the Pablum of which reader series are popularly accused. These are the works of major children's authors . . ." (from *Teaching Elementary Reading* by Miles A. Tinker and Constance M. McCullough, published by Appleton-Century-Crofts). Obviously, no basal reader can hope to consistently measure up to the quality of the writing of an Ezra Jack Keats or a Robert McCloskey. What we often forget, however, is that many of the standard works we use to measure the quality of the basal's content were written to be read *to* children, not *by* them. There's a big difference.

Skills to be developed

No matter what the nature of the content, the strength of the basal reading series lies in its well-planned skills program.

In order to read successfully, the child must be able to recognize words quickly, apply phonetic principles to decode unknown words, identify new words through structural analysis, and use context clues to figure out word meanings. In addition to being able to read the words, a child must see the relationship between words in different parts of the sentence in order to understand and interpret the total meaning of what he reads. When this comprehension is followed by mental reaction, the reading act is complete. Close attention to these fundamental and basic reading skills is the basal's forte.

The skills program of a basal reading series is both comprehensive and balanced. Modern basal programs are designed by experts who know the field of reading and know it well. A total inventory of the skills needed to deal with all phases of reading, both silent and oral, is almost assured. These skills are carefully graded. Provision is made at each grade level for the introduction, sequential development, gradual reinforcement and systematic review of appropriate basic skills.

Basal series provide for skill development through supplementary materials. Specific techniques and suggestions for developing each skill are built into the lessons in the teachers' manuals, guides designed to assure that these important skills will not be handled haphazardly or overlooked completely. Workbooks provide professionally designed exercises for the development and diagnosis of these basic skills.

The skills programs of all basal series are by no means the same. Vocabulary varies considerably from series to series. Since skills are developed in conjunction with vocabulary, there will be differences in the manner and the level at which these skills are introduced. The emphasis and focus on skills will vary from series to series as well. For example, one series will have a heavy emphasis on phonics early in the program, while the focus of another will be more oriented toward the whole-word approach. In general, however, there is a core of skills systematically developed throughout a whole basal reading program.

A feature that one finds in the skills program of modern basal readers is the re-emphasis on reading as a language skill. While no one ever openly denied its status as such, it was usually separated for instructional purposes. Reading is one of the language arts, closely related to listening, speaking and writing in the total communication process. This relationship is highlighted and built upon in more up-to-date basal programs. The prodigal son of the language arts is finally returning to his rightful place in the classroom.

The key to success

Most automobile accidents are caused by "the nut behind the wheel." Most successful reading programs are caused by the teacher before the class. Much of the criticism leveled against basals might be more justifiably leveled at the way in which they are used. As with any tool—teacher's, artist's, or craftsman's—the key to success is in the way in which it is used.

Categorically, the basal should not be the total reading program in any class. As complete as a basal tries to be, it cannot provide all the practice that children need in recreational reading, news reading or reading in content areas. It's up to you as a teacher to provide a balance, to put the basal reader in its proper perspective, to supplement it with materials that your class needs.

Do some of the stories in the basal "turn your pupils off" because the subject matter is out of line with their interests and background? Then it's up to you to work with the kids in finding material that is in line with their interests and to set aside some classroom time each week when they can read this material on their own.

Is the vocabulary load in the basal too confining, especially at the early levels? You can use experience charts to support and supplement the basic developmental program.

Are the workbooks turning into busy work? Let the kids skip the skills they are good at and concentrate in areas where they really need help.

Are you bored to death with the same old lessons in the manual? Look at the lessons with an eye for variety. Start with the suggestions of the expert and take off according to the needs of your own group.

Is the basal aimed at the mythically average child, only three of whom you have among your 30 pupils this year? But isn't every book? And isn't adjusting instruction to meet individual differences your most difficult challenge as a teacher? (Take a peek at the manual. Many new manuals have very concrete suggestions for adjusting lessons to meet individual differences.)

The basal has some shortcomings. It is not the "be all and end all" of reading instruction, but it does provide a solid foundation for your basic developmental reading program.

Reading problems are not automatically solved by doing away with basals. Before we expel the basal from school, let's make sure what we put in its place will be better.

IRVING H. BALOW

Does Homogeneous Grouping Give Homogeneous Groups?

Homogeneous grouping for reading instruction in the elementary schools is often based on several assumptions. One assumption is that homogeneous groups are secured by classifying pupils on the basis of their scores on achievement tests and by limiting each group to a narrow range in test scores. According to this assumption, once pupils have been placed into such groups individual differences in achievement have been severely limited. Hence the teacher will need to provide only one set of materials and prepare only one lesson to teach the group. In short, the teacher can concentrate on the entire group rather than on individuals in the group.

A second assumption made by many advocates of homogeneous grouping is that increased achievement is an automatic result of homogeneous classes. That is, homogeneous grouping automatically leads to greater gains in reading achievement than heterogeneous classes that have a wide range of reading ability. The grouping itself is assumed to be the significant factor.

The study reported here was concerned with testing these assumptions. More specifically, the study was directed to answer the questions: Are homogeneous groups homogeneous? Do homogeneous groups make greater gains in reading achievement than heterogeneous groups?

In October, the principal of a school in southern California, in consultation with his fifth-grade teachers, decided that homogeneous grouping for reading instruction would result in greater gains for the children and would make the teaching of reading easier for the teachers. It was decided that a comprehensive test of reading achievement should be administered to the four fifth-grade classes and that the composite score would determine which group the child would enter.

In November, Form AM of the Iowa Silent Reading Tests, New Edition, was administered to the ninety four fifth-graders. The median grade equivalent for the children on the total test ranged from 2.0 to 9.0.

The children were divided into four classes on the basis of their grade equivalent. Children in Class A had grade equivalents that ranged from 5.7 to 9.0. Grade equivalents of children in Class B ranged from 4.6 to 5.6, in

ELEMENTARY SCHOOL JOURNAL, October 1962, vol. 63, pp. 28-32.

Class C from 3.6 to 4.6, and in Class D from 2.0 to 3.6.

Table 1 shows the number of children in each homogeneous class, the range in grade equivalent for each class, and the median grade equivalent for each class.

Table 1 suggests that this organization resulted in more homogeneous classes. Under heterogeneous grouping each class would have had a range of

As Table 2 shows, on any one subtest there was a tremendous overlap in scores from one homogeneous class to another. In fact, on most of the subtests classes B, C, and D have grade-equivalents from second-grade level to sixth-grade level.

In Class A, the "above grade level" class, the smallest range (four years) is on word meaning and the greatest range (ten years and six months) on

TABLE 1. *Median and Range in Grade Equivalent in Reading for Four Fifth-Grade Classes after Homogeneous Grouping*

	Class A	Class B	Class C	Class D
Number of pupils...	21	29	26	18
Range............	5.7–9.0	4.6–5.6	3.6–4.6	2.0–3.6
Median...........	6.7	5.2	4.0	3.3

TABLE 2. *Range in Grade Equivalent in Reading for Four Homogeneous Fifth-Grade Classes That Took the Eight Subtests of the Iowa Silent Reading Tests*

Subtest	Class A	Class B	Class C	Class D
Rate....................	2.1–12.7	1.8–12.7	1.8–12.7	1.8–7.4
Comprehension...........	3.8–11.1	2.5–11.1	2.0–6.5	2.0–6.0
Directed reading..........	2.5–11.8	1.8–7.0	1.8–5.7	1.8–5.2
Word meaning............	4.5–8.5	2.9–7.9	1.9–6.1	1.9–3.8
Paragraph comprehension...	3.7–10.2	1.9–9.4	1.9–8.6	1.9–5.6
Sentence meaning..........	4.4–10.3	2.9–8.4	1.9–7.5	1.9–9.5
Alphabetizing............	3.1–12.4	3.1–8.1	3.1–9.8	3.1–5.9
Use of index.............	4.7–11.3	1.9–8.0	1.9–6.5	1.9–6.0

seven years (2.0 to 9.0) in reading ability. Under homogeneous grouping, two classes had a range of one year; another, a range of one and a half years; and the last, three and a third years. But such data reveal only a small part of the picture.

The Iowa Silent Reading Tests consist of eight subtests that measure rate, comprehension, directed reading, word meaning, paragraph comprehension, sentence meaning, alphabetizing, and use of index. Table 2 shows the range in each homogeneous class for each subtest.

the rate test. On rate, the children in this class ranged from more than three years below grade level to almost seven and a half years above grade level. On the word meaning test, the scores in Class A ranged from more than a half year below grade level to more than three years above grade level. On each of the eight subtests, some children in Class A scored below grade level.

In Class B, the smallest range in grade equivalent was five years, and this range was found in the alphabetizing tests; in each test the scores ranged from almost two years below grade level to more than three years above grade level. The greatest range was on the rate and the comprehension tests. On the rate test, children ranged from more than three years below grade level to almost seven and a half years above grade level. On the comprehension test, scores ranged from more than two and a half years below grade level to almost six years above grade level.

Classes C and D had more restricted ranges, but the scores in each class were so divergent that only by stretching the term could any of these classes be considered homogeneous with respect to any of the subtests.

Table 2 presents evidence that groups designated as homogeneous in reading ability may in fact be extremely heterogeneous. Classification on the basis of standardized test scores does not necessarily result in homogeneous groups.

The second assumption tested in this study is that once the pupils have been grouped, the problem of teaching reading is solved and greater gains in reading achievement will result.

To test this assumption, the sixth-grade classes in three other schools in this community in southern California were tested. One school was using homogeneous grouping for reading instruction for the second year. The experience of the previous year had been evaluated informally, and the teachers were convinced that the children had made greater gains in reading as a result of homogeneous grouping. The sixth grades that served as the control group were selected because no special grouping methods had been used in these schools. Each sixth-grade teacher had a random selection of the sixth-grade children in the school.

In October, Form B, Intermediate Battery—Complete, of the Metropolitan Achievement Tests, was administered to all the children in the two groups. The results of this test were immediately given to the teachers of the experimental group so the scores could be used for grouping.

In the school that used homogeneous grouping three groups were organized. The pupils whose scores were above grade level went to one teacher for an hour each day for reading instruction. Pupils whose scores in reading were average went to the second sixth-grade teacher. Pupils whose scores in reading were below average went to the third sixth-grade teacher.

In January, the California Short-Form Test of Mental Maturity was administered to all children in the two groups, and the intelligence quotients were secured. In June, Form A, Intermediate Battery—Complete, of the Metropolitan Achievement Tests, was administered.

The average intelligence quotient for the homogeneously grouped classes was 103.5 and for the control classes 103.9. The variance of the intelligence quotients of the two groups was tested and no statistically significant difference was found. A *t* test of the difference between means resulted in a *t* value of .175, which has a probability greater than .80 with 164 degrees of freedom. These findings strengthened our assumption that the two groups of pupils were of equal intelligence at the beginning of the experiment.

The variances of the reading test scores at the beginning of the experiment were tested and found to be statistically equal for the two groups. The mean raw score of the homogeneous group was 23.80 and of the control group, 20.97, a difference of 2.83 points. When this mean difference was tested by using the *t* test, a *t* value of 2.64 was found, a value which is significant at the 1 per cent level of probability. The hypothesis that the two groups were equal in reading abilities at the beginning of the experiment was therefore rejected. At the start of the study, the reading achievement of the homogeneous group was significantly higher than the reading achievement of the control group.

Growth in reading from October to June was determined by subtracting the October score from the June score for each child in the study. The difference was the gain as measured by the Metropolitan Achievement Tests —Reading. The mean gain for the children in the homogeneous groups was 5.078 points and for the children in the heterogeneous groups, 5.157 points. The variances of the growth scores for the two groups were tested and found to be statistically equal. The mean difference was tested using the *t* test and a *t* value of .10 was found. The probability of a *t* value of .10 with 164 degrees of freedom is greater than .90. Consequently, the hypothesis of no difference in growth between the two groups was accepted.

The first assumption, that a homogeneous group may be secured by classifying children according to a reading test score, would seem to be untenable. The evidence presented here tends, instead, to substantiate the belief that reading growth, in all its aspects, varies with each child. Reading ability is made up of many skills. The child in the fifth-grade who secures a grade equivalent of 4.5 on a reading test may be scoring below grade level because he is poor in word analysis. He may use context clues well, have high intelligence, and answer all questions on the test. Another child with the same score may be very good at word analysis, but he may not comprehend well, and he may read too slowly to complete the test. These two children cannot be considered equal in reading skills even though they received the same score in reading. If test results are used as the basis for grouping, however, these two children would be placed in the same homogeneous class.

The second assumption, that greater gains in achievement will necessarily result from homogeneous grouping, was also rejected by the evidence presented in this study. The difference in mean growth scores was in favor of the control group, not the homogeneous groups, though the difference was not significant. The results show, however, that in this study the homogeneous grouping did not lead to greater measured gains.

There may be advantages which accrue to classes that are homogeneously grouped for reading instruction, but these advantages are not automatic. Procedures more sophisticated than achievement testing are required to secure a reasonably homogeneous class. But homogeneity is not enough. Once homogeneity is secured, to justify the grouping, a program must be devised that will result in greater reading growth.

Fifteen Flaws of Phonics

Patrick Groff

In spite of recent promises to put "phonics in proper perspective" (1), and to separate the "fact and fiction about phonics" (2), a survey of present-day books, parts of books, and journal articles on phonics shows that such is not accomplished. It is more realistic to say that current phonics writings, in fact, fail to organize the relevant data of phonics into their meaningful relationships. Then, too, the errors of past writings on phonics that stain the pages of recent texts hardly support the claim that the age of truth has emerged for this matter.

Several of these weaknesses in the prevailing phonics writings are mere foibles. That is, they consist of slight mistakes, mostly harmless, often amusing and eccentric-sounding (especially to linguists). Appearing as such, rather than as the result of any conscious or dogmatic wrongdoing, they can be excused. Other defects in these writings on phonics cannot be so easily ignored, however, since they appear to have a ring of truth about them. It is these latter kinds of errors that need exposure to criticism. They truly are dangerous since if phonics instruction followed their advice it is likely children's learning to read would be interferred with. It is axiomatic, then, that phonics (that knowledge of the certain sound-spelling relationships a child can learn to use as he masters reading and spelling), to be taught to properly function, must be based on sound evidence and/or logical thinking.

Patrick Groff is Professor of Education at San Diego State University, California.

The important faults in phonics

A *primary* failing in the writings on phonics is the role some of these books say perception plays in phonics "readiness." It is claimed that the child to be "ready" for phonics should first participate in both visual and auditory "readiness" activities. The fact is that relatively low correlations have been found between the present measures of children's power of *auditory* discrimination and their beginning reading achievement (3). Then, children when they enter school *produce* (obviously *know*) all but four or five of the phonemes (sounds). They exhibit few problems discriminating these few. Moreover, the evidence that indicates there is little growth in children's so-called auditory discrimination abilities after the age of seven (4) gives scant support to the notion that six-year-olds do not have enough auditory discrimination to learn phonics. As for the powers of visual discrimination needed for success in phonics lessons there seems little evidence from either theories of reading (5) or from the research on the relation of visual perception and reading (6) to support the idea that children need pre-phonics training programs in this matter.

A *second* widespread weakness of phonics writings is the comment there that the child should learn a certain number (50-

ELEMENTARY ENGLISH, 1973, Vol. 50, No. 1, pp. 35-40.

100?) of "sight" words before he begins his instruction in phonics. There is no evidence (7), however, to indicate that any such sequence of teaching is based on the research in perception. From the moment they are first recognized, words are differentiated by their distinctive, individual features *and* by their overall structures (parts larger than letters). A teacher may report a child to be reading by "sight." In actuality, however, this child is responding to letter cues, and to structure cues of the word (and very likely to the syntax, as well).

This brings us to a *third* fault of a great number of current phonics texts, that is, the lack of attention given there to the role of syntax as a cue to the recognition of individual words. In brief, the prevailing phonics books seldom consider the vast differences between teaching phonics with isolated words and teaching it through sentences. The beginning reader is a sophisticated user of language (teachers who think five- and six-year-olds don't speak "complete" sentences, to the contrary notwithstanding). The sentences he tries to read therefore relay to him syntactic and semantic information he needs to make wise guesses as to the meaning (therefore the spelling) a word in a sentence is likely to have. This expectation helps the beginner identify the letter cues this word contains. In this way the child also develops some strategies for correcting his expectations about words, whenever they prove to be wrong.

Fourth, prevailing phonics books rarely consider the differences for teaching phonics that the different parts of speech entail. Teaching nouns, verbs, adverbs, and adjectives is not the same as teaching function words (the remaining parts of speech). Function words are more difficult to decode for several reasons. They are less predictable in their spelling than are words in general. They have less lexical meaning, by and large. They do not form inflections or derivations. And they occur in all writings regardless of the content of the piece. Accordingly, function words particularly should never be taught in isolation.

A mistreatment of the element of dialect, that particular style of speech a child uses, whether this is standard or nonstandard for the speech region in which he lives, is the *fifth* shortcoming of almost all current phonics. Either this matter is avoided by the book on phonics, or worse yet, the teacher is told the child first must learn to speak the "standard" dialect given by the phonics book (often a strange dialect even to the teacher who speaks the standard dialect of a given speech region) before he can learn to read. A safer assumption is that the task of learning phonics is basically one of relating the child's *peculiar* phonological system (whatever that is) to the spelling system (which is standard for all dialects). Since the teacher cannot change the child's dialect (therefore should not try to), above all he cannot teach the child to "say" the spelling system. That is, there is no best-spelled dialect, a dialect a child should learn to speak in order to spell well, although the illusion of its presence continues to be raised (8).

A *sixth* shortcoming of all conventional phonics writings is their support of the way the traditional dictionary syllabicates words, particularly the separation of words according to the formulas: VC-CV *(but-ter),* and V-CV *(ma-rine).* These and other rules of dictionary syllabication, accepted by popular phonics texts, are not based on the true nature of the syllable as described by phoneticians. Dictionary syllabication, in fact, is based on neither theories of the syllable nor on scientific findings regarding this phenomenon (9). Little wonder, then, that teaching dictionary syllabication to children does not have its special intended purposes, to help them read and spell better, than otherwise would be possible. The results of studies of phonics generalizations, that employ dictionary syllabication, are widely quoted in contemporary phonics. The use of dictionary syllabication in such studies makes their results highly doubtful, however, and therefore inapplicable for word-structure analysis.

Notable in many standard phonics writings is the plea for spelling reformation, a *seventh* fault of these books. An explicit weakness of such advice is a lack of understanding of the morphophonemic nature of spelling. Little if any comment is found in recent phonics regarding the fact that the boundaries of morphemes (smallest units of meaning) in certain words must be known in order for the reader to predict the spelling-to-sound correspondence of these words. For example, the first vowel sound in *national* is conditioned by the presence of the morpheme *al*. The double consonants of mi*dd*ay and le*tt*er respectively are given two and one sounds because *midday* has two morphemes, and *letter* has one. This morphophonemic nature of English orthography leads prominent linguists to suggest our present spelling system "comes remarkably close to being an optimal" one (10).

An *eighth* defect of virtually all existing phonics texts is their assumption that polysyllabic words and monosyllabic words are equally proper material for beginning phonics teaching. Such a decision violates a cardinal principle of learning and teaching reading: move from the simplier, more-easily learned, and more common elements to the complex, the difficult to learn, and the infrequently seen. Polysyllabic words in general are more difficult for children to read and spell than are monosyllabic ones. Measures of readability attest to this, as does a test of the relative spelling difficulty of various words (11). It takes over twice as many vowel spelling-to-sound correspondence rules to read vowel letters in two-syllable words as in one-syllable words (12). The critical problem for the reader given by the polysyllabic word is that it introduces the unaccented (schwa) sound which is spelled in a variety of ways. Although about two-thirds of little word (accented words) found in bigger words can be pronounced without appreciably violating the sounds of the bigger words (13), this only lessens to a degree the problem of the relatively greater difficulty of polysyllabic words. And, it illustrates the need for a reader's prior skill in pronouncing monosyllabic words.

The wrongly-held belief of typical phonics books that certain sounds in words "blend" with each other to a unique degree is a *ninth* blunder of these books. For example, according to this erroneous idea the two sounds /kr/ as represented by *cr* seen in *crawl,* for example, are called a "blend." It is the impression of these phonics writers that the /k/ and /r/ "blend" with each other "more" than they do with the vowel sound in *crawl.* Or more so than the vowel sound here blends with /l/. This is a false impression, however, which has no basis in phonemics nor phonetics. Teaching such fallacious material to children is not only a waste of time. It presents the inherent danger to learning common with all misleading teaching. Too, phonics books to date have not presented a rational order in which to teach these more properly-called "consonant clusters" (e.g., *cr*). Such a sequence, based on the spelling and reading difficulty of words in which such clusters appear, and on the frequency of use of such words, is now available (14).

A significant number of present-day phonics books support a *tenth* misconception about their subject, that the teaching of the meaning of affixes (prefixes and suffixes) gives children a special assistance in learning to read. The only piece of relevant research regarding this denies such is the case (15). Logically the idea will not stand up. Over the years many affixes in words have lost their autonomous meanings (e.g., *re*ceive). Knowledge of the "meaning" of an affix so used therefore is worthless. Too, for a child to apply his knowledge of the meaning of affixes (assuming such can be taught so well as to be retained until the exact needed moment) he must remember (a) which of the multiple meanings of the affix to apply, (b) identify the base word and its meaning, (c) apply the affix to the base word, and (d) integrate the dual meaning this supposedly gets at. Surely such a complicated act is beyond the grasp of most elementary school children.

The recommendations generally made by existing phonics texts as to how to teach vowel spelling-to-sound correspondences is an *eleventh* imperfection of these books. Often it is suggested that the vowel letter(s) that represents a sound be isolated so that the isolated vowel sound then can be identified. The child here is taught the "rules" about sounding "long" and "short" vowels (h*o*p*e*-h*o*p). Teaching children to identify isolated spelling-to-sound correspondences is undesirable, however, since the sounds of our language can only be spoken within syllables. A different, preferable, approach to this that keeps sounds within syllables has the child identify phonograms and their sounds (e.g., *at, et, it, ot, ut*) within words (16). This phonogram approach also rules out the need to try to teach children about dipthongs, a teaching also usually recommended by existing phonics texts, but one much too difficult for children to understand. This system is also better than teaching children to read consonant-vowel combinations, e.g., *ha—t*, which some phonics texts suggest. This latter *CV-C* reading is an inefficient one, however, since the reader cannot read many vowel letters in words without knowing ahead of time the vowel and/or consonant letter(s) that follow these vowel letters. For example, one cannot read *ho—* until he sees what follows: *hope, hop, honest, hour,* etc.

A *twelfth* doubtful practice, approved nonetheless by some prevailing phonics texts, is that of teaching children to mark the accented syllable in polysyllabic words. Logic would compel one to question what possible gain could come from this practice. For to do this a child *first* would have to read the word in question. And if he can do this successfully without marking the accented syllable, what value could there be in his marking of the accented syllable *after* this successful reading? From the only study made of this matter Winkley (17) reported that children who "received instruction in applying accent generalizations to unfamiliar words" developed "greater 'power' in *(a)* ability to attack unknown words, *(b)* vocabulary development, and *(c)* comprehension." The report of this study is incomplete, however. One cannot learn from it whether these two instructed groups were comparable in intelligence and reading ability, and most importantly, whether the differences in "power" in reading so found were statistically significant differences. Neither is any description given as to how intensive the two instructional programs were. So, at this point the logical objection to this practice should prevail.

Extreme statements as to the specialized uses of phonics for spelling as versus reading is a *thirteenth* fault of contemporary phonics writings. Most of these imply that a knowledge of phonics has value only for reading. Others go to the other extreme contending that phonics is only learned as a spelling skill (18). Some insist phonics does not affect the learning of spelling (19). The truth of the matter lies among these extreme statements. It is that phonics has more usefulness for reading than for spelling, but it does provide some help for the latter. The process of spelling, having to recall both sound and its graphic equivalent obviously is more difficult to learn than reading. The sound associations a child can make to a printed word are many fewer than the graphic units that conceivably could be used by him to spell a spoken word. This explains how we can read many more words than we can spell, and why phonics is of greater help in reading than to spelling.

A *fourteenth* error in the usual phonics books is the trust they place in the use of popular tests as tools to evaluate children's growth in phonics. A recent analysis of popular standardized diagnostic reading tests revealed otherwise, however: they "cannot be used to determine a child's chief area of skill deficiency" (20). A like analysis of well-known standardized survey tests of reading indicated these tests "do not measure and/or measure well the skills and abilities that inhere in the reading process" (21). Moreover, it was found elsewhere that "all criteria employed in the IRI [Informal Reading Inventory] need further verification" (22). Such evidence forces one to conclude that at present the phonics teacher must be the one to evaluate his pupils' growth.

A *final* defect in many of today's phonics books seems to stem from the small knowledge of phonemics (sounds) and graphemics (their spellings) authors apparently have. Of late, linguistics have had a field day plucking out of phonics books a host of erroneous interpretations of phonemics and graphemics. It has been shown that some writers of phonics are not even sure of the distinctions between these two fields of knowledge. For example, they talk of diagraphs as phonemic phenomena, and about listening to graphemes. Their confusions as to the character of diphthongs, their notion that "long and short" are apt terms for vowel sounds, their conclusions that letters have sounds, and that consonants are simpler to pronounce than vowels, all are examples of a lack of knowledge. Even worse is their habit of strewing about meaningless statements on their subject. For instance, one such writer says, "The vowel sounds and meanings of the words *mat* and *mate* differ as much as the vowel sounds and meanings of the words *mat* and *mut*" (23). This is a senseless statement about the vowel sounds in these words since it in no way reflects the information about their different intensities and durations, their different distributions in words, their different articulatory characteristics—position, lip and tongue movement, nor their different values as universal phonetic models—only one is a cardinal vowel. Such unverifiable statements do little more than confuse teachers and infuriate language specialists.

Hopefully this description of some of the critical flaws in current phonics (in no particular order of their importance) can have a usefulness. If these criticisms will be kept in mind by teacher-buyers of phonics books, and by the reviewers of future phonics books, the process of eliminating phonics books that pass along discredited information surely will be speeded up. Obviously, the time has come to stop congratulating phonics books that perpetuate erroneous information and methodology as, "contributions to their field." The present list of criticisms provides a basis for chastising any book on phonics which perpetuates, for whatever reason, the cliches of bad phonics.

References

1. Arthur W. Heilman. *Phonics in Proper Perspective.* Columbus: Charles E. Merrill, 1964.
2. Roma Gans. *Fact and Fiction about Phonics.* Indianapolis: Bobbs-Merrill, 1964.
3. Robert Dykstra. "Auditory Discrimination Abilities and Beginning Reading Achieve-

ment," *Reading Research Quarterly*, 1966 (1) 5-34.
4. Mildred Templin. "A Study of Sound Discrimination Ability of Elementary School Pupils," *Journal of Speech and Hearing Disorders*, 1943 (8) 127-132.
5. Frank Smith. *Understanding Reading*. New York: Holt, Rinehart and Winston, 1971.
6. Ruth Waugh and Zana Watson. "Visual Perception and Reading," *Education*, 1971 (91) 266-269.
7. Eleanor J. Gibson. *Principles of Perceptual Learning and Development*. New York: Appleton-Century-Crofts, 1969.
8. Gertrude A. Boyd and E. Gene Talbert. *Spelling in the Elementary School*. Columbus: Charles E. Merrill, 1971. p. 26.
9. Patrick Groff. *The Syllable: Its Nature and Pedagogical Usefulness*. Portland, Oregon: Northwest Regional Educational Laboratory, 1971.
10. Noam Chomsky and Morris Halle. *The Sound Pattern of English*. New York: Harper and Row, 1968. p. 49.
11. Harry A. Greene. *The New Iowa Spelling Scale*. Iowa City: State University of Iowa, 1955.
12. Bruce Cronnell. *Annotated Spelling-to-Sound Correspondence Rules*. Inglewood, California: Southwest Regional Laboratory for Educational Research and Development, 1971.
13. Patrick Groff. "Should Children Read Little Words in Bigger Words?" submitted for publication.
14. Patrick Groff. *New Phonics*. Boston: Allyn and Bacon, 1973. (in press)
15. Lois M. Otterman. "The Value of Teaching Prefixes and Word-Roots," *Journal of Educational Research*, 1955 (48) 611-616.
16. Richard E. Wylie and Donald D. Durrell. "Teaching Vowels through Phonograms," *Elementary English*, 1970 (47) 787-791.
17. Carol K. Winkley. "Which Accent Generalizations Are Worth Teaching?" *Reading Teacher*, 1966 (20) 219-224.
18. Jeannette Veatch. *Reading in the Elementary School*. New York: Ronald, 1966.
19. Walter T. Petty. "Phonic Elements as Factors of Spelling Difficulty," *Journal of Educational Research*, 1958 (51) 209-214.
20. Carol Winkley. "What Do Diagnostic Tests Really Diagnose?" in *Diagnostic Viewpoints in Reading* (Robert E. Liebert, editor). Newark, Delaware: International Reading Association, 1971. pp. 64-80.
21. Howard F. Livingston. "What the Reading Test Doesn't Test—Reading," *Journal of Reading*, 1972 (15) 402-410.
22. William R. Powell and Colin G. Dunkeld. "Validity of the IRI Reading Levels," *Elementary English*, 1971 (48) 637-642.
23. Carl J. Wallen. *Word Attack Skills in Reading*. Columbus: Charles E. Merrill, 1969. p. 21.

Linguists and phonics

ROBERT EMANS

Emans heads the Early and Middle Childhood Education Department at Ohio State University. In this article he summarizes possible misconceptions and reservations about linguistic approaches and phonics teaching.

A NUMBER of articles have been written by various linguists on the topic of distinguishing between the terms phonics and phonetics. Whereas the authors have seemingly explained phonetics well, some seem to have misconceptions about the term phonics. At the heart of the confusion are the notions that phonics implies a primacy of written language over oral language, and that phonics refers to specific procedures for teaching children to read.

The first apparent misconception is that there are only two possible and mutually exclusive approaches for teaching beginning reading, phonics and look-say. Those expressing this philosophy intensify their misconceptions by polarizing the two aspects of beginning reading. Either procedure used alone for beginning reading instruction has certain disadvantages. Look-say may fail to give children techniques for reading independently. Phonics may result in slow, laborious readers. However, in most reading programs today phonics and look-say are used together. Each approach tends to compensate for the other's weaknesses. Therefore, any serious attempt to analyze modern reading instruction must look at how phonics and look-say function together —not separately.

Phonics is actually not a method for teaching beginning reading; it is a goal: to give children the ability to associate oral and written language (Cordts, 1965). Look-

THE READING TEACHER, 1973, Vol. 26, pp. 477-482.

say can also be accurately described as a goal: to have children recognize words instantaneously. Within either phonics or look-say there are many and varied teaching methods. In this view, the so-called "linguistic procedures" for teaching reading are actually ways for teaching phonics.

Other perceptual goals

In addition to phonics and look-say, there are other perception goals in teaching beginning reading. The use of context clues is one; the use of structural analysis is another; the use of the dictionary is a third. Some linguists have greatly oversimplified beginning reading instruction by looking only at the first two of these goals, and viewing them as two opposing approaches.

Those critical of "phonics" programs contend that "phonics" teaches children how to pronounce words as though they were learning language all over again. Such criticism may have been valid a hundred years ago when reading instruction was used as a means for teaching English to children of immigrant parents. Such is not the case today. As Heilman (1968) states, "the purpose of phonic instruction is to teach the child to associate printed letter-symbols with known speech sounds." (p. 99)

In probably the best known book on teaching word analysis, Gray's *On Their Own in Reading* (1960), oral language is given central importance. In Chapter One, the first paragraph, we read:

> A child who is ready to read knows the sound and meaning of hundreds of words, and he knows how these words are put together in phrases and sentences to convey ideas. In short, he expresses and receives ideas through the medium of spoken language. Soon he will learn to respond to these same words in print, a process known as reading.

The work of the late W. S. Gray has had a very important and extensive influence on phonic instruction. He understood the importance of oral language in reading instruction and preceded many of the linguists in recognizing the importance of the relationship between oral language and reading.

Sounds in isolation

One of the major misconceptions held by some linguists and those who advocate a "linguistic" approach to beginning reading is that phonic methods isolate speech sounds. The linguist Bloomfield (1961) stated, "The authors of these methods tell us to show a child a letter, for instance *t*, and to make him react by uttering the t-sound." (p. 28) Another linguist has stated, "Children are taught that the letter g has a /g/ sound, and so on through the alphabet." (Rystrom, 1965, p. 266) Still another example, "Children would then produce a series of pretaught sounds, and the resulting chain of sounds was supposedly a word." (Seymour, 1969, p. 100) As stated previously, phonics is a goal: any number of different procedures can be used to achieve it.

Most reading programs today use procedures like those developed by Gray and Cordts. Children are taught to substitute sounds represented in words that they can already read for the values of symbols in words they cannot read. Such a procedure is very similar to those advocated by Bloomfield and by Fries (1962). This approach is referred to as analytic phonics, as opposed to synthetic phonics—the approach used more than a generation ago and the one Bloomfield and other linguists have attacked.

Surprisingly, many linguists advocate the teaching of letter names. The distinction between teaching "letter names" and "letter sounds" in isolation is a fine one since most "letter names" contain within them commonly associated "letter sounds." For example, is there any real difference for the young child between associating the letter name /be/ and associating the letter sound /buh/ with the symbol *b*? The child is still learning a commonly associated sound for the symbol. Thus, it would appear that teaching letter names is very similar to teaching "letter-sounds" in isolation, a practice to which many linguists object.

The "linguistic" procedure often advocated in teaching beginning reading is similar in certain respects to procedures in the substitution techniques of the analytic phonic procedure found in many reading programs today. In both procedures children are expected to note likenesses and differences in hearing and viewing words. Similarly, the tight vocabulary control found in "linguistic" readers is much like the vocabulary control found in readers more than one hundred years ago. For example, note the similarities in this passage taken from a McGuffey reader (1879) to those in some of the linguistic readers:

See Rob! See Ann!
See: Rob has the hat.
Can Ann catch Rob?

Of course, there are differences. However, any idea that "linguistic" procedures are a panacea must be tempered by the realization that similar procedures were used in the past.

"Linguistic" reservations

Just as there is no one "phonic" approach to teaching reading, neither is there any one "linguistic" approach. Thus, any consideration of reservations must recognize that they may not be true for all the various "linguistic" procedures. Some linguists recommend that children should learn to read by reading sentences. This, they claim, gives proper emphasis to the structure of language. Their claim is that meaning is carried by larger units than the word and that the emphasis on word recognition is unwarranted. They cite examples of children crippled in reading because they read word by word and cannot glean meaning from the printed page. Thus, they believe emphasis must be placed on intonation, stress, juncture, and pitch.

In many respects the linguists who advocate greater emphasis on sentences are probably right. However, to ignore the word in reading instruction and to cite the word by word reading of young children as evidence of poor instruction is not well founded. Even mature readers will read word by word under certain circumstances.

What is especially strange about the stress that some linguists place on the importance of the sentence, over the importance of the word, is the linguists' inability to define either a word or a sentence. Both concepts represent man's attempt to describe his language; both concepts are probably related more to describing written language than oral language. Therefore, some linguists' attempts to say that meaning is carried more by sentences than by words seem to contradict their own theory. If one would carry their argument further, one would have to argue that meaning is expressed more by complete paragraphs than by sentences, and more by books than by paragraphs.

No linguist is advocating teaching reading by using the paragraph or book as the unit instead of the word. Words, phrases, sentences, paragraphs, and books all carry meaning. In written language one of the perceptual units is the written word. Thus, it seems logical to stress the word in reading instruction as well as giving importance to the larger units.

Grapheme-phoneme approaches

Among the linguistic approaches which are very different, almost opposite, from a sentence approach, is that which assumes that the child learns to read by responding to words by associating phonemes and graphemes. The limitation of such an approach is that readers, even young readers, do not read in this fashion. Research studies on eye movements indicate that children learning to read make about two fixations per word, not one fixation for each grapheme. In addition, readers use many clues in word identification other than grapheme-phoneme correspondence including word length and context. Thus, such "linguistic" teaching procedures may inhibit the use of other devices that readers require and may conflict with the child's spontaneous disposition towards learning to read.

Some linguists advocate teaching only regularly spelled words. However, many English words are not spelled regularly. Thus, various linguists have advocated using nonsense words or have used words which are likely to be relatively unfamiliar to many children. For example, in one program (Fries, Wilson, and Rudolph, 1966) words used early in the program include: *van, fit, lit, bin, rim, fig, jig,* and *rut*. Even when comparatively unfamiliar words are used, authors of materials have had to use contrived sentences which have resulted in stories of little interest to children (Emans, 1969).

There is another limitation in using regular spelling patterns. The child is given no method of recognizing words unfamiliar to him in print which do not follow the regular spelling patterns. The only way a child is taught to recognize irregular words is by sight. As Bloomfield states, "when it comes to teaching irregular and special words, each word will demand a separate effort and separate practice" (Bloomfield and Barnhart, 1961, p. 206). Some sound clues can be used with most irregular words; it may be only a beginning consonant sound with context. Children need to learn to recognize the many words which do not follow regular spelling patterns. Various linguistic approaches give children no way of figuring out such words for themselves.

The practice of introducing only regularly spelled words may also result in the child developing a mind set for reading only such words. He may develop the notion that all words are spelled regularly and be confused when he discovers that they are not. This possibility is given support by a study by Levin and Watson (1963), who found that introducing words early with variable grapheme-phoneme correspondence helped in later learning.

Modifying practices

Some control of the variability of spelling patterns may be desirable. If spelling patterns were not controlled as rigidly as some linguists have advocated, more natural language could be used, resulting in more interesting stories for children. Meaning would not have to be sacrificed nearly to the extent that it is in some linguistic materials.

This would make possible the use of context in recognizing words, something which some linguists would object to but which may still be desirable. In addition, it might be desirable to plan for some study of speech sounds in isolation. Although linguists and many reading specialists object to isolating speech sounds, the results of the study by Chall (1967) and the twenty-seven first grade studies (Bond and Dykstra, 1967) indicate that a strong and early emphasis on some type of phonics is desirable. It is hard to imagine how phonics could be emphasized early without isolating some speech sounds.

Most children require systematic instruction. It would appear that the regular spelling approach may fail to emphasize letter-sound relationships to the degree necessary. Perhaps Bateman and Wetherell (1964) have a useful idea when they state, "Isolating the speech sounds is only the beginning in perfecting a skill which is part of the process of learning to read." (p. 102) Other procedures can help children apply what they learn in words and contextual reading. An either-or approach is probably unnecessary.

Linguistics is the scientific study of oral language. Adults are able to read words which are not within their oral language vocabulary. Most people can learn to read more proficiently than they listen. Thus, there is more to teaching children how to read than applying linguistic principles which stress oral language.

How children learn

The study of how children learn and how teachers can best teach must be considered along with linguistic principles. For example, more study is required before it is known if children require a specific knowledge of phonic generalizations for efficient reading or if a habitual response to symbols as advocated by some linguists is all that is required. Even though phonic generalizations may have limited application, they may be better than no clue.

Teachers are sometimes criticized for teaching that there are five vowels when there are actually about fourteen; and for teaching that there are long and short vowels when some of the short vowels actually have a longer duration in oral language than some of the long vowels. Although it may be untrue in respect to oral language, five vowel letters do generally represent the various vowel sounds in written language. The difference between the duration of the various vowel sounds is infinitesimal. Children probably do not associate the terms long and short with duration of sound, and, even if they do, it probably would make little difference in their learning of them. If particular practices help in pupil-teacher communication, why should they not be used, even if they are not exactly lawful from a linguistic viewpoint?

Linguists have much to offer to the teaching of reading; they can help in describing the phonology and structure of language, in developing understanding of how children acquire language. They can help to stimulate debate and force reading specialists to take a new look at what they are doing. However, linguists can also help by knowing what really is happening in the teaching of reading today and understanding that their theories must be modified by theories from other disciplines and by generally effective practice in the classroom.

References

Bateman, Barbara and Wetherell, Janis. "A Critique of Bloomfield's Linguistic Approach to the Teaching of Reading." *The Reading Teacher*, 8 (November, 1964), pp. 98-104.

Bloomfield, Leonard and Barnhart, Clarence. *Let's Read: A Linguistic Approach.* Detroit, Michigan: Wayne State University Press, 1961.

Bond, G. L. and Dykstra, R. "The Cooperative Research Program in First Grade Reading Instruction." *Reading Research Quarterly*, 2 (Summer, 1967), entire issue.

Chall, Jeanne, *Learning to Read: The Great Debate.* New York: McGraw-Hill Book Co., 1967.

Cordts, Anna D. *Phonics for the Reading Teacher.* New York: Holt, Rinehart and Winston, Inc., 1965.

Emans, Robert. "For Beginning Readers—What Kind of Materials?" *The Elementary School Journal*, 70 (November, 1969), 91-98.

Fries, Charles C. *Linguistics and Reading.* New York: Holt, Rinehart and Winston, Inc., 1962.

Fries, Charles C., Wilson, Rosemary G., and Rudolph, Mildred K. *Merrill Linguistic Readers.* Columbus, Ohio: Charles E. Merrill Books, Inc., 1966.

Gray, William S. *On Their Own in Reading.* rev. ed. Glenview, Illinois: Scott, Foresman and Co., 1960.

Heilman, Arthur W. *Phonics in Proper Perspective.* 2nd ed. Columbus, Ohio: Charles E. Merrill Publishing Co., 1968.

Levin, Harry and Watson, J. *The Learning of Variable Grapheme to Phoneme Correspondence: Variations in the Initial Consonant Position.* Cornell University Cooperative Research Project No. 639, 1963.

McGuffey's First Eclectic Reader. New York: American Book Co., 1879, p. 11.

McKee, Paul. *Reading: A Program of Instruction for the Elementary School.* Boston: Houghton Mifflin Co., 1966.

Rystrom, Richard. "Whole-Word and Phonics Methods and Current Linguistic Findings." *Elementary English.* XLII (March, 1965), pp. 265-68.

Seymour, Dorothy Z. "The Difference between Linguistics and Phonics." *The Reading Teacher.* XXIII (November, 1969), pp. 99-102. 111.

The effective reading teacher

WILLIAM R. POWELL

Originally presented as part of a speech, this article moves from a broad question to six criteria offered as a partial answer to the question. Professor Powell is on the faculty in elementary education at the University of Illinois at Urbana-Champaign.

SOMETIMES when I talk with my colleagues about "The Effective Reading Teacher," I feel as if I am bringing in the minority report. While some individuals spend their time and energies in the "lures" and "false images" of the endless controversies of

—grouping methods for teaching reading
the ungraded school
team teaching
Joplin plan
family grouping
middle schools, etc.

—this approach or that approach to teaching reading
sight (look and say)
phonics
linguistics
language-experience
CAI, etc.

—this type of material versus that type of material
phonovisual
i.t.a.
unifon
Distar
PKR
SRA
EDL
rebus, etc.

I say we can begin to possess the skill of becoming an effective teacher of reading if we prepare ourselves with the basic and fundamental knowledge about the mission. That is where our source of strength and power emanates in the effective teaching of reading. Only after the "land has been possessed" should we as teachers concern ourselves with the related, but secondary, areas: grouping, approaches, materials, and the

THE READING TEACHER, 1972, Vol. 25, pp. 603-607.

like. We must first, however, establish a baseline from which to launch our later priorities.

The basic issue

The most fundamental of basic questions: What are the first-order understandings that prepare us to be effective reading teachers? The same question stated with a little different perspective but with the same intent is: What makes a reading teacher unique—whether he is a classroom teacher of reading, a remedial reading teacher, a reading consultant, or an English teacher? What makes any teacher who teaches with and through written verbal material unique, that is, anyone who uses print at that teachable moment as the main avenue to learning? What distinguishes him from other teachers?

In these days of accountability, both fiscally and professionally, we had best be about the business of answering such a fundamental question. What follows is my own idiosyncratic reply to this crucial question.

Generally, there have been three approaches to the resolution of this issue. One approach is through studying, defining, and describing the characteristics of "effective" classroom teachers. Another approach for describing teacher behavior is through the technique of interaction analysis. The third alternative is to define and describe the basic competencies of such individuals. These three options are not necessarily mutually exclusive although past research efforts have tended to treat them as such. Neither are the approaches without their limitations. Perhaps the direction of research needed in this area is to design and conduct studies which include all three categories.

How do the people who pursue the characteristic approach describe the effective teacher? They say he or she is a person who is warm, friendly, understanding, responsive, businesslike, systematic, stimulating, and imaginative. But are these not descriptions of capable individuals regardless of their vocational field?

The "interactionists" attempt to describe the teacher through the manner in which communication is processed and facilitated in an instructional setting. They characterize their effective teacher as one who is focusing, accepting, controlling, extending, clarifying, ignoring, and the rest. While these characteristics are certainly qualities of a teacher, indeed, do they not equally describe an effective physician, minister, advertising man, lawyer, sociologist, or salesman?

Yet, aren't all teachers generalists and salesmen, too? So what makes us unique? Perhaps it is time we got around to the serious business of asking what it is we are selling and what leads us into the competence approach. What is it that we as reading teachers are supposed to be competent with or to master?

Competencies

First, we must have some conception of what makes up diagnostic teaching. For me, the effective reading teacher is one who teaches diagnostically. I view diagnostic teaching as a four-dimensional process. It involves the discriminating ability to collect data in the teaching-learning situation. (Oh, how the powers of observation become a most critical factor in effectively diagnosing.) Diagnostic teaching also includes clinical thinking. But to think clinically, one has to have something to think about and think with. In this second dimension, we need to have a clear-cut conception of the nature of and the components of the task we are to do. We have to develop conceptual maps of those items which are related to the task: the sound system, the cognitive system, the symbol system, the affective system, the error system, and the notion of syndromes. Unless one knows where he is going, a map is of no value; but once the destination has been identified, the accuracy of that map is of vital concern.

A third part of diagnostic teaching is the ability to design and devise effective strategies for teaching. These strategies are based on the data from the other two previously mentioned dimensions. This involves our ability to match the performance level of the child, the difficulty level of the material, the valence of the interest value with the task, and the teacher's instructional ways and means of perfecting the match. Undergirding these three dimensions of diagnostic teaching is the development of a diagnostic attitude—the skill and technique which brings the other three major parts into congruence and consonance.

Second, the effective reading teacher knows how to determine the various reading levels inherent in each child in her charge—most important of which is the child's instructional reading level. This is indeed a unique characteristic of a reading teacher. Further, this technique encompasses a frame of reference for the reading teacher, a way to monitor oral reading behavior constantly, and a way to measure daily growth in reading.

Third, the effective reading teacher appreciates the value of, knows how to determine, and how to interpret accurately the potential of each student he has in his class. If we really believe in the development of each individual child to his fullest extent, then we must know something of his parameters. How do we know whom we should encourage greatly? With whom to act a bit more forcefully? Which youngster has a disability and to what degree? What is the range of individual differences we must attempt to meet? For whom is which mode of instruction most appropriate?

Fourth, we need as effective reading teachers to have a conceptual system of the organic nature of comprehension (cognitive system). We need to know the relationship between reading characteristics, the language basis for comprehending, the elements of the materials to be comprehended, and the specific comprehension skills we wish to develop. Instructional control of this vital skill area demands a conceptual map and even then any lack of knowledge about the process will lessen our effectiveness. Further, we need to see the direct effect of our ability to frame and present discriminating spiralling questions on the results of our instructional control.

Fifth, an understanding of the concept of readability (symbol system) is fundamental to an effective diagnostic teacher of reading. We need to know those message characteristics which influence the difficulty of the material and we need to be able to utilize this information on-the-spot. Diagnostic teaching demands instant replay and we do not have time to resort to specialized formulas from which our knowledge may have been derived.

Sixth, the basic ingredients of phonics, structural analysis and, more recently, linguistic patterns must clearly be perceived in our repertoire of knowledge and skills. We need to see the relationships between the auditory (phonic) and the visual (structure). Further, we should know the relationship between these two subreading tasks and linguistic patterns. Hopefully, we will have some idea of what constitutes the minimal requirements in this conceptual area.

These six competencies are basic, though I could mention one or two more. How, for instance, can we put it all together for teaching purposes, that is, the teaching of a reading lesson? Do we know the distinctive characteristics of that operation?

I cannot stress too much the importance of the completeness and the accuracy of these conceptual maps we hold concerning the primary systems of reading. A teacher who hasn't any conception or a very limited notion of these primary areas has untrained and uncontrolled perception. Faulty diagnostic teaching is probably related strongly to the incompleteness or the inaccuracies in conceptual maps.

As teachers we can operate at various levels of effectiveness. We can function at a verbal level, a performance level, or an automatic level.

At the verbal level of functioning, the correct words and jargon of the field are used. Unfortunately, people operating solely at this level often do not have the vaguest notion what those terms really mean nor how they are related. They just give the appearance of knowing.

A higher level of functioning is the performance level, of which there are two stages. At the preferred stage the teacher knows the primary systems, but they are applied only with conscious effort. The lower stage of this level occurs more frequently than we would like to admit. In the lower stage, the teacher has the knowledge and the maps but does not use them. This represents the most serious limitation to the competency approach. To know a task does not guarantee that the knowledge will be applied. Such reading teachers are not unlike the critic of whom James Russell Lowell wrote in 1848:

It would be endless to tell you
the things that he knew,
All separate facts undeniably true,
But with him or each other they'd
nothing to do;
No power of combining, arranging,
discerning
Digested the masses he learned,
into learning
A reading machine all wound up
and going,
He mastered whatever was not
worth his knowing.

The highest level of functioning is truly the effective diagnostic teacher of reading. This is the automatic level. The knowledge, the maps, the strategies, and the attitude all become blended into one and become a part of the person. This teacher does correctly what comes naturally without conscious effort, but not without careful organization and preparation.

The humanistic touch

One can only hope the automatic teacher of reading will combine her more generalistic and humanistic qualities in arranging and conducting a teaching-learning environment. To do less may be to render their high levels of functioning ineffective. To paraphrase an old adage, "It is not only what you do, but how you do it."

This humanistic touch probably is achieved, in a large part, through the quality of the covenant between the persons involved. In every teaching situation, there is a covenant, implicit though it may be, between the student and the teacher. The student comes expecting, however covertly, to give and receive. The teacher senses and accepts this responsibility and does likewise. The youngster has a right to expect to move progressively up a spiralling curricular ladder, commensurate with his potential, to new and more challenging levels of learning. When a teacher knowingly accepts a child he cannot and will not be able to help, implying that he will help, the covenant is made in bad faith. For maximum learning, a teacher must have the professional right and opportunity to enter into all covenants with his students in good faith.

Perhaps this Arabic proverb summarizes best:

He who knows not and knows not he knows not,
he is a fool—shun him;
He who knows not and knows he knows not,
he is simple—teach him;
He who knows and knows not he knows,
he is asleep—wake him;
He who knows and knows he knows,
he is wise—follow him!

EARLY READERS—REFLECTIONS AFTER SIX YEARS OF RESEARCH

Dolores Durkin

For the past six years I have been working on two longitudinal studies of children who learned to read at home, prior to their entering first grade. The first of the studies began in September 1958. The subjects were children who just started first grade in the Oakland, California, public schools. The second study was begun in September of 1961, with first grade children enrolled in New York City public schools as subjects.

In June of 1964 both studies were concluded. The California children were then completing sixth grade; the New York children were spending their last month in the third grade.

Over the years central questions in the research have focused on the frequency of preschool readers in the population, on the factors that encourage early reading, and on the future advantages—or problems—of an earlier start.

Data in the studies have been collected from a variety of sources. Many findings have come from tests designed to assess intelligence, creative thinking ability, memory, perceptual skills, personality characteristics, and, of course, reading achievement. Other data have come from home interviews and teacher rating scales.

Since the research was first begun, periodic reports have been published. Some of the reports concentrated on research findings (*1, 2, 3, 4, 7, 10, 11*). Other reports were more concerned with the possible implications of these findings for the kindergarten curriculum (*5, 6, 8, 9*).

Now I would like to comment on some of the accidental and incidental things I have learned and noticed as I worked on the studies. There is no pretense about the profundity of these comments. For many of you, in fact, the comments and observations might only recall what you learned and noticed a long time ago.

Attitudes Toward Earlier Reading Instruction

In 1957, when plans for my research were still somewhat vague and indefinite, the general response to the topic selected for study was an unenthusiastic response to say the least. It was as if to think about the possibility of earlier reading instruction was to encourage a return to the era of child labor abuses. Consequently it has been very interesting to observe, over a period of only seven years, the great change in attitude and acceptance. Today, the climate that surrounds educational thinking and decision-making is so full and heavy with demands that cry, "Let's have more and let's have it sooner" that a matter like teaching reading in th

THE READING TEACHER, 1964, Vol. 18, pp. 3-7.

ndergarten is now a very popular pic. One might even call it a dan- rously popular topic because its opularity often discourages the care- l and objective probing that is ne- ssary for intelligent decisions about ndergarten. Too often, today, intel- gent decisions are replaced by the ish to be modern or, on the other and, by the rush to defend what is aditional.

When the topic is reading and the indergarten, the "rush to be mod- rn" sweeps along with a point of ew that assumes all five-year-olds re ready to learn to read. For the w children who might not be ready, interested, the remedy usually of- red is the use of reading readiness orkbooks.

In this particular rush, the picture f reading instruction itself looks very uch like a typical first grade pic- ire. The job is simply to transfer to indergarten what is now in grade ne.

The rush in the opposite direction –that is, the rush to defend what has een traditional for kindergarten— ften moves along a road marked by ostalgic thinking and sentimentality. On this road the youngness of young hildren is highlighted, as is their eed for social and emotional devel- pment. Overlooked, very often, is e obvious presence of preschool hildren who are very much aware f the written language in their vorld, and who are curious about it. Overlooked, too, are the preschool hildren who want to write, who ask ow to spell, and who could learn to ead with ease and enjoyment.

However, for the traditionalists the entrance of reading into the kinder- garten marks the inevitable entrance of a formal program. And, though the term "formal" is almost never defined with preciseness, it is com- monly used to denote instruction that is book-centered, group-centered, and rigid—and, therefore, most inappro- priate for five-year-old children.

To think about the practices pro- moted either by those who want to be modern or by those who are tra- ditional is to face the temptation of supporting the opposite position. Kin- dergartens that are cluttered with workbooks and that are noisy with phonics certainly tempt one to urge, "No reading in the kindergarten, please!" On the other hand, kinder- garten programs that are totally emp- ty of opportunities to learn to read but which, very often, are full of ac- tivities that some children abandoned even before they came to kindergar- ten—these programs, too, tempt one to move quickly away and to the opposite extreme.

But these extremes are the easy re- actions. They should remind us, nonetheless, that extreme and oppos- ing positions in education do not na- turally counteract one another in such a way that they are then re- placed by a more sensible and bal- anced position. Instead, it would seem, the position that makes sense is one that emerges only after the important questions are asked, and when these questions then get atten- tion that is as full of objectivity and scholarship as it is empty of bias and sentimentality.

Important Questions

What are some of the important questions that need to be considered in any discussion about reading and the kindergarten? I personally feel the initial questioning should concentrate on the total kindergarten curriculum before the focus ever shifts to one possible piece. Otherwise the emphasis will be on curriculum patchwork rather than on fundamental questions about the purpose and appropriateness of the whole.

If one accepts, as a fact, that the kindergarten program today is almost exactly like the earliest of the American kindergarten programs—even though the pre-kindergarten life of children has changed—then it is both fair and fundamental to ask whether this is as it ought to be.

Implications for Kindergarten Programs

In the parent interviews I have done for my research (in the second study the interviews were with parents of both early and nonearly readers) it became commonplace to hear about five-year-olds who had expressed disappointment with what they found in kindergarten. For the children who had attended nursery school, kindergarten was often either a repetition of the previous year or, in a few instances, a year of reduced challenge and interest. For the children who had not attended nursery school, the kindergarten program which offered them games and coloring and singing and storytelling was interesting for a while, but not for a year.

Very often, when the content of kindergarten programs was compared with the preschool activities of the children, there was either very little difference or, if there was much difference, the preschool activities generally looked better in variety and challenge. When differences favored the kindergarten, it was because the abilities the children brought to school were recognized, and the kindergarten program then moved on to extend them.

The few kindergarten programs that offered challenge certainly showed no scorn for the importance of social and emotional development. Instead, it seemed, they reflected the assumption that maturity is not accomplished in a vacuum. In the case of these better programs, the vacuum was filled with a curriculum that neither bored nor frustrated the children.

If kindergartens, as a whole, are to avoid both boredom and frustration, and if they are to build on the abilities the children bring to school, then at least some kindergarten programs should offer opportunities to learn to read, either because the children arrive with the beginnings of reading ability or because, over time, they show an interest in learning. For other five-year-olds other kinds of learning opportunities should be provided because these children show special interest and ability in art, for example, or because they are fascinated with simple arithmetic.

Within this framework, then, reading in the kindergarten becomes one possibility. Within this framework, too, kindergarten instruction in reading becomes one of the possible ways in which differences among five-year-olds are both recognized and utilized.

Kindergarten Instruction in Reading

Were I to try to put into kindergarten programs the kinds of things that encouraged the early reading ability of children in my research, I would begin with a kindergarten teacher who not only answers questions about written language but who also plans ways to increase the questioning. In the research, the preschool questions of children were frequent; and the questions were about street signs and car names as often as they were about words appearing in books. When books did help, it was generally while a parent read to a child and, on occasion, pointed out words that were of special interest or importance.

Actually, more than half of the preschool readers in the research were interested in writing before they ever showed any interest in reading. For these children writing seemed to be the extension of a still earlier interest in scribbling. Over time, the scribbling changed to the drawing of people and things; later, to the drawing of letters of the alphabet. Here, small blackboards were often used for "practice."

Still other early readers, according to their parents, showed interest in playing with oral language and with sounds. For some of the children this interest resulted in the ability to respond to requests like, "Tell me a word that begins the way 'bird' begins." For a very few children the interest in sounds and in letters eventually led to some independence in spelling.

Were I to try to move from research findings to kindergarten programs, I would also be quick to remind teachers that the preschool children who were interested in reading, or in writing, were not necessarily interested every day. On some days, according to their parents, the children would be occupied for an hour or even longer with the kinds of questioning and with the kinds of pencil and paper activities that can lead to skill in both reading and writing. On other days the interests of the children were very different, and might go in the direction of playing house or of building with blocks. But even here, playing house occasionally included attempts to make out a grocery list, while block building sometimes included the making of signs to identify what had been built. In both instances, interests of the children were made productive by parents who gave help when help was requested.

If kindergarten education is also to give help—whether with reading or with something else—then there is work to be done. Immediately needed, for example, is more research that will tell us in detail about the preschool years of children who are living and learning in the 1960's. Hopefully, this research will have an excellence that leads to an increase in the number of facts about young children and, in turn, to a reduction in the number of myths.

With these facts, it seems safe to predict, our conception of the role of kindergarten education will be broadened to include much more variety in the curriculum and, consequently, much more need for small-group and individual activities. And this immediately suggests what all kindergarten teachers know: If a truly worthwhile job is to be done, kindergarten classes must be reduced in size and, in some instances, extended beyond a two- or three-hour period.

If a "worthwhile job" *is* made possible, one can also predict an attitude toward kindergarten which views it as an integral and very important part of the total elementary school program. For too long, now, kindergarten has been either isolated or put on the sidelines. It has been—as I heard a parent say just the other day—"a good time for catching measles and mumps because not much of importance goes on there." This is unfair to kindergarten children, and to kindergarten teachers.

References

1. Durkin, Dolores. "A Study of Children Who Learned to Read Prior to First Grade," *California Journal of Educational Research,* 10 (May 1959), 109-13.
2. Durkin, Dolores. "The Precocious Reader," *California Journal for Instructional Improvement,* 2 (Dec. 1959), 24-28.
3. Durkin, Dolores. "Children Who Read Before Grade One," *Reading Teacher,* 14 (Jan. 1961), 163-66.
4. Durkin, Dolores. "Children Who Learned to Read at Home," *Elementary School Journal,* 62 (Oct. 1961), 14-18.
5. Durkin, Dolores. "Some Unanswered Questions About Five-Year-Olds and Reading," *Changing Concepts of Reading Instruction,* pp. 167-170. IRA Conference Proceedings, 1961.
6. Durkin, Dolores. "Kindergarten and Reading," *Elementary English,* 39 (Mar. 1962), 274-76.
7. Durkin, Dolores. "An Earlier Start in Reading?" *Elementary School Journal,* 63 (Dec. 1962), 146-51.
8. Durkin, Dolores. "Reading Instruction and the Five-Year-Old Child," *Challenge and Experiment in Reading,* pp 23-27. IRA Conference Proceedings 1962.
9. Durkin, Dolores. "Should the Very Young Be Taught to Read?" *NEA Journal,* 52 (Nov. 1963), 20-24.
10. Durkin, Dolores. "Children Who Read Before Grade I: A Second Study," *Elementary School Journal,* 64 (Dec. 1963) 143-48.
11. Durkin, Dolores. "A Fifth-Year Report on the Achievement of Early Readers," *Elementary School Journal,* in press.

SECTION VI

SCHEDULING: ADMINISTRATIVE PRACTICES AND PROGRAMS

Beginning an activity-centered classroom

MARCIENE MATTLEMAN

EVERYONE has his own teaching style—special ways in which he operates best. How then do teachers who are used to being "directive" handle activity-type programs in their classrooms, recognizing that more activity in the classroom takes more structure and more resourcefulness on the part of the teacher? The following plan, developed to provide practice in reading skill areas for the elementary school child, might be of help.

First, select a group of activities. Choose enough so that no more than four children will usually be clustered in one area: for thirty-two children, eight "games" are sufficient. Teach each activity to the entire class over several days so that all the children know how the "games" work. When all "games" are learned, select a place where each will be housed. "Games," of course, can be played anywhere, even on the floor, as long as the children know where activities are located. Work out simple rules with your class such as: each person stays at his activity place for the entire period.

Write the names of all activities on the chalkboard and assign the children to different places each day. Each morning the children must find their names or ask for help. (List names alphabetically.) In making assignments use activities differentially to give needed skill practice. Select a forty-five minute block of time for activities, and list this time on the daily schedule on the chalkboard, and always circulate among the children during games activities to ob-

THE READING TEACHER, Feb. 1972, Vol. 25, pp. 424-429.

serve what is being learned—and how.

Once procedures are smooth and the children know the alternatives, they will be able to decide for themselves where to sign up for each day. After a month or so add new "games," delete unpopular or unproductive activities, have the children make up their own.

The following list of activities, some teacher-made and some commercial, may offer interesting learning situations for pupils.

Teacher-made

Alphabet Bingo. Make a spirit master containing twelve spaces by drawing three vertical and four horizontal lines. Print fifteen capital or lowercase letters on the board. Have children fill their twelve spaces with any twelve letters. Have a caller randomly select letters to call. Have children cover letters called with paper squares (cut in advance). The first to get "bingo" wins.

Sentence Game I. Put words from books or experience charts on separate 3x5 inch cards. Give a pack to each child. In varied "rounds" have children put cards together to make up 1) the longest sentence, 2) the shortest sentence, 3) the funniest sentence, 4) a sentence beginning with a name, etc.

Word Bingo I. Same as Alphabet Bingo using, instead, words from either reading books, experience charts, or word lists (Dolch).

Color Match. On individual 3x5 inch cards make colored circles, one on each card. Print the names of each color underneath the circle. On another set of cards print the color names, (one on each) omitting the circle. Have children match the color names. When played by two children, one times the other to see who can finish more quickly. (Use the second hand on a clock.)

Alphabet Concentration. Print any alphabet letters on ten 3x5 inch cards, one on each. Make up a second set to match. Have children place cards face down in random order. Turn two cards at a time. If they match, remove them and gain two points. If they do not, put them back. Keep playing, each player taking one turn until all matches are found.

Numeral Concentration. Same as Alphabet Concentration using as many numerals as children can recognize independently,

Clay Alphabet. Print letters of the alphabet on separate 3x5 inch cards. Have each child make the letters in clay, matching his product to each card.

Sandpaper Alphabet. Print alphabet letters on separate 3x5 inch cards. Cut out the same letters from sandpaper and have the children match the cards by covering each with the identical sandpaper letter.

Shape Match. Same as Color Match using instead a circle, a square, a rectangle, a triangle, an X, and a check mark.

Pipe Cleaner Alphabet. Print letters of the alphabet on separate 3x5 inch cards. Have each child make each letter using pipe cleaners, matching his product to each card.

Sentence Game II. Same as Sentence Game I, at primary level, substituting harder words and more complex directions, as, 1) a sentence beginning with a vowel, 2) a sentence beginning with a consonant, 3) a sentence containing a describing word.

Word Bingo II. Same as Alphabet Bingo I, at primary level, substituting harder words, words from Dolch list.

Sentence Slot Game. Write out simple paragraphs on 3x5 cards. John .... to school. On the way he saw a .... The .... was .... John was .... Have children insert words that fit into slots. (Encourage humor!)

How many Words? Put several long words on separate 3x5 inch cards. Examples: encyclopedia, democracy, arithmetic, dictionary. On separate sheets, have children list as many smaller words as they can get from each.

Expansion Game. Write single simple sentences on 3x5 inch cards. Have children expand them on separate sheets in any way. (Encourage humor!) Example: The boy ran home. The tall, sad, young boy ran to his sister Jane's home.

Substitution Game. Place simple sentences on separate 3x5 inch cards. Examples: Our team *beat* the Phillies.
John *hit* Mary.
Jack *talked* to Frank.
Have children use the same construction substituting other words for the ones in italics, without changing the intent of the sentence.

Describing Game. Put names of objects on separate 3x5 inch cards. Examples: fruit, people, room, hair, girl, boy. Have children list any modifiers for each word on separate sheets.

Commercial

Learn the Alphabet — $2.25
Milton Bradley Company
Springfield, Mass.

Doghouse Game (Fun with Phonics) — $1.50
Kenworthy Educational Service, Inc.
Buffalo, New York

Five First Steps and Pop Words — $1.80
Kenworthy Educational Service, Inc.
Buffalo, New York

Stand Up and Sound Off — $2.75
Charles A. Merrill Co.
Columbus, Ohio

Word Prefixes — $ .85
Kenworthy Educational Service, Inc.
Buffalo, New York

Pairs Word Game — $1.25
Milton Bradley Co.
Springfield, Mass.

Vowel Lotto — $2.10
Garrard Publishing Co.
Champaign, Ill.

Basic Sight Vocabulary Cards — $1.60
Garrard Publishing Co.
Champaign, Ill.

Sentence Builder — $1.25
Milton Bradley Company
Springfield, Mass.

Link Letters — $1.25
Milton Bradley Company
Springfield, Mass.

Picture Word Builder — $ .65
Milton Bradley Company
Springfield, Mass.

Sight Phrase Cards — $1.10
Garrard Publishing Co.

Champaign, Ill.

The Syllable Game $2.60
Garrard Publishing Co.
Champaign, Ill.

Consonant Lotto $2.10
Garrard Publishing Co.
Champaign, Ill.

Quizmo (consonants, blends) $2.25
Milton Bradley Co.
Springfield, Mass.

The New Phonetic Word Drill Cards
Kenworthy Educational Service, Inc.
Buffalo, New York

Word Blends $ .85
Kenworthy Educational Service, Inc.
Buffalo, New York

Phonics Rummy A, B, C, D, E $1.50
Kenworthy Educational Service, Inc.
Buffalo, New York

Word Suffixes $ .85
Kenworthy Educational Service, Inc.
Buffalo, New York

Speed Up $2.75
Charles E. Merrill
Columbus, Ohio

This plan was developed as the author saw a need to help teachers who wanted to diverge from the teacher-centered classroom, yet were reluctant to start for fear of chaos. Innercity teachers who initiated change in these ways have enjoyed the resulting opportunity to observe their students in such guided learning experiences.

This, then, is a first step toward freeing teachers and children. As we watch the British experience, examine the findings and gain more insights, hopefully we will move toward helping children discover ways to maximize their own chances for school success.

Reference

Scheffler, Israel. *The Language of Education*. Springfield, Ill.: Charles C. Thomas, 1960.

Group instruction in a language-experience approach

EDMUND H. HENDERSON

Henderson directs the McGuffey Reading Center at the University of Virginia. In this article he recommends that teaching comprise many styles of leadership, including autocratic, democratic, laissez faire. This, he notes, is often overlooked by enthusiasts for both open and grammar school curriculum models.

IN A time when all are seeking better ways to teach, there is often a tendency to champion one strategy over another and to hope or claim the belief that one device or another will satisfy this educational mission. Today, for example, there is a rising chorus of approval for the open classroom organization, one which is similar to the exciting "progressive" schools of the twenties. Enthusiasts for this management design tend to see themselves as opposed to the teacher-centered or autocratic styles of leadership generally characteristic of the traditional grammar school curriculum.

Midway between these positions lies the "democratic" or small group interaction design, and it is this model of pupil management that is highlighted in this article. It is my belief that all three group instructional models are necessary for effective teaching, and the small group plan is the quintessential model for teaching certain basic processes of reading behavior. This harmony of management design has been remarkably well effected in the language-experience approach (Stauffer, 1970).

Misconception

There are two fairly general misconceptions about the language-experience approach itself. Surprisingly, some think that this method applies only to beginning reading instruction, specifically to the use of chart stories to initiate a sight vocabulary. The use of both group and individually dictated accounts is, of course, a part of the language-experience approach, but

THE READING TEACHER, 1973, Vol. 26, pp. 589-597.

this is only part of a much larger scheme, each stage of which functions consistently under a single theoretical model.

Learning to read requires this global view because it is not thought of as a simple, single event phenomenon. Rather it is conceived to begin with the child's first responses to his environment and conclude, if it ever concludes in a lifetime, with the behavior of a mature adult dealing selectively and purposefully with graphics in all forms.

The term "language-experience approach" is a pedagogical label denoting a particular way of directing the learner as he moves toward the attainment of a mature reading facility. The term implies that reading competence advances as the learner's internalized language experience evolves into increasingly complex and functionally adequate schema, and that this occurs as a function of the pupil's activity in his own terms upon a relatively natural and minimally distorted language environment. Stages of development are identified and a variety of different teaching strategies is used. These are recognized, however, as events and teaching acts which are distinct from the complex individual cognitive development of the learner.

When pupils are directed in a routine of perusing or perhaps choral reading a dictated account, they are following a particular procedure of the language-experience approach. When a pupil can name some words at random from an account not seen for twenty-four hours, this new attainment may be thought of as a stage. It is not thought, however, that the beginning reader who "knows" ten or twenty words indeed knows these words in any complete or final sense. Rather, his internalized concept of word forms is thought of as merely sufficient at that point for him to identify these particular words on request. To the degree that he continues to learn, however, his concept of words is conceived of as growing in complexity until a mature word-identification facility is attained. Thus the abilities of naming letters or words, differentiating phonic or structural elements, answering questions about something read, or drawing conclusions about it, are seen as surface elements.

In psychological terms, the language-experience approach fits under the theoretical framework of cognition. In general, its procedures and strategies for teaching are consistent with the ideas of psychologists like Guilford (1959), Bruner (1962), and Piaget, and of psycholinguists like Miller (1965), Chomsky (1970), Goodman (1968), and Smith (1971), for example. On the other hand, the approach is a set of practical field techniques, a methodology, and in that sense it is distinct from the substantive theory from which it derives.

Programed approach

Contrasting with the language-experience approach is a sharply different methodology which might best be labeled as a programed or structural approach. In this, most teaching strategies are roughly consistent with the paradigm of stimulus-response and could be psychologically termed a behavioral approach. Pedagogically, the emphasis of this approach is upon the surface elements of progress, and the assumption is made that enough can be known about the ordering and chaining of these responses to effect an underlying competence in language and in reading.

Teaching in a programed approach requires that one anticipate the required set of responses, compose and order the stimuli that will produce these, and then apply them to each pupil according to an optimum schedule of repetition and reward. In practice, the selective sequencing of events, the programing, is carried out by an outside expert, and the teacher concentrates upon a heightening of motivation, (that is, obtaining the highest possible level of response) and upon tallying the results. Ideally, the teacher will also readjust sequences and recycle or advance individual pupils according to their success or failure in the various phases of the prescribed program.

It is this model that characterizes nearly all formal reading instruction conducted in our schools for the past seventy-five years. The current label of programed reading is merely a Skinnerian variation on a theme that holds equally true for the so-called traditional basal readers, for most "linguistic" programs, and so on. Thus it is important to recognize that the language-experience approach is not one or two procedures confined to a particular level of instruction, nor is it a simple variation on the common instructional theme. Rather, it is a distinctly different method, capable of countless internal variations and subject only to the overlying rationalistic or cognitive model from which it is derived.

Second misconception

The second major misconception of the language-experience approach stems from the first and lies in the tendency of some educators to delimit their concept of methodology by specific practices or strategies rather than by the model from which it stems. A few examples may illustrate this point.

Individualized reading instruction as a pedagogical label and as a teaching strategy has enjoyed a brave and stormy history over the past several decades. Typically it denotes a teaching plan in which children select different trade books to read and the teacher directs their progress through these by individual conferences. This procedure does in fact fit within the rubric of the cognitive model. Programed vocabulary and preconceived sequences are avoided, learning advances by the action of the pupil upon relatively natural material.

Thus it is not surprising that proponents of this technique are also generally sympathetic with an individualized word acquisition strategy like that followed in the language-experience approach. In fact, they are and have been among the principal leaders in this movement (Veatch, 1966). The difficulty comes when a teacher accepts a limited set of practices within a theoretical framework but denies others which have an equal right to belong. It is not uncommon, however, to find an advocate of individualized reading denying the propriety of small group instruction where pupils share a common book (Groff, 1970). Obviously, the latter procedure can be managed in other than a programed system and thus may and should be a part of a global and theoretically consistent approach.

The recent wave of enthusiasm for the open classroom (Silberman, 1970) poses very much the same problem. Here, what would appear to be a single managerial option, albeit palpably within the cognitive domain, is equated with an overall methodology whose repertoire of possible strategies is vastly larger and more flexible.

Obviously, open classroom settings are useful for certain purposes, and individualized reading instruction for others. Moreover, it would be perfectly reasonable in an Alice in Wonderland sense that either of these labels serves to denote the distinct global approach termed language-experience (Stauffer, 1971). Regardless of label, however, it must be recognized that pedagogical differences cannot be discussed intelligibly, let alone evaluated, if different random pieces of the same approach, or worse, of different approaches, are championed indiscriminately. It is like arguing that a beaver's forefoot is better than his hindfoot, or that either of them is superior to those of a dog or a kangaroo.

Group behavior insights

True eclecticism must involve neither an arbitrary limitation of procedures within an approach nor a hodgepodge of procedures from different approaches. Rather, what would seem to be required is an elaboration and orchestration of strategies consistent with a central theme. The science of group behavior offers some insights to guide in this task.

The study of group behavior has proven to be a rich field of interest to research psychologists during the past two decades. In both natural and laboratory settings, using a wide variety of tasks, they have examined group effectiveness as a function of size, composition or membership, communication network, style of leadership and a host of similar variables. The five volume *Handbook of Social Psychology* edited by Lindsey and Aaronson (1969) is a tribute to the vigor of this area of study. Moreover, in this edition a chapter (Getzels) has been introduced for the first time to deal with the implications of social psychology for education.

Conclusions

From this work at least two very general conclusions can be reached. The first is that the variables of size, membership, communication network, and style of leadership do make a difference experimentally, and this difference bears a complex but predictable relationship to group effectiveness as a function of the task performed and the objective or goal to be attained. The second generalization, equally obvious, is that these neatly defined parameters of group behavior have real life counterparts that are easily recognized and a part of the ordinary parlance of laymen and of educators.

The familiar terms *lecture*, *recitation*, and *seminar*, for example, depict conditions in which very different styles of leadership are employed and in which different communication networks obtain. When, however, these settings are viewed, not as good or bad ways of teaching, but rather as experimental variables, one is better able to appraise the assets and liabilities of each. In the well known study of autocratic, democratic and laissez faire styles of leadership (White and Lippett, 1962), the experimenters found greater effectiveness for the democratic style, given a specific task and a specific set of dependent measures. These findings, however, do not serve as a blanket endorsement of the democratic posture for all cases and conditions, nor do they deny the viability of autocratic or laissez faire styles in other settings. A researcher's view of leadership, in short, conforms to the rules of generalizability and attempts to see each variable in relation to the other. It is important that educators follow a similarly disciplined approach to their work. A set of hypothetical studies may serve to illustrate this point.

Competition

Suppose that there are competing groups, each with leaders who are known to understand the routines by which a fairly complex mobile may be assembled. The goal is to get the job done correctly and quickly in order to win a prize.

In group one, the leader urges all to have a go at it. He answers questions readily, but initiates no strategies for solution (laissez faire). In group two, the leader begins with "Now folks, how do you think we should proceed—That's a good idea—Can anyone think of another way it might be done?" (democratic). In group three, the leader plays the enlightened autocrat by saying "Okay, fellows, I know how this thing works. You two guys start putting the long pieces together while the rest of us sort these" (autocratic). Needless to say, group three will win the race hands down. Moreover, the group will probably enjoy greater cohesiveness—that is, class spirit, be higher in group esteem, and, one would suspect, be better informed about mobile assembly than their ill led peers.

In this circumstance, one notices that the goal is external and concrete, the motivation structure extrinsic, and that the enlightened despot, an autocratic style of leadership, is clearly most effective. By the same token, the effective teacher must at times assume the autocratic role as, for example, when she lays down the ground rules of operation that make activity possible and efficient for the group. It is held, therefore, that an authoritarian teacher role is appropriate in a language-experience classroom, provided that conditions and objectives warrant it.

Now, however, change the experimental goal bit by bit. Instead of a prefabricated mobile to be assembled in record time, decree that the objective is to create a mobile from some common materials. Which style of leadership would suit this new objective best? Also, what group size would be optimal? Next, change the goal on a continuum as follows: Which group can create 1) the most mobiles? 2) the most different kinds of mobiles? 3) the most unique mobiles? Finally, the dependent variable might be this: Which group one year from now will score highest on a test of creativity? Clearly, as the goal is changed, the source of information shifts from the leader to the membership, and the character of the objective changes from concrete to abstract, from a product to a process. Motivational forces shift from extrinsic to intrinsic—that is, for the group to attain the latter goals, its members must be moved by an inner force. A summary of these relationships is suggested in the table.

All approaches needed

In a language-experience classroom, all styles of leadership are needed and are employed. Here, there are open pupil centered settings where things are pretty much allowed to happen, and there are also strictly teacher centered, teacher dominated settings where, as it were, the teacher is both the medium and the message. Somewhere about midway on this continuum lies a territory where the small group, open network, teacher agitator model (Stauffer, 1968) is most appropriate and effective.

When the thing to be learned is a process, when the source of the information lies in the action of learners upon a task, the small group setting is needed. The language-experience approach, moreover, does concentrate upon those processes that emerge through learner action rather than upon a predetermined set of teacher initiated responses. It is for this reason that small group settings are seen as indispensable to this method.

Murray study

A recent study by Murray (1971) dealing with the effects of training upon preoperational children illustrates the small group interaction model and its possible effects. As is well known, the habits of mind of the preoperational child are, in Piaget's terms, highly resistant to direct teaching. The child who maintains that the flattened ball of dough must be heavier as a consequence of its change in form, may be conditioned to give the correct response, that is, to say weight remains constant. He will err again, however, when the principle of conservation is tested in another form, or so the weight of research evidence suggests.

In Murray's study a small group instruction learning model was employed for training in the conservation principle. After identifying conservers and nonconservers among kindergarten children, he placed each nonconserver in a group with two conservers and directed them to solve various conservation problems. The children argued, persuaded, reasoned and ultimately agreed upon correct solutions to each task. On posttests involving different tasks, the nonconservers changed significantly and positively toward the conservation response. So surprising were the findings that a replication of the study was conducted, but again, the nonconservers appeared to have learned the principle.

Murray's conclusions were properly cautious. He suggested that the effects might be accounted for, or seen as similar to, those in the Ash studies where subjects tended to conform to a group consensus despite palpable evidence to the contrary. Yet one notes that in the posttests there was no pressure to conform. Further, Piaget himself has suggested that the transition from stage to stage in cognitive development occurs through social interaction. One is strongly tempted to believe that those subjects who were ready to do so, did in fact change in their approach to the task as a consequence of the group interaction method used.

Small group settings

Numerous examples could be given to illustrate small group strategies used in a language-experience approach. Two settings might serve as overt examples, one dealing with word recognition, the other with reading comprehension.

Knowledge of words is conceived in this approach to emerge not simply by means of a sequence of letter-sound or whole word associations (Gibson, 1970), but through

Table
Teaching style as a function of academic goal

	Autocratic	*Democratic*	*Laissez Faire*
Pedagogical Term	Lecture and Recitation	Seminar	Open Classroom
Communication Network	Closed	Open	Undirected
Group Size	Large (30 +)	Small (7-9)	Moderate (30)
Motivation	Largely Extrinsic	Extrinsic & Intrinsic	Largely Intrinsic
Task	Concrete	Relatively Abstract	Abstract
Goals	Specific Response	Integrated Behavior	Creative Production
Source of Information	The Teacher	The Group	The Individual

the acquisition of increasingly elaborate indexed rules that order written language and permit the rapid and, largely, subliminal cue-response of the adult reader. It is not enough that the learner commit to memory a limited set of responses; he must act upon the material, generate hypotheses about how words work and then test these directly for goodness of fit. Right answers are not the significant matter, and indeed they need not emerge at the conscious or verbal level at all. Who among us, for example, can recite the rules that govern the final sound of *k* in English spelling? Yet we act in this regard with great certainty. It is this process, one that yields a knowing behavior, that the teacher seeks to elicit in a small group interaction setting. The stuff itself lies in the actions of the learner, and it is this that is shared and assimilated.

As an illustration, consider this situation. The teacher sits in a circle of seven children. She writes on the chalk board the word *bake*. Then she says, "Look in your word banks. See how many words you can find that are like the word *bake* in some way." One child may choose *book, banana,* and *banjo*; a second, *bacteria, sack,* and *lake* Still another picks out *stove, eat,* and *cook,* and so on. As what is produced is shared and defended by the children, the "ways of looking at words" are illuminated, and from this experience an increasingly versatile and productive way of "looking" may be adopted by each group member.

Perhaps the most notable characteristic of the so-called dyslexic child is his tendency to make almost random passes at a word, to look away and guess wildly out of fear of failure, or to persevere in a single strategy of letter naming or sounding. To the degree that this behavior is not irrevocably based in some neurological impairment, mechanized conditioning to words of similar configuration and to segmented letter parts would be ideally suited to produce this kind of aberrant word perception. Small group settings of the kind just described provide a very different and, for some children, a critical range of experience with words.

A second example of the small group interaction model where the goal is process rather than product can be seen in the comprehension teaching strategy which Stauffer (1968) has designed and labeled a "directed reading-thinking activity". In this procedure the teacher sets in motion what Goodman (1968) has called "the psycholinguistic guessing game" and illuminates pupil action through oral sharing of hypotheses, tests for proof, and the formulation of judgments and conclusions.

In a recent session with a group of second graders, a fine interaction emerged. The story to be read came from a standard basal reader. All pupils could handle the text, attacking an occasional unfamiliar word on their own or with help if needed. The story involved a child who wished for a dog—and eventually got one. The joys of ownership soon paled, however, when he found he must take care of the pet. When he failed to keep Fido from tracking up his mother's newly polished floor, she made him clean the floor himself. Dejected at the close of the sequence, the boy contemplated finding another owner for his pet.

From the title and picture the children predicted as a group that the boy wanted a dog and would get one. With the focus of this hypothesis, they read quickly and silently to test its truth. At the end of two pages they affirmed their prediction, and, after a quick look at the next illustrations, one of which showed Fido prancing on the floor, they divided in their opinion about what would happen next. One said that Mike would teach his dog tricks (a good possibility); another, that he would feed the dog (a rather pedestrian thought). A third said, "I don't know!" and finally a fourth suggested that the dog was going to get Mike into trouble. When asked why, he replied, "Because Mother said he'd have to take care of him and that always means trouble."

This demonstrates a range of critical thinking skill and an illumination of the basis for that thinking. It is this, emerging from different children and tested by them, that is the thing to be learned and internalized if they are to become efficient readers. Herein lies the self-generated semantic thrust that lifts the reading act from the crude, mediated, word by word responding, to a sweeping, mind constructed apprehension signaled by minimal cues (Smith, 1971).

Again, silent reading achieved the object. The fourth child's idea was affirmed, and the chapter completed. Then the teacher asked, "What do you think about the way Mother handled Mike and his dog?" Six of the children chorused at once that she had done the right thing. One could almost feel the force of the Puritan ethic and the group's conformity to it. When asked why they thought so, however, there was a moment of silence. At last one child advanced the "eye for eye, tooth for tooth" rationale: "he messed up the floor, so he ought to clean it up." And this drew general approval. But then another hand went up. It belonged to a rather shy little girl. "I don't know," she said. "You know, that boy really did want that dog and now he doesn't, and that's a shame. And besides, he's just a little boy. He couldn't clean the floor up right anyway."

What a marvelous movement away from mindless conformity! How indeed *should* punishment fit a crime? Here was an act, an act of reason, mildly subversive perhaps; but so be it, for it is inquiry, not answers, that is the business of education. This was the thing to be shared and learned, and there is no more effective strategy for doing so than by directing the interaction of ideas as children read and think.

Conclusions are anticlimactic when they follow the ideas of children in the act of learning. Yet a summation will be made. To the degree that the language-experience approach is conceived as a global cognitively based methodology, all variations of group management will be required. At times the teacher must structure the activity precisely and manipulate directly a sequence of punishment and reward. At other times an open classroom strategem is needed—free exploration in reading and writing, in science and sound and art where children have the time and space to find themselves and savor their own capacity to wonder and create. Central, however, to this approach and firmly grounded in the substantive theory that underpins it, stands the small group interaction model. It is in this setting that the wise teacher may elicit from children their range of language experience and guide them to test its merit day by day.

References

Bruner, Jerome S. *The Process of Education.* Cambridge, Mass.: Harvard University Press, 1962.

Chomsky, N. "Phonology and Reading." *Basic Studies on Reading,* Eds. H. Lewin and Joanna P. Williams. New York: Basic Books, Inc., 1970.

Gibson, Elinor J. "The Ontogeny of Reading." *American Psychologist,* Vol. 25, No. 2 (1970), pp. 136-43.

Goodman, K. S., Ed. *The Psycholinguistic Nature of the Reading Process.* Detroit: Wayne State University Press, 1968.

Groff, P. "Jeanne Chall Revisited." *Phi Delta Kappan,* Vol. 52, No. 3 (Nov. 1970), pp. 162-65.

Guilford, J. P. "Three Faces of the Intellect." *American Psychologist,* Vol. 14 (August 1959), pp. 469-479.

Lindsey G. and Aaronson, Eds. *Handbook of Social Psychology,* 5 Vols. Reading, Mass.: Addison-Wesley Publishing Co., 1969.

Miller, G. A. "Some Preliminaries to Psycholinguistics." *American Psychologist,* Vol. 20 (1965), pp. 15-20.

Murray, F. "The Acquisition of Conservation through Social Interaction." Paper presented to the American Educational Research Association, New York City, 1971.

Silberman, C. *Crisis in the Classroom.* Baltimore: Random House, Inc., 1970.

Smith, F. *Understanding Reading. A Psycholinguistic Analysis of Reading and Learning to Read.* New York: Holt, Rinehart and Winston, 1971.

Stauffer, R. G. *Directing Reading Maturity as a Cognitive Process.* New York: Harper and Row, 1968.

Stauffer, R. G. "Integrating the Language Arts." *Elementary English,* Vol. 68, No. 1 (Jan. 1971), pp. 22-26.

Stauffer, R. G. *The Language-Experience Approach to the Teaching of Reading.* New York: Harper and Row, 1970.

Veatch, Jeannette. *Reading in the Elementary School.* New York: The Ronald Press, 1966.

White and Lippett. "Leader Behavior and Member Reaction in Three 'Social Climates.'" *Group Dynamics Research and Theory,* Eds. D. Cartwright and A. Lander. New York: Row, Peterson and Co., 1962,

WHAT IS INDIVIDUALIZED READING?

Emmett Albert Betts

Time flies when Jimmy reads a book of his own choice and drags when he is bored by meaningless "seat-work". Monday morning cannot come soon enough when he is comfortable in his reading. To develop and to maintain this kind of interest, plans for individualizing reading have been used.

In many classrooms today, teachers are experimenting with different ways of individualizing basic reading instruction. Briefly, individualized reading is independent reading *plus* "skill" development. It is a plan to provide for individual differences in reading, not a reading method. It is individualized teaching to support learning, which has always been individual.

Plans for individualizing basic reading instruction which set the pattern for today's programs were reported in the early 1930's. Since then, the term *individualized reading* has been given different meanings in different classrooms.

In some classrooms, for example, individualized reading is merely free, or independent, reading — without skill development — during a given time every day or several times a week. While independent reading of this type is an important part of any child's reading program, it is no substitute for basic reading instruction.

THE READING TEACHER, 1973, Vol. 26, pp. 678-679.

In these instances, the teachers have set the stage for wide reading—for pure enjoyment.

Independent reading is for those who can read. To derive pleasure from reading calls for a mastery of those word perception and thinking skills and abilities needed to do it. There is some truth in the statement: "The only way to learn to read is to read." The tricky term in that statement is *learn.* Through interesting reading the pupil learns to enjoy reading; he applies the reading skills he has been taught, but he does not necessarily learn new reading skills.

In other classrooms, teachers make a sincere effort to individualize basic reading instruction. They guide the independent reading study activities of each pupil, giving help on phonic and thinking skills in individual conferences and small group meetings.

Individualized reading study activities may include:

1. each pupil reading at his independent level
2. each pupil reading (silently) a different book—a trade book, a textbook, a reference book, magazine, or newspaper
3. each child searching for "the right book" — interesting and readable for him
4. each pupil reading a book of his own choice
5. each pupil reading at his own rate, without pressure
6. each pupil receiving individual help on skills during an individual conference with the teacher
7. each pupil asking for individual help as the teacher moves about the room
8. each pupil deciding how he will report to the group

A very important individual activity is browsing until the pupil can find a book he can convert to his own use. Reading here and there in a book to sample its contents is a freedom that is denied to no one. This freedom to select a book, magazine, or other material places the emphasis where it belongs: relaxed reading because it is interesting and serves a personal purpose.

Individualized reading and study also may include group activities:

1. help on word perception skills (need groups)
2. cooperative study of a topic of interest to two or more pupils (interest groups)
3. help on thinking and other aspects of comprehension (need group)
4. reports on reading to a group
5. discussions of a book read by different pupils in order to share it with the rest of the class or a small group
6. creative activities such as plays and dramatizations
7. reading or rereading a book, an article, or other material to a small group interested in it
8. discussion of news based on reports in *My Weekly Reader, Read, Junior Scholastic, Young America, Reader's Digest,* and other periodicals
9. organizing information for a report
   a. note taking
   b. outlining
   c. summarizing
   d. preparing charts and graphs
   e. preparing a booklet for the room library

Individualized reading, then, is a plan for capitalizing on the wide range of individual differences within the classroom. It is an approach to classroom management that places a premium on individual differences. However, the secret to the success of the plan is the professional competence of the teacher. Plans do not work, and methods do not work, but competent teachers make the best use of plans and of methods.

The goal of basic reading instruction—group or individualized—is to teach all pupils how to read efficiently, within the limits of their abilities and needs. To achieve this goal teachers help pupils by giving them painstakingly thorough, day-by-day help on specific skills—with as much individual attention as possible.

Games reinforce reading skills

FLORENCE V. SHANKMAN

GAMES can be used to reinforce many different reading skills. They are an incentive for learning vocabulary, phonics, word structure, and sight words. Most of the major professional texts on the teaching of reading recommend using games to reinforce the reading skills in an interesting way. Roma Gans (1963) tells us that ". . . the way in which children manage their own learning reveals the importance of games." The teacher can plan for a greater variety in drill by using games to reinforce the skills that she introduces in the regular lesson. Strang (1957) found games ". . . especially valuable in providing practice for individuals deficient in certain specific word recognition, vocabulary, paragraph reading and other skills. Harris (1961) found that "Many kinds of drill can be disguised as games, becoming play rather than distasteful work." In studying the interests of children, Witty (1966) found that girls prefer the quieter games while boys prefer highly organized games.

There are many things that a teacher can do in connection with games. She should encourage the creative efforts of the children to help them develop original games, riddles or puzzles to aid them in remembering certain words or principles in reading. Time for practice must be planned carefully to give all children the opportunity to reinforce skills in an interesting way. The children can often devise variations that are helpful. Although many games can be purchased, those made by the classroom teacher to meet the particular needs of her children are of greater use in the classroom. Teacher-created games and work type exercises should be made out of durable material in order to be used over again with different groups or individuals.

In visiting many different classrooms and observing both student teachers and master teachers, it was noted that certain characteristics were found in the games that were best liked by the children. The directions for playing the games were clear and simple enough to be played with a minimum of supervision. They were fun and gave the child a sense of satisfaction. The children were stimulated to learn and found personal recognition that helped to build a better self-image and morale. Young children had to experience immediate success while developing a respect for serious effort, rather than just fast achievement. Games could be used to test one's own adequacy, if individuals were competing with themselves to improve their own record. Team games involved the par-

THE READING TEACHER, December 1968, pp. 262-264.

ticipation of more children and encouraged cooperation among the older children. Action games often added zest to learning and satisfied many basic psychological drives. Learning was facilitated while formal instruction was reinforced.

There are certain characteristics that are essential for the games used in the classroom. They must have a real learning value that reinforces or teaches a reading skill. The mechanics of the game should not take much learning time and should not overshadow the skill it is supposed to reinforce. The fun of the game should center around the *reading skill*, rather than in the *game itself*. Each game should have a specific purpose that is meaningful to the child, but reinforces or enriches a classroom goal. Children should be able to act as leaders in most of the games or they should be self-checking. They should be adaptable to the needs, abilities and interests of the children involved. The teacher can often learn to understand individual children as she observes them playing a game. Good sportsmanship can be developed through games.

At the same time, while advocating games to give practice in reading skills, one must be aware of their limitations. They can be busy work *or* just a play activity. Often, it is difficult to evaluate the effectiveness or value of the game. Many games are limited to practice on words in isolation, unless a special effort is made to use the words in context or to use a wide variety of supplementary reading materials, where the child can find the words in context. Smith (1963) emphasized considering the interest and pleasant association while avoiding contrived games that are far removed from the original activity. She considered these unrelated games an insult to the intelligence of any child. Well-planned games, carefully selected, can be used with individuals, small groups, or the whole class. The materials needed are inexpensive and can be prepared by any classroom teacher quickly. Betts (1957) states that "When used with discretion, games tend to improve social relationships among the group and stimulate interest in reading."

Games involving word recognition should not be used until pupils have met these words in a meaningful situation. There are many listening games that can be used to develop auditory discrimination. A game shelf should be part of each classroom library. Good sportsmanship should be stressed whenever playing a competing game. Children should be required to stop playing a game while they still have the desire to continue. This will motivate them to want to use the same games on other occasions.

Games are not a bag of tricks, but a means to an end. A good reading teacher is aware of why a particular game is appropriate and how it will meet the unique needs and interests of the individual or group using it. The teacher should continually evaluate the effectiveness of games being used and should make necessary changes to adapt them for her own needs. Some children acquire a particular reading skill the first time it is introduced, while others may need to have it explained in several different ways before they grasp it. A wide range of games can help to meet the individual's need for extra practice on a particular skill. If games are kept interesting and challenging, they can contribute a great deal.

REFERENCES

Betts, E. A. *Foundations of reading instruction.* New York: American Book Company, 1957. P. 518.

Gans, Roma. *Common sense in teaching reading.* Indianapolis: The Bobbs Merrill Company, 1963. P. 86.

Harris, A. J. *How to increase reading ability.* New York: Longmans, Green and Company, 1961. P. 290.

Smith, Nila B. *Reading instruction for today's children.* Englewood Cliffs, New Jersey: Prentice-Hall, 1963. P. 174.

Strang, Ruth, and Bracken, Dorothy K. *Making better readers.* Boston: D. C. Heath and Company, 1957. P. 177.

Witty, P. A., Freeland, Alma M., and Grotberg, Edith H. *The teaching of reading.* Boston: D. C. Heath and Company, 1966. P. 236.

Individualized Reading—A Revisit and Review

By Irene Allen and Richard Thompson

If you are in a rut, you need a lift. If you are tired or dispirited using a basal reader approach to teach reading, why not kick the habit? One way to do this is to try individualized reading. If you enjoy your rut, perhaps you should remember the only difference between a rut and a grave is the distance. If you feel in need of a stimulant, why not read further? You may climb upward and guide your students along, too.

Individualized reading, as an approach to the teaching of reading, has stimulated much discussion and controversy since it came into prominence at the turn of the century. It was developed by a teacher for her classroom based on her students' needs and her understanding of the reading process. Much of the misunderstandings come from disagreements concerning certain aspects of this approach.

The following question-and-answer format was developed in order to give you a better understanding of the individualized approach and to encourage more thinking along the lines of individualized instruction.

What Is Individualized Reading?

Essentially, individualized reading is an approach which utilizes the interests of the pupils and permits them to select their own reading material, allowing them to read independently instead of in organized groups. In choosing their own books, the pupils have different books as opposed to all pupils having the same lesson at the same time. Reading is not considered a separate subject, but is considered a process to be used in all learning situations. The philosophy underlying this approach is directed toward self-evaluation and self-growth.

Crosby (2) states that individualized reading differs from traditional programs because the children read different books, receive different instruction from their teacher, select their own reading material and are grouped at irregular intervals for specific skill instruction.

This approach is not a commercially prepared kit of books. It is a way of learning based on interests and needs of each pupil utilizing books and materials that were self-selected.

What Are the Advantages And Disadvantages Of Individualized Reading?

Children do more reading because they are able to self-pace themselves. Selfselection of material meets the interests of the students, and the reading material level of difficulty tends to match the child's reading ability level. Individualized reading avoids the possibility of stigmatization sometimes unavoidable when reading groups are formed on the basis of reading ability. Individual conferences insure individualized attention for each student. Individualized reading, then, is likely to meet the needs and interests of all pupils regardless of their reading level.

Besides advantages there are some disadvantages to individual reading. One weakness is that skills are not systematically taught except when the teacher provides instruction during individual conferences or sets up groups for sequential skill instruction. Without considerable thought, planning, and skill on the part of the teacher, these skills may be unlearned or underdeveloped. Without question, keeping track of each pupil's progress and sequentially programming skill needing instruction, requires managerial competence coupled with systematic record keeping. Not all

THE MICHIGAN READING JOURNAL, Spring 1972, vol. 6, no. 2, pp. 29-32.

teachers are capable of handling this. For these potential problems to be minimized or eliminated, the teacher contemplating immersion of her students into individualized reading must plan carefully and in advance.

Why Use Individualized Reading?

The logic of individualized reading instruction rests on the premise that the use of reading materials only with maximum ranges of readability levels will meet the divergent reading range of any group of students.

As Austin (1) states, on the first day of school we can expect a four-year range of mental maturity among the children. The longer the pupils are in school the wider the range becomes. By the seventh grade, the range is from third to eleventh grade.

You can expect the range of reading abilities within a class to be at the very least approximately two-thirds of the mean chronological age of the pupils in the class. If the average age is eight the range may be five years, while among twelve-year-olds there is usually an eight-year spread or more between the best and the poorest reader (1). Therefore, individualized reading seems to be the most logical approach in meeting such diverse differences.

For What Grade Level Can Individualized Reading Be Successfully Used?

Individualized reading can be achieved at any level. Most schools use it above first grade, but some teachers have found it successful in first grade. Warford (13), Spencer (8,9), Johnson (4,5), and many others have compared individualized reading at various grade levels with other approaches, but mainly the basal reader approach. The evidence seems to indicate that individualized reading is equal to or superior to the approaches with which it is compared at any level. The implication is evident. A teacher who uses individualized reading will not likely curtail the reading power of her students; quite the contrary, she will more than likely get better results or at least comparable achievement gains.

How Should You Get Ready?

The teacher should get a variety of books, five or more for each child, that will meet the reading abilities and interests of the class members. To meet the independent reading level of most of your students, approximately two-thirds of the books should have a readability level below your grade level. Set up a notebook with a page for each child to record events of individualized conferences. Read available materials on individualization and adapt it to your students needs. Veatch's (11) book is a classic on this approach.

It is helpful and informative to give group diagnostic tests and/or an Individual Reading Inventory to each child to determine his instructional level and to know in what skill areas he needs help. The Bond-Ballow-Hoyt *Diagnostic Reading Tests* or *The Stanford Diagnostic Reading Test* are good examples of group tests to use. Analysis of the data collected will help you understand the strengths and weaknesses of each of your students. This information is necessary regardless of the reading approach you use.

It takes a creative and flexible teacher to do these things well. She must be cognizant of the sequential development of skills and recognize when the optimum time arises to present particular skills to the pupil.

What Is Your Role In The Individualized Reading Program?

Your role would be primarily that of consultant and resource person to your students, a manager of the classroom environment, and a supplier of materials. You would help pupils learn to plan, evaluate, and consider alternatives. You would provide students with ego support, give first aid when needed, and facilitate the learning environment so that students might direct their own learning.

You would meet the children individually or in groups for evaluation, ascertaining needs, and teaching skills when they were needed. You would guide children so they could grow creatively and learn at an exhilarating pace.

The success of your program will depend upon your diagnostic abilities in identifying children's needs in the areas of reading skills, selection of materials and in your ability to evaluate the pupil's progress.

How Does The Child Select An Appropriate Book For Individualized Reading?

Care must be taken to insure that each child is selecting books on his independent reading level. Veatch (11) says, by "Rule of Thumb," have the child choose a book on a topic he likes and have him open the book near the middle to a page with many words on it. Ask him to read it silently and when he comes to a word he doesn't know, he should put his thumb on the table. If he meets another he doesn't know he puts down his next finger, and so on. If he uses up all the fingers on one hand, that book is too hard for him. He should put it back and choose another one. The child's independent reading level is his instructional level.

Dolch (3) says that ideally, the child should not miss more than three words per page. If the books chosen are too hard, skipping will inevitably result and wrong habits will be cultivated.

The books should suit the purposes of each child either for his own enjoyment or for specific purposes worked out during a conference. Motivation results from meeting needs, interests or both.

Can Group Activity Be Utilized In The Individualized Reading Program?

Yes! According to Vite (12) and your authors, individual reading need not place limitations on good group experiences. There are many wholesome, meaningful, sociable, enjoyable and fruitful group experiences inherent in such programs. Some types of grouping suggested are: grouping for conference, social purposes, spontaneous social grouping, grouping for audience reading, grouping for skill needs. If more than one student needs to learn a skill, grouping is logical.

As Wilson (14) says, "Grouping makes sense only in terms of immediate purpose in an individualized approach, as in bringing a small group together to teach a certain skill."

How Much Time Should Be Devoted To Individual Conferences With Pupils? How Do You Know What Is Going On And Keep Track Of It?

You have student-teacher conferences lasting as little as three to five minutes daily, ten minutes a week, or more if the pupil needs more help. Spache (6) recommends two to four conferences per child per week. Some teachers meet this situation by making a schedule which insures that all pupils will have conferences in turn. Others offer a schedule sheet on which children may write their names when they feel the need for a conference or wish to report on a book they have read. A combination of these types of schedules may be more effective to meet the needs of the children.

You cannot keep everything in your head; so you need to keep simple recor[ds]. If the teacher follows Spache's (6) suggestions, she will collect five basic types of records for each child. These may be placed in a notebook , a card file, or a folder. The first records include the facts acquired from the school's cumulative record-keeping system. These should include the child's age, I.Q., mental age, reading interests, and scores from recent standardized and informal reading tests. A record of the child's instructional, independent, and potential reading levels will be obtained during the initial inventory conference or from initial testing. A third record will be that of his oral reading behaviors. A fourth record will contain an analysis of the pupil's oral reading errors as observed during the inventory conference and several subsequent conferences during which the child reads orally. The final set of records will include those notes that each teacher deems adequate for judging and guiding the progress of the pupils. These may include such items as titles of books read, degree of any type of comprehension shown, child's reaction to the book, plans for sharing his selections and the like.

On reporting to the teacher the child's record should include only the name of the book, the author, a brief comment and sometimes a notation about the size or length of the book. To truly individualize, each teacher, in cooperation with her students, must set up records that are informative yet simple to avoid consuming unnecessary time and energy.

Summary

If you are still with us, you now realize that we have reviewed much information concerning individualized reading. We have described what it is, its advantages and disadvantages, why it meets pupil needs, how you can get ready, and how you can run an individualized reading program. If you feel some eagerness, move forward and upward by trying this exciting approach to teaching reading. Should you discern no enthusiasm, release your finger grips and fall back into your rut. We are sorry to have bothered you.

SELECTED BIBLIOGRAPHY

1. Austin, Mary C. "Promising Practices in the Teaching of Reading." *The Florida Reading Quarterly*, (March, 1965), 2-8.
2. Crosby, Muriel. "Organization for Reading Instruction," *Elementary English*, XXXVII (March, 1960), 169-173.
3. Dolch, E.W. "Individualized Reading vs. Group Reading," *Elementary English*, XXXVII (December, 1961).
4. Johnson, Rodney H. " Individualized and Basal Primary Reading Programs," *Elementary English*, XXXXII (December, 1965), 902-904.
5. Johnson, Eleanor M. *Individualized Reading*. Department of School Services and Publications, Middletown, Connecticut.
6. Spache, George D. *Toward Better Reading*. Champaign: Gerrard Publishing Company, 1963.
7. Spache, George D. *Reading in the Elementary School*, Allyn and Bacon, Inc., Boston, 1967.
8. Spencer, Doris U. "Individualized First Grade Reading vs. a Basal Reader Program in Communities," *The Reading Teacher*, XIX (May, 1966), 595-600.
9. Spencer, Doris U. "Individualization Versus a Basal Reading Program in Rural Communities — Grade One and Two," *The Reading Teacher*, XXI (October, 1967) 11-17.
10. Talbert, Dorothy G. "The Relative Effectiveness of Two Approaches to the Teaching of Reading in Grade V," *The Reading Teacher*, XIX (December, 1965), 183-186.
11. Veatch, Jeanette, "A Reply to the Critics of Individualized Reading," *The Florida Reading Quarterly*, IV (December, 1967), 2-10.
12. Vite, Irene W. "Grouping Practices in Individualized Reading," *Elementary English*, XXXVIII (February, 1961), 91-98.
13. Wardord, Phyllis. "Individualized Reading in First Grade," *Elementary English*, XXXVII (January, 1960), 36-37.
14. Wilson, Richard C. *Individualized Reading. A Practical Approach*, Wm. C. Brown Book Co., Dubuque, 1965.

Reading instruction through the multi-station approach

MARILYN J. NAYLOR

CRUCIAL to teacher planning and effectiveness is the range of dissimilarity and similarity within the classroom. The realistic possibility of providing adequately for these differences within typical classrooms has been questioned. This is the report of a program in which these differences have become the springboard for unique developmental reading opportunities.

A century ago the assignment of children to grade levels was hailed as "the" way to reduce the range in a group and ensure teaching-learning success. As testing materials and analysis procedures became available to classroom teachers, the wide individual range within classes was revealed. Analyses of intelligence and achievement test results suggested classroom ranges equal to two-thirds of the median student age. Thus the teacher of twelve year olds might expect an eight year variation in measured ability and achievement (Cook and Clymer, 1962).

Intra-individual differences have frequently proven as striking as inter-individual variations (Goodlad, 1966). Hopes of attaining significant similarity through homogeneous grouping have not been fulfilled (Sartain, 1968). Promotion and retention policies have frequently proven more effective in creating social and behavioral problems than in reducing the academic range. Effective, challenging teaching has further increased this dissimilarity (Cook and Clymer, 1962).

Recent educational adjustments have favored the adaptation of the learning environment to the individual. Continuous progress, individually prescribed instructional programs are typical of this tailoring emphasis. The purpose of this article is to describe the initial phase of an evolving program designed to incorporate the strengths of numerous known approaches to meet the individual needs of intermediate grade students.

ASSUMPTIONS OF THE MULTI-STATION APPROACH

The multi-station approach—so named because materials

THE READING TEACHER, May 1971, vol. 24, no. 8, pp. 757-761.

are located at various learning areas or stations within the classroom—was designed to develop those basic reading skills needed by each student. Reading areas reflecting basic skills were identified as vocabulary, word recognition, comprehension, oral reading, application, and appreciation. Choices of organization, material, and method for each learning assignment resulted from continuous evaluation of these areas.

This program made several assumptions about readers and reading:

1. Each learner has a unique reading profile;
2. Adjustment can and should be made to the level, rate, material, method and organizational pattern most effective for each learner;
3. The learner should be personally and activity involved in reading activities throughout the reading period;
4. Self-direction, personal options and immediate feedback should be part of each program;
5. Individual assignments must be constantly revised through continuous evaluation;
6. There is no one best method of teaching reading to all children, nor need all instruction be teacher-centered;
7. Students are concerned about their progress and, given the opportunity, will share responsibility for their learning.

PREPARATION FOR THE PROGRAM

Preceding assignment to specific activities it was necessary to determine the specific strengths and weaknesses of each student. Individual informal reading inventories, group standardized tests, and cumulative records provided these data. Sight vocabulary, phonic knowledge, comprehension of literal and inferred meanings, oral reading, and personal reading interests were evaluated and analyzed.

On the basis of these preliminary data it was possible to arrange discussion groups and special skill groups mutually existent with pupil teams and individual study. The functioning of a student in these early assignments provided additional information concerning his optimal placement. Observation of the efficiency of various methods and materials confirmed or altered the initial prescription.

Basic to the organizational pattern was the desire that each student be actively and purposefully involved throughout the reading period. Each student had a scheduled reading period of approximately one hour per day. This hour was subdivided into twenty or thirty minute modules, accommodating from one to three station placements. These assignments were flexible, changing as initial needs diminished, and others became apparent.

Depending on specific requirements, weekly station listings accommodated opportunity for group discussion, teamed oral reading, individual study, specific skill instruction, and individual pupil-teacher conferences. Some time was provided each week for self-selected reading activities. School library and multi-media facilities were available to students daily.

To accommodate various modes of learning, several methods were available. These approaches included kinesthetic, linguistic, basal, language experience, programmed instruction, and individualized reading. Student operated multi-media offered direct and indirect learning opportunities.

Materials were chosen, adapted or designed to meet specific learning needs. Transparencies, tapes, filmstrips, records, and various game-type manipulative materials provided flexible reading involvement opportunities. Located in a specific area of the classroom, each station was identified and assigned by number.

Utilizing maximum student involvement, these materials were largely self-instructional and self-correcting. The advantages of immediate feedback and acceptance of responsibility far outweighed problems of incorrect grading. Levels of academic and social-emotional expectation were investigated for the child who could not accept personal errors.

PROGRAM IMPLEMENTATION

Once materials and assignments had been prepared, program implementation was gradual. Through demonstration, discussion and role playing, the total group was introduced to such multi-range materials as individualized reading and comprehension laboratories. Students were then gradually drawn from this nucleus for initiation into new stations. Using student-to-student explanation of new materials provided a check on adequacy of directions, while fostering positive student interaction.

Although constant supervision was provided by the teacher and student teacher, self responsibility and peer assistance were stressed. The teaching role included supportive assistance, observation, discussion group leadership and individual conferencing.

Ongoing evaluation was essential to individual prescription preparation. After initial placement, data were obtained from five sources: observation; daily progress; conferences; station-coordinated tasks; and periodic formal evaluation. Individual record folders, maintained by each student, reflected achievement in tasks of increasing difficulty. Thus the total program was self-evaluative as the presence or absence of growth at various stations was noted.

During weekly individual conferences, the student and teacher cooperatively evaluated progress, set goals and readjusted schedules. The attitude of the student toward various stations and his own progress reflected degrees of acceptance of himself and the program.

PROGRAM EVALUATION

Preliminary evaluation of the multi-station program was made in terms of the students, student teachers and teacher. Results were based on data obtained during the first complete year of operation, with data collection scheduled to continue. Lack of complete longitudinal data made comparison of growth rates difficult.

Individual grade equivalent scores on the *Iowa Tests of Basic Skills* for Fall, 1968 and Fall, 1969 were compared. Vocabulary development changes were positive for 96 per cent of the students, while 89 per cent recorded a gain in Paragraph Comprehension. The majority of those gains were from 1 to 1.9 grade levels.

Changes in student attitude and involvement were assessed more subjectively. Conference comments and attitude survey responses indicated a continuing preference for this type of reading experience, while acknowledging heavy demands on student effort. The lack of discipline problems suggested low student frustration. Both peer assistance and self reliance were increasingly noticeable.

Student teachers rated their experience as unusual and rewarding. The smaller ratio of large group instruction was balanced by the opportunity to gain familiarity with a wide variety of student groupings, methods and materials. Involvement of university students in mini-teaching and observation was minimally disruptive.

The teacher noted several improvements in her role. The frustration of requiring equal goals for unequal students was gone. The teacher-student relationship was increasingly positive. Busywork tasks were replaced by tasks of genuine and immediate importance. In short, the teacher had a chance to teach.

As in any evolving plan, much remains to be done. Refinements in evaluative techniques are needed. Materials and methods must be continually revised or developed. The purpose and the challenge continue—to meet the specific needs of individual students to the highest possible degree.

REFERENCES

Cook, W. W., and Clymer, T. Acceleration and retardation. Individualizing instruction. *Yearbook of the National Society for the Study of Education*, 1962, *61*, 179-208.

Goodlad, J. I. Diagnosis and prescription in educational practice. *Education Digest*, 1966, *31*, 8-11.

Sartain, H. W. The research base for individualizing reading instruction. Paper presented at the International Reading Association Conference, Boston, April, 1968.

SECTION VII

READING: DIAGNOSIS AND PRESCRIPTION

Diagnose the reading program before you diagnose the child

MORTON BOTEL
ALVIN GRANOWSKY

Professor of education at the University of Pennsylvania, IRA past president Morton Botel is the author of numerous reading texts, tests, and professional publications. Alvin Granowsky directs the Diagnostic Reading Center for Greensboro (North Carolina) City Schools.

SOME educators look at reading failure as the child's failure. This way of thinking explains our current involvement with individual diagnosis of the child's learning needs and prescription of specific materials, activities and instructional settings.

However, it would seem to be more productive first to examine the instructional program as a basic source of reading failure before attempting to diagnose and prescribe for deficits in the individual child.

We are not able today to tell how any given child learns best. No combination of tests presently available does that job. But, experience has shown that there are particular deficits in the learning environment that produce reading failure. These deficit conditions include a frozen instructional hierarchy in decoding, ho-hum stories, and dead-end questions.

Frozen hierarchy

It would be hard to find anyone today who is against helping children learn to decode at the earliest possible time. However, we also know that children are not pigeons. They cannot be placed in a controlled environment and paced through a single hierarchy of phonic rules. While this approach may be successful for some, it will result in failure for others. Imagine the speech failures that would occur if we used a frozen hierarchal approach of oral language patterns to teach all children to speak.

It is probable that children learn the important idea that letters

THE READING TEACHER, 1973, Vol. 26, pp. 563-565.

stand for sounds in a variety of ways—if they are allowed to use their own learning styles. Insistence on all children learning by any one basic method actually creates learning failures for some students. It is necessary, therefore, that the instructional program provide for a guided discovery of the connection between letter and sound patterns through diverse experiences. These include systematic presentation of spelling patterns, spelling pattern games, learning words and sentences the child wants to know, and reading stories (including those that play on spelling patterns). This variety of approaches provides the needed quantity and alternatives in materials and activities from which children can induce the needed rules—in their own way and in their own time.

Ho-hum stories

Reading as an activity apart from the story to be enjoyed or content to be learned is rather sterile and meaningless. Used to the excitement of television, Walt Disney movies and the emotion-filled traumas of their own lives, many children find the materials facing them in many basal readers relatively dull. They are materials to be read solely for the act of reading. Because of this fact, many students develop negative attitudes about reading. It's something that they have to do, like eating vegetables, rather than something they want to do. Salvation for these students often comes in encounters outside of the school with comic books, riddles or joke books — materials whose content excites them and makes them want to read.

Even at the first stages of speech, there is an impelling content to be communicated, causing the child to struggle with his first sounds and sentence forms. If the content to be communicated were dull and of little interest, there might be many children who would never become adept in speech.

Admittedly, many teachers attempt to bring "interesting" materials into the classroom. But, "interesting for whom" is a very basic question. It's a rare book or activity that excites all children, or needs to be experienced by everyone. Variety of reading content, coming from a quantity of inexpensive books and activities available to all students is needed. While we don't know which book will excite a child, he does. The point is to make books and activities available, and provide time and encouragement. In this setting, children will read many books, even books they are supposedly not able to read.

Dead-end questions

Anyone who has spent an afternoon with a child at a zoo or circus knows the excited reactions that arise from within the child himself—what we may term the organic response. The questions, especially, are endless and seemingly disconnected. But this is the way children think and learn in a natural setting. They need to talk a lot to get in touch with their thinking and feeling.

Not having the patience or ability to observe the logic in the child's approach, we fall into traps of imposing a more "logical" or "productive" way of thinking on the child. This practice often results only in ending the child's interest in the discussion. If we don't concern ourselves with the child's perceptions and questions, if we regard his thoughts as trivial, if we attempt to shortcut the child's "seeming" ramblings and fumblings toward understanding by simply forcing him into the adult's logic, then the child is just as likely to turn us off as we have turned him off.

Teachers realize the need for open-ended questions which promote discussion, thought and involvement. They know the limitations of close-ended questioning eliciting a response that draws only from the memory. These insights represent real growth in our understanding of children's thinking and personal motivation. The open-ended question, however, can also lead to a dead end unless it fits the pupil's frame of reference. The key concern should be: What does the answer or discussion supply for the child? How does it fit into his perceptions and understandings of the world?

In short, open-ended questions in themselves will not achieve the environment that leads to pupil involvement and growth of thought and language. The teacher must also set up interaction situations based on the reading experiences that stimulate organic responses from within children, allowing a flow of observations and feelings to emerge in speech and writing.

The way to arrange the classroom setting to provide the quantity of time needed by each pupil for this language flow is in small interaction groups of three to five students. For the teacher accustomed to directed reading activity of the basal reader, this concept may be difficult to visualize. Today, however, new interaction-oriented reading materials have been designed to make the teacher management of this process easy to facilitate.

Check your program

In conclusion, many students are able to overcome the minimal mileage program characterized by a frozen hierarchy for learning decoding skills, ho-hum stories and activities, and dead-end questions. These children usually bring to the reading setting sufficient strength in the other language arts areas to operate successfully. Combined with personal motivation, that strength allows them to overcome meager instructional offering. Many students, however, are not able to rise above the minimal mileage instructional setting.

The basic prescription of a quantity of materials, activities and settings for the reading program can well bring the cure for many learning failures. These include 1) providing a variety of approaches for helping children induce their own decoding strategies, 2) providing a wide selection of exciting activities and stories from which children make choices, and 3) providing many opportunities in interaction settings where children talk and write about their reading experience as a basis for getting in touch with their thinking and feeling.

Diagnosis and prescription are solid concepts. We don't question their worth. We simply suggest that before we focus on the notion of diagnosis of children and prescription for their learning failures, we first diagnose the instructional program.

Evaluation and reading: perspective '72

A. N. HIERONYMUS

Hieronymus presents an overview of current issues and answers in the area of evaluation, with an eye toward further progress in the 70's. Professor of education and psychology at the University of Iowa, he coauthored the Iowa Tests of Basic Skills.

IN READING, the problems and issues in evaluation closely parallel those in instruction, because evaluation is an integral part of the instructional process. In a good instructional system, it is difficult to determine where instruction leaves off and evaluation begins. Both teacher and pupil are constantly monitoring the effects of their efforts.

Many generations of teachers, authorities in curriculum and method, researchers, and measurement specialists have worked jointly toward a common goal of improving instruction in reading. In spite of efforts by a host of dedicated and creative professionals, there is little consensus on a common curriculum or a universal instructional model. To the contrary, the result has been diversity—diversity of goals, methods and materials, and procedures. While such a state of affairs is not very satisfying to those who want simple solutions to complex problems, diversity of attack holds the greatest promise for progress. It is also the sign of a live and dynamic profession.

The purpose of measurement is to provide information which can be used in improving instruction. Measurement has value to the extent that it results in better decisions which directly affect the pupil. In general, these decisions apply to the selection of objectives and learning procedures, to the creation of the physical and social environment in which reading is taught, and to how the teacher attends to various needs and characteristics of her pupils. Reorientation of the role of measurement in

THE READING TEACHER, 1972, Vol. 26, pp. 264-267.

relation to reading has resulted in the development of a variety of instruments to serve a variety of purposes, all of which lead directly to the improvement of instruction in reading. Among these purposes:

1. to determine the pupil's level of reading development in order to better adapt materials and instructional procedures to his needs and abilities

2. to diagnose specific qualitative strengths and weaknesses in a pupil's reading development

3. to indicate the extent to which individual pupils have specific readiness skills and abilities needed to begin reading instruction or to proceed to the next step in the instructional sequence

4. to provide information useful in making administrative decisions in grouping or programing to better provide for individual differences

5. to diagnose strengths and weaknesses in group performance (class, building, or system) which have implications for change in curriculum, instructional procedures, or emphasis

6. to determine relative effectiveness of alternate methods of reading instruction and the conditions which determine effectiveness of various procedures

7. to assess effects of experimentation and innovation

8. to monitor constantly the progress of individual students with respect to specific behavioral objectives in order to make immediate instructional decisions

9. to monitor constantly the effectiveness of instructional procedures in order to modify them as the need arises

10. to provide a model for the pupil to show what is expected of him and to provide feedback which will indicate his progress toward goals which are suitable for him.

It is obvious that no single test can ever be designed to accomplish all of these purposes. Different kinds of evaluation procedures are implied by each purpose.

Issues and answers

Approaches to measurement center mainly along two lines:

1. development of measuring instruments designed to implement a concept of reading development as a continuous process in which individual differences in readiness, expectations, and needs are recognized, and differences in rates of progress are maximized;

2. development of measuring instruments designed to define specific, common, immediate behavioral objectives; to monitor the effectiveness of procedures designed to attain the objectives; and to determine when the objectives have been mastered and when the pupil is ready for the next step in the instructional sequence.

These two approaches are not mutually exclusive, nor do they necessarily conflict. Rather theirs is a complementary relationship; each is essential to improvement of instruction.

Should a reading test be independent of method of instruction or intimately related to method? Should a test be sensitive or relatively insensitive to intervention?

This issue relates to immediacy of goals in reading. All of us have certain ultimate or long range goals which we hope to attain in the next year, or in the next ten years, or in our lifetime. We also have more or less immediate goals for the next hour, week, or semester.

We need two kinds of measures. One reflects progress toward the ultimate objectives of reading. Ideally, this first test contains 1) passages representative of the whole range of reading materials which a pupil at a given level of development could reasonably be expected to comprehend; and 2) questions which represent the *extent* of his understanding. This test should be relatively independent of instructional methods used to develop understanding. Such a test is useful not only in assessing individual pupil progress, but also in providing evidence on the general effectiveness of method.

The other type of measure is designed to measure attainment of immediate goals. Built to specifications of highly specific, immediate behavioral objectives, this second test corresponds very closely to method. In fact, the test is a *part* of method in that information from the test is used to monitor and modify method continuously. It is thus highly sensitive to intervention.

Should tests be designed to emphasize qualitative individual differences, or to determine mastery of common objectives?

This issue is closely related to the first. Many objectives must be mastered to a relatively high degree of proficiency before instruction can proceed. However, there are many higher order concepts which can be attained only by the most talented pupils. Types of learning should be differentiated and considered before instruction begins.

Should the same tests be used with all pupils, or should testing be individualized?

Teachers often underestimate the extent to which they provide for individual differences. It is impossible to treat every child exactly alike; teachers inevitably set different expectations for different pupils. Expectations are by nature judgmental, and involve consideration of both objective and subjective evidence. Procedures teachers use in evaluating students, both formal and informal, also differ. When the instructional emphasis of one student is on decoding skills, and of another on higher order comprehension processes, the evaluation procedures are, of necessity, different.

One application of individualized testing has evolved from the use of instructional systems such as Individually Prescribed Instruction, and Project PLAN. In such systems, children work toward different objectives at different rates, and require different tests to monitor progress.

Today's standardized tests are used to implement a nongraded or continuous progress philosophy of instruction. Such tests are constructed to represent a wide range in reading proficiency. Each pupil is assigned a test level most appropriate to his needs and level of reading development. Thus, different pupils in the same classroom may be taking several different levels of the test at the same time —tests which are more relevant, more accurate, and less frustrating than tests intended for the "average" pupil in the "grade".

Other promising developments include tests for children of different linguistic or cultural backgrounds, and for those whose developmental level in reading is markedly different from their age and interest levels.

Should reading readiness tests be primarily diagnostic or predictive?

Reading readiness tests have proven useful practice for a variety of purposes. Present emphasis in interpretation is not so much on prediction, or on determining whether a child is or is not ready, but on the extent to which he has acquired the specific readiness skills necessary to further progress.

Should diagnostic tests be primarily descriptive or prescriptive?

This issue is similar to the last. Reading may be measured and described in terms of different subtests or traits which may be represented in a profile. One approach to the organization of a diagnostic test battery is primarily statistical, and is intended to maximize the reliability of measurement of trait differences. The other approach is largely through judgment—the nature of each subtest prescribes the action to be taken to remedy the particular deficiency. Ideally, diagnostic test batteries have both characteristics. They should provide accurate diagnosis which is of maximum usefulness in followup.

Who should be accountable? To whom? For what?

Whereas accountability is a concept of the 70's, it has always been with us. Teachers have generally regarded their responsibilities seriously and have tried in the face of indifference to communicate problems and progress to parents and to the community as a whole.

The most important aspect of accountability is the teacher's responsibility to the child. This involves getting to know the child—his needs, readiness, strengths and weaknesses, level of mental and educational development, interests, learning styles, and so forth. It also involves knowledge of methods and materials and the ability to match them to the characteristics of the child.

What of the future? Progress will depend, as it has in the past, on the ability of those representing the various specialties — curriculum, instruction, and evaluation—to communicate and cooperate. We are of the same profession and we share a common goal.

Criterion referenced measurement: an alternative

JASON MILLMAN

A familiar name in testing and evaluation, Jason Millman is professor of educational research methodology at Cornell University. He formerly edited the Journal of Educational Measurement *and* Educational Researcher.

SOME school tests are tests of *typical* performance; others are tests of *maximum* performance. Interest, attitude, and personality inventories are included in the former category and will not be discussed here. Maximum performance tests can be further subdivided into diagnostic, norm referenced (NR), and criterion referenced (CR) tests.

Diagnostic tests contain items intended to discriminate between individuals who have some learning deficiency (for example, letter reversals) and those who do not. NR tests contain items intended to discriminate more able students from less able ones. Standardized reading tests and those teacher-made tests used as a basis for assigning school marks almost invariably fall into this category. Since the purpose of NR measures is to discriminate among students, test questions that all students can answer correctly or questions so hard that no student can answer are of no value. Rather, the questions used on such tests should have moderate difficulty and be answered correctly more frequently by those students judged to be higher achievers or more able.

Although test experts do not agree on a single definition of *criterion referenced* tests, all variants have in common their emphasis, in interpretation, on what a child can do relative to the subject matter of the test. Unlike NR tests, in which scores get meaning from norms indicating how well other students have performed on a test, CR measurement meaning comes from a comparison of the student's

THE READING TEACHER, 1972, Vol. 26, pp. 278-281.

performance relative to the skills being assessed by the test questions.

Perhaps the most fruitful concept of a CR test, also called a domain referenced test, is one whose questions are a representative sample from some *identifiable and limited domain.* A sight vocabulary test composed of a representative sample of all words in a given reading book presented out of context would be an example of a domain referenced test. In this example a child's test score would represent an estimate of all the words in the book he can read out of context.

There exist several other notions of what a CR measure is. For a very few, such measures are synonymous with mastery tests in which the test questions measure those very important facts and skills which all students need to learn. For others, any test is CR if it has a criterion, by which is meant some standard or passing score. For most people, a CR test is defined not by the composition of the questions but by the interpretation given to the scores of such tests. With NR measures, a student's score is compared with those of others taking the test; with CR measures as defined in this paragraph, performance is judged against a specified criterion score without reference to the distribution of scores of others.

It follows that if a competency interpretation of a test score is to be possible, the questions must measure a restricted set of skills. A CR test of general reading is not possible because, from a person's total score on such a test, the teacher would not be able to identify what the child can and cannot do.

Thus questions on a CR test are chosen because they represent examples of a given task which the teacher wants to determine if the child can accomplish. In contrast with NR measures, CR test questions may properly be selected without regard to their difficulty level or ability to discriminate among examinees.

Which type of test is best?

The answer to the "is best" question depends on the purpose of the testing. When a child has a specific learning problem, a diagnostic test can be helpful. For example, if a perceptual problem is suspected as the cause of a reading disability, a series of tests can be given in an effort to pinpoint the difficulty.

Although perhaps overused, there are definitely times when NR testing is valuable. Teacher-made tests composed of questions selected on the basis of their difficulty or discrimination power indicate how a student's performance compares with that of others in the class and thus are capable of yielding local norms. Standardized tests with national norms indicate how the student's performance compares with students on whom the test was standardized. Although one must be careful in interpretation, NR tests do provide a basis for judging whether a student has gained in achievement as much as other children and whether the child has achieved or is achieving at a level expected on the basis of his measured scholastic aptitude.

We do live in a competitive society. When demand for certain programs or other benefits exceeds available resources, decisions are necessary. Discrimination, even among young children, must occasionally be made. NR tests, constructed to maximize the sensitivity with which individual differences are measured, are best for such purposes.

When are CR tests best? Since CR tests are usually composed of groups of questions designed to measure particular instructional objectives, they are ideal for the situation in which a teacher wants to know if a student has acquired a particular skill or knowledge. Many of us hope that decisions about future instruction are made on the basis of what a child can do now. CR information seems indispensable to making such instructional decisions. This seems especially critical in a skill area such as reading, in which later tasks often depend upon having more basic skills. CR measures provide the needed assessment of these prerequisite skills. As a by-product, it forces attention on instructional objectives and on the specific student behaviors and skills which the teacher seeks to develop.

Grading

The distinctions between and roles of CR and NR tests are highlighted when the question of school marks is considered. Traditional grades are devices for comparing the performance among children. Teacher-made tests which discriminate among the achievements of students are well suited for the purpose of assigning such grades. Going, say, from a grade of B to a grade of A would indicate progress. Since each grade, such as A, is given to a relatively fixed proportion of the students, few children are able to earn higher and higher school marks without other children receiving lower grades. Traditional grades are poor indicators of the progress a child may be making. They are devices for *ranking*, not *rating*.

Another approach to grading involves reporting to students and their parents which instructional objectives of the curriculum have been achieved. When CR measurement is used to guide and monitor the instructional program, it is a logical next step to have the learners' grades consist of check marks opposite instructional objectives which indicate which skills and understandings have been acquired. As more skills are learned, more check marks (with appropriate dates) are entered, and the progress which has occurred is made very visible. Such a reporting scheme has been described in more detail elsewhere by the author (1970) and by Airasian and Madaus (1972). Some reading programs (for example SRA Reading Laboratory) use a similar approach.

Are CR tests available?

Some existing reading series have CR tests built into them for purposes of assessing student progress. The "check tests" of the SRA Reading Laboratory are such an example. Infrequently, some subtests of standardized tests can be used as CR tests (for example, the oral reading tasks of the Standard Reading Inventory, 1966). The Instructional Objectives Exchange[1] is now developing an extensive set of CR tests in reading from which a school can select those which match its instructional objectives. CR tests are used by one firm[2] in its materials to improve the teaching of reading and to evaluate reading instruction. Educational

Testing Service (1971 p. 2), as part of the Right to Read effort, is developing criterion referenced test items ". . . predictive of competent performance on a set of adult reading tasks selected to have favorable returns to the individual and to society in general."

Few would argue against the claim that every child has the right to read. CR tests can play an important role in assessing whether each child is enjoying that right and in guiding future instructional decisions made on the child's behalf.

Footnotes

1. P.O. Box 24095, Los Angeles 90024.
2. Instructional Appraisal Services, P.O. Box 24821, Los Angeles 90024.

References

Airasian, Peter W. and Madaus, George F. "Criterion-Referenced Testing in the Classroom." *Measurement in Education*, Vol. 3 (May 1972), pp. 1-8.

Educational Testing Service. "ETS Takes Part in Nation Right to Read Effort." *ETS Developments*, Vol. 18 (Spring 1971), p. 2.

Millman, Jason. "Reporting Student Progress: A Case for a Criterion-Referenced Marking System." *Phi Delta Kappan*, Vol. 52 (Dec. 1970), pp. 226-30.

Criterion referenced tests—let the buyer beware!

GRAYCE A. RANSOM

The author directs the USC Reading Centers in Los Angeles. As part of her long-range study for the Ransom Reading System, she has researched for the past eight years in public schools to devise components.

IT SEEMS that a new band wagon has appeared on the American reading scene. The Flesch-Phonics and other "saviors" have turned a corner, and the performance objectives, detailed test oracles are here. How are teachers to make sound judgments in the decision making that now occurs in their midst with rapid acceleration? As with any problem, it is wise first to face the fundamental issues involved.

The first issue centers on the performance objectives which are at the heart of the tests. Are these objectives carefully and practically conceived, set in a well-founded theory of learning, part of a well-delineated model of the reading process? Do the objectives represent a true progression from early learning experience spread across all skill-attitude strands, spiraling into good reading attitudes, skills and behaviors as a final outcome (in other words, a skill-attitude reading taxonomy)? Terminology for such strands is not as important as the fact that the undergirding objectives must reflect all of the important aspects of learning to read, liking to read, reading to learn processes.

Delineation of performance objectives that represent pathways to capable and eager readership is only a first step. Then, skillful judgment must be used about which behaviors, skills, and attitudes can best be assessed by paper and pencil tests. Such careful spelling out becomes the framework or overall map for good cri-

THE READING TEACHER, 1972, Vol. 26, pp. 282-285.

terion referenced tests. *A good framework for reading will always have more delineated skills, attitudes, and behaviors than are reflected in its written tests.* In other words, criterion referenced tests are only a part of the diagnostic approach essential in giving children appropriate challenge, involvement, success, and joy in the process of learning.

Types of assessment

There are, of course, many levels and types of diagnosis to be used by classroom teachers. The most important thrust is the gaining of accurate information about the learning needs of each pupil. At primary reading levels, this implies assessment of breadth and depth of concept formation, the child's facility in listening and speaking, visual and auditory perception, phoneme-grapheme understandings, and perceptual-motor skills relevant to the reading process.

Diagnostic approaches imply at all levels the need for usable information about the cognitive processes of each child. Is he a slow learner? Highly creative? Which modalities are favored for learning?

Since a learner is one who has a positive set for acquiring new understandings, skills or enjoyment, diagnostic and prescriptive teaching implies accurate assessment of the child's feelings and interests. Informal picture and story interpretations aid in achieving this goal. Can we help a child find a match of instructional material to his feelings about himself and his world? Cloze tests and application of readability formulas will help the teacher and child find appropriate utilitarian, pleasure, reference, and instructional reading sources.

As soon as suitable instruction is in progress, the question of skill mastery must be faced. Where does each child stand in vocabulary and concept development? In decoding skills? In linguistic understanding of print? In levels of comprehension as he reacts to print with thought and feeling? In adaptive reading? In reference and study skills?

Need for specific answers to these questions has led to development of informal and formal batteries of criteria based tests as well as standardized diagnostic tests. In addition, the classroom teacher can gain much insight into each child's strengths and weaknesses by interpreting his "miscues" in oral reading while pupil pairs are reading to each other in the instructional period. Other informal diagnostic procedures are outlined by DeBoer (1970) and Leibert (1971).

We then come to some other crucial questions about criterion referenced tests. Will mastery of such a succession of specific tests make adequate and *eager* readers? Our answer is "perhaps"— if other conditions are right. There are some real concerns in this area. How can an objective test assess the spirit of a child as he gets turned on about one book and not by another? Can it tell us about prescriptions involving many manipulative modes so needed by some of our culturally different youngsters? Equally crucial: Is the plan of administration of such tests so lacking in realistic classroom application that most teachers attempting to utilize them would be crowded beyond endurance?

Critical considerations

Then, a potpourri of cautions: vocabulary differences and difficulties, matters of balance, questioning about effective implementation. In other words, many batteries of reading support systems now appearing on the market are woefully lacking in evidence of wrestling with ways in which a testing program can be well-related to content and classroom management of a total communication skills program.

The content of test items should also be open to question. Do the items truly test what they purport to measure? Types of questions should be carefully analyzed for adherence to the type of task involved, as well as suitability of level.

Also relevant are possible vocabulary differences between the tests and the rest of the reading program, especially at primary levels. No matter how much we honor decoding—and rightfully so—there are certain words and morphemes of our language which demand instant recognition. In a test emphasizing comprehension, a struggle to decode beclouds comprehension assessment.

Other critical aspects are the physical and mechanical elements of the proposed tests. Even though the tests accurately embody carefully considered objectives, physical aspects of the tests may raise blocks to true measurement of reading skills. Some typical relevant questions are: Does the average child easily get lost in trying to follow page and test sequences? Are there simple aids built into the tests which help him maintain his place? Do examiners' directions reflect true understanding of children's ability to listen and follow directions? Do directions include confusing conceptual terms not understood by numbers of children who are responding?

A deep concern about format revolves around the use of efficient planning as an aid to finding and recording test results. Some test batteries do not incorporate features that would save time and money, such as 1) answer sheets and scoring masks; 2) provision for use of small optical-scanning test-scoring devices; 3) planning for possibilities of tying in with available computer facilities.

There are other cost factors. Are the test booklets reusable? If there are carbon recording devices on the test, how much does one pay for them? Actually the total question of costs must be raised in relation to balance with costs of the rest of the reading program.

But probably the greatest stumbling block of all is the "dangling" involved in most criterion referenced systems about the teacher's *use* of the results of skill testing. Instructions with a number of tests on the market make few comments on how to incorporate realistically useful profiles into the everyday life of the school.

As a teacher, I would quarrel with the concept that all skill experiences must be done in solitary fashion in order to be individualized or personalized. Rooms of children working along in lonely, isolated paths of drill-test-drill do not portray the same picture as the enthusiastic learning to be seen in classrooms with flexible skill groups engaged in multimedia and multimodal experiences. The author's research over several years has repeatedly shown the values of small flexible skill groups and joyous interaction and involvement. It has also shown that teachers need much help in effectively managing such arrangements.

Each teacher should ask herself: "What are the grouping needs of my particular classroom? What common skill needs are identified for small groups? How can we provide for communication of feelings? How can we organize to stimulate problem solving? Creative experiences in art, music, writing, speaking, dramatics? What curriculum objectives are best reached through use of pupil pairs, crossgrade tutoring and other working teams?" And as district or school personnel look at reading support systems, the question should be asked, "How would this extraneous system help *the teacher* with classroom management?"

Conclusions

During the past eight years the author has completed several series of field studies in diagnostic and prescriptive teaching of reading in nine school districts serving 13,500 elementary students (K-8) and 450 teachers. Several conclusions from these studies are relevant to our closing thoughts:

1. Diagnostic and prescriptive components were used successfully for varied developmental reading programs (linguistic, programed reading, basal reader, language-experience, i.t.a.).

2. Teachers need to be assured that easily accessible, skill-labeled varieties of prescriptive materials are available, in order for them to become enthusiastic about diagnostic materials.

3. When teachers experience the furnishing of well-organized, varied media, their creativity is stimulated and desire to share new ideas with others is tremendously increased.

4. Most teachers need help with classroom organization — flexible skill grouping—before they can fully implement diagnostic and prescriptive components of teaching reading.

5. Periodic group testing of the total school, using criterion referenced placement tests, accomplished by each teacher testing one level of the tests, is a more manageable plan for classrooms without aides than room based or completely individualized procedures. Informal administration of one-skill mastery tests works out well on the basis of small group needs.

6. Children are greatly aided in prescriptive learning by use of multimedia learning stations.

7. Provision of a resource teacher for leadership and demonstration in all of the above areas has been of inestimable value.

8. Prospective users of a diagnostic-prescriptive system have been greatly aided by viewing research schools in action, as well as participating in high involvement workshops.

9. The use of diagnostic-prescriptive procedures with provision of varied learning modes and media has decreased need for special education classes, reduced percentages of absenteeism and vandalism, and has increased numbers of involved, enthusiastic learners and their parents.

References

DeBoer, Dorothy L., Ed. *Reading Diagnosis and Evaluation.* Newark, Del.: International Reading Association, 1970.

Leibert, Robert E., Ed. *Diagnostic Viewpoints in Reading.* Newark, Del.: International Reading Association, 1971.

SECTION VIII

READING FOR THE "DIFFERENT LEARNER"— THE MINORITY STUDENT, THE BI-LINGUAL STUDENT AND THE DISADVANTAGED STUDENT

Seven fallacies: reading retardation and the urban disadvantaged beginning reader

S. ALAN COHEN
THELMA COOPER

An authority on learning problems of the socially disadvantaged, S. Alan Cohen is director of the Educational Systems Division, Random House, Inc. Thelma Cooper, a doctoral candidate at Yeshiva University, is an executive assistant for the New York City Board of Education. Their article emphasizes that quality teaching can overcome the stumbling blocks of a disadvantaged background.

RESEARCH findings consistently indicate that some of our most cherished excuses for not reaching Black and Puerto Rican urban children are fallacious. This report summarizes research done at Yeshiva University's Reading and Language Arts Center and elsewhere on seven fallacies about language and its relationship to beginning reading instruction.

FALLACY #1: *Urban Black children tend to be less verbal than middle class children.*

What does it mean to be less verbal? Study after study has demonstrated that amount of verbal output depends upon the social context in which the speaker finds himself (Horner and Gussow, 1970; Labov, Cohen, Robbins and Lewis, 1968; Labov, 1969). This is true of Whites as well as Blacks. Houston for example, describes how Florida Black children verbalized less in "formal situations" than in "informal situations." One classic demonstration of the reinforcing effect of social context was Salzinger's clown puppet whose nose lit up each time a kindergarten child talked to it (1962). That simple positive reinforcement was enough to control the speech rate of the children. Socioeconomic status (SES) was, of course, a discriminant of language rate and quality, but the important point was that children became more verbal when they perceived the

THE READING TEACHER, 1972, Vol. 26, pp. 38-45.

social context as positively reinforcing of verbal output. The child is the same organism, but the environment that provides certain kinds of positive reinforcers is different from the environment in which these reinforcers are absent.

Like other fallacies in the behavioral sciences, this fallacy is related to the kinds of measurement certain researchers use to observe verbal output. The nature and conditions of the observation technique are at least as powerful as the phenomenon observed in determining the research findings. Thus, for example, intelligence is what the researcher measures on a WAIS in a test booth, and it may be barely related to making an intelligent business decision. In a similar vein, reading may be performance in a classroom with a soft lead pencil making dark lines on an IBM answer sheet ancillary to a test booklet. It is not, in this case, a visceral response to the centerspread of this month's *Mad Magazine*. And being verbal is talking a lot to an authority figure in a school setting that is often hostile to the talker.

No wonder Labov *et al* (1968) found verbal capacities in urban Blacks far above what previous investigators found. He changed the social context (the contingencies) in which he assessed verbal output. He measured language in peer groups outside home and school. He reports that the urban Black child participates in a highly "verbal subculture where he is involved in verbal stimulation and verbal contests from morning to night."

Nonverbal indeed! Perhaps a better explanation would be that people who find themselves in a threatening, degrading social context tend to keep their mouths shut. When the environment provides positive reinforcement of verbal output, the organism is verbal; when it provides negative reinforcement, the organism shuts up. That's not nonverbal behavior. That's *smart* behavior.

FALLACY #2: *There is little verbal interaction between the disadvantaged child and his mother or other adults who are psychologically significant to him.*

Most of these conclusions were based on inferences from studies of institutionalized children (Goldfarb, 1955; Rheingold, 1956; Spitz, 1945). This overextension from urban disadvantaged conditions to institutional conditions may not be racist so much as it is just plain unfortunate.

More substantive is Baratz's criticism of the fallacy (1970b). She points out that this fallacy, like so many psychological and educational conclusions, is based on correlational rather than experimental studies. Kagan (1968) reports that urban Black children get as much or even more verbal stimulation than White middle class children.

No matter. We need simply to read Horner's study (Horner and Gussow, 1970) to throw out most of the previous literature on this point. Once again the issue is what was observed under what conditions. Horner sewed a button-size CIA-type radio transmitter into the linings of preschool urban Black children's clothes and simply recorded the typical day's verbal intercourse. No one has ever documented language production in such a natural, "real life" state without effects of observer intrusion. From this study we can conclude with maximum assurance that urban Black preschoolers have enormous amounts of verbal interaction with adults who are psychologically significant in their lives.

FALLACY #3: *Black English is a substandard, inferior form of Standard English.*

Black English exists. Without belaboring the psychodynamics involved in critics who deny its existence as an identifiable language form, it is, nevertheless, disconcerting to some of us to witness the passionate denial of some Black educators that a legitimate Black English — not a Southern dialect — exists. Baratz (1969a, 1969b, 1969c), Labov *et al* (1968, 1969a, 1969b) and Stewart (1969) have documented this language form, but no one has done a more scholarly and readable description of Black English than Dillard (1970). The authors' own work in the Cape Cod area of Massachusetts with Blacks who did not trace their ancestry to the South and with Black children all over the country indicates that the incidence of certain syntactic patterns in Black children is quite high, and that these patterns are Black, not Southern.

The degree of incidence, however, is not at issue in considering this fallacy. What is at issue is the fallacy that Black children speak an inferior, error-ridden form of "low" English. Assuming a close relationship between language and cognition, that inferior form would contribute to poor cognitive development. Ironically, however, if Dillard and our own observations are reliable — that Black English is prevalent in young Black children — then Black English would result in high cognitive development. Why? Because Black English is at least as complex as Standard English and in some respects markedly more sophisticated than Standard as evidenced by the young child's correct use of the extended duration form of predication described under Fallacy 4, below. In other words, the young Black child's nonstandard form, when that form is Black English, is a well-ordered, highly structured, highly developed, sophisticated language system.

FALLACY #4: *The mismatch between Black English (BE) syntax and Standard English (SE) syntax requires the Black child to translate written SE into spoken BE. That translation process increases the opportunity for a communications breakdown. Therefore, beginning reading books for Blacks should be written in BE to minimize that breakdown (Baratz, 1970a; Goodman, 1969; Stewart, 1969).*

So many absurdities abound in this position. Almost all of them derive from a misassumption implicitly made by some linguists: language output is a close approximation of language input. That error is not unique to linguists; reading specialists have made the same misassumption for decades. They assume that a child's oral recitation is a direct reflection of what he decodes (reads). Reading diagnosticians call this operation "an oral reading test."

Certainly encoding and decoding are related, but not directly. On the aural-oral communications level, Baratz unwittingly demonstrated this point in her study (Baratz, 1969a) when she asked Blacks to repeat what she said. Black subjects translated Baratz's SE into BE, and what she demonstrated was the Blacks' ability to decode and understand SE. Proof of their ability to comprehend was their ability to translate SE into BE. Some kinds of subtle meaning mismatches showed up, but they involved high level tense changes that would not make a difference at the beginning reading stage.

On the visual-to-oral communications level we see the same process. A Black child may orally recite, "they Black" for the written message *They are Black.* That translation proves his ability to get the written message which is, after all, what reading is really about. This is linguistically analogous to the American child who takes a written page of French and recites it in English. He is proving his ability to read French. In fact, he does not have to answer comprehension questions as would be required in an English-to-English oral reading task. French-to-English direct translation implies some sort of phonic decoding and demonstrated comprehension, while English-to-English oral reading demonstrates phonic decoding but leaves open the question of comprehension which is why we ask him "comprehension questions." In other words, the oral reader could be a "word caller" but the translator must be a "comprehender."

That some reading teachers confuse how the Black child speaks with how he reads is not sufficient reason for writing basal readers in BE. Perhaps a better solution is to reeducate teachers.

Second, the kinds of meaning changes that occasionally occur in SE to BE translation do not make a difference in light of the kinds of comprehension demands schools make on beginning readers. The mismatches in meaning and communications among "He is my dog," "He my dog," and "He be my dog" will not matter in Scott Foresman basal readers and even in "fat cat sat on a hat" basals. The BE use of "be" in the third sentence represents an extended duration which becomes a comprehension problem in Aristotle's *Poetics* but not in *Dick and Jane*.

Third, the syntax of linguistic and sight preprimers and early readers is markedly dissonant from the oral language of middle class children as well as low SES Black children. If we use the "syntax mismatch" theory to explain low SES Black children's reading retardation, then we should expect to see a similar problem with White middle class children. We do not see that. (Weber, 1970)

Fourth, most Black and Puerto Rican urban children are exposed to SE consistently and early in life. TV and their teachers give them more or less SE models, and while they may not be intensive enough to change encoding patterns, they are certainly intensive enough to train their auditory decoding abilities.

We could, of course, rationalize basal readers in BE to achieve a Hawthorne effect or to get teachers to accept BE as a legitimate sophisticated version of English. But if we do this, let us recognize that results of this technique would derive from "novelty" rather than linguistic factors, in which case we might consider a less expensive novelty to achieve an equal effect. Perhaps we could try better methodology before we burden the world with yet another version of *Dick and Jane*.

FALLACY #5: *The disadvantaged urban child's deficient conceptual and usable vocabulary interferes with his learning to read in the beginning grades.*

Plenty of evidence exists to demonstrate that lower SES children have more deficient vocabularies than middle class children (Figurel, 1964; John and Goldstein, 1964). But it does not necessarily follow that these deficiencies interfere with beginning reading success. Indeed, our investigations of this issue demonstrated that to the contrary, urban Black children have sufficient conceptual and usable vocabulary to handle the materials we use in schools to teach them to read in the beginning grades. Cohen and Kornfeld (1970) discovered that most previous studies of Black disadvantaged children's usable vocabularies underestimated their verbal repertoire. Nevertheless, given these conservative, underestimated vocabularies, a vocabulary analysis of the most widely used beginning reading books showed that urban Black disadvantaged children had sufficient vocabulary to handle those materials. Even that underestimated assessment of vocabulary matched, pretty well, the vocabulary in their reading books.

FALLACY #6: *If we improve oral language patterns of disadvantaged children we will be able to teach them to read better.*

Wrong again! Rystrom tells us so, not once but twice (1968; 1970). First in California and then in Georgia, he trained young children in "good" oral language. And in both studies the trained pupils did no better in reading than the untrained.

Of course the language we read and write is similiar to the language we speak. But how we speak is not directly related to how we read, and if one needs more evidence to be convinced see Martin (1955), Winter (1957), Wilson (1938), Bougere (unpublished), Strickland (1962), Labov (1969b), Fleming (1968) and, in summary, Weintraub (1968).

FALLACY #7: *Poor articulation contributes to auditory discrimination deficiencies and, therefore, to deficiencies in learning phonic skills among disadvantaged urban Black and Puerto Rican children.*

We often forget that low SES, independent of ethnicity, correlates with poor performance across the behavioral spectrum. So it is no surprise to find that urban Black disadvantaged children perform poorly on tests of auditory discrimination (Cohen, 1968). However, the conclusion that this discrimination deficiency is causally related to urban Black children's "misarticulations" is not justified by the data. Studies at Yeshiva University's Reading and Language Arts Center indicate that dialect and articulation, an encoding (output) behavior, and discrimination of word sounds, a decoding (input) behavior, are not causally linked.

Investigating the relationship between pronunciation and auditory discrimination, Gross (1968) could not find sufficient data to posit a cause and effect relationship. Six sounds most often poorly discriminated (input) by Black children in the study were the same sounds most often poorly articulated (output). But many other sounds poorly articulated by Black children in the study were *not* poorly discriminated. Furthermore, the kinds of misarticulations of those six sounds made by Black underachievers appear to be high frequency misarticulations of White achievers and underachievers in reading as well.

Sardy (1968) found the usual significant correlations between auditory discrimination and ethnolinguistic group membership. But she also found that the best auditory discriminators and phonic decoders were not middle class Whites, but lower class, urban Puerto Ricans whose teachers were providing a thorough auditory discrimination-phonics program to these bilingual children. This jibes with an early unpublished study by this author (Cohen) and Steve Knight at Mobilization for Youth in 1964, in which it was demonstrated that two fifteen minute training sessions on a Wepman test-like task could teach most urban disadvantaged elementary school children on New York's Lower East Side to discriminate a sound in words.

In other words, misarticulation or not, most children can learn to discriminate sounds in words if they are taught to do so independent of their articulation.

Conclusion. The literature has continued to encourage more and more armchairing about etiological factors that contribute to reading retardation. These "contributions" derive from two misassumptions about psychosocial, psychophysical, psychodynamic and psycholinguistic factors related to reading instruction. These misassumptions have led to the seven fallacies discussed in this paper. Perhaps it is worth considering these misassumptions in the hope that the number of fallacies that we use to explain underachievement in reading of urban disadvantaged children will decrease. These misassumptions are discussed in more detail elsewhere (Cohen, 1971).

First, etiology is generally irrelevant to reading instruction. The psychosocial, psychophysical, psycholinguistic and psychodynamic effects of racism and poverty are irrelevant in the light of intensive, thorough pedagogy. Albert Harris's CRAFT project in beginning reading (1968) was just one research that showed in the three year followup, a grade level mean at placement for grade three for hard core poverty children across a number of different beginning reading programs. Why? Harris did not change linguistic patterns. He did not solve the problems of racism and poverty in New York City. In order to compare the relative effects of different beginning reading programs, he gave the teachers more than the usual training and supervision in the respective beginning reading programs they taught. Quality of pedagogy made a difference.

Second, correlation does not mean a cause and effect relationship. Psychosocial, psychophysical, psycholinguistic and psychodynamic factors correlate with poor reading achievement, but that does not mean we must teach to the correlated factors to get a change in reading behaviors. To put it bluntly, we are all for eradicating racism and poverty and the effects of those social diseases. But we do not have to wait for these diseases to disappear before we can teach urban disadvantaged children to read. Good pedagogy can do that job all by itself.

References

Baratz, J. "A Bidialectal Task for Determining Language Proficiency In Economically Disadvantaged Children." *Child Development*, 40, No. 3, (Sept. 1969a), 889-901.

Baratz, J. "Linguistic and Cultural Factors in Teaching English to Ghetto Children." *Elementary English*, 46, (1969b) 199-203.

Baratz, J. "Teaching Reading in an Urban Negro School System." *Teaching Black Children to Read*, Eds. Joan Baratz and Roger Shuy. Washington, D.C.: Center for Applied Linguistics, 1969c, 92-116.

Baratz, J. "Ollie, Friends, Old Tales." (Experimental Edition) Washington, D.C.: Educational Studies Center, 1970a.

Baratz, J. "Social Science Research Strategies for the Afro-American." *Black America*, Ed. J. Szwed. New York: Basic Books, 1970b.

Bougere, M. B. "Selected factors in oral language related to achievement in first grade reading." Unpublished doctoral dissertation, University of Chicago, (in progress).

Cohen, S. Alan. "Research and Teaching Reading to Disadvantaged Learners: Implications for Further Research and Practice." Speech delivered at International Reading Association Convention, Boston, Mass., 1968.

Cohen, S. Alan and Kornfeld, G. *Oral Vocabulary and Beginning Reading in Disadvantaged Children*. Reading and Language Arts Center, Yeshiva University, 1970.

Cohen, S. Alan. "Dyspedagogia As a Cause of Reading Retardation: Definition and Treatment." *Learning Disorders, Vol. 4, Reading*, Ed. B. Bateman. Seattle: Special Childhood Publications, 1971, 269-96.

Dillard, J. *Black English In the United States*. New York: Random House, 1970.

Figurel, J. "Limitation in the Vocabulary Development of Disadvantaged Children: A Cause of Poor Reading." *Improvement of Reading Through Classroom Practice*, Newark, Delaware: International Reading Association, 1964, 160-75.

Fleming, J. "Oral Language and Beginning Reading: Another Look." *The Reading Teacher*, 22, No. 1, Oct., 1968, 24-29.

Goldfarb, W. "Emotional and Intellectual Consequences of Psychological Deprivation In Infancy: a Re-evaluation." *Psychopathology of Childhood*. Eds. Dr. P. H. Hoch and J. Zobin. New York: Grune and Stratton, 1955.

Goodman, K. "Dialect Barriers to Reading Comprehension." *Teaching Black Children to Read*, Eds. Joan Baratz and Roger Shuy. Washington, D.C.: Center for Applied Linguistics, 1969, 14-28.

Gross, R. *Dialect, Pronunciation, Auditory Discrimination and Reading*. Doctoral Dissertation, Ferkauf Graduate School of Humanities and Social Sciences, Yeshiva University, 1968.

Harris, A., Morrison, C., Serwer, B. L., and Gold, L. *A Continuation of the Craft Project: Comparing Reading Approaches with Disadvantaged Negro Children in Primary Grades*. January, 1968, Project No. 5, 0570, 2, 12, 1, Division of Teacher Education, The City University of New York, New York, Contract #OE 6-10-063, 143-50.

Horner, V. and Gussow, J. "John and Mary: A Pilot Study in Linguistic Ecology." Draft chapter to appear in *Functions of Language in the Classroom*. Eds. Cazden, John and Hymes. New York: Teachers College Press, (In press).

John, V. and Goldstein, L. "The Social Context of Language Acquisition." *Merrill-Palmer Quarterly*, X, (July, 1964), 165-76.

Kagan, J. "His Struggle for Identity." *Saturday Review*, (Dec. 1968).

Labov, W., Cohen, P., Robbins, C. and Lewis, J. "A Study of the Non-Standard English of Negro and Puerto Rican Speakers in New York City." Cooperative Research Project #3288, New York: Columbia University, 1968, 339-48.

Labov, W. "Some Sources of Reading Problems of Negro Speakers of Non-Standard English." Eds. J. Baratz and R. Shuy. *Teaching Black Children to Read*. Washington, D.C.: Center for Applied Linguistics, 1969a.

Labov, W. "The Logic of Non-Standard Dialectic." Ed. J. Alatis. *School of Languages and Linguistics Monograph Series*, 1969b.

Martin, C. "Developmental Interrelationships Among Language Variables in Children of the First Grade." *Elementary English*, 32, (1955).

Rheingold, H. "The Modification of Social Responsiveness in Institutional Babies." *Monograph of Society for Research and Child Development*, 21 (2), Serial No. 63. (1956).

Rystrom, R. "Effects of Standard Dialect Training on Negro First Graders Being Taught to Read." Report Project No. 81-053, US Dept of HEW, 1968.

Salzinger, S. "Operant Conditioning of Continuous Speed in Young Children." *Child Development*, 33, (1962), 683-95.

Sardy, S. "Dialect, Auditory Discrimination and Phonic Skills." Doctoral Dissertation, Ferkauf Graduate School of Humanities and Social Sciences, Yeshiva University, 1968.

Spitz, R. "Hospitalism: An Inquiry into the Genesis of Psychiatric Conditions in Early Childhood." *Psychoanalytic Study of the Child*, 1945, 1, 53-74.

Strickland, R. G. "The Language of Elementary School Children: Its Relationship to the Language of Reading Textbooks and the Quality of Reading of Selected Children." *Bulletin of the School of Education*, Indiana University, 38, (1962).

Weber, Rose-Marie. "Some Reservations on the Significance of Dialect in the Acquisition of Reading." *Reading Goals for the Disadvantaged*, Ed. J. A. Figurel. Newark, Delaware: International Reading Association, (1970), 124-31.

Weintraub, S. "Research: Oral Language and Reading." *The Reading Teacher*, 21, (1968), 769-73.

Wilson, F. T., Flemming, C. W., Burke, A., and Garrison, G. "Reading Progress in Kindergarten and Primary Grades." *Elementary School Journal*, 38, (1938).

Winter, C. "Interrelationships among Language Variables in Children of the First and Second Grades." *Elementary English*, 34, (1957).

Role of Teacher Attitude in Educating the Disadvantaged Child

HAROLD A. HENRIKSON

THE failure of the disadvantaged child in the classroom has been documented and studied with increasing concern through the 1960's. Considerable evidence reported by Harlem Youth Opportunities Unlimited, Inc. (1964) has indicated the progressive deterioration of performance and IQ of the culturally disadvantaged child as he advances from the third to the sixth grade in the nation's schools. Various reasons have been cited for this failure.

Bernstein (1960) has attributed the restrictive language pattern of the lower class family to school failure. Sexton (1961) has equated income and education, finding a strong correlation between family income and school achievement. In her study, when the average family income was below $7,000, the achievement level of the child dropped below grade level.

Charters (1963), following an exhaustive review of the literature, confirmed that social class position determined or predicted all school-related success to the extent that it could be regarded as "empirical law."

EDUCATIONAL LEADERSHIP, January 1970, vol. 28, no. 4, pp. 425-429.

The nationwide concern for the failure of the disadvantaged child in the classroom has led to the development of compensatory education programs directed at changing the status of failure in the classroom through various educational processes. These educational processes have held in common the belief that the failure of the disadvantaged child in the school rests within the child himself, and that the child must be compensated to offset the progressive retardation observed in him within the classroom.

Compensatory education programs have used the middle class home environment as a standard in the belief that this environment nurtures achievement motivation, and the development of the learning and language skills which appeared to be lacking in the disadvantaged child.

Compensatory education programs have demanded new procedures and new materials at a considerable expenditure of money, yet they have not been recognized as unqualified successes. The Westinghouse Report (1969) indicated that results from testing in Head Start programs had not shown retention of the initial gains by the children in these programs. This report also questioned whether long range help for the disadvantaged child lay in the direction of helping him obtain middle class standards, or perhaps whether the influence of the child's home environment was such that school programs could not hope to compensate for its influence.

Many researchers have taken a position opposed to compensatory education. These men have placed the responsibility for the failure of the child directly on the school, indicating that it is the school that must change to meet the needs of the child, not the child who must be compensated to meet the needs of the school.

A study of Chicago schools by Becker

(1952) found that teachers (a) used different teaching techniques in slum schools than in middle class schools, (b) had a conflicting middle class value system that alienated them from lower class students, (c) wanted to transfer to a better school as soon as possible, and (d) were prone to expect less from lower class children.

Goldberg (1967) stated that the school and the teacher were two of the recognized causes of academic retardation of the disadvantaged, as the school had no expectation for the child to learn, and the teacher was failing to do an adequate job of teaching him. Kozol (1967) and Holt (1969) have also placed a great share of the blame for the failure of the child on the schools and the teachers. Kozol emphasized the degree of hostility toward the disadvantaged child that he had seen in many school situations, while Holt accused the schools of adopting a deliberate failure strategy, stating that too many teachers have a conviction that the poor children in the cities cannot be taught.

Wilson (1963) indicated that it is in part the variation of teachers' expectations and standards that contributed to the pupils' later attainment and aspirations, and that the standards set in lower class schools were set lower than those in middle class schools. Glasman (1970) indicated that many teachers with a middle class outlook experience difficulty in working with, and understanding, disadvantaged children. He stated that such teachers have serious misconceptions of the pupils' preschool experience, and display a highly pessimistic view of what the school can do to help the disadvantaged learner.

Asbell (1963) visited many schools in the large cities and reported that teachers were more concerned with what to expect from disadvantaged children than with what they might effect with these same pupils.

Deutsch (1963) has charged the school with the responsibility for the disadvantaged child's negative attitude toward learning. Davidson (1960) reported a study in which teachers rated the classroom behavior of disadvantaged children as undesirable even when their academic achievement was good. The children in his study acquired lower perceptions of themselves as they became aware of the teachers' critical attitudes and subsequently achieved less and behaved less satisfactorily.

Does attitude play the crucial role in the classroom that these men have assigned to it? Is the teacher's attitude so pervasive, as indicated by many of these researchers, that it can actually be a cause of the child's success or failure in school? If so, what responsibility must the school and the teacher carry for the failure of the disadvantaged child in the classroom?

Self-Fulfilling Prophecy

The concept of the self-fulfilling prophecy—that one person's expectation about another's behavior may contribute to a determination of what that behavior actually will be—has been illustrated in sports by Whyte's well-known *Street Corner Society* (1943). In Whyte's study, the "self-fulfilling prophecy" of the gang acted upon one member's ability at bowling: the night the gang "knew" the member would bowl well, he did so, and vice versa.

The concept of self-fulfilling prophecy has been demonstrated in the field of education by Rosenthal and Jacobson in *Pygmalion in the Classroom: Teacher Expectation and Pupils' Intellectual Development* (1968). This study dealt with children in grades one through six in a school that served the lower socioeconomic segment of a community. In *Pygmalion*, approximately 20 percent of each class in the school was randomly selected, and teachers were given an expectancy advantage for those children (were told that the children could be expected to "bloom" academically). After one year a significant expectancy advantage was found, through post-testing, with those children who were expected to "bloom."

The critics of *Pygmalion* are many: those such as Jensen (1968) who question that such a concept even exists, and others such as Snow (1969) and Gumpert and Gumpert (1968) who, while accepting the presence of such a concept, point out the need for a different analysis of the data for more concise evidence of it within the study.

Clasen (1970) and Aiken (1969) are among those critics who accept the concept but suggest further research with it; Clasen, in the area of other racial backgrounds, and Aiken, in research studies with larger sample sizes, indicating his concern that the significant differences in the *Pygmalion* study might have been obtained through the extreme scores of only a few children.

Attempts to replicate and adapt the *Pygmalion* study to other research have been carried out with varying results. Research by Beez (1967), reported by Rosenthal and Jacobson (1968), supported the concept of the self-fulfilling prophecy in a study with 60 pupils in a Head Start program. Seventy-seven percent of the children in the study alleged to their teachers to be good symbol learners did learn five or more symbols, while only 13 percent of those children alleged to be poor symbol learners learned five or more symbols. The teachers in Beez' study who had been given favorable expectations about their pupils generally saw them come true, while those teachers who were given unfavorable expectations also found what they had expected to find.

A quasi-replication of the *Pygmalion*

study was done by Conn and others (1967), and reported in Rosenthal and Jacobson (1968). The study was carried out with children from a middle or upper-middle class community, and teachers in the study were led to expect gains in intellectual development after having a full semester's contact with the pupils prior to being given the expectancy advantage. In this study, the expectancy advantage noted with the "special" children was small, approaching only marginal statistical significance ($p < .10$).

A replication of the *Pygmalion* study by Claiborn (1969) assessed teacher-pupil behavior following communication to the teacher of the intellectual potential of certain pupils. The results of this study, too, were in contrast to those of Rosenthal and Jacobson (1968), since there were no significant differences between those pupils designated as "bloomers" when compared to the remaining pupils in the class. The expectancy advantage was given to the teachers approximately five months after the beginning of the school year, a time lapse which, as in Conn's study, had perhaps already given the teachers a considerable basis for forming certain expectations of the pupils.

Preliminary results of a study conducted by Evans (1968), reported in Rosenthal and Jacobson (1968), again failed to show significant differences. This study was conducted with middle class pupils whose teachers were given an expectancy advantage concerning their intellectual ability.

Results of a study by Henrikson (1970), however, supported the findings of the study by Rosenthal and Jacobson in *Pygmalion*. Some striking differences were found in achievement gain scores of the experimental and contrast groups of a sample composed of disadvantaged kindergarten children. The generation of an expectancy advantage for the children of the experimental group in the study was given to teachers at the beginning of the school year. Post-test results at the end of the school year saw differences of +17.1 points between the experimental and contrast groups in achievement mean gain scores manifest across all conditions and significant ($p < .005$).

The concept of the self-fulfilling prophecy as it is applicable to education demands further research to clarify its applicability to the classroom. The possibility that teacher attitude plays as significant a role in the classroom as some of the studies have indicated is of great importance to further planning in education for the disadvantaged child. It challenges the belief that the child who is disadvantaged in both home and school is so because one environment is working irrevocably against the other. It asks whether it is not possible that the disadvantaged status of the child, as viewed by the teacher, itself creates the disadvantage for the child within the classroom.

It is possible that the Kerner Report (1968), asking for more preschool intervention programs for the disadvantaged child, overlooks a basic premise—that a change in the quality of the child's education can be effected through nothing more than a change in the teacher's expectations of his abilities in the classroom.

References

Lewis R. Aiken, Jr. "Book Review of *Pygmalion.*" *Educational and Psychological Measurement* 29: 226-27; Spring 1969.

B. Asbell. "Not Like Other Children." *Redbook* 121: 65, 114-18, 120; October 1963.

H. S. Becker. "Social Class Variations in the Teacher-Pupil Relationship." *Journal of Educational Sociology* 25: 451-56; April 1952.

Basil Bernstein. "Language and Social Class." *British Journal of Psychology* 11: 271-76; 1960.

W. W. Charters, Jr. "The Social Background

of Teaching." In: N. L. Gage, editor. *Handbook of Research on Teaching.* Skokie, Illinois: Rand McNally & Company, 1963. pp. 715-813.

Robert E. Clasen. "Book Review." *The Journal of Educational Research* 8: 378, 381; April 1970.

Helen H. Davidson and Gerhard Lang. "Children's Perceptions of Their Teachers' Feelings Toward Them Related to Self-Perception, School Achievement and Behavior." *Journal of Experimental Education* 29: 107-18; December 1960.

Giacinto De Lapa. "The Slosson Intelligence Test—A Screening and Retesting Technique for Slow Learners." *Journal of School Psychology* 6: 224; Spring 1968.

Martin Deutsch. "The Disadvantaged Child and the Learning Process." In: A. H. Passow, editor. *Education in Depressed Areas.* New York: Bureau of Publications, Teachers College, Columbia University, 1963. pp. 163-70.

Judy Evans. *Preliminary Report of a Study.* Reported in Rosenthal and Jacobson, 1968.

Naftaly S. Glasman. "Teachers' Low Expectation Levels of Their Culturally Different Students: A View from Administration." *Journal of Secondary Education* 45: 82-94; February 1970.

Miriam L. Goldberg. "Methods and Materials for Educationally Disadvantaged Youth." In: A. H. Passow, Miriam Goldberg, and Abraham J. Tannenbaum, editors. *Education of the Disadvantaged: A Book of Readings.* New York: Holt, Rinehart and Winston, Inc., 1967. 503 pp.

Peter Gumpert and Carol Gumpert. "The Teacher as Pygmalion: Comments on the Psychology of Expectation." *The Urban Review* 3: 21-25; September 1968.

Harlem Youth Opportunities Unlimited, Inc. *Youth in the Ghetto.* New York: HARYOU, 1964.

Harold A. Henrikson. "An Investigation of the Influence of Teacher Expectation Upon the Intellectual and Achievement Performance of Disadvantaged Kindergarten Children." Unpublished doctoral dissertation, University of Illinois, 1970.

John Caldwell Holt. *The Underachieving School.* New York: Pitman Publishing Corporation, 1969. 209 pp.

Arthur R. Jensen. "How Much Can We Boost IQ and Scholastic Achievement?" *Harvard Educational Review* 39: 1-123; Winter 1968.

Jonathan Kozol. *Death at an Early Age.* Boston: Houghton Mifflin Company, 1967. 240 pp.

Robert Rosenthal and Lenore Jacobson. *Pygmalion in the Classroom.* New York: Holt, Rinehart and Winston, Inc., 1968. 240 pp.

Patricia C. Sexton. *Education and Income.* New York: The Viking Press, 1961.

Richard E. Snow. "Unfinished Pygmalion." *Contemporary Psychology* 14: 197-99; April 1969.

United States National Advisory Commission on Civil Disorders. (The Kerner Report.) Washington, D.C.: Superintendent of Documents, U.S. Government Printing Office, 1968. 425 pp.

Westinghouse Learning Corporation. *The Impact of Head Start.* Bladensburg, Maryland: Westinghouse Learning Corporation, April 1969.

W. F. Whyte. *Street Corner Society.* Chicago: University of Chicago Press, 1943.

A. B. Wilson. "Social Stratification and Academic Achievement." In: A. H. Passow, editor. *Education in Depressed Areas.* New York: Bureau of Publications, Teachers College, Columbia University, 1963. pp. 217-35.

Ability to "read a picture" in disadvantaged first grade children

NICHOLAS C. ALIOTTI

AMONG THE various learning skills that first graders bring with them into the classroom, the ability to interpret or "read a picture" has been suggested as an indicator of school readiness (Torrance, 1967). Indeed, according to Monroe (1951, P. 75) "a child's verbal interpretation of a picture gives the teacher the opportunity to observe several aspects of language in a single, very simple, informal test." Additionally, Porter (1968) recommends that teachers provide varied opportunities for reading and interpreting pictures in order to prepare children for the necessary visualizations required in reading.

Torrance (1967) reported that among a group of older disadvantaged black children over 60 per cent of them made gross misperceptions of a picture used in the oral administration of the Ask-and-Guess test (Torrance, 1966). Similar analyses of data obtained from a sample of disabled readers at the fourth and fifth grade levels and another sample of disadvantaged black children at the same educational level again revealed errors in 60 per cent of the cases. Such errors were practically non-existent among advantaged children of similar ages and grade level. Studies conducted in Europe (source undetermined) have provided additional clues. Children reared in African cultures in which books have been inaccessible, until quite recent times, made the same kind of misperceptions or perceptual errors as the disabled readers.

Bruner (1966), Hunt (1964), and other educators have also noted the correlation between early social and cognitive deprivation and perceptual impairment. Hunt (1966, P. 90) observed that compared to most middle class children disadvantaged children show perceptual deficiencies in their ability to recognize objects and situations. M. Deutsch (1963) reported perceptual deficits in both visual and auditory channels among New York City's black and Puerto Rican children. More recently, Cohen (1969) administered the *Frostig Developmental Test of Visual Perception to* 120

THE READING TEACHER, 1970, Vol. 24, pp. 3-6, 57.

first graders from the lower East Side of New York City. The perceptual quotients obtained were consistently below the expected average perceptual age. Moreover, white and Chinese children scored higher than Puerto Rican and black children.

TESTING TECHNIQUE

To test the significance and implications of these clues, an objectively scored, "true-false," picture interpretation test was developed and pre-tested with children from kindergarten through sixth grade. Since the skills involved in learning to "read" a picture are apparently learned through examining pictures in books and other sources, asking questions about them, and being stimulated to make judgments about these pictures, disadvantaged black children and other children often have not yet developed these skills when they enter the first grade. The data collection instrument is based on the drawing used in Verbal Form B of the *Torrance Test of Creative Thinking Ability* (Torrance, 1966). The subject is shown the picture and asked to answer the following questions "Yes" or "No":

1. Is the girl carrying the pot?
2. Is the boy carrying a rabbit?
3. Is the boy stepping on the girl's feet?
4. Does the boy have on any kind of shirt?
5. Are the children standing still?
6. Is the bird cage hitting the boy in the back?
7. Is the boy carrying an elephant?
8. Is the girl carrying the bird cage?
9. Is the girl holding onto the pot?
10. Is the writing on the wall English?
11. Do the children have on shoes?
12. Is the boy carrying a dog?

Additional information concerning this instrument is reported elsewhere (Torrance, 1967; Torrance & Aliotti, 1968).

Ss were ninety-four white, middle-class advantaged first grade children enrolled in the Lillie B. Suder School in Clayton County, Georgia, and ninety-six black, disadvantaged first grade children enrolled in the Jeremiah S. Gilbert School in Atlanta, Georgia, and the East Athens School in Athens, Georgia. *The Picture Interpretation Test* (Form 1) was individually administered to the advantaged and disadvantaged first grade *Ss* as part of a warm-up task for a verbal creative thinking test.

RESULTS

Table 1 presents the means, standard deviations, and *t*-ratios for advantaged and disadvantaged first grade children in *The Picture Interpretation Test.* A pooled estimate of the standard error of estimate was employed.

Table 1 Means, standard deviations, and *t*-ratios for advantaged and disadvantaged first grade children on *The Picture Interpretation Test*

		Advantaged	*Disadvantaged*	*t-Ratio*
	N:	43	55	
Girls	X:	7.16	5.89	9.23**
	SD:	2.17	1.99	
	N:	51	41	
Boys	X:	7.17	6.00	8.95**
	SD:	1.79	2.20	
	N:	94	96	
Total	S:	7.17	5.94	4.35**
	SD:	1.97	2.08	

**$p < .001$

Inspection of the *t*-ratios for boys, girls, and the combined group indicate that in each case the mean performance of the advantaged *Ss* is favored. All of the tests of the mean difference were significant at more than the .001 level of confidence by a two-tailed test. Clearly, the advantaged first grade children were superior to their disadvantaged peers on this test measure (advantaged mean =7.17 versus disadvantaged mean=5.94.) In fact, the disadvantaged male first-graders scored at a chance level (six correct) while the disadvantaged female first-graders scored slightly below chance.

Table 2 reports means, standard deviations, and *t*-ratios for first grade males and females. A pooled estimate of the standard error of estimate was employed.

Table 2 Means, standard deviations, and *t*-ratios on *The Picture Interpretation Test* for first grade boys and girls from an advantaged and a disadvantaged social class

Classification		*Boys*	*Girls*	*t-Ratio*
	N:	51	43	
Advantaged	X:	7.17	7.16	.009
	SD:	1.97	2.17	
	N:	41	55	
Disadvantaged	X:	6.00	5.89	.330
	SD:	2.20	1.99	

$p < .05$, NS

Inspection of the means for boys and girls revealed only slight differences in performance and in each case statistical significance was not obtained. Thus sex did not appear to be a relevant variable with respect to performance on *The Picture Interpretation Test.*

DISCUSSION

These findings appear to be consonant with a number of studies pointing up the general perceptual impairment found among disadvantaged groups. A recent replication of this study with Mexican children revealed similar results. Walker (1969) administered *The Picture Interpretation Test* to advantaged and disadvantaged Mexican boys. Consistent differences were found at each grade level which favored urban male advantaged children over their disadvantaged peers. All of the differences were significant at better than the .025 level of confidence. Interestingly, the performances of the Mexican first grade boys, both advantaged and disadvantaged, are below those of the male American first grade children in the present study. Moreover, it is noteworthy to consider that only by the sixth grade does the mean performance of the disadvantaged Mexican males begin to approach the performance of advantaged first grade children in the United States.

What these tentative clues may be suggesting is a need for educators to be sensitive to children's visual literacy or ability to "read a picture." The present study indicates that disadvantaged children fare relatively poorly on this skill. In view of the large number of pictures found in school textbooks, it is interesting to speculate how ability to "read a picture" may account in part for reading performance, particularly comprehension. Correlational analyses indicate this skill subserves more than simple visual discrimination. Language components measured by intelligence tests, particularly the child's fund of verbal concepts and his ability to express and comprehend verbal material, play an important role in this skill (Torrance and Aliotti, 1968; Buccellato, 1969).

REFERENCES

Aliotti, N. C. The effects of warm-up activities on the verbal creative thinking abilities of disadvantaged first grade children. Unpublished doctoral dissertation, University of Georgia, 1969.

Bruner, J. S. The cognitive consequences of early sensory deprivation. In J. L. Frost and G. R. Hawkes (Eds.) *The disadvantaged child: issues and innovations.* New York: Houghton Mifflin, Co., 1966. Pp. 137-144.

Buccellato, L. A. Verbal intelligence and "picture reading ability." Master's thesis, University of Georgia, 1969.

Cohen, S. A. Studies in visual perception and reading in disadvantaged children. *Journal of Learning Disabilities*, 1969, 2, 498, 503.

Deutsch, M. The disadvantaged child and the learning process. In A. H Passow (Ed.) *Education in depressed areas.* New York: Bureau of Publications Teachers College, Columbia University, 1963. Pp. 163-174.

Hunt, J. M. The psychological basis for using preschool enrichment as ar antidote for cultural deprivation. *Merrill-Palmer Quarterly*, 1964, *110*, 209-248.

Monroe, Marion. *Growing into reading*. New York: Scott, Foresman and Company, 1951.

Porter, P. Pictures in reading. *The Reading Teacher*, 1968, 22, 238-241, 291.

Torrance, E. P., and Aliotti, N. C. *The picture interpretation test: selected test correlates*. Athens, Georgia: Research and Development Center, Educational Stimulation, 1968. *(mimeo)*

Torrance, E. P. *Torrance tests of creative thinking: norms-technical manual*. (Res. Ed.) Princeton, N. J.: Personnel Press, Inc., 1966.

Torrance, E. P. Influence of an experimental pre-primary program upon ability to "read a picture" upon entry to first grade, Athens, Georgia: Research and Development Center, Educational Stimulation, 1967. (*mimeo*)

Walker, P. C. Creativity among Mexican children. Unpublished doctoral dissertation, University of Georgia, 1969.

As I see Spanish-speaking students

RUTH H. MATTILA

Drawing upon twenty-six years' experience in teacher education, and her work with Spanish-speaking students in the Southwest, Ruth Mattila compares Spanish-speaking children with Anglos of similar background, age and intelligence Her description here is based solely on personal observation. The author is professor of education at New Mexico Highlands University.

THE tendency toward uncritical acceptance of expert opinion frequently lulls teachers into operating in an atmosphere of pedagogical stereotypes. Teacher insight then gives way to guided observation—a concentrated effort to see what the experts say should be there—and, accordingly, contrary evidence is discounted. The case of the disabled reader provides excellent examples. Three widely accepted generalizations responsible for much formula teaching will serve to illustrate the point. These are:

- Nearly all children come to school wanting to learn to read.
- Children who fail to learn to read soon develop emotional reactions which then become barriers that further complicate and impede the learning process.
- Children who fail at reading develop numerous symptoms which reflect their difficulty and enable teachers, specialists and counselors to identify them quickly and provide the help they need.

Perhaps these generalizations once held true for large groups of middle class children but it may be argued that there are today many middle class children to whom the generalizations do not apply and certainly there are many others to whom the generalizations never applied.

Middle class bias

An examination of the three assumptions reveals their obvious middle class bias. Education has long been revered by the middle class as the road to upward mo-

THE READING TEACHER, 1973, Vol. 26, pp. 605-608.

bility and no group in our society has been more strongly set on the path of upward mobility than the solid middle class. Furthermore, the ability to read—literacy—is recognized by all members of this group as the first giant step on the educational ladder.

However, it may be contended that this pattern is now being broken for many reasons. First, the middle class value system is seriously threatened, as the strong middle class following in drug culture, commune living and draft evasion quite dramatically attest. Second, today's society is increasingly mobile. This mobility is reflected in changing goals—goals which are set in terms of peer group orientation. Thus, today's youth tends to be much less single-minded with regard to school achievement and much less willing to accept adult evaluations of achievements, whether it be from teachers or other adults.

Third, independent thinking among even the very young is today a reality. Children are much less docile about accepting the way to do anything, in school or out of school. Fourth, television and other mass media have increased the expectation for being entertained and for enjoying any pursuit in which one chooses to engage. Fifth, civil rights measures have changed the complexion of the schools, loosening community pressures and controls over students, clouding issues of accountability for both faculty and students, and, for the time being at least, confusing all as to goals and sense of direction.

Sixth, complexities of today's problems, at home and abroad, have eroded confidence levels and have frequently paralyzed constructive action in schools and in school communities. Consequently, teachers and administrators are no longer sure where they are or should be going and children, sensing the faltering leadership, drop out.

Reexamination required

In this milieu, then, it seems reasonable to assume that student needs and the reading programs designed to serve them require reexamination. To date at least, the writer's experience with Spanish-speaking students in northern New Mexico has served to reinforce this conclusion. It should be emphasized that the conclusions drawn here apply to children of middle class background who are of normal intelligence, are from fifth to eighth grade level in school and have reading disabilities.

In comparing Spanish-speaking children who fit this description with English-speaking children of similar socioeconomic background the writer has noted some interesting contrasts and comparisons:

1. The Spanish-speaking children are not disturbed in their social adjustment. Not being able to read is accepted as normal. Many of their friends, as well as many adults whom they respect and admire, either cannot or do not read. Therefore, Spanish-speaking retarded readers have friends at school and relate well to their peers. Lack of reading ability, at least well into the junior high school levels, does not cut them off from normal social participation. (At the senior high school levels the picture tends to change but that, of course, depends on the high school attended.)

2. There is a notable absence of nervous symptoms—bitten finger-

nails, nervous ticks—commonly noted among so-called Anglo children who are retarded readers. However, clowning and distractive techniques designed to pull attention away from reading and toward other activities are tactics common to both groups.

3. Spanish-speaking children are more social in their relationships to adults than are children of the Anglo middle class. Apparently, the extended family relationships which most Spanish-speaking children enjoy has made them more accepting of adults and given them a better base for establishing friendships with adults.

4. Spanish-speaking students are strongly aware of themselves as Spanish-speaking citizens and on the alert for any reaction, particularly any note of disapproval or reservation in accepting them or their culture. They reject any teacher who does not like them, whether or not that teacher speaks Spanish. They work well with teachers who like them and not at all with teachers who do not, but they seem to have a special hostility for the Spanish-speaking teachers who do not like them.

5. They are less verbal than their Anglo counterparts—less fluent in all areas of language, less aware of what reading is all about and, consequently, much less strongly motivated toward improvement in reading.

6. They work well together and poorly alone. The immediate social application of learning is seemingly much more important to them than to their Anglo middle class peers.

7. They are supersensitive to changes in social climate. A new member of a group must be assimilated before work can move forward. A new teacher must be assessed as a person before his suggestions can be fully accepted.

8. Spanish-speaking students are politically more astute, showing much stronger interest in government at all levels—local, state, national—than their Anglo counterparts.

9. Though reading may seem relatively unimportant to them, speech does not. The Spanish-speaking person who can speak out in public, make himself heard and show himself to be forceful and fluent in public meetings is much admired. The substance of his speech is often less important than the fact of his speaking and his persuasiveness is gauged by his ability to hold his own against English speakers in English-speaking groups.

10. Spanish-speaking students are authoritarian and male-oriented in their leadership expectation. Consequently, permissiveness tends to be interpreted as weakness and the verbal, positive leader who knows what *he* wants is easily accepted. Women teachers are all right; women principals are suspect.

11. Spanish-speaking students are more strongly tied to ritual and protocol than their Anglo counterparts. Form is important. Knowing the right thing to say and the right thing to do counts for much. Forms are also useful to hide behind. Sometimes they are useful for delaying unwanted action.

12. Once they have assessed the reading task and set goals for themselves Spanish-speaking students show patterns of ups and downs in motivation and attitude that are indistinguishable from patterns shown by Anglo children. There is the early cockiness with initial progress, the slump when

the realization of how far behind they really are strikes them, the leveling off and digging in when they decide that the job can be done after all and the growing self-assurance as they hit their stride and begin to make steady progress.

13. Once they are on the road to success, Spanish-speaking students are just as competitive as their Anglo counterparts but probably more responsive to praise and more sensitive to criticism. Their sensitivity to loss of face in front of a group is far greater than that of the typical Anglo student and they are less likely to have a ready defense against sarcasm or unfair criticisms.

It should be reemphasized that the above generalizations are meant to apply only to those children who have developed a middle class orientation. However, with this particular group there are strong teaching-learning assets available to the teacher. Perhaps the greatest of these assets is a refreshing absence of generation gap. Seemingly these students have not yet been turned off by adults and they offer both a challenge and friendship to teachers who sincerely want to help them.

Cultural constraints in teaching Chinese students to read English

AN-YAN TANG WANG
RICHARD A. EARLE

Probably few RT readers will teach native Chinese to read English. Yet, the observations and comparisons in this article not only are clear and interesting; they also enlighten our perceptions of our own native language. An-Yan Tang Wang is a doctoral student at Indiana University, where Richard Earle serves both as assistant professor of education and assistant director of ERIC/CRIER.

IT IS nearly universally accepted that a person's language not only reflects his culture but contributes to it in large measure. This is true of subcultures within the United States, where linguistic differences very clearly identify an individual's subculture. Incredibly enough, however, not until recently have we recognized the need to change our methods and materials for teaching reading to such diverse groups. Instead, it was commonly assumed that both text and technique should be held constant, while an all-out attack was mounted to change the person's linguistic traditions—that is, to wrench from him a most intimate part of his cultural heritage.

Given this natural intimacy of language and culture, there is often a tremendous cultural shock when one sets out to learn to read a foreign language. This is particularly true of the Chinese student in his attempt to master English. This article will attempt to explain some of the differences between English and Chinese that we feel bear directly on several important considerations in teaching speakers of Chinese to read English. In each case, we make recommendations which may be helpful in dealing with these sociolinguistic constraints.

Formal instruction

In China (Taiwan) formal language instruction in English begins in the seventh grade, just as the child enters adolescence. By this time, the students have been quite thoroughly "acculturated," with the

THE READING TEACHER, 1972, Vol. 25, pp. 663-669.

following results. First, they have learned to be constantly aware of their manners and facial expressions—too many facial expressions, as well as exaggerated expressions, are both considered improper. Learning outlandish sounds often involves eccentric facial contortions. Adolescent or adult students often find this embarrassing in front of the class.

Perhaps the only way not to embarrass the students, and to teach the language effectively at the same time, is to employ informality and a relaxed atmosphere. However, in most places in China, informality is frowned upon. In the classroom a teacher is expected to maintain his prestige and status by not getting on too familiar terms with his students.

Secondly, Chinese adolescents in general are well-behaving students, in the sense that they are very quiet in the classroom; they do not fall asleep in class; they do not open their mouths unless asked by the teacher to do so; they seldom ask questions; and they keep in mind the wise saying of Chinese philosophy: "Hide your brilliance and never outshine others." All these virtues are generally formed when the child is growing up in Chinese society, and become hard to break barriers to learning foreign language. Perhaps Chinese students should begin to learn English before these attitudes are well developed.

This discussion suggests that, when possible, instruction in English begin much earlier for speakers of Chinese, perhaps between the ages of three and ten, ages suggested by several experts as optimum for students from any culture (Brooks, 1960; Moulton, 1966).

Orthography

Unlike many other written languages, including English, Chinese orthography is composed of characters instead of letters; thus, it is "ideographic" rather than "alphabetic" in nature. Each character has a unique shape. The child has to learn the shape, sound, and meaning of thousands of characters in order to be able to read and write.

Chinese characters are written in vertical columns from top to bottom, and from right to left of the page. Being used to such word arrangements, a Chinese student, in beginning stages of reading English, will find it difficult to follow the horizontal lines from left to right. However, the recent appearance of some Chinese texts printed horizontally from left to right may diminish this kind of difficulty.

Another problem the Chinese student may encounter in reading English is the irregularity of word length. Shifting from the neatly printed, equal sized, square Chinese characters to "chicken-bowels"—as the Chinese sometimes call the English script—the student often finds this irregularity quite disturbing, even to the point of causing a lot of strain on the eyes.

Since Chinese script differs almost completely from English, students should be constantly reminded that the alphabet letters are symbols representing the sounds of the spoken language. It is also essential to teach students to recognize the letters in the English alphabet.

Beginning reading materials written in words of about equal length might be useful in reducing problems caused by irregular word length. This could be accomplished through word selection and by applying printing techniques similar to what is called "chunking" in longer linguistic units. As the student improves his reading ability, the words in the reading material can become more varied in length. For the purpose of directional training, the controlled reader, speed reading pacers, typing practice, or any other method which guides reading from left to right would be very useful.

Sequence in language learning

Since speaking precedes reading and writing in the language learning process of a native speaker, linguists assert that the same sequence should be followed in learning a second language. A few linguists and educators have gone as far as to say that a language cannot be read until it can be understood and produced orally. Finocchiaro (1968) says that learners should be able to say the material with reasonable fluency before they are permitted to see it. Many other authorities have made the same conclusion from their research and observations.

This may not be true for Chinese students. As presently practiced, instruction in English is usually provided for adolescents or adults,—that is, students who are already literate, and whose purpose is not to become conversationally fluent. Stern read a paper concerning this problem at the International Conference on Modern Foreign Language Teaching held in West Berlin in 1964. He pointed out that once a child has learned to read and write it is fictitious to treat him as a nonreader. Lipton (1969-70) experimented with two groups of students learning French: the control group was taught with pure oral-aural approach, while teachers in the experimental group introduced reading activities in addition to listening and speaking. Results showed that the experimental group was superior to the control group when tested on auditory comprehension in French, with a difference in performance significant at the .01 level.

Doman (1971), in *Teaching Your Baby to Read,* says that young children can actually learn to read earlier than they can learn to speak. Hughes (1971) asserts that in learning a foreign language, instruction in reading can accelerate the mastery of that language. Given the condition as stated here, this research seems to support the point of view expressed earlier by psycholinguists Bever and Bower (1966), Kolers (1969), and others.

From ideograph to alphabet

In any event, nearly all research of an "aural vs. visual" nature was done in situations where the learners are Spanish, German, or French. These students' native languages all belong to the same Indo-European language family as English. Like English, their languages are based on the alphabetic principle—a grapheme-phoneme correspondence. It is quite a different matter when the students are Chinese, since the Chinese written symbols are self-contained ideas, ideographs which directly convey meaning. Chinese students, when learning to read Chinese, are shown visually the written symbol, its meaning, and its sound. It is important to understand that the latter may or may not be the same as the corresponding word in the listener's spoken language. Take as example the character for *man*. When a Mandarin speaker learns to read it he memorizes the shape of the character, the meaning "man," and the sound "jen" which is identical to the sound for man in his speaking dialect. However, when a child from Fuchien Province learns to read the word, he must not only memorize the shape of the character and its meaning, but also its sound, "jin," which is completely different from the sound, "lang," which he uses for man in his speaking dialect. Such training gives much stress on visual recognition, and consequently requires of the Chinese student a strong visual memory for written symbols. Many Chinese students find themselves recognizing English words visually much easier than auditorily. (This is based on general observation. Whether it is true or not needs to be proved by factual research.) Perhaps this strength should be made use of more frequently in learning a second language.

Based on the observation that Chinese students are particularly strong in visual memory and direct association of symbol with meaning, and taking into consideration the above-mentioned studies which suggest that there are students who learn a foreign language faster with the incorporation of reading, we should venture to assume that the theory that learning to read English should begin by aural-oral practice is not applicable to Chinese students. Instead, a synthesized aural-oral reading approach should be employed at the earliest stage of instruction.

Pronunciation and oral interpretation

Many Chinese students have neither the opportunity nor the inclination to develop oral English skills. A college education, for example, demands the ability to read English, not speak it. Hence, it is by no means certain that perfect pronunciation and fluent oral interpretation is a goal worthy of much time and effort. Nevertheless, if such goals are desirable, certain additional factors become prominent.

In learning English pronunciation, Chinese students may actually have one advantage over students whose native languages use alphabetic systems of writing. German, Spanish, or French students may obstinately stick to the sounds which are assigned in their native languages to the same symbols in English. For example, a Spanish student says to his English teacher, "Sir, would you listen to my bowels (vowels)?" and a German student persists in saying, "My father drives a Folksvagon." Since Chinese students usually have never had any previous experience with the alphabetic principle, they do not have a preconceived idea as to how a word *should be* pronounced, and thus are more ready to accept English pronunciation as it is.

The teacher should take care to see that the student learns to pronounce a written word vocally, and to spell a spoken word. Intensive training in these tasks will prevent Chinese students from devoting themselves merely to memorizing the word by its shape and meaning, forgetting the basic sound element. Then through an analysis of oral reading miscues, the teacher can find out how well the student can pronounce a word.

A second purpose of oral reading is to master the intonation. Linguists have described the significant structural contrasts of the intonation of American English, but a foreign student will often transfer his native tonal difference to reading English. Consequently, to a native speaker of English, a Chinese seems to be singing rather than reading.

It is clear that the case for a very considerable amount of properly directed and properly used oral reading from the very beginning stage rests primarily on the need to develop, along with the automatic responses to the bundles of contrastive graphic shapes that actually are present in writing, the ability to supply or produce the appropriate set of intonation and stress patterns that fit and display evidence of a total cumulative understanding. In other words, we agree that mastery of spoken English becomes essential to fluent oral reading. The following way of oral reading suggested by Lloyd and Warfel (1956, p. 418) might be very useful:

> The next step is to read aloud, using the eyes in a somewhat different way. Instead of looking at a small group and saying it, pick up with your eyes the longest stretch you can, look up and away from the book, then say what you have seen. This is what speakers do who are speaking from a prepared text. . . . They do not mumble what they have written with their eyes down. . . . Keep pushing for longer and longer segments—whole lines . . . or even whole sentences. . . . Be careful to speak in your usual conversational tones, without the reading monotone. . . .

Chinese students are fond of reading aloud. Since their language has different tones and other characteristics that make it musical, they have developed a keen ear for pleasing rhymes and meters. This fortuitous cultural fact suggests that poetry reading, as well as other expressive reading, such as plays and stories, can be introduced at an early stage of learning.

Oral reading can be correlated with dictation—a good practice to reinforce the student's ability in transforming oral sounds into written words. In China most English teachers practice dictation on seen materials. Instead of testing student's ability with sound-letter association, they are testing how well a student can memorize a word by shape or by other contextual connections. At the earlier stages, dictation should be administered on unseen materials, which may even include nonsense words. The purpose would be primarily to reinforce pronunciation and spelling. The exercise would proceed most effectively from simple to increasingly more complex tasks, and would lead to more and more effort on the part of the student.

Reading as thinking

English sentence structures are very different from those in Chinese. English texts and writings, too, are organized in different ways. The differences are largely due to the differences between the thought patterns of the English and the Chinese.

The thought pattern which speakers and readers of English appear to expect as an integral part of their communication is a linearly developed sequence. An

English expository paragraph usually begins with a statement of the topic. Then a series of substatements of that topic, each supported by examples and illustrations, proceeds to develop that central idea, relate it to all the other ideas in the whole essay, and employ it in its proper relationship with other ideas, in order to prove or to argue something. Preciseness and succinctness are considered most important to achieve coherence and unity. Contrarily, the English paragraph may use just the reverse procedure. It may state a whole series of examples and illustrations, and then relate them into a final statement at the end of the paragraph. These two types of development represent the most common inductive and deductive reasoning which the English reader expects to be an integral part of any formal communication.

Much Chinese writing, on the other hand, is characterized by what may charitably be called an approach by indirection. In this kind of writing, the development of the paragraph may be said to be turning around a gyre. The circles or gyres turn around the main subject and present it from a variety of tangential views, but the subject is never "straightforwardly" stated. Thus the students have to learn to follow the way English writers customarily develop their thoughts. They should be able to trace the author's purpose, how he organizes his essay; to discover key words, main sentences, and central ideas; to find out the attitude of the author and evaluate his statements; and to reject or assimilate what they have read.

Chinese students are very imaginative, but never very analytic. They often tend to read passively and too acceptingly. Questioning ability and critical insight will have to be developed through intense practice.

Classroom practice

At the beginning stages the teacher can suggest questions and let the students look for answers given in the material. Later, students can develop these questions themselves. To achieve this, the teacher can direct the students' attention to the title of the reading material, the table of contents, and the sectional titles, then show them how questions can be formed from these.

There should be periods assigned for individual silent reading, such that students with common interests can get together in groups to discuss their opinions and reactions. One or two students with more initiative or ability can join each group to start the discussion when these activities are first introduced.

In order to suit the requirements of different reading materials, students should be able to read with flexibility of speed and various degree of comprehension: rapid scanning as when searching a newspaper for the latest news; relaxed reading to gain pleasure from recreational reading; quick scanning to glean salient points of a chapter or book; serious analytic (reflective) reading—study reading—for abstracts and reports. Many Chinese students cannot adjust their reading to different materials. The lack of variety in English reading materials now available in most Chinese schools is one major cause of this problem. These materials are invariably narrative writing.

Narrative writing is based on a simple chronological organization, one that is used in most cultures, and students find it easy to comprehend. Although the narrative is a natural starting place, and students may find it more interesting, story reading should only be continued as exercises in vocabulary building, idioms, faster reading, and perhaps cultural understanding. If our goal is to prepare students to study history, philosophy, science, and other courses in the English language—then the use of narratives seems limited, and should be cut short. Analytical reading exercises should be shifted to expository prose as soon as possible.

Certainly in an expository reading selection, the vocabulary and sentence structures will have to be controlled at first and geared to the specific level of the students. Also, readings will have to be selected to teach the various organizational patterns the students will encounter within classes. This again points out the need for specially prepared materials—a task urgently waiting to be done. It may be that the teacher will have to prepare his own materials for instruction until special, more appropriate ones are developed.

Many Chinese students have never learned to use the library, or to use the preface, introduction, table of contents, footnotes, indexes, and the bibliography of a book for initial and further information. Ninety percent of Chinese books are printed without footnotes, indexes, or bibliographies even today. The English teacher can help the students use book parts, build their own library in the class, make catalogs, teach them how to look for information and how to use dictionaries effectively but not superfluously. Remind them that in learning a new word, the dictionary should be the last source to look for pronunciation and meaning.

Conclusions

Many linguistic and other cultural phenomena are intimately related to the teaching of English to speakers of Chinese. Some of these suggest considerations especially crucial to the teaching of reading. Perhaps the critical attribute of the teacher is a fair understanding of important differences between Chinese and English in terms of spoken and written language, educational philosophy, instructional methods, and other aspects of the two cultures. This paper attempts to begin that understanding by presenting some ideas that may be useful. Clearly a lot more needs to be done.

References

Bever, Thomas G. and Bower, Thomas G. "How to Read Without Listening," *Project Literacy Reports,* No. 6, Cornell University, Ithaca, New York, January, 1966.

Brooks, Nelson. *Language and Language Teaching: Theory and Practice.* New York: Harcourt, Brace & World, Inc., 1960.

Doman, Glenn. *Teach Your Baby to Read.* London: Jonathan Cape, Ltd., 1971.

Finocchiaro, Mary. *Teaching English as a Second Language in Elementary and Secondary Schools,* rev. ed. New York: Harper & Row, 1968.

Hughes, Felicity. *Reading and Writing Before School.* London: Jonathan Cape, Ltd., 1971.

Kolers, Paul A. "Reading is Only Incidentally Visual," in Goodman and Fleming (Eds.), *Psycholinguistics and the Teaching of Reading.* Newark, Delaware: IRA, 1969.

Lipton, Gladys C. "To Read or Not to Read: An Experiment on the FLES Level," *Foreign Language Annals,* III (1969-70) 241-46.

Lloyd, Donald J. and Warfel, Harry Redcay. *American English in Its Cultural Setting.* New York: Knopf, 1956.

Moulton, William Gamwell. *A Linguistic Guide to Language Learning.* New York: Modern Language Association of America, 1966.

Teaching Reading to Disadvantaged Children

S. ALAN COHEN

HERE are two hunches and 12 conclusions about teaching socially disadvantaged children to read and write. Cold data back the conclusions. The hunches are on thinner ice.

Hunch One: Most of the characteristics listed in the literature on socially disadvantaged youth echo textbooks on the adolescent. Certain language patterns are peculiar to slum children. But many psychosocial characteristics associated with socially disadvantaged youth are, in fact, characteristics of adolescents in general, disadvantaged or not.

Hunch Two: Suburban kids sit still, read "Look Jane! Look!", get in line in a hurry, and do their homework no matter how meaningless the task. Slum kids are not as acquiescent; unless it is really meaningful, they are less likely to play according to school rules.

Now, to safer grounds—conclusions based on data.

Conclusion One: Compensatory programs for socially disadvantaged children have not proved successful. The reasons appear to be that the persons involved have not specified goals; they have not delimited goals (they usually bite off more than they can chew); they have not controlled relevant variables; they have not measured outcomes accurately.

Conclusion Two: Most Puerto Rican, Negro, Mexican-American, and Appalachian white children are retarded in reading. Not *many*, but *most*. Many educational administrators are kidding themselves by not recognizing and accepting the magnitude of the problem. When they kid themselves, there is little chance of effecting significant change in reading instruction for these unfortunate children.

Conclusion Three: Most children learn to read, write, and do arithmetic in spite of psychosocial problems. Psycho- or sociotherapy does not need to precede reading instruction.

Conclusion Four: Culturally deprived children learn to read *before* their emotional problems are solved. Many learn to read while they continue to live in slums with

THE EDUCATION DIGEST, May 1967, vol. 32, pp. 40-42.

prostitutes for mothers and narcotics addicts for fathers.

Conclusion Five: Phonics in any form by any name will not win the War on Poverty. Nor will it solve the reading problems of culturally deprived children. However, we do know that retarded readers, socially disadvantaged or not, lack word attack skills, including phonics skills. We do know that training in these word attack skills is one necessary component in a remedial program.

Specifically we know that most socially disadvantaged retarded readers in seventh grade do not know the alphabet. We know, further, that most do not discriminate sounds in words accurately. Most Negro and Puerto Rican children who are retarded in reading in the early grades do not discriminate letters accurately. We know that auditory discrimination of sounds in words and visual discrimination of letters are two prerequisites to successful reading for all children regardless of ethnic background or socioeconomic level.

Conclusion Six: Most socially disadvantaged retarded readers tend to be visual rather than auditory or phonic readers. This is probably true of middle-class retarded readers as well. Their visual memory scores are low, but they are significantly higher than their scores for auditory discrimination of sounds in words. We also know from abundant experience that once hooked on a sight approach to reading, these children are extremely difficult to move to a phonic and structural approach to word attack. This suggests that a linguistic-phonic skill should be built into the beginning reading program early in formal and informal reading instruction—as early, perhaps, as kindergarten. This explains partially why blending sounds is so difficult to teach to retarded readers and leads this author to suggest that sounds in words or diagraphs be taught without blending.

Conclusion Seven: The perceptual development of culturally deprived children at the beginning reading grades (K through three) is severely impaired. Since these children have so little going for them in other areas, these perceptual dysfunctions preclude the possibility that most of them will learn to read well. One major component of a Head Start or kindergarten program should be perceptual training.

Conclusion Eight: Compensatory programs for culturally deprived children are usually more of the same. Most ESEA Title I projects attack quantity rather than quality. More services, longer hours devoted to reading instruction, more basal readers, more time with the teacher will not solve the problem of reading retardation in socially disadvantaged children. New programs utilizing new methods and materials geared to changing quality rather than quantity are what is needed.

Conclusion Nine: One particular approach to teaching reading to all culturally deprived children is not the answer to their reading retardation. Culturally deprived children are human beings, and must be taught as individuals.

Conclusion Ten: Thorough, continuous, quality instruction will teach culturally deprived children to read. A high intensity learning program in which content, level, and rate are adjusted to individual needs has worked every time this author has tried it with socially disadvantaged children and youth.

Conclusion Eleven: Most teachers do not know what materials and methods are available for teaching socially disadvantaged children. They do not read journals and are unaware of research and programs conducted in many sections of the country. Like lawyers and physicians, teachers blame (with good reason) their poor professional training for their deficiencies. But unlike most lawyers and physicians, teachers often do not make up these deficiencies once they enter the field.

Conclusion Twelve: The culturally deprived child depends more on the school for language development and general verbal intelligence than does the middle-class child. In fact, the latter learns most of his verbal behavior, including reading, informally through his home environment. Thus the school has never really had to teach reading and language development. A sort of quick and dirty glossing over has been enough to get middle-class children "on grade level." Now the culturally deprived child has been discovered and we educators are on the spot.

I hope we can deliver. Right now I have my doubts. If we do not deliver, we will be replaced, and by "we" I mean the public schools. Perhaps that gradual replacement has already started under the aegis of the War on Poverty. Look closely and you will see what I mean. •

SECTION IX

ORAL READING *VS.* SILENT READING

READING WITH THE INDIVIDUAL TOUCH

Richard A. Thompson

INTERMEDIATE GRADE TEACHERS frequently say to me, "I recognize that my students have different reading needs, but I don't know how to individualize my reading program." Recognition of the problem is the first step in problem solving. It is the purpose of this article to help with the second part of the question by suggesting a way to meet the reading needs of these students.

Most teachers today know that children at any grade level have a multiplicity of differences. Besides mental ability and experiential background differences, each student varies widely in his ability to comprehend each subject and most certainly the sub-skills within each subject. Reading competencies of students fluctuate widely because reading ability depends upon skillful use of the many word recognition and comprehension sub-skills.

Reading achievement scores at the beginning of the sixth grade typically vary from second to the ninth reading level. By the end of the sixth grade, it is usual to find reading levels from third grade to the eleventh. With each successive year of schooling, students' achievement levels widen as greatly in reading as in any other skill area, or perhaps even more because there are more sub-skills in reading than in other skill subjects. Every teacher realizes that students arrive in the classroom exhibiting several reading achievement levels and many different skill needs. It is no wonder that these teachers ask frequently how they can individualize their reading programs.

Opening the basal reader and using the recipe provided is not the answer. Although admittedly some teachers follow the basal program explicitly and instruct the whole class as if each student needed what is offered one page's worth after another, this kind of reading instruction will not meet the varied needs of students. A procedure such as this meets the reading skill needs of students about as effectively as pellets scattered from a shotgun can drop a whole bevy of ducks. Of course, a few may be hit in either case, but most will escape unscathed.

The alternative to shooting the whole class with the same instruction or to teaching the same lesson to everyone and hoping the instruction "takes" with a few is to instruct students according to their skill needs. Individualizing your reading instruction by focusing on students' specific needs

THE CLEARING HOUSE, January 1973, vol. 47, vo. 5, pp. 296-300.

should provide a similar expectancy. The implication is that a more effective means of teaching reading is to take the trouble to find out the specific reading needs of students and instruct each group of students having similar weaknesses.

The natural question is, "How do I find out these needs?" Teachers have different methods for assessing needs of students. Some are informal, such as skill checklists; and others are formal, such as standardized instruments. The following personal experience in a split class of 44 fifth and sixth graders may provide clarification.

Within the first week of school a group diagnostic reading technique was employed. Each student read three to five lines in the basal reader, and as they read, I noted those who read fluently without errors and those who omitted, repeated, substituted, or didn't know a word. By using this group diagnostic procedure, the students were classified into two groups: those who could read satisfactorily in their basal reader and those who could not.

To those students who had erred on the group diagnostic, I administered the Bond, Clymer and Hoyt, *Silent Reading Diagnostic Tests—Form D-A*,[1] a valuable diagnostic instrument which identifies specific weaknesses and strengths for each student. These were detailed when plotted on the profile which graphically portrayed skill needs and strengths of the students.

Out of 44 fifth and sixth grade students, nine needed work on vowel sounds, and these students formed the first specific skill need group. This group met fifteen minutes daily utilizing the Durrell-Murphy, *Speech-To-Print Phonics*[2] as instructional material. This phonic material proved to be a real asset in sustaining interest because it was easy enough material for these students to meet with success, and the use of the cards required oral responses which helped the students to become active learners.

Besides meeting for fifteen minutes daily in a special skill group, these students were given second, third, and fourth reading level trade books for individualized reading. Their reading levels had been determined by the results of *The Stanford Achievement Test*. Evaluation was carried on by student-teacher conferences, and the information was recorded on each student's record sheet.

Another group was formed from the fifth grade students who read well when given the informal group diagnostic and whose reading achievement test score was between 4.9 and 5.8. Their basic instructional material was the fifth level basal reader and workbook. In the usual five-reading-period-week, three periods were usually reserved for basal reader instruction while recreational reading consumed the remaining two periods.

A sixth grade basal group was formed on a similar basis. The arbitrary criteria was successful reading from the informal group diagnostic and reading achievement test score between 5.9–6.9. Only five sixth grade students had reading achievement scores above 6.9, and they too read independently in individualized reading materials, receiving teacher attention about once a week.

To recapitulate, the fifth grade students were formed into two groups, a basal reader group and individualized readers. The students who had reading achievement test scores below 4.9 and above 5.8 were in individualized reading. The sixth graders also were either in the sixth grade basal group or in the individualized program. Sixth graders whose reading achievement test scores fell between 5.9 and 6.9 formed the sixth grade basal group, while students whose scores were below 5.9 and above 6.9 utilized individualized reading. A score-

[1] G. Bond, T. Clymer, and C. Hoyt. *Silent Reading Diagnostic Tests, Form D-A*. Chicago: Lyons and Carnahan.

[2] Donald D. Durrell and Helen A. Murphy. *Speech-To-Print Phonics*. New York: Harcourt Brace Jovanovich, Inc., 1964.

FIGURE 1

A TYPICAL WEEKLY READING SCHEDULE

Monday	Introduce Story to A 10 Minutes	→	Provide Skill Instruction to B 20 Minutes	→	Meet S for Phonics Instruction 15 Minutes	C Reads Independently
Tuesday	Meet S for Phonics Instruction 15 Minutes	→	Students Work Individually 45 Minutes		A & B Recreational Reading	
Wednesday	Discuss Story and Questions with A 20 Minutes	→	Introduce Story to B 10 Minutes	→	Meet S for Phonics Instruction 15 Minutes	C Reads Independently
Thursday	Meet S for Phonics Instruction 15 Minutes	→	Work Individually with C Students 45 Minutes	→	A & B Recreational Reading	
Friday	Skill Instruction A 15 Minutes	→	Discuss Story and Questions with B 20 Minutes	→	Meet S for Phonics Instruction	C Reads Independently

A = Fifth Grade Basal Group
B = Sixth Grade Basal Group
C = Individualized Group
S = Special Needs Group

board would read: one fifth grade basal group, one sixth grade basal group, one individualized reading group (composed of both fifth and sixth graders), and a special skill group for phonics instruction who were also using individualized reading. Reading was scheduled for one hour daily, and the grouping arrangement followed this pattern, although deviations were made at times.

The basal reader groups were taught rather traditionally following the teachers' manuals, taking from three to five days to present the story and accompanying skill instruction. At times additional materials such as games and ditto sheets were injected (skill practice) to increase the dosage when necessary, and, of course, workbooks were used occasionally for skill reinforcement.

By the time a month had passed, routines were established and things were going reasonably well when it became necessary to make some adjustments. It became necessary to change the reading program because a goal had been met.

If grouping is to facilitate achievement, it must be flexible and modifiable because students' needs and achievements are changeable. The original groupings had to be changed within a month since the special skill group had learned the vowel sounds sufficiently well enough to be disbanded. When grouping by skill needs, it is imperative that the skill need group be disbanded as soon as the members have attained their goal.

The next skill need group was organized on the basis of those students who needed structural analysis skill development. As might be expected, many members of the first group also were included in the new grouping as well as some new members. The structural analysis group came to 15 pupils. A few of this number were very good readers, but they were diagnosed as being in need of this kind of work by having them attack unknown words in their individualized reading. Other members came from the basal groups who had been discovered to need this work during their basal skill developmental activities. Thus, the new skill group was organized. Because the new skill group members came from previous groups, more adjustments necessarily followed which required new groupings. Necessary, too, were new materials.

Those students who were reading on the third reading level formed a group who read Dolch books of the appropriate readability. The major reason for selecting these materials was that these books provided much repetition of the basic 220 words, serving to establish well the students' sight vocabularies, Furthermore, members of this group were participants in the special skill group for structural analysis.

Another group was composed of students who were reading at the fourth reading level, and their books were *Ben Hur, King Arthur,* and *From the Earth to the Moon. Ben Hur* was read first and was followed by the others, one after another as the group completed each selection. For *Ben Hur* and *King Arthur,* I made up questions to be used as purposes for reading and to be used as comprehension questions. *From the Earth to the Moon* came with questions in the back of the book, which was convenient.[8]

The fifth and sixth reading level students continued in the basals respectively, but had supplementary materials for use when warranted. For example, crossword puzzles, scrabble, word origins, and the SRA *Reading For Understanding* kit were used as well as *Gates-Peardon* comprehension exercises.

Those fifth and sixth graders whose reading achievements were above their grade placement levels formed the individualized readers who read independently, self-pacing themselves.

A typical week's reading is approximated in Figure 2.

[8] The Globe Publishing Company's Classics contain comprehension questions.

FIGURE 2

A Typical Weekly Reading Schedule

Monday	Meet S for Structural Analysis Skill Development 15 Minutes	Discuss *Ben Hur* with X 10 Minutes	→ Assist Group A with Creative Enrichment (Dramatization) 15 Minutes →	Present Skill Development Exercise to B 5 Minutes	Assist C Members Individually 15 Minutes
Tuesday	Introduce Story to B 10 Minutes →	Meet S for Skill Development 15 Minutes →	Continue *Ben Hur* story with X 10 Minutes	Group A Continues Enrichment Activity Independently	Group C Recreational Reading
NOTE: 25 minutes is left for general supervision. A good time to provide additional EGO support.					
Wednesday	Group A Performs for Everyone Else 15 Minutes →	Discuss Story and Questions with B Group 15 Minutes →	Meet S for Skill Development 10 Minutes →	See Group C Members 10 Minutes →	Group X Continues Assignments without Help
Thursday	Introduce Story to Group A 10 Minutes →	Present Skill Exercise to Group B 15 Minutes →	Meet S for Discussion of Dolch Book 15 Minutes →	Group C Reads Independently →	Group X Recreational Reading
Friday	Discuss Story and Questions with Group A 15 Minutes →	Meet Group X for Discussion 15 Minutes →	Meet S for Skill Development 15 Minutes →	See Group C Members Individually 15 Minutes	Group B Recreational Reading

A = Fifth Grade Basal Group comprised of fifth reading level students
B = Sixth Grade Basal Group comprised of sixth reading level students
C = Individualized Reading for students reading above grade level
S = Special Needs Group (Structural Analysis Development and Reading Dolch Books—third reading level)
X = Students Reading at 4th level in *Ben Hur, King Arthur,* and *From the Earth to the Moon*

The preceding description was one way that I individualized reading instruction when faced with a split grade of 44 students. Immersion of all these students into basal readers would have been a catastrophe because many of them had met with defeat in basal readers in previous years principally because the readability level of their instructional materials had been too high and provision for specific skill needs were not made. By using multi-level reading materials and a variety of supplementary materials to meet specific reading needs, reading progress of all students was a reasonable expectancy.

Individualization of instruction can be done in many different ways. The principles to follow are: (1) Find specific reading needs of students and program instruction to meet these needs. (2) Find students' instructional reading levels and provide reading materials commensurate with those levels. Reading with the individual touch *is* possible!

Oral reading as a communication process

A. STERL ARTLEY

A. Sterl Artley, past president of IRA; has developed reading programs and directs graduate programs at the University of Missouri, Columbia. In this article, he stresses communicative aspects of oral reading, and suggests ways to make oral interpretation more than a gauge of word perception.

LITERALLY any periodical or textural reference to oral reading either states or implies that the major function of oral reading is to communicate to listeners by voice the thoughts and feelings of a writer. The author usually proceeds to explain how oral reading should be taught to carry out that mission.

The fact that a substantial number of teachers either do not accept the above purpose as the reason for teaching oral reading, or, if they do, fail to see its implications, was indicated recently in an analysis of the responses of over 800 teachers to statements dealing with oral reading found in the *Inventory of Teacher Knowledge of Reading* (Artley 1971) which had been administered as part of an extensive in-service education program. On this instrument, 37 percent indicated that the major justification for oral reading instruction was to stress precision in word perception. In an item asking for a choice among possible reasons why a teacher would have children take turns reading portions of a story sequentially, 47 percent, or almost one half, marked as the one desired, ". . . it gives all children the opportunity to practice word recognition skills." On another item, 44 percent said that the most acceptable way to determine the effectiveness of oral reading was to ". . . take note of the number of word recognition errors the reader makes."

Coupled with such attempts to justify oral reading as a check on word perception is the practice

THE READING TEACHER, 1972, Vol. 26, pp. 46-51.

one finds so frequently in actual teaching situations — that is, of using oral reading chiefly as a test of the reader's ability to pronounce words, while little, if any, attention is given to the communicative aspects of the act. Children frequently engage in "round robin" or around-the-group oral reading of a selection, paragraph by paragraph, frequently in a high pitched unnatural voice. Hawk-like, the teacher and the other members of the group sit waiting to pounce upon the reader at the first word miscalled. Apparently something still needs to be said about oral reading — its purpose and its teaching.

Purposes for oral reading

An article that remains almost a classic in the area of oral reading is one by W. S. Gray, "Characteristics of Effective Oral Reading" (1955), presented as a paper at the Eighteenth Annual Reading Conference at the University of Chicago. The major portion of the paper discusses oral reading as a "unique art in communicating ideas to others."

The reason for Gray's emphasis of the communication aspect of oral reading should be obvious when one considers just what real-life purpose or function oral reading serves, regardless of where and when it is done. Emphatically it is not to demonstrate the reader's ability to pronounce words. Word perception, though necessary, is only peripheral or incidental to the main and only reason for reading aloud—which is to interpret to interested listeners the ideas, information, feeling, mood or action that is in printed or written form. *It is an act of interpretation.* Obviously the interpretation is more effective when the words are perceived rapidly and accurately, but pronouncing words is only the means to the end of communicating a message that a writer has to convey and a reader wishes to transmit.

There will be occasions when a teacher or clinician wishes to test a child's ability to perceive words in context. This may be done through the use of an informal inventory. In this case the teacher wants to diagnose the kinds of reading errors made and the nature of the thinking process the child uses when he comes to a word not perceived instantaneously. But that is a test situation engaged in for a specific purpose and not the real-life reason for teaching oral reading. In fact, Heilman (1967, p. 178) questions whether oral reading for diagnostic purposes represents a true oral reading situation "since pupil purpose, informing an audience, is not paramount." Oral reading as an exercise in word pronunciation is one of the most useless instructional practices that a teacher can carry out. It is the perseverance of a practice from the past that has no justification in a modern classroom.

Oral reading and silent

One can hardly discuss oral reading or oral interpretation, as we shall refer to it from here on, apart from silent reading. Each serves a particular function — silent reading to reconstruct the writer's ideas, to sense the mood or feeling; oral, to interpret what the writer says or feels to concerned listeners. Figuratively speaking, one is a "getting" task, the other a "giving," and the two should not be confused as to purpose.

Gray, in the paper already alluded to, states that there are four significant tasks involved in effective oral interpretation: 1) grasping an author's intended meaning, 2) sensing the mood and emotional reactions which the author intended to produce, 3) conveying the author's intended meaning to a listener, and 4) conveying the mood and feeling. In other words, silent reading serves as a foundation for oral interpretation, for it is there that the reader concentrates on meaning, on the reconstruction of the writer's ideas, on the mood or emotional tone that is implied. This the reader must do before he can transmit those ideas to others.

Sensing fully through silent analysis what the writer wishes to say, the reader is now prepared, if the occasion requires it, to convey it to others, hopefully, in the same manner that the writer himself would do were he present. The oral interpreter, in a figurative sense, serves as a stand-in for the author, and through appropriate inflection, emphasis, pauses, and expression, conveys to others the feeling, action, or information that he has already secured for himself.

Occasions for oral interpretation

Many legitimate situations arise during the course of a school day, both in and outside the reading period, to interpret material aloud. The following are only examples:

- dramatizing informally a story or portion of a story
- conveying the step-by-step directions for playing a game or performing an experiment
- interpreting an exciting passage from a book being read as personal reading
- reading a news article
- choral reading
- interpreting a portion of a story that the reader likes best
- interpreting the mood or feeling expressed in a poem
- proving a point or offering evidence for an idea
- reading a joke or riddle
- interpreting the characterization or action of a play
- entertaining children on a lower grade level.

In each situation the reader has an honest to goodness reason for interpreting the story, poem, or textual material to someone else. In some cases the reader is the only one who has the book or poem being interpreted.

Many linguists are pointing out that a special purpose for oral interpretation exists in the early stages of learning to read. That is to develop the concept that printed symbols stand for and may be turned into speech. This reason, however, in no way negates what has been said about functional reading.

The point being made is that the young child comes to school already having attained a high level of performance in communicating orally. As he begins to meet written language he needs to understand that the words that comprise it symbolize spoken words. The teacher usually begins to develop this concept by having the child dictate words, phrases, or sentences which the teacher writes on the chalkboard or beneath a picture as a caption or title. As the teacher reads his sentences aloud the child can see his spoken words become written symbols which, in turn, become spoken words. Further understanding of this concept takes place as the child is given an opportunity to speak the words he meets in his early reading books. Hence, as many linguists have pointed out, there is a need for more oral reading experiences at this level than at any other time.

This is not to be taken, however, as a justification for oral round robin reading in the first grade. Even on this level the reading should be a purposeful activity — reading to find out and interpret. In teaching a story on an early reading level the teacher might say, "The first sentence under the picture tells what William did. Read it to yourselves. Now, who would like to read it aloud?" She queries as she guides the novice reader from sentence, to sentences, to paragraphs. In this way reading becomes the act of making the black marks talk.

Oral reading is always a purposeful activity of interpreting what a writer says to someone who has occasion to listen. If no good purpose exists, if the others in the group already know what the writer has said, then there is no occasion for oral reading. There is no rule in the book that says that every child must read aloud every day.

Developing ability to interpret orally

Standard texts of reading methods frequently list the competencies that contribute to effective oral interpretation. Lists frequently include such abilities as

- facility in the perception of words
- flexibility in voice pitch, volume, and rate
- ability to phrase or group words in thought units
- ability to identify with story characters and give proper expression to action and feelings
- ability to pronounce and articulate acceptably
- ability to use appropriate body movements and facial expressions.

In general such abilities can be developed more effectively by an indirect approach than by a direct one. That is to say rather than teaching a "style" of dramatic expression the teacher might more profitably spend his time helping readers comprehend the writer's ideas and perceive the dramatic quality, feeling, emotion, or the mood and tone of the passage.

On the playground and in the home children have no difficulty in expressing very dramatically and effectively through voice and action such feelings as surprise, anger, indecision, distrust, fear, or sorrow. In no uncertain terms they are able to make statements of fact. They think and feel in a variety of ways, and experience has taught them how to express their ideas and emotions appropriately and convincingly. Hence, in interpreting printed material aloud the reader needs to understand that in a sense, words are being placed in his mouth by a writer to express a particular idea or emotion. He needs to do in a make-believe manner what he does normally all the time. Gray confirms this contention in these words:

> The training of pupils to convey meaning effectively is an insightful but subtle art. The teacher should have a good understanding of the techniques or skills involved. However, he does not center attention on them as such. . . . The teacher relies far more largely on helping the child to grasp clearly the idea to be presented than on formal directions concerning modes of expression. (p. 9)

Further in the article Gray adds:

> . . . If the reader senses mood and feeling vividly and appropriately and is eager to read to others, he will need little guidance in these techniques. (p. 10)

Instructional implications

The instructional implication is to direct the reader's attention to what the writer is saying, to the ideas he is trying to express, and, in the case of a story or poem, to the feeling or emotional tone he desires to convey. For example, assume that the instructional group has just completed the silent reading of "Henry and Ribs" from Beverly Cleary's *Henry Huggins* (1950). Because the story has a great deal of dramatic conversation it lends itself admirably to interpretive reading.

To enhance the action and humor of the story the teacher asks the children if there is a part they would like to interpret to the others. One child selects the episode showing Henry in the phone booth talking to his unenthusiastic mother, trying to convince her to let him keep a mangy dog with whom he has just shared his ice cream cone. Though in his reading he identifies all the words correctly, he interprets the action in only a matter of fact manner.

At this point the teacher says, "Have you ever done what Henry is trying to do to convince your mother that you wanted something badly? Maybe you know she's not going to be easy to convince. Now, how will you read that part to make it sound real? Let's try it now."

The reader tries again. Though his phrasing and inflection have improved, the teacher thinks he can do still better. So, he says, "That was much better, but I don't believe you have convinced your mother. Imagine yourself in the phone booth. Hold an imaginary receiver to your ear and *say* the line, 'He's a good dog, and I'd feed him and wash him and everything. Please, Mom.' Don't *read* it; just *say* it, and remember, you just must have the dog."

Following the teacher's suggestion and divorcing himself from the words of the book, the reader's voice takes on a natural quality, even to the pleading, whining, "Please, Mom." "Good," the teacher says, "Now you have it. Now *read* it just the way you *said* it."

One could have additional fun with this episode by asking several children to interpret the same passage to see which could make his voice sound more convincing. A tape recorder would also be a useful device in this situation, for children like to hear their own voice. One child might record the same passage several different ways, so that he could note how much more effective one was over another. Any kind of activity that would help the reader identify with the situation and provide an opportunity to project the action and feeling through his voice would be useful and effective — puppetry, informal dramatization of a story with children volunteering for "parts," choral reading where the shy child can lose his voice with those of others, turning a story into a play with stage instructions for action and interpretation, are all variations of this technique.

Taught or caught?

Since so much of what children learn is caught rather than taught, and since children are such skillful imitators (Have you ever seen yourself in a group of children playing school?), another effective way of teaching oral interpretation is through the model the teacher presents through his own interpretative reading. Seldom should a day pass, certainly not a week, without the teacher on any of the elementary levels doing interpretive reading in connection with some event, project, or situation, if for no reason other than to provide an opportunity for children to experience good literature, well read.

Obviously the teacher must prepare for this reading as meticulously as though he were preparing a presentation before a group of discerning adults. Though not necessarily a goal in the reading of *Charlotte's Web,* for example, one should not be surprised to have children applaud when Wilbur wins the special prize at the county fair, or to hear sniffles and see misty eyes at the death of Charlotte.

Frequently a teacher can give additional effectiveness to his interpretation by "reading-telling" a story, that is by reading several paragraphs and then by telling in his own words the next dramatic episode, changing voice to characterize the various speakers. The story goes that a teacher was reading-telling the story of the three little pigs to a group of young children. Apparently she was giving a very dramatic rendition as she said, "The bad, old fox crept up to the first little pig's house, and do you know what he did? He huffed and he puffed (she illustrated) and he blew that little pig's house all to pieces." Whereupon she heard one little ragamuffin say disgustedly, "That damned old fox!"

The concept of oral reading as a check on word perception should be replaced by oral interpretation as a process of communicating to interested listeners a writer's ideas, thoughts, and feelings. Accurate word perception, though certainly a legitimate teaching objective, can be tested by more effective means than by having children engage in round robin reading. Oral interpretation is not unlike art, the dance, or music in providing children with the opportunity for creative self-expression. As such, it becomes in its own right an extremely important objective in a well rounded reading program.

References

Artley, A. Sterl, and Hardin, Veralee. *Inventory of Teacher Knowledge of Reading.* Columbia, Mo.: The Missouri Store Co., 1971.

Cleary, Beverly. *Henry Huggins.* New York: William Morrow, 1950.

Gray, W. S. "Characteristics of Effective Oral Reading." *Oral Aspects of Reading.* Ed. H. Robinson. Supplementary Educational Monographs, No. 82, December 1955. Chicago: University of Chicago Press, 1955.

Heilman, Arthur. *Principles and Practices in Teaching Reading.* Columbus: Charles Merrill, 1967.

Subtleties of the reading group

WALLACE RUSSO

AS NEW METHODS of teaching reading are developed, educators are forced to re-evaluate the old. However, the re-evaluation is oftentimes confined to specific salient goals of the new; the supplementary and subtle values of the old are discounted, ignored, or overlooked. The small reading group method used in elementary schools for years has many of these values that should be considered at this time, for it is being measured against such methods as programmed, completely individualized, and mass homogenous class instruction.

CONSIDER THE ARRANGEMENT

When the elementary school teacher calls for a reading group to assemble at the side or back of the classroom, children in the group move into a small circular seating pattern that facilitates maximum verbal communication. In this face-to-face pattern the teacher who is an opportunist can incidentally alert listeners when a group member augments his contribution with facial expressions or body movements. Likewise, the speaker can be made aware of the worth of spontaneous reactions of his listeners. With practice, children should soon be able to look beyond words they hear for enriching shadings in oral communication.

In kindergarten and grade one when children tend to have polarized emotional concepts (to them one appears unhappy unless he is laughing or smiling broadly) the teacher can stress basic supplementary actions, such as a forehead stretched into an unmistakable frown and clapping indicating joy. Children with greater maturity can learn to interpret such shadings as eyebrows raised in disbelief and the emergence of a slight smile.

While strengthening oral communication, the teacher cannot help improving reading comprehension. For example in almost all basic reading series, the authors suggest that the teacher encourage children to form conclusions about story characters from pictures or words describing character actions and reactions. Students have observed and used in their discussions many of the facial expressions and body movements pictured or described in their readers;

THE READING TEACHER, February 1970, vol. 23, pp. 429-431.

consequently, they should require very little, if any, special instruction to apply real life experiences to find meaning in semi-abstract and abstract situations.

If pupils do need help, the teacher can employ one of the tried and true methods: having children give spontaneous dramatizations of story action with subsequent pupil-teacher evaluations to determine whether the author's intent was revealed. Having grouped children according to reading problems, the teacher can use effectively this and other horizontal reinforcement activities. He is freed from the fear of boring some students and losing others as frequently happens when an entire class must sit through several variations of a lesson that has been mastered by or is too complex for a sizeable segment of children. He can take necessary pauses in the program for firm step-by-step reading development.

The face-to-face relationships in the reading group make possible direct, immediate exchanges between student and teacher and student and student. Few educators will attempt to refute the commonly held belief that children seem to learn as much (if not more) from one another as from the teacher.

Therefore, the teacher who believes this will promote student to student communication during discussions. One of the simplest methods is for the teacher to yield to the students, whenever possible and practical, his discussion leadership role. When a student makes an observation about a situation in a story, he should be allowed the courtesy of defending or clarifying his observation as it is challenged or questioned by fellow group members. *He* should recognize students who wish to speak directly to him while his remarks are under fire. Thus, the teacher is partially removed from his standard position as the intermediary through whom students find it necessary to speak to one another. Children can place more concern on fellow students rather than teacher opinions about their contributions.

The circular arrangement, also, may be a factor in preventing students from "tuning out" the teacher, providing the teacher learns that his words have better reception if he decreases the volume of his voice several notches below that of his normal fullclass delivery. Following the teacher's practice, children will make similar adjustments in volume appropriate for their distances apart. Delicate meanings of impromptu statements need not be modified by the speaker's annoyance over having to repeat his words to wayward listeners, for lower voices not only reduce the strain on the listener's ear but also tend to give an atmosphere of privacy to conversations.

And how expressive the soft voice can be! Pupils can be encouraged to read in a real whisper passages to be whispered. They can savor the tenderness of a faint sigh. They can sense the alarm apparent in the sound of the gentle but sudden inhalation of air.

ESPRIT DE CORPS AND RESPECT FOR THE INDIVIDUAL

"Now *my* group is going to read," might well be the thought of each student during the first few fleeting moments when his reading group is finally settled and poised to begin work. Children enjoy the security of the group's separation from the rest of the class and, knowing they are all on the same reading level, sit with little fear of embarrassment. A feeling of group cohesiveness can be developed if the teacher enlists students to help students as reading problems arise, and views as significant each student's contribution, whether it is simply the identification of an initial consonant sound or a conclusion reached about a main idea of a story. Students receiving such treatment will be willing to assist one another to reach common goals.

In the absence of the threat of ridicule and in the presence of a co-operative spirit in discussions, children can develop sound concepts about truth, value, and reality. When the teacher encourages children to evaluate what they believe to be the underlying reasons for the behavior of a story character, they are afforded opportunities to identify with the character.

To be sure, students' perception of people, objects, and situations in the character's environment will vary, and the reading group soon becomes a dynamic market place for perceptions. Vicarious experiences are bought and sold so long as tolerance, a critical element for this free trade, is practiced by all the merchants. The teacher, mainly by his example, promotes sincere respect for each individual's judgments. Each contributor must enjoy the privilege of having his views aired, even when he constitutes a minority of one. It is the listener's job to attempt to see things from the speaker's point of view. Only when minds are held open can the group, guided by the teacher, arrive at a consensus that will be honestly accepted by almost all.

In this process children are *really* learning from one another about one another and about themselves. Also, as children reveal—through the medium of story characters, their attitudes, beliefs, and pressing perplexing problems—the teacher is able to construct a sensitive mosaic of each child, a mosaic that enables him to become more empathetic toward each of his students. What greater values could any method of instruction have?

Therefore, any educator contemplating replacing the small reading group would do well to take a second look at secondary considerations. He should weigh all the values of each method with regard to the total educational program, not just within the narrow boundaries of subject-centered objectives.

IMPLEMENTING AN INDIVIDUALIZED READING PROGRAM

Richard A. Thompson

Classroom teachers are becoming increasingly interested in individualized reading. Recent studies seem to indicate that the individualized approach to teaching reading tends to produce favorable results. With teacher interest being abetted by positive evidence that individualized reading is worthwhile, teachers want to know how the individualized reading approach is implemented. How to implement, conduct, and evaluate individualized reading instruction is the focus of this article.

What is the teacher's role in the individualized reading program?

According to Witty et al. (1959), the teacher's role would be primarily that of consultant and resource person to the student. She would be a manager of the classroom environment, supplying a variety of materials and at times initiating new experiences. She would help pupils learn to plan, to evaluate, and to consider alternatives. The main focus of her activity would be self-direction.

She would meet the children individually or in groups for evaluating, diagnosing needs, and teaching skills when they are needed. The teacher must be able to see the children growing creatively rather than moving ir predetermined paths.

The whole program depends upon the teacher's diagnostic skills in identifying children's needs relative to reading skills, in selecting reading materials, and in evaluating the progress o pupils.

How should reading materials for the classroom be selected?

Cook (1965) recommends that a minimum of ten books be available fo each child at various levels of diffi culty. Although most authorities rec ommend a minimum of five books pe child, ten books per student provide a greater flexibility than five an should be strived for.

Tradebooks, textbooks, librar books, a variety of graded readers and other printed materials are sug gested. Another source of material i the students themselves. They ca write experience stories and compil them in a booklet.

By providing youngsters with a wid range of books for, about, and b minority groups as well as those tha feature the urban environment, th teacher immediately removes som barriers to reading (Keener, 1967 This suggestion is particularly valuab for the disadvantaged.

Veatch (1967) says the best boo being published are the trade book Help should be sought from the l

INDIANA READING QUARTERLY, April 1971, vol. 3, no. 3, pp. 6-9.

brarian to find appropriate materials. Paperbacks and children's book clubs provide inexpensive books. Supplementary books published by basal publishers and a few copies of basal readers are good to have in the classroom library.

In any system of teaching reading, you need special workbooks, games, charts, and so on to teach phonics and other skills. Individualized reading does not lessen the necessity for having many suitable materials available.

How does the child select an appropriate book for individualized reading?

Care must be taken to insure that the child is selecting books on his instructional reading level. Inappropriate reading level materials will defeat the purpose of any reading program.

Veatch (1967) says by "Rule of Thumb", have the child choose a book on a topic he likes. Have him open the book near the middle to a page with many words on it. Ask him to read it silently. When he comes to a word he doesn't know, he puts down his thumb on the table. If he meets another he doesn't know he puts down his next finger, and so on. If he uses up all the fingers on one hand, that book is too hard for him. He should put it back and choose another one. The child's independent reading level is his instructional level.

Dolch (1961) says that ideally, the child should not miss more than three words per page. If the books chosen are too hard, skipping will inevitably result and wrong habits will be cultivated.

Careful selection of appropriate, readable materials is essential for pupil success in an individualized reading program.

How are the skills taught?

Grouping children for the teaching of basic skills may be used for the children who indicate common needs. For example, if some students need to acquire word attack skills, they may be grouped for instruction. Whenever the skills are sufficiently learned, the student returns to reading independently.

Some persons wish to use workbooks to practice on separate skills in individualized reading. Formerly the whole class practiced the same thing whether some individuals needed this practice or not. With the individualized method, the teacher, in conferring with a single child, can see just what skill he needs and can assign him just the practice pages she thinks he needs.

According to Dolch (1961) sight vocabulary can be learned through the interest in games. Games have built-in motivation which should be capitalized upon.

What is the role of group activity in the individualized reading program?

Group activity should allow the teacher to teach the pupils what they don't know at the time she discovers they need it. Children following mutual interests can be grouped together. The psychological brutality of ability grouping is not desirable and is avoidable if grouping by interests or needs is used (Veatch, 1967).

According to Vite (1961), individualized reading need not place limitations on good group experiences. There are many wholesome, meaningful, sociable, enjoyable and fruitful group experiences inherent in such programs. Some types of grouping she suggested were: grouping for conferences, social purposes, spontaneous social grouping, grouping for an audience reading, grouping for special interests and grouping for skill needs.

Wilson (1965) says that grouping makes sense only in terms of immediate purpose in an individualized approach, as in bringing a small group together to teach a certain skill. A particular skill development should be the basis of grouping in an individualized reading program.

Does the basal reader have a place in the individualized reading program?

Basal readers can be used on a self-selection basis or to teach certain skills, such as oral reading of a conversation, a single copy or in small groups; but as a series, with manual, hitting all the pre-planned processes would violate the basic philosophical principles of self-selection (Veatch, 1967).

How does the teacher evaluate comprehension and other reading skills?

Just as in any other program, evaluation can be made with standardized achievement tests and by following outlines set up for individual conferences.

Emans (1965) conducted a study where twenty teachers in a graduate course in remedial reading each judged the skills of two children. The teachers were asked, for each of the two children with whom they had worked individually an hour every day for five weeks, to rank fifteen reading skills in the order in which the children needed help. The findings indicate that the twenty teachers involved in the study were unable to distinguish the skills on which the children needed help unless they determined them by a well-accepted reading test. As this study brings out, evaluation should be systematic and include check lists, standardized achievement tests, diagnostic reading tests, and anecdotal record keeping.

How much time should be devoted to individual conferences with pupils?

It may be as little as three to five minutes daily, ten minutes a week, or more if the pupil needs more help. Spache (1967) recommends two to four per child per week. Some teachers meet this situation by making a schedule which insures that all pupils will have conferences in turn. Others offer a schedule sheet on which children may write their names when they feel the need for a conference or wish to report on a book they have read.

What records should be kept on each child?

If the teacher follows Spache's suggestions, he will collect five basic types of records for each child. These may be placed in a notebook, a card file, or a folder. The first records include the facts acquired from the school's cumulative record-keeping system. These should include the child's age, I.Q., mental age, reading interests and general comments on his interest, progress, and difficulties. Scores from recent standardized and informal reading tests may be included. A record of the child's instructional, independent, and potential reading levels will be obtained during the initial inventory conference. A third record will be that of his oral reading behaviors. A fourth record will contain an analysis of the pupil's oral reading errors as observed during the inventory conference and several subsequent conferences during which the child reads orally. The final set of records will include those notes that each teacher deems adequate for judging and guiding the progress of the pupils. These may include such items as titles of books read, degree of and types of comprehension shown, child's reaction to the book, plans for sharing his selections and the like.

On reporting to the teacher, the child's record should include only the name of the book, the author, a brief comment and sometimes a notation about the size or length of the book.

Can any teacher successfully direct an individualized reading program?

Veatch (1967) answers affirmatively that any teacher can learn to individualize to the extent he envisages the approach.

Spache (1967) says some teachers are capable of planning and organizing the procedure rather readily while others find it difficult to adjust to a relatively large number of individualized or small group activities. But it is quite feasible for all teachers to develop a personal program at their own pace beginning at first with a few of the better readers. Later the approach may be extended to more of the superior group and then gradually to the average pupils as the teacher's skill in planning and directing the program increases.

A flexible teacher with a positive attitude toward individualized reading should be able to use this approach if sufficient and appropriate materials are available.

REFERENCES

Cook, Opera. "Individualized Reading: Another Look," *The Florida Reading Quarterly,* I (March, 1965).

Dolch, E. W. "Individualized Reading vs. Group Reading," *Elementary English,* XXXVIII (December, 1961).

Emans, Robert. "Teacher Evaluation of Reading Skills and Individualized Reading," *Elementary English,* XLII (March, 1965), 258-260.

Hunt, Lyman C., Jr. *The Individualized Reading Program: A Guide for Classroom Teaching,* I.R.A. 1966-1967.

Keener, Beverly M. "Individualized Reading and the Disadvantaged," *The Reading Teacher,* XX (February, 1967) 410-412.

Spache, George D. *Reading in the Elementary School,* Allyn and Bacon, Inc., Boston, 1967.

Veatch, Jeanette. "A Reply to the Critics of Individualized Reading," *The Florida Reading Quarterly,* IV (December, 1967) 2-10.

Vite, Irene W. "Grouping Practices in Individualized Reading." *Elementary English,* XXXVIII (February, 1961) 91-98.

Wilson, Richard C. *Individualized Reading—A Practical Approach,* Wm. C. Brown Book Co., Dubuque, 1965.

Witty, Paul, Anne Coomer and Robert Sizemore. "Individualized Reading—A Summary and Evaluation," *Elementary English,* XXXVI (October, 1959) 401-412.

Wolfson, Bernice J. "Pupil and Teacher Roles in Individualized Instruction," *The Elementary School Journal,* LXVIII (April, 1968) 357-366.

SECTION X

READING AND THE AFFECTIVE DOMAIN

Affective growth through reading

MARGARET GREER

Arguing for reading as an affective experience, the author offers numerous ideas and techniques to move toward that goal. A teacher for twenty-three years, she now coordinates the Hoover Middle School Project, Albuquerque Public Schools in New Mexico.

THE children sit on the "reading rug" in a tight circle about the teacher listening to the reading of *Old Yeller*. Now they lean closer to catch the description of Yeller's battle to save the mother and brother from a rabid wolf. Travis shoots the wolf, saves his dog, and expresses his relief that all are safe, thanks to the bravery of Old Yeller.

The teacher's voice breaks as she reaches the part where Travis realizes that he must destroy his dog because Old Yeller has been bitten by a rabid animal. Silence follows as she attempts to regain sufficient composure to continue reading. Then, from the back of the group comes a soft "Oh, God! I wish they had rabies shots then."

This teacher and her children are engaged in an affective reading experience.

The need for affective development and the school's responsibility for meeting this need have been well established by others (Combs and Snygg, 1959; Henry, 1963; Goodman, 1964; Friedenberg, 1959; Krathwohl, 1956; Raths, 1966; and Rogers, 1961). The classroom reading program is a context which offers many opportunities for affective growth. Such a program reflects an equal concern for both skills and affective development. There is recognition that the same content—stories, poems, plays—can be used as a means to both types of growth. Finally, selection of affective learning experiences is based on knowledge and understanding of the way in which affect develops.

THE READING TEACHER, 1972, Vol. 25, pp. 336-341.

Affective development

The basic element in affective development is *feeling*, the direct experiencing of any phenomena at a given moment. As a process, feeling is the energy system, the force which makes possible all affective growth. Feeling has two dimensions, depth and breadth. Depth refers to the intensity, the degree of experiencing at a given moment, while breadth denotes that which is felt, the products of feeling—emotions.

Through the continuing process of feeling, each individual gradually acquires an expanding store of emotions. Values are formed when certain emotions begin to cluster about and to be associated with given objects, people, states, events. The role of feeling in a developing affective system is, therefore, a crucial one.

An interrelationship exists among feeling, emotions, and values. At every state of development, each shapes and is shaped by the other. The ability to feel more deeply influences the quality and quantity of emotions produced; the larger the store of emotions available to one, the broader the plane for feeling; the number and types of emotions associated with a given value determine the individual's commitment to that value.

Affective dvelopment is seen as a continuum of growth involving three basic elements, feeling-emotions-values, and a dynamic relationship among them. Individual growth along the continuum requires the active participation of the learner. The child who whispered a prayer for rabies vaccine as he listened to the reading cited earlier was fulfilling this requirement. He could not have been told how or what to feel about the incident. The response he made was the result of his feeling, his own experiencing of the drama being described in the story. Emotions are not passed from one individual to another; each produces his own through the process of feeling. Values belong to those who have built the emotional store necessary to generate and sustain them.

Active involvement in affective experiences in reading provides for individual growth in sensitivity, identification, and empathy, all of which are necessary to the full development of affective potential. Sensitivity emerges as a result of the ability to feel and the presence of a context for feeling; it is a readiness to participate in the affective process. Readiness involves an awakening, an awareness, a tuning in, an ability to receive.

Identification is a focusing on, a clarification of that which exists only as a vague sensation in the initial stage of involvement. The process of feeling is activated, and a match is made between emotions and events, states, objects, people. Sensitivity and identification are both products isolated within the individual, and the potential of each as a force in affective development is limited until provision is made for empathy, a sharing of emotions and the feeling process by those engaged in an affective experience.

Promoting affective development

The foregoing description of affective development suggests useful guidelines for planning a classroom reading program in which each learner has the opportunity to move toward fulfillment of his own affective potential.

1. Learning experiences are selected to provide a balance between skills and affective development.
2. Activities, materials, environment, and teaching strategies required for affective growth are systematically planned and incorporated into the reading program throughout the year.
3. Activities are structured a) to create a context for feeling in increasingly greater depth, b) to expand the store of emotions available, c) to stimulate analysis of emotions and values, d) to provide for sharing of the entire affective process.

Affective learning through reading

Many stories in reading texts provide for examining emotions. Where fear is a dominant theme, the teacher may ask, "Have you ever been really afraid?" Children probe their own experience backgrounds to locate incidents that portray the appropriate emotion. As each recounts an event, he recreates for himself and for listeners, the opportunity to feel, to generate the emotion. As a member of the group, the teacher may offer stories from her own experiences.

Any number of emotions may be explored by following this procedure; bringing the activity to a close presents the only difficulty, for telling personal experiences has its own dynamics in which hearing about one event reminds each listener of other experiences he is eager to recount.

Opportunities to share

A broad range of activities, that provides for exchange of personal responses to reading content, should be included in the reading program. The very act of sharing denotes active involvement, direct participation in the feeling process. The context in which the exchange takes place offers an additional dimension for affective growth. Whether the medium is discussion, a form of dramatization, or an artistic production, each provides a setting in which an affective tone develops as the result of interaction among participants focused on a theme, an idea.

Small groups, formed periodically to discuss a particular book read by members of the group, make possible the exchange of viewpoints, attitudes, emotions generated by the content. Through similar encounters over a period of time, each individual's affective store is enriched by exposure to attitudes and values different from his own. He may gain a better understanding and greater acceptance of the views and feelings of others, thus establishing a base for further affective development. The act of exchange itself is a means for growth.

Expressive activities

A student may present a book or story to the entire class by using any one of a variety of techniques. He may prepare special materials: a mural depicting a dramatic scene, a set of drawings following a story sequence, or three dimensional characters done in clay or papier-mache. He may use live pets for demonstration or dress as the main character and role-play a scene. Bulletin boards using a variety of materials to portray events in a story or a book may be prepared by an individual or a group. A shoe box turned on its side to form a "theater" may be used for three dimensional representations of scenes, events, or characters from a favorite story. Instead of "theaters," shoe boxes may become peep boxes with three dimensional scenes inside.

Such activities offer a number of avenues to affective growth. For children less proficient in verbal skills, drawing, building, and dramatization are excellent alternatives for expressing emotional reactions. For the more articulate child, depicting affective responses in a less verbal medium can become a special challenge, as the act of creating, regardless of the medium, is an affective experience.

Sharing "creations," whether in terms of artistic productions or dramatic presentations, should be expanded to include environments and others outside one's own classroom. Children's work may be displayed in the library, office, teachers' lounge, cafeteria, hallways—even the custodian's closet if he would like to brighten up the place.

Across ages

Interaction across age levels is an additional means for extending the sphere of affective influence. Upper grade children may share affective reading experiences with children in lower grades in several ways. Some may go to lower grades to read to small groups; others may develop skills as storytellers for younger children; still others may prepare different types of dramatic presentations such as plays or puppet shows based on stories and books appropriate to children of a younger age level.

Cross-age associations through these activities can result in marked changes in interpersonal relations among children involved. Older children have an opportunity to see younger ones in a different perspective as they share emotional experiences through reading content.

These mutual changes in perspective begin to be reflected in behaviors of children from both age groups. They begin greeting each other by name right out in public places like hallways, the playground—even the principal's office. Older children have less need to ignore little ones, and the latter suffer fewer pangs of approach-avoidance in their encounters with the Big People. With barriers that often separate age groups removed, each can view the other as truly human, despite differences in size and age.

Reading to children

Perhaps no experience provides greater possibilities for nurturing affective growth through involvement in the feeling process than does listening to the teacher read a story or book. Oral reading makes possible the setting of an affective tone not available in silent reading. Through pitch, stress, rhythm, and intonation, the reader can "play" the content much as a fine pianist interprets a musical score.

The teacher becomes a model as she reveals by her responses an emotional involvement in that which is being read. Children see that showing of emotions is acceptable, even desirable. Freedom to feel and to express that which is felt is a necessary condition for affective growth; the teacher provides the means by example and by acceptance of emotions as they surface in the group.

Through active involvement in group listening, children have the opportunity to develop the types of sensitivity, identification, and empathy that are crucial factors in affective development. Each child brings to the listening situation a unique sensitivity derived from his capacity to feel and his openness to receive. His level of "readiness" to participate in the affective process through listening will differ from others, but the oral context and the story content provide the means for involvement at a variety of levels.

As he listens, the feeling process is activated. Descriptions of places, events in the story, and the emotions associated with them come to represent similar situations from his own experience. He feels with the characters being portrayed, relives story experiences being described. Once he has identified with the emotional theme of the story, he is capable of participation in a broader dimension of the affective process—empathy.

Now he can share with other listeners what he feels about the story situation. Whereas sensitivity and identification are personal matters between himself and the story content, empathy is a group sharing of that which each has derived on his own through the former two. The process of sharing establishes a different atmosphere for feeling, a new direction for relating one to another.

Affective growth: a goal

Facilitating cognitive and physical growth through a systematically planned and sequentially developed program has long been a goal of educators; it is imperative that equal emphasis also be given to affective growth. This area of development is too important to be left to chance or to incidental learnings, for one is a "fully functional individual" (Combs, 1962) only to the extent that all his potentials for growth are met. Just as cognitive growth may be fostered by a comprehensive program of experiences designed to elevate thinking to higher levels, so may affective potential be developed by a program rich in a variety of affective experiences so structured as to elicit greater and greater depth of feeling and to produce an expanding repertoire of emotions.

The classroom reading program can become a major source for growth along the affective continuum. The content of reading materials provides the affective substance; the use of the content determines whether or not it serves affective goals. The reading teacher who structures reading content to provide a broad program of affective experiences as described herein makes possible the achievement of a major educational objective—the full development of affective potential for all children.

References

Combs, A. W. (Ed.) *Perceiving, Behaving, Becoming.* A New Focus for Education. Washington, D.C.: Association for Supervision and Curriculum Development, 1962.

Combs, A. W., and Snygg, D. *Individual Behavior.* (Rev. ed.) New York: Harper & Brothers, 1959.

Friedenberg, E. Z. *The Vanishing Adolescent.* Boston: Beacon Press, 1959.

Gipson, Fred. *Old Yeller.* New York: Pocket Books, Inc., 1957.

Goodman, Paul. *Compulsory Mis-Education.* New York: Horizon Press, 1964.

Henry, Jules. *Culture Against Man.* New York: Vintage Books, 1963.

Krathwohl, D. R., et al. *Taxonomy of Educational Objectives:* Handbook II: Affective Domain. New York: David McKay Company, 1956.

Raths, L. E., et al. *Values and Teaching.* Working with Values in the Classroom. Columbus: Charles E. Merrill, 1966.

Rogers, C. R. *On Becoming a Person.* Boston: Houghton Mifflin Company, 1961.

Dragons I have known and loved

NORMA J. LIVO

A lifelong love of dragons prompted Norma Livo to "drag in" this information about the famous and fabulous creatures. Her whimsical account may just brighten your day, or it may encourage you to take a closer look at these perennial child favorites. The author is an associate professor at the University of Colorado, Denver.

A train is a dragon that roars
through the dark.
He wriggles his tail as he sends
up a spark.
He pierces the night with his one
yellow eye,
And all the earth trembles when
he rushes by.*

JUST as no two people are alike, no two classes are alike. Interests differ. Points of humor differ. Tastes differ.

I remember fondly one class as being a Winnie the Pooh class. Another class was dinosaur mad and yet another class was dragon happy. That was the year of the song "Puff the Magic Dragon." I guess as Confucius or somebody else said, "One good dragon deserves another" and so the year went.

Since that year, I have a very special spot in my heart for dragons, though as a child I dearly loved the song, "I'm a Reluctant Dragon," so maybe my love for dragons really started then.

References to dragons are found in such diverse places as the *Bible*, collections of children's poems, books of literature, cartoons, books of children's literature, in technical psychiatric discussions and in the *Wall Street Journal*.

In checking through sources of information on dragons such as *Dragons, Unicorns and Other Mag-*

*"*A Modern Dragon" from* Songs from Around A Toadstool Table *by Rowena Bennett. Copyright © 1967 by Rowena Bennett. Copyright © 1930, 1937 by Follett Publishing Company. Used by permission of Follett Publishing Company, division of Follett Corporation.*

THE READING TEACHER, 1973, Vol. 26, pp. 566-571.

ical Beasts (Palmer, 1966), *The Beasts of Never* (McHargue, 1970), *The Dictionary of Folklore: Mythology and Legend* (Leach, 1950), and the *New Larousse Encyclopedia of Mythology* (Graves, 1968), a lively picture of dragons is presented. For instance, their personalities are unique whether you are concerned with the benevolent beast a Chinese schoolboy knows or the horrid carnivorous beast an English schoolboy knows. If you can't differentiate between a fire breathing dragon, a mist breathing dragon, a five toed one, one with whiskers and a pearl growing under his chin, or a miserly dragon, you might not do very well on a dragon IQ test.

Red hot dragon

One example of a Chinese dragon at work is "The Terrible Tempered Dragon" (Palmer). In this story a thousand foot long fiery red dragon named Ch'ien T'ang is chained to a huge pillar at the bottom of Lake Tung T'ing for lashing his tail so hard that a great wave rose from the lake and destroyed whole villages.

The hero, a poor student, dejected because he has just failed his examinations, helps the niece of the fiery dragon. As a result of the fiery dragon's great bravery, he redeems himself, and the poor sad mortal student wins the lifetime gratitude of a dragon plus the dragon princess even after modestly confessing his unworthiness to become the son-in-law of a dragon king. However, the dragon king's solution to his horrendous defect (failing his university examinations) is simple—a tutor.

If we have not read certain books and stories, we do not have the meanings for common literary allusions. Such common expressions as sour grapes, the sky is falling in, jousting a windmill, and Cheshire grin illustrate this point. Another example of literary allusion with an origin in children's stories is the lovely, happy word *serendipity*.

"Serendip" is another name for the beautiful island of Ceylon, and from Serendip came the word *serendipity*. Horace Walpole, an English author who lived from 1717 to 1797, coined this word, which means finding valuable or agreeable things not sought.

The Three Princes of Serendip (Hodges, 1966) describes another group of Eastern dragons. King Jaiya asked wise men from his own country and from other lands to come to teach his three sons. However, very few from abroad dared approach his island because great dragons inhabited the wide ocean lanes around the island.

The king and the wise teachers therefore decided the princes must travel in the great world to perfect their education and also find the solution to one of the most serious problems of Serendip. This problem was a magic formula named "Death to Dragons" which contained the secret of a potent liquid which would destroy all dangerous monsters if poured into the ocean.

Needless to say, the three princes were successful in their quest and they all lived happily ever after.

Mythological heroes

A modern example of a ferocious beast as found in Norse and Greek mythology is the dragon Smaug in *The Hobbit* (Tolkien, 1964). Older dragons are found in the *Iliad*. By the Middle Ages dragon slaying was an accepted occupation and had such heroes as Siegfried, Beowulf, King Arthur and King Lodbrok of Denmark. Another Tolkien dragon fighter is Farmer Giles who encountered Chrysophylax in "Farmer Giles of Ham" (1966).

A Good Knight for Dragons (Bradfield, 1967) deals with the typical destruction of dragons by knights. However, this story is not the usual dragon slaying story. Prince Cedric is a beguiling and peace loving prince who must rid the kingdom of a new dragon. His father had long ago driven every last dragon from the kingdom but is now stiff in his joints and rides no more. Florence, the old king's horse, is so deaf and blind that no one knows if she knows where she is going. And so this book centers on the problem of how Cedric will become a good knight for dragons

New twist on old tale

Our dragon class adapted a modern fable of St. George, *The Reluctant Dragon* (Grahame, 1938, 1968), to a skit for presentation to school and parents. Kurt, playing the role of dragon, decided spontaneously during the performance that this time the dragon would beat St. George and not just play-act as in *The Reluctant Dragon.* That surely added new flavor to an old story. Our St. George was taken completely by surprise!

St. George wasn't the only famous dragon slayer. One of the world's great sagas is the Persian epic poem the *Shah-Nameh* (the *Book of Kings*). The hero Rustem is perhaps the most famous figure in this cycle and symbolizes the struggle of the Iranians or Aryans with the savage people of the East. In a lovely Persian miniature of 1486 Rustem is seen killing a dragon which had attacked his horse. This miniature can be found in the *New Larousse Encyclopedia of Mythology* (Graves, p. 325).

Seemingly dragons have always been in danger. Maybe that is why they are extinct today. Even the *Bible* mentions aggression on the dragon by the Lord in Isaiah: "In that day, the Lord shall punish the piercing serpent. . . . And he shall slay the dragon that is in the sea."

Sometimes the dragon is just simply part of a story, to be slain by the knight, having no personality or bearing on the story, as in *The Silly Knight* (Pascal, 1967). Then again, the dragon or dragons may have a distinct personality of their own and may be individuals of importance as in *The Fourteenth Dragon* (Seidelman and Mintonye, 1968). In this book thirteen dragons are not hard to find but you and you alone can find the fourteenth dragon.

Then there are dragons just for fun. Many stories and books have dragon characters; and dragons are like any other self-respecting individuals. They are all unique and different. An example is an Ukrainian folktale, *Ivanko and the Dragon* (Bloch, 1969). In this translation, Ivanko is a little boy brought to life from a stick of wood (compare this with the tale of *Pinocchio*) by the love of his parents who want a child desperately. When Ivanko grows up, he goes fishing and each day is menaced by a lady dragon who eventually captures him. However, the lady dragon learns to hate the day she took Ivanko, for he figures out how to outsmart her. She meets her fate in a manner remindful of the witch in *Hansel and Gretel.* If you are interested in a new dragon tale about old Russia, investigate *Branislav the Dragon* (Masey, 1967).

A humorous story of how a new royal cook is able to keep the king happy provides the plot for *Dragon Stew* (McGowen, 1969). Since the king loved to eat and also had a hard time staying out of the kitchen, dragon stew had to be quite an inventive dish.

There is also a collection of three very different dragons in the book, *The Three Dragons* (Sebby, 1968). These dragons represent the Yantze, early Roman and Viking cultures. Another collection of dragon stories is *A Cavalcade of Dragons* (Green, 1970).

A Sky Full of Dragons (Wright, 1969) deals with the very current topic of a child's acceptance by other youngsters. In this story, which includes colorful kites, a sensitive grandfather helps the young boy.

Some lazy animals capture a baby dragon and put him to work in the story, *My Father's Dragon* (Gannett, 1948). One monster book which never gets cold on the shelf is Peet's *How Droofus the Dragon Lost His Head* (1971).

The 1969 Honor Book of the Children's Spring Festival contains another unique dragon. This book, *Dominique and the Dragon* (Tamchina, 1968) is about a dragon who swims swiftly down the Rhone River and terrifies all the villagers except little Dominique. After the villagers attempt to destroy the monster, Dominique finds a solution to the problem that pleases everyone, even the dragon.

Dragons as housepets

In *The Dragon of an Ordinary Family* (Mahy, 1969) an ordinary family wants a pet. In the course of the conversation Mrs. Belsaki calls Mr. Belsaki a "fuddy-duddy" and the challenge has been delivered. It's no surprise that the family pet is no ordinary family pet.

Another great fun book is *The Dragon in the Clock Box* (Craig, 1962). Joshua said he had a dragon's egg in the clock box but of course nobody was allowed to peek because baby dragons don't like to be bothered. One day Josh announced that the dragon had flown away to where dragons go. The question remains, what did his dragon look like if he really was there? This book was used with a class of second grade children with examples to illustrate their ideas. A clock box was sealed, with a hole in one end. The children were curious about this clock box sitting on the teacher's desk. When given egg-shape pieces of construction paper they created many exciting pictures of what they thought a baby dragon looked like.

The song "Puff the Magic Dragon" as sung by Peter, Paul and Mary (Warner Brothers Records, 1962) was played to a group of third graders accompanied by an overhead transparency presentation of graphic impressions of this song. This included transparencies that "did things." For instance, using overlays it is easy to lower pirate flags and to pour green punch-holes on the transparency of a sad dragon to show the green scales falling like rain. This was followed by a presentation of the dragon picture play *The Dragon's Tears* (Hamada, 1964). The class then compared how the boys in "Puff" and *The Dragon's Tears* were alike and different. Also discussed were different ways dragon stories could be presented, such as through music, transparency presentations, picture plays, books, poems, stories in a collection of stories, and so forth. The subsequent work of individual children and groups of children was a rich smorgasbord of approaches and ideas.

In the Caldecott award winning book, *Sam, Bangs and Moonshine* (Ness, 1966) the imaginative heroine practices moonshine regularly. One of Sam's favorite moonshine activities is to sit in her chariot and be drawn by dragons to faraway secret worlds. Ness illustrates this activity delightfully.

Author's favorite

My favorite dragon story is *The Fifty-First Dragon* (Brown, 1968). It is the story of a not too promising pupil at knight school and how his professors decide to train him to slay dragons. It isn't until Gawaine kills his fiftieth dragon that he learns about the magic of self-confidence.

Several recent cartoons and comics have considered various aspects of dragon-lore. Included among them are several from the *Wizard of Id* (Parker and Hart, 1970), one from *Broom-Hilda* (Myers, 1970) and one from the *Shortribs* comic strip.

You could also include in this category the wordless picture book, *The Winner* (Ringi, 1969). This is a story told only in pictures, with an unexpected and ingenious ending. It was created for children ages three to six but has been found to be especially funny to children ages twenty to sixty.

Dragon etiquette

Sendak illustrates several fanciful dragons in two books on children's manners, *What Do You Do Dear?* (Joslin, 1961) and *What Do You Say Dear?* (1958). In *What Do You Do Dear?* author Joslin poses the problem of the arrival of a large and hungry dragon. Sendak's pictorial dragon is really a charming guest.

In *What Do You Say Dear?* a fierce dragon gets his knightly just rewards as Joslin questions the mannerly thing for the rescued damsel in distress to do at this point.

Another book by Joslin and Haas is a collection of correct forms for letters called *Dear Dragon* (1962).

Samples of dragons are evident in fables such as the Chinese fable the *Lord and the Dragons* (Ch'iu, 1967). In this fable, Lord Yeh was so fond of dragons that he had them painted and carved all over his house. When the real dragon in heaven heard about this, it flew down and put its head through Lord Yeh's door and its tail through one of his windows. Predictably, Lord Yeh left in a hurry. My household may also be tempting the real dragon to test our fondness since painted and carved dragons decorate the entire house.

Dragons in verse include "The Toaster" by Smith (1961) and several poems by the late Ogden Nash. Nash must have enjoyed dragons if his poems "The Tale of Custard the Dragon" and "Dragons Are Too Seldom" are any indication (1956). Two illustrated books are also available, *Custard the Dragon* (1959) and *Custard the Dragon and the Wicked Knight* (1961).

If your curiosity concerning dragons has been whetted, it is not too late to include firsthand experiences with dragons to add to your experiential background. For $1,048 you can obtain an economy round-trip air fare from California to Bali. Another $1,000 or so will get you a chartered cabin cruiser. This will get you to Komodo, an Indonesian island where you can investigate the little known Komodo dragon as advertised in the *Wall Street Journal* (Pinkerton, 1971).

And finally, following a presentation of "Dragons I Have Known and Loved" to a group of librarians I received something I never expected to see from a librarian; three pages torn from a book. There was a note with these pages from this very special librarian: "These dragons are from *Artie and the Princess*" by Marjorie Torrey published in 1945 by Howell. It is most likely out of print but such appealing dragons ought to be revived!" Yes, as Confucius or somebody else said. "One good dragon deserves another" or something to that effect.

References

Bennett, Rowena Bastin. "A Modern Dragon." *Songs from Around A Toadstool Table.* Chicago: Follett Publishing Co., 1967.

Bloch, Marie Halun. *Ivanko and the Dragon.* New York: Atheneum, 1969.

Bradfield, Roger. *A Good Knight for Dragons.* New York: Young Scott Books, 1967.

Brown, Heywood. *The Fifty-First Dragon.* Englewood Cliffs, New Jersey: Prentice-Hall Inc., 1968.

Ch'iu, Kathy, Ed. *Chinese Fables.* Mt. Vernon, New York: Peter Pauper Press, 1967.

Craig, M. Jean. *The Dragon in the Clock Box.* New York: W. W. Norton and Co., 1962.

Gannett, Ruth Stiles. *My Father's Dragon.* New York: Random House, 1948.

Grahame, Kenneth. *The Reluctant Dragon.* Ill. Ernest H. Shepard. New York: Holiday House, 1938.

Grahame, Kenneth. *The Reluctant Dragon.* Ill. Gregorio Prestopino. New York: Grosset and Dunlap, 1968.

Graves, Robert. *New Larousse Encyclopedia of Mythology.* New York: Prometheus Press, Hamlyn Publishing Group Limited, 1968.

Green, Roger Lancelyn, Ed. *A Cavalcade of Dragons.* Ill. Krystyna Turska. New York: Henry Z. Walck Inc., 1970.

Hamada, Hirosuke. *The Dragon's Tears.* Rutland, Vermont: Charles E. Tuttle, 1964.

Hodges, Elizabeth Jamison. *The Three Princes of Serendip.* New York: Atheneum, 1966.

Joslin, Sesyle and Irene Haas. *Dear Dragon.* New York: Harcourt, Brace and World, 1962.

Joslin, Sesyle and Maurice Sendak, Ill. *What Do You Do Dear?* New York: Young Scott Books, 1961.

Joslin, Sesyle and Maurice Sendak, Ill. *What Do You Say Dear?* New York: Young Scott Books, 1958.

Leach, Maria, Ed. *Funk and Wagnalls Standard Dictionary of Folklore: Mythology and Legend.* New York: Funk and Wagnalls Co., 1950.

Mahy, Margaret. *The Dragon of an Ordinary Family.* New York: Watts, 1969.

Masey, Mary Lou. Ill. Helen Basilwsky. *Branislav the Dragon.* New York: David McKay Co., 1967.

McGowen, Tom. *Dragon Stew.* Chicago: Follett Publishing Co., 1969.

McHargue, Georgess. *The Beasts of Never.* New York: Bobbs-Merrill Co., 1970.

Myers, Russell. "Broom-Hilda." Chicago Tribune-New York News Syndicate, Inc. (Oct. 24, 1970).

Nash, Ogden. *Custard the Dragon.* Boston: Little, Brown and Co., 1959.

Nash, Ogden. *Custard the Dragon and the Wicked Knight.* Boston: Little, Brown and Co., 1961.

Nash, Ogden. "The Tale of Custard the Dragon," and "Dragons Are Too Seldom." *Verses From 1929 On.* New York: The Modern Library, 1956.

Ness, Evaline. *Sam, Bangs and Moonshine.* New York: Holt, Rinehart and Winston, 1966.

O'Neal, "Shortribs." Newspaper Enterprise Association. (Oct. 15, 1970).

Palmer, Robin. *Dragons, Unicorns and Other Magical Beasts.* New York: Henry Z. Walck, Inc., 1966.

Parker, Brant and Hart. "Wizard of Id." Millers Service, Ltd. (Oct. 2, 1970).

Parker, Brant and Hart. "Wizard of Id." Millers Service, Ltd. (June 28, 1970).

Pascal, David. *The Silly Knight.* New York: Funk and Wagnalls, 1967.

Peet, Bill. *How Droofus the Dragon Lost His Head.* Boston: Houghton Mifflin Co., 1971.

Pinkerton, W. Stewart. "The Komodo Dragon, Big Mean and Hungry, Is Eager for Visitors." *Wall Street Journal,* Pacific Coast Edition, (Oct. 7, 1971), p. 1.

Ringi, Kjell. *The Winner.* New York: Harper and Row, 1969.

Sebby, Sam R. *The Three Dragons.* New York: Grove Press Inc., 1968.

Seidelman, James E. and Grace Mintonye. *The Fourteenth Dragon.* Long Island City, New York: Harlin Quist, Inc., 1968.

Smith, Jay. "The Toaster." *Time for Poetry.* May Hill Arbuthnot. Chicago: Scott, Foresman and Co., 1961.

Tamchina, Jurgen. *Dominique and the Dragon.* New York: Harcourt, Brace and World, 1968.

Tolkien, John R. R. "Farmer Giles of Ham." *The Tolkien Reader.* New York: Ballantine Books, 1966.

Tolkien, John R. R. *The Hobbit.* Boston: Houghton Mifflin, 1964.

Torrey, Marjorie. *Artie and the Princess.* Howell Publishing Co., 1945.

Wright, Mildred Whatley. *A Sky Full of Dragons.* Austin, Texas: Steck-Vaughn Co., 1969.

Toward positive self-concept

DONALD M. QUICK

In addition to editing the Wisconsin State Reading Association Journal, *Donald M. Quick directs the Reading Clinic at the University of Wisconsin, Oshkosh. Here he notes influences in the development of self-concept and suggests strategies for promoting positive self-concept through reading instruction.*

EDUCATORS are continually gaining insight into the necessity, relevance, and importance of promoting positive self-concepts among young learners in the classroom. Studies by Wylie (1961), Coopersmith (1967), Combs (1962), and Purkey (1970), as well as several others, have strongly suggested that there are both positive correlations and a multitude of ramifications associated with promoting positive self-concepts and providing an educational setting which will stimulate achievement motivation and the academic progress of the learner.

How is self-concept developed?

Self-concept (what an individual believes he is) is learned. Wylie has suggested that the self-concept is learned through a combination of rewards and punishments related to one's actions and characteristics. The individual learns about himself through success or failure and from others' reactions to him. That is, the young child learns who he is and what he is from the treatment he receives by those who surround him in the process of maturation (Combs). The child, therefore, begins to develop a self-concept in reference to the feelings which are reflected by those individuals who mean something to the child. This results in continuous feedback and the eventual formation of personal attitudes which comprise the personality of the child.

Anderson (1965) suggests that the individual behaves compulsive-

THE READING TEACHER, 1973, Vol. 26, pp. 468-471.

ly, once the psychological self-image has been formed. Because of this, a child may behave in a certain way in order to receive the kind of treatment to which he has adjusted. The child who views himself as successful will most likely continue to function that way and be treated that way, while the child who views himself as a failure will function in that way and be looked upon as a failure.

Self-concept and achievement appear to be interrelated—that is, poor achievement usually promotes a depreciation of one's self-concept, which, in turn, leads to continued poor achievement. To a lesser degree, successful achievement leads to an enhanced self-concept, which, in turn, leads to improved achievement (Alexander, 1964). Because of these factors, a child's behavior, to a large extent, becomes a function of the expectations of others—those who play a significant part in the child's life. The particular behavior evoked becomes the child's emerging self.

Teacher influence

How can teachers influence the development of positive self-concepts? According to Combs and Snygg (1959), teachers can be most influential in developing positive self-concepts within a child by providing a democratic classroom atmosphere wherein each pupil can think of himself as a responsible citizen, a contributing member of the group—where there is respect for each person in the class, and where each pupil feels free to express his opinions frankly and openly. The teacher can also provide a wide variety of opportunities for success and self-appreciation through productive learning situations where the child *can* and *will* achieve.

To develop positive self-concepts, therefore, it is the primary task of the teacher to promote a positive atmosphere within the classroom to enable the child to gain a positive yet realistic image of himself as a learner. In developing this climate for learning it is necessary, of course, to avoid the negative whenever possible.

Combs (1969) also found that the teacher's attitudes toward himself and others are as important as, if not more important than, his techniques, practices, or materials and that effective teachers can be distinguished from ineffective teachers on the basis of their attitudes toward themselves and others. In short, a teacher with positive attitudes can promote a positive classroom atmosphere, while a teacher with negative attitudes promotes a feeling of negativism to the children.

How the teacher feels about his pupils has been found to be especially important. If a teacher believes that his students can and will achieve, then the students will be more successful. Conversely, if the teacher believes that pupils cannot achieve, then this will influence their performance negatively.

This phenomenon has been especially well illustrated through some recent research completed by Rosenthal and Jacobson (1968). Rosenthal's experimental treatment involved nothing more than giving teachers the names of children who could be expected to make unusual intellectual gains in the year ahead. The children were chosen at random. Teachers working with elementary children revealed tendencies of differential treatment to the subjects who were said to be bright or who would be expected to make great gains. It was hypothesized that the teacher's tone of voice, facial expression, touch, and posture projected his expectancies to the pupils. Rosenthal's experiments clearly indicated that children from whom teachers expected greater intellectual gains showed such gains.

What are some specific strategies a teacher can utilize to promote more effectively the development of positive self-concepts through reading instruction?

Strategies for building self-concept

Personalize your reading instruction.

1. Demonstrate a sincere liking for each child by developing empathy; give each child the feeling that he is liked, understood and appreciated.
2. Let each child know you are aware of him as a person, that you are willing to listen to him and help him when necessary.
3. Take some time during your busy schedule to establish opportunities to communicate with each child privately or semiprivately about his interests and concerns.
4. Serve as a model of respect and self-respect. Treat each child as if he were the most important person you know.

Guide each child through the reading process.

1. Set the *purpose* of instruction. Let each child know what is expected in performing a given task or in his effort to learn a particular skill. Let each child know what your expectations are and promote the feeling that you are confident that he *can* accomplish the given task, that he *can* learn and can succeed.
2. Find the instructional reading level of each child and locate reading material at his reading and interest level. Make certain that each child experiences success; organize and plan instructional activity to meet each child's range of challenge—neither above nor below his instructional level.
3. Guide each child toward having as many successful experiences as possible. Make units of improvement small enough to record the child's progress at frequent intervals; enable pupils to have some immediate feedback—to realize they have mastered the smallest step. Children learn from success, not failure!

Establish a positive instructional setting.

1. Evaluate pupil progress in reference to previous accomplishments—compare each child's progress only with his own past performance. What improvements has he made?
2. Generally put positive comments on written work. Negative remarks and a great many checkmarks pointing out mistakes only reinforce the child's feeling of inadequacy, and discourage positive attitudes and any further attempts to improve.
3. Take special opportunities to praise pupils for their successes. Tell children when they have done well and encourage this kind of work to be continued. Send notes to parents letting them know their children do well.

Provide for flexibility in planning and in learning.

1. Involve each child in planning his educational program, in

charting his progress, and in evaluating his performance. Children need this responsibility and the feeling of belonging.

2. Give each child some freedom to explore, discover, and make some mistakes. These opportunities can include creative and recreational reading activity.

John W. Gardner (1961) has said in his book, *Excellence: Can We Be Equal and Excellent Too?*, "What we must reach for is a conception of perpetual self-discovery, perpetual reshaping to realize one's best self, to be the person one could be" (p. 136). By promoting a positive self-concept in each child, this goal can be reached. We can move forward towards eliminating illiteracy, enabling each child to become that person he can and should be.

References

Alexander, Eugene D. "The Marking System and Poor Achievement." *Teachers College Journal*, 36, (Dec. 1964), pp. 110-13.

Anderson, Camilla M. "The Self-Image: A theory of the dynamics of behavior." *The Self in Growth, Teaching, and Learning*, Ed. Don E. Hamachek. Englewood Cliffs, N.J.: Prentice-Hall, Inc., (1965), pp. 1-13.

Cohn, M., and Kornelly, D. "For Better Reading; A More Positive Self-Image." *Elementary School Journal*, 70, (Jan. 1970), pp. 199-201.

Combs, Arthur (Ed.), *Perceiving, Behaving, Becoming: A New Focus For Education*. Washington, D.C.: Association for Supervision and Curriculum Development, 1962, p. 84.

Combs, Arthur and Snygg, Donald. *Individual Behavior*. New York: Harper and Brothers, 1959, p. 378.

Combs, Arthur W. et al. *Florida Studies in the Helping Professions*. Gainesville: University of Florida Press, 1969, pp. 3-9.

Coopersmith, Stanley. *The Antecedents of Self-Esteem*. San Francisco: W. H. Freeman and Company, 1967, pp. 25-44.

Gardner, John W. *Excellence: Can We Be Equal and Excellent Too?* New York: Harper & Row, Publishers, 1961, p. 136.

Purkey, William Watson. *Self Concept and School Achievement*. Englewood Cliffs, New Jersey: Prentice-Hall, Inc., 1970, pp. 43-65.

Rosenthal, Robert and Jacobson, Lenore. "Teacher Expectations for the Disadvantaged." *Scientific American*, 218, (April 1968), pp. 19-23.

Sebeson, Lucille. "Self-Concept and Reading Disabilities." *The Reading Teacher*, 23, (Feb. 1970), pp. 460-64.

Wylie, Ruth C. *The Self Concept*. Lincoln: University of Nebraska Press, 1961, pp. 184-200.

Motivation: What? Why? How?

Here's what 10 reading experts have to say about turning children on to books and helping good readers become better readers

By IAN ELLIOT

Mo'ti•vate (mō'tĭ•vāt), *v.t.* To provide with a motive; to impel; incite.—**mo'ti•va'tion** (-vā'shŭn), *n.*—*Webster's New Collegiate Dictionary.*

THAT'S ALL very well—but, despite Mr. Webster's best intentions, it's rather abstract. Sure, motivation means to impel, to incite. But come down to the word as it is applied to the teaching art in a particular curriculum area—let's say, reading. What does motivation mean when applied to reading instruction? How important is it? How can a teacher make it happen?

These are some of the questions GRADE TEACHER asked a panel of reading experts recently. (For a rundown on who was asked and their contributions to reading instruction, see box on page 95.) What follows is a synthesis of what they said:

Is motivation the key to making good readers become better readers?

There is general agreement among the panelists that while motivation may not be the only key to better reading, it is at least one of the most important keys. Dr. Lynette Gaines believes, for example, that motivation is particularly important in today's society because there are so many alternatives to reading. Does a child want facts? He can watch television. Does he wish to be entertained? He can listen to his record player.

Prof. Margaret Early sees the importance of motivation in a somewhat different light. She believes that "without it, the child's natural curiosity and ability are damaged, stifling his growth and maturity. The best reading program in the world can be dull without motivation."

What is motivation?

Although several panelists offered succinct definitions—"a set of conditions which produces a need or desire to act in certain ways" (Dr. Theodore Clymer); "the mobilization of individual energies toward a particular goal or goals" (Dr. Albert

GRADE TEACHER, 1971, Vol. 89, pp. 94-96.

Harris)—many of the experts felt that the word itself was so vague as to defy accurate definition.

This vagueness lies not so much in the meaning of "motivation," as it does in who supplies it. The teacher, through a series of classroom strategies or through her own personality? Or the student, by summoning up from within himself some spark which impels him to read? Dr. Roach Van Allen, for one, believes that it is both. He says, "Motivation is essentially a releasing, a tapping of what already exists. It's raising an awareness that it *does* exist."

The existence of some kind of motivation (whoever is responsible for bringing it into play) is disputed by none of the reading experts. They warn, though, of a very real danger that teachers will take it too lightly. Says Dr. Harris, "Motivation must not be general and vague, as in such concepts as 'liking reading.' It must be specific and linked to the improvement of specific skills. A child, for example, must have the motivation to read more, or to read in greater depth, or to read faster, or whatever is his particular goal."

How can motivation be achieved in the elementary school classroom?

There were as many different answers to this question as there were different reading experts to give answers.

Prof. William K. Durr believes that in helping children become better readers, teachers are often guilty of asking the wrong questions to begin with. Instead of teachers asking how they can motivate children, they should be trying to find out what kinds of things motivate children and what can be done to utilize the motivations the children already have. Honest answers to such questions might provide teachers with a long list of possible techniques and strategies that could be applied in a kind of shotgun approach.

Several members of the panel—Drs. Gaines and Harris in particular—believe that the teacher's own enthusiasm for reading is a big plus factor in achieving proper reading motivation in the classroom. Enthusiasm is a contagious thing and if a teacher can show that she is really excited by reading, she can go a long way towards turning children on, too.

How does a teacher show her genuine enthusiasm? Not necessarily by sweeping gestures and fulsome praise. Often, it's more a matter of the little things a teacher says and does. Prof. John Manning, for example, believes that the problem of motivation is closely bound up with the set of values held by either the teacher or the child. (Some children come to school with a set of values that make them want to read and make reading easy to learn; some teachers have a set of values which children respect and admire.) A teacher who is respected and admired for her values can be tremendously effective by suggesting, in a subtle way, that reading is an exciting and rewarding venture.

Two other things a classroom teacher can do to achieve motivation for better reading came in for practically unanimous mention by the reading experts:

First, the teacher can make sure that the children are given a positive learning situation in the classroom. Says Dr. Eleanor Carlson, "The teacher must provide an environ-

Who's who

Here are the reading experts who were queried by Grade Teacher on the role played by motivation in better reading:

Eleanor Carlson, senior editor; and Theodore Clymer, senior author of Ginn's Reading 360 Series.

William K. Durr, professor of education at Michigan State University; senior author of The Houghton-Mifflin Reading Program.

Margaret Early, professor of education and associate director of the Reading and Language Arts Center, Syracuse University; senior author of Harcourt Brace Jovanovich's Bookmark Reading Program.

Lynette Gaines, professor of education at University of South Alabama; author and consultant for Harper and Row's Design for Reading program.

Marie Hackett, assistant professor of educational psychology at Florida State University; author of Criterion Reading (formerly Hackett Reading System) for Random House-Singer.

Albert J. Harris, professor emeritus of education at City University of New York; senior author of basal readers for The Macmillan Company.

John Manning, professor of elementary education, University of Minnesota and co-author of Scott Foresman Reading Systems.

Lew Robins, author of the Grolier Creative Reading Program; adviser to Bank Street College of Education.

Roach Van Allen, professor of elementary education, University of Arizona; author of *Language Experiences in Reading* and consultant to Encyclopaedia Britannica Educational Corp.

ment conducive to learning—where the child wants to learn and where he is able to apply what he is learning."

Second, the teacher must provide the children with some method of self-evaluation. Drs. Carlson and Clymer sum it up this way: A successful program must be one in which a child can see his progress—in which he can be led to believe in himself.

Prof. Harris lists three other things of a practical nature that a classroom teacher can do, in addition to the points already mentioned: *1.* She can make sure that the available reading material is interest-arousing and easily accessible to all children: *2.* She can schedule classroom time exclusively for individual reading (that is, giving the children a chance to read the things *they* want to read); and *3.* She can explain to the youngsters the importance of certain reading skills.

And Prof. Early provides a fourth: Don't set your sights too low. The child's natural (i.e., instinctive) curiosity must be safeguarded at all times. Too often, teachers have unintentionally tried to kill this curiosity by leading the children "on a plane that is lower than their potential."

What role does reading material play in achieving or thwarting the child's motivation?

Considering the fact that all of the panelists are either authors of or consultants to reading programs put out by major publishers, their answers to this question may come as something of a surprise. They were almost unanimous in their belief that a child needs something more than a steady diet of readers and reading programs.

Says Prof. Early, "I must caution the teacher to spread out and break out of the book rut. Good readers will reject reading if their only outlet is the book itself. Give them less formal arrangements of the printed word—newspapers, magazines and so on. Sure, there are values to books, but we're turning the child off by overemphasizing books as the only printed form."

Dr. Hackett puts it another way. She says, "Children know where they are and where they're going—that's what motivation is all about to me. And they have many routes to get there. That is what produces a competent reader."

Prof. Manning believes that—at least as far as competent readers are concerned—certain kinds of technical publications can play a role in creating reading motivation. Children whose families subscribe to periodicals such as yachting or gardening magazines frequently develop an interest in those subjects and a distinct competency in reading about them.

Such a change of pace is often all to the good. Prof. Manning, for one, feels that many reading programs today suffer from what can be called a "narrative style" to the exclusion of all other styles. A primary reading program, let's say, features little stories about children—where they live, how they play, etc. Readers on an intermediate level feature almost exactly the same thing by highlighting children of foreign lands. The names may be different and the vocabulary may be more complex, but students are still reading about where children live and how they play, etc. Most important, the students are reading in exactly the same way and in the same pace that they were in the primary grades; indeed, it is difficult to get them to read in any other way.

If variety has anything to do with reading motivation—and most of the panelists believe that it does—then it is probably valuable for a teacher to get her students to sample other forms of writing, such as how-to pieces, fantasy, etc.

Mr. Robins offers a detailed analysis of the part played by materials in motivating youngsters to become better readers. He lists three essential ingredients:

1. There must be no extensive background required of the child. When the material requires a child to have background knowledge before he comprehends what he is reading, there is a good possibility that he will be turned off. (Background can always be included in the material, of course, and in a pinch can be supplied by the teacher before the child begins to read.)

2. The material must contain memorable ideas. So much of the material that is given to children today consists of ideas or facts that are in no way memorable. With such unappetizing fare, it is difficult to turn anyone on.

3. The material must be well written—which is decidedly not the case in many reading programs today. Children should not be expected to have to struggle with faulty sentence structure, words outside of their experience, etc. The problem here, Lew Robins believes, is that all too few authors of these programs bother to write through the eyes of their young readers.

Mr. Robins sums up the entire problem of motivating good readers to become better readers by pointing out that "there's no simple solution to any of this. There's no magic wand that will automatically solve the problems presented by motivation or the lack of it."

Right. But nevertheless it's a problem that has to be faced. As Prof. Durr says, "A teacher can force a child to read, but she can't make him like it."